I ALONE AM LEFT

I Alone Am Left

ELIJAH AND THE REMNANT IN LUKE-ACTS

Jeremy D. Otten

◥PICKWICK *Publications* • Eugene, Oregon

I ALONE AM LEFT
Elijah and the Remnant in Luke-Acts

Copyright © 2021 Jeremy D. Otten. All rights reserved. Except for brief quotations in critical publications or reviews, no part of this book may be reproduced in any manner without prior written permission from the publisher. Write: Permissions, Wipf and Stock Publishers, 199 W. 8th Ave., Suite 3, Eugene, OR 97401.

Pickwick Publications
An Imprint of Wipf and Stock Publishers
199 W. 8th Ave., Suite 3
Eugene, OR 97401

www.wipfandstock.com

PAPERBACK ISBN: 978-1-6667-0135-7
HARDCOVER ISBN: 978-1-6667-0136-4
EBOOK ISBN: 978-1-6667-0137-1

Cataloguing-in-Publication data:

Names: Otten, Jeremy D., author.

Title: I alone am left : Elijah and the remnant in Luke-Acts / by Jeremy D. Otten.

Description: Eugene, OR: Pickwick Publications, 2021 | Includes bibliographical references and index.

Identifiers: ISBN 978-1-6667-0135-7 (paperback) | ISBN 978-1-6667-0136-4 (hardcover) | ISBN 978-1-6667-0137-1 (ebook)

Subjects: LCSH: Bible. N.T. Luke—Criticism, interpretation, etc. | Bible. N.T. Acts—Criticism, interpretation, etc. | Elijah (Biblical prophets). | Remnant (Theology)—Biblical teaching.

Classification: BS2589 O87 2021 (print) | BS2589 (ebook)

Unless otherwise indicated, Scripture quotations are from New Revised Standard Version Bible: Catholic Edition, copyright © 1989, 1993 National Council of the Churches of Christ in the United States of America. Used by permission. All rights reserved worldwide.

Quotations marked NETS are taken from *A New English Translation of the Septuagint*, ©2007 by the International Organization for Septuagint and Cognate Studies, Inc. Used by permission of Oxford University Press. All rights reserved.

To Christy Joy, my partner in life and ministry

"I have been very zealous for the LORD, the God of hosts; for the Israelites have forsaken your covenant, thrown down your altars, killed your prophets with the sword. *I alone am left*, and they are seeking my life, to take it away."

—1 Kgs 19:10 (NRSV, emphasis added)

Contents

Preface ix

Abbreviations xi

Abstract xv

1. Introduction 1
History of Research 2
Present Study 6
Summary 15

2. A Theology of Remnant 16
History of Research 17
The Remnant Concept in the Old Testament 19
The Question of Remnant Theology in Second Temple
   Jewish Literature 25
Summary 27

3. Elijah and the Remnant in the Old Testament 29
Elijah in 1–2 Kings: A Model Remnant Figure 30
Turning the Hearts of Israel (Malachi 3:23–24) 45
Conclusion 50

4. Elijah and the Remnant in Later Jewish and Christian Literature 51
Second Temple Jewish Literature 51
New Testament Literature 61

5. Elijah and John the Baptist in Luke   71
The Spirit and Power of Elijah (Luke 1:5–17)   71
A Prophet of the Most High (Luke 1:67–79)   76
The Prophet Preparing the Way (Luke 3:1–20)   78
The One about Whom It Is Written (Luke 7:18–35)   89
Summary and Conclusions   95

6. Elijah and Jesus in Luke-Acts   97
A Prophet without Honor (Luke 4:16–30)   98
The Widow and the Gentile Officer (Luke 7:1–17)   107
Some Say Elijah (Luke 9:1–62)   114
The Ascension (Luke 24:51; Acts 1:1–11)   130
Summary and Conclusions   137

7. Elijah and the Disciples in Luke-Acts   139
Messengers Ahead of Him (Luke 9:52; 10:1–16)   139
Philip and the Ethiopian Official (Acts 8:26–40)   143
Peter with Tabitha and Cornelius (Acts 9:32–43; 10:1–48)   147
Paul and Eutychus (Acts 20:7–12)   155
Summary and Conclusions   159

8. Conclusion   162
Summary   162
Implications   165

Appendix   169

Bibliography   175
Author Index   203
Scripture Index   209
Extra-Biblical Index   226

Preface

LUKE-ACTS IS, AMONG MANY other things, an exemplar of Christian reflection on and appropriation of the Old Testament. Although the Third Evangelist is firmly convinced that "the things accomplished among us" mark something radically new in God's work of salvation, at the same time, he is consistent in highlighting the ancient roots that support it. In his Scripture quotations, his echoes and allusions, and even his Greek syntax, Luke is pointing his readers back to the Old Testament (for him, the Septuagint), guiding them through both the oldness and the newness of the Christian faith. Or in other words, he is teaching them how Israel's Scriptures can be fulfilled in a messiah who dies and in a salvation that is for all people. It was when I first began to see this complex network of allusions, patterns, and themes from the OT that I became fascinated with the Lukan prose. This book seeks to trace one key OT motif out of the many woven through the Lukan narrative, and in so doing, to offer a deeper appreciation for Luke's use of OT Scripture and of all Scripture as the living and active word of God.

I would like to acknowledge my debt to the many academic mentors who have shaped my thinking over the years, especially those who taught me to love Greek prose by inviting me into the texts of the New Testament and the Septuagint. I am particularly indebted to my doctoral supervisor, Nicholas Perrin, as well as to Richard Schultz, for their oversight and guidance through many iterations of this project. They have provided invaluable insight (and occasional sparring!) on everything from exegetical methodology to my use of commas. Thanks also goes to my cohort at Wheaton, with whom it was my privilege to share this journey. I am also grateful to my colleagues at the ETF Leuven, who have encouraged me in my continued growth as a scholar. Finally, I would like to thank my wife

Christy for believing in me from the very outset of this project, as well as Malachi, Caleb, and Samuel, who have joined us along the way.

Abbreviations

AB	Anchor Bible
ABRL	Anchor Bible Reference Library
AnBib	Analecta biblica
Ant.	*Jewish Antiquities.* Josephus
ApOTC	Apollos Old Testament Commentary
ArBib	Aramaic Bible
AUSS	*Andrews University Seminary Studies*
BBR	*Bulletin for Biblical Research*
BECNT	Baker Exegetical Commentary on the New Testament
BETL	Bibliotheca ephemeridum theologicarum lovaniensium
Bib	*Biblica*
BIS	Biblical Interpretation Series
BKAT	Biblischer Kommentar, Altes Testament. Edited by M. Noth and H. W. Wolff
BN	*Biblische Notizen*
BR	*Biblical Research*
BSac	*Bibliotheca sacra*
BTB	*Biblical Theology Bulletin*
BZ	*Biblische Zeitschrift*
BZAW	Beihefte zur Zeitschrift für die alttestamentliche Wissenschaft
BZNW	Beihefte zur Zeitschrift für die neutestamentliche Wissenschaft und die Kunde der älteren Kirche
CBQ	*Catholic Biblical Quarterly*
CBR	*Currents in Biblical Research*
CTR	*Criswell Theological Review*
CurBS	*Currents in Biblical Research*
DSD	*Dead Sea Discoveries*

EBib	*Etudes Bibliques*
EdF	Erträge der Forschung
ETL	*Ephemerides theologicae lovanienses*
ExAud	Ex Auditu
ExpTim	Expository Times
FB	Forshung zur Bibel
GTJ	*Grace Theological Journal*
HALOT	Koehler, L., W. Baumgartner, and J. J. Stamm. *The Hebrew and Aramaic Lexicon of the Old Testament.* Translated and edited under the supervision of M. E. J. Richardson. 4 vols. Leiden, 1994–1999
Hermeneia	Hermeneia: A Critical and Historical Commentary on the Bible
HNT	Handbuch zum Neuen Testament
HTKNT	Herders theologischer Kommentar zum Neuen Testament
HTR	*Harvard Theological Review*
ICC	International Critical Commentary
Int	Interpretation
ITC	International Theological Commentary
JBL	*Journal of Biblical Literature*
JBQ	Jewish Bible Quarterly
JETS	*Journal of the Evangelical Theological Society*
JITC	*Journal of the Interdenominational Theological Center*
JSJ	*Journal for the Study of Judaism*
JSJSup	Supplements to the Journal for the Study of Judaism
JSNT	*Journal for the Study of the New Testament*
JSNTSup	Journal for the Study of the New Testament Supplement Series
JSOT	*Journal for the Study of the Old Testament*
JSOTSup	Journal for the Study of the Old Testament Supplement Series
JTI	*Journal of Theological Interpretation*
JTS	*Journal of Theological Studies*
J.W.	*Jewish War*, Josephus
LNTS	Library of New Testament Studies
LTQ	*Lexington Theological Quarterly*
LXX	Septuagint
MAJT	*Mid-America Journal of Theology*
MNTC	Moffat New Testament Commentary

MT	Masoretic Text
NAC	New American Commentary
Neot	*Neotestamentica*
NIBCNT	New International Bible Commentary on the New Testament
NICNT	New International Commentary on the New Testament
NIGTC	New International Greek Testament Commentary
NovT	*Novum Testamentum*
NovTSup	Supplements to Novum Testamentum
NTL	New Testament Library
NTS	*New Testament Studies*
NTT	New Testament Theology
OBS	Österreichische Biblische Studien
OTL	Old Testament Library
OTP	*Old Testament Pseudepigrapha*. Edited by James H. Charlesworth. 2 vols. New York, 1983–1985
PCNT	Paideia: Commentaries on the New Testament
PEGLMBS	*Proceedings: Eastern Great Lakes and Midwest Biblical Societies*
Per	*Perspectives*
PiNTC	Pillar New Testament Commentary
PRSt	*Perspectives in Religious Studies*
RB	*Revue biblique*
ResQ	*Restoration Quarterly*
RevQ	*Revue de Qumrân*
RTP	*Revue de théologie et de philosophie*
RTR	*Reformed Theological Review*
SAC	Studies in Antiquity and Christianity
SANT	Studien zum Alten und Neuen Testament
SBFLA	*Studii biblici Franciscani liber annuus*
SBLDS	Society of Biblical Literature Dissertation Series
SBLEJL	Society of Biblical Literature Early Judaism and Its Literature
SBLSP	*Society of Biblical Literature Seminar Papers*
SBLSPS	Society of Biblical Literature Seminar Papers Series
SBLSymS	Society of Biblical Literature Symposium Series
ScEs	*Science et Esprit*
SJLA	Studies in Judaism in Late Antiquity
SJT	*Scottish Journal of Theology*

SNT	Studien zum Neuen Testament
SNTSMS	Society for New Testament Studies Monograph Series
SNTSU	*Studien zum Neuen Testament und seiner Umwelt*
STJ	Second Temple Judaism
TDNT	*Theological Dictionary of the New Testament*. 10 vols. Edited by Gerhard Kittel and Gerhard Friedrich. Translated by Geoffrey W. Bromiley. Grand Rapids: Eerdmans, 1964–1976.
Tg. Ps.-J.	*Targum Pseudo-Jonathan*
TJ	*Trinity Journal*
TS	*Theological Studies*
TWOT	*Theological Wordbook of the Old Testament*. Edited by E. Jenni, with assistance from C. Westermann. Translated by M. E. Biddle. 3 vols. Peabody, MA, 1997
TynBul	*Tyndale Bulletin*
VT	*Vetus Testamentum*
WBC	Word Biblical Commentary
WTJ	*Westminster Theological Journal*
WUNT	Wissenschaftliche Untersuchungen zum Neuen Testament
WW	*Word and World*
ZAW	*Zeitschrift für die alttestamentliche Wissenschaft*
ZNW	*Zeitschrift für die neutestamentliche Wissenschaft und die Kunde der Älteren Kirche*

Abstract

IN EXAMINING LUKE'S MULTIPLE appeals to the figure of Elijah through the lens of a literary motif, this study not only provides clarity to a fascinating but often misunderstood element of the Lukan narrative, but also provides a helpful model for understanding an even more perplexing question in Lukan studies, namely, the presentation of the nation of Israel. No NT author takes more interest in the figure of Elijah than Luke, who may allude to the Elijah-Elisha narratives as many as 40 times. While the other Synoptics appear to limit interest in Elijah to typology with John the Baptist, Luke appeals to the OT prophet not only in connection with John, but also with Jesus, Peter, Paul, and the other disciples. However, critical scholarship has failed to reach a consensus on the nature or significance of this interest in Elijah. This study pushes past questions of typology and one-to-one correlation that have stalled scholarly discussion on the topic, examining the theological significance of the figure of Elijah as a literary motif in Luke-Acts. It is argued that, in drawing on a common association between Elijah and the OT concept of remnant (cf. 1 Kgs 18:22; 19:10, 14), Luke appeals to Elijah at key moments in the narrative in order to develop his remnant theology. For Luke, as in the days of the prophets, the concept of remnant holds in tension God's irrevocable promises to Israel with the widespread rejection of God's new work of salvation; the faithfulness of a few with a hope for the nation as a whole; and the particular election of Israel with the message of salvation for all nations.

1

Introduction

"When dogs howl, the Angel of Death has come to a town. But when dogs frolic, Elijah the prophet has come to a town."—*b. Kam.* 60b

WHEREVER HE APPEARS, ELIJAH stands alone: a solitary prophet of Yahweh challenging a thousand pagan priests; a lonely figure on Mount Horeb, standing before the fire of God; a single zealous prophet snatched away from even his closest disciple as he is taken up to heaven in a whirlwind. Elijah is unique also in his radical contrasts: summoning heavenly fire on his enemies but also tenderly summoning back the spirit of a poor widow's dead son; bringing about the wrath of God on an apostate nation, but also turning back God's wrath on the last day as he gathers the eschatological remnant (cf. Sir 48:10). It is little wonder that both Jewish and Christian writers were so captivated by him.[1] In the NT, no author takes greater interest in Elijah than does Luke, who draws on the OT Elijah traditions through dozens of quotations, allusions, and echoes.[2] Moreover, while the other Synoptics seem to limit interest in Elijah to typological connections with John the Baptist (e.g., Mark 1:6; 9:11–13// Matt 17:9–13; Matt 11:14), Luke's Gospel develops strong parallels not

---

1. See esp. ch. 7 of Ginzberg, *Legends of the Jews*.

2. For the purposes of the present study, we shall use "Luke" to designate the implied author of Luke-Acts (see esp. Tannehill, *Narrative Unity*, 1:6–7; cf. Robbins, "Social Location," 303–32).

only with John, but also with Jesus and even the disciples. Furthermore, his interest appears not to be primarily typological. Rather, drawing on long established associations between Elijah and the remnant of Israel, Luke appears to employ the figure of the Tishbite to get at the heart of one of the most pressing theological questions his work addresses: the relationship between Israel and the church.

History of Research

Typology/Fulfillment Models

Much of the scholarly discussion regarding Luke's use of Elijah has focused on prophecy fulfillment and typology and has thus revolved around the question of which figure Luke associates with the OT prophet, whether Jesus, John, or perhaps both.[3] The first position, best represented by Hans Conzelmann and Walter Wink, sees a deliberate denial of any connection between John the Baptist and Elijah in favor of an Elijah-Jesus association.[4] Pointing to Luke's notable omissions of synoptic material that connects John to Elijah (esp. Mark 1:6; 9:9–13//Matt 17:10–13; Matt 11:14), Conzelmann argues that Luke omits John's role as Elijah or the Messianic forerunner as both theologically unnecessary and salvation-historically inaccurate.[5] The evangelist is aware of the John-Elijah connection from his sources and even retains some of it in the prologue (1:17), but he makes clear "by what he omits and by what he adds" that he sees no such connection himself.[6] Building on Conzelmann, Wink argues more positively that Lukan additions (esp. Luke 4:23–27; 7:11–16) develop a strong Elijah-Jesus connection, while downplaying any residual relationship with John, as part of Luke's "desire to assimilate all honorific and exalted titles to Jesus Christ."[7] However, this position fails to take

---

3. Biblical typology may be broadly described as an escalating coherence between an OT figure (person, event, or institution) and an NT figure. In the divine unfolding of salvation history, this correspondence is often thought to have a prophetic element, especially when viewed in retrospect. See esp. Davidson, *Typology in Scripture*, 390–98; Treier, "Typology," 823–27; Beale, *Handbook*, 13–27; Bock, *Proclamation*, 49–50.

4. Conzelmann, *Theology of St. Luke*, 20–27; Wink, *John the Baptist*, 42–45.

5. "John is not the precursor, for there is no such thing, but he is the last of the prophets" (Conzelmann, *Theology of St. Luke*, 25).

6. Conzelmann, *Theology of St. Luke*, 22.

7. Wink, *John the Baptist*, 45.

seriously those passages which Luke retains or even adds that maintain a connection with John, most notably from the birth narratives (1:17, 76; see also 7:27; cf. Mal 3:1).[8] On the other hand, a minority of scholars sees Luke connecting Elijah with John and not Jesus, pointing especially to those points in the Lukan narrative which appear to distinguish Jesus from the OT prophet (esp. 9:8, 19, 52–56). The most common explanations pertain to christological concerns on Luke's part, although some also note a concern to preserve the John-Elijah typology found in Luke's sources.[9] R. E. Brown even suggests that Luke portrays Jesus as the Elisha to John's Elijah, a suggestion which, though intriguing, fails to account for some critical parallels with Elijah, such as Jesus's ascension (cf. Luke 9:51; 24:51; Acts 1:2, 9–11).[10] Ultimately, the Jesus-Elijah connections are too numerous to be dismissed.

In an attempt to better account for both sets of data, Fitzmyer proposes a "double Elijah theme" in which John initially identifies Jesus as Elijah *redivivus* (Luke 3:16; 7:19; cf. Mal 3:1), though Jesus rejects the title for himself, attributing it instead to John (7:27).[11] Luke himself prefers the Jesus-Elijah typology, but he also retains the connection with John because of its emergence in Christian tradition.[12] In a similar attempt to account for these multiple associations, some scholars suggest that Luke is associating Jesus with the Elijah of 1 & 2 Kings, and John with

---

8. Conzelmann acknowledges that he is not taking Luke 1–2 into account in his study, as the view presented in these chapters "plainly contradicts" Luke's own view of both John and Elijah (Conzelmann, *Theology of St. Luke*, 22n2, 24). Though Wink acknowledges 1:17, he nevertheless insists that "Luke has retained nothing of John's role as Elijah" (Wink, *John the Baptist*, 42, 45). However, the tide of scholarship has rightly shifted towards an appreciation of "the homogeneity of the infancy stories within Luke's two-volume work," based on consistency of vocabulary, idiolect, literary features, and theological emphases (Minear, "Luke's Use of the Birth Stories," 111–30. See also Fitzmyer, *Luke*, 1:83, 309–11; Marshall, *Gospel of Luke*, 59; Müller, *Mehr als ein Prophet*, 4).

9. E.g., Rowe, *Early Narrative Christology*, 124–25; cf. Fitzmyer, *Luke*, 1:827. Rindoš, *He of Whom It Is Written*, 231, though he recognizes parallels between Jesus and Elijah, sees the link with John to be stronger and more explicit.

10. Brown, "Jesus and Elisha," 85–104.

11. Fitzmyer, *Luke*, 1:213–14; cf. 319–20, 664–66, 672–73; cf. Robinson, "Elijah, John and Jesus," 263–81. Much of Fitzmyer's complicated proposal hangs on his identification of "the one who is coming [ἔρχεται]" (3:16; cf. ὁ ἐρχόμενος in 7:19) as Elijah. While he is right to see an echo of Mal 3:1 ("Behold, he is coming [ἰδοὺ ἔρχεται]," as we shall see in subsequent discussion, the subject of ἔρχεται in Mal 3:1 is best understood to be either Yahweh or the angel of Yahweh.

12. Fitzmyer, *Luke*, 1:672–73.

the Elijah of Malachi.[13] However, such artificial distinctions between two Elijahs are unlikely to have occurred to Luke or his readers, nor does this proposal account for John's similarities to the Elijah of 1 Kings (e.g., Luke 3:19–20). Marshall suggests the much simpler solution that Luke develops an Elijah typology in connection to both figures, but does so "freed from any literalistic misunderstanding," so that both John and Jesus may be typologically linked to Elijah "without any sense of logical impropriety."[14] While this helpfully avoids the false dilemmas that other views fall into, Marshall does not adequately explain what Luke is accomplishing through a double typology. More significantly, this view (along with those above) fails to account for the connections between Elijah and the disciples (esp. Luke 9:52; 10:1; Acts 9:32–43; 10:1–48). To have so many different characters in a single narrative all typologically linked to Elijah in different ways greatly reduces the effectiveness of any one of the parallels. Though it does appear that Luke retains some understanding of John at least as the fulfillment of Elijianic expectation (cf. 7:27), it becomes evident that the overall phenomenon of Luke's use of Elijah is best explained with different categories than those of typology or fulfillment.

Literary Models

Various more recent studies have helpfully redirected the conversation away from one-to-one correspondence towards more literary discussions. Most notably Thomas Brodie's numerous works on the Elijah-Elisha Narratives argue for what he calls "literary imitation" or "*imitatio*," by which the narratives themselves (rather than the individual characters) are linked through thematic elements, such as the role of prophecy, and structural elements, such as the centrality of the ascension.[15] However,

---

13. Croatto, "Jesus, Prophet like Elijah," 454. See also Miller, "Messenger," 1–16; Clark, "Elijah as Eschatological High Priest," 2. Kaiser, *Malachi*, 107–8, makes a similar assertion (though for slightly different reasons), arguing for a distinction between "Elijah the Tishbite" in Kings and "Elijah the Prophet" in Malachi. This distinction is especially dubious in our present discussion, given that LXX Mal 3:22 (Luke's presumed source) reads Θεσβίτην rather than προφήτην. In Luke's mind, the Elijah expected was connected to the "historical" Elijah.

14. Marshall, *Historian and Theologian*, 147. So also Bock, *Luke*, 1:902, who posits that John is only "like Elijah" for Luke, perhaps to avoid an over-realized eschatology that could result from misreading Matthew or Mark.

15. Brodie, "Luke the Literary Interpreter"; Brodie, *Birthing of the New Testament*, 84–96; Brodie, "Luke's Use of the Elijah-Elisha Narrative," 6–29; Brodie, "Luke-Acts as

Brodie's model of "structural analogy," particularly his hypothesis of a "proto-Luke" based literarily on the Elijah-Elisha Narratives, has been called into question by most scholars.[16] Rather than structure, therefore, Markus Öhler appeals to the function of the characters within the narrative, arguing that John, and especially Jesus, fulfill the function of a miracle-working prophet (*Wunderprophet*) who is rejected by his people.[17] However, the majority of passages that connect Jesus to Elijah show him enjoying relative popularity rather than rejection (esp. 7:1–17; 9:8, 7–18, 19; though cf. 4:25–27). Moreover, John, though a rejected prophet (3:20–21), is not seen to do miracles, and is more frequently connected to Elijah's role as messenger rather than *Wunderprophet* (Luke 1:17, 76; 7:27; 9:52; 10:1; cf. Mal 3:1). John Nolland suggests more generally that Luke employs an "anthological style . . . which is concerned not with the fulfillment of prophecy but with the interpretation of God's present acts in line with those of the past."[18] However, an anthological style tends to refer to the reemployment in a single passage of "words or formulas" from various parts of Scripture, a style which Luke does employ in the *Benedictus* (1:68–69) and the *Magnificat* (1:46–55), but which fails to describe the appeals to Elijah, which are generally conceptual rather than verbal, refer to a select number of Scripture passages, and are spread throughout a two-volume work.[19] Undeniably, Luke's use of Elijah has the effect of presenting the deeds of John, Jesus, and the disciples "in line with" those of the OT hero, yet this explanation fails to explain why the consistent interest in Elijah in particular.

C. A. Evans attempts to offer such a theological explanation, arguing that "where the Elijah/Elisha references and allusions are clearest, the

---

an Imitation," 78–85; Brodie, *Crucial Bridge*, 83. This approach is taken up by Denova, *Things Accomplished among Us*, 29.

16. See discussion in Kloppenborg and Verheyden, *Elijah-Elisha Narrative*. In particular, his structural model causes him to find otherwise improbable correlations, based primarily on the location of episodes within the narrative structure, such as parallels between Zechariah and Elizabeth and Ahab and Jezebel (Brodie, *Birthing of the New Testament*, 284–89).

17. Öhler, *Elia im Neuen Testament*, 183–84, 237–44. See similar approach in Litwak, *Echoes of Scripture*, 92–94.

18. Nolland, *Luke*, 1:322. This is similar to Wink's suggestion of an "Elijah-midrash" (Wink, *John the Baptist*, 43–45).

19. Robert, "Littéraires (Genres)," 5:411 (my translation). See also Robert, "Les attaches," 42–68; Wright, "Literary Genre Midrash," 105–38; Wright, "Literary Genre Midrash (Part Two)," 417–57.

theme of election is present, if not paramount."²⁰ Because his thematic approach is not tied to one-to-one correlation, Evans is free to consider a variety of passages broadly under the "Elijah" motif, including those showing potential contrast, those evoking Elisha in addition to or instead of Elijah, and those connecting John or the disciples to the prophet instead of Jesus.²¹ Evans uses "election" in the broadest sense, and his thesis would be strengthened were he to delve further into the nature of this theological theme in order to give it greater precision. However, he is successful in demonstrating that a theological theme connected to "participation in the kingdom of God" surfaces whenever the narrative appeals to Elijah.²² Though he does not use the term, what Evans envisions is best described as a literary motif.

Present Study

The Elijah Motif

The present study will examine the major references to Elijah throughout Luke-Acts as a literary motif. Robert Alter defines a motif as "a concrete image, sensory quality, action, or object [that] recurs through a particular narrative; . . . it has no meaning in itself without the defining context of the narrative; it may be incipiently symbolic or . . . a means of giving formal coherence to a narrative." By contrast, a theme is "an idea that is part of the value-system of the narrative . . . [that] is made evident in some recurring pattern," and "may also be associated with a motif."²³ More simply put, a motif is something concrete, which, though it does not carry a particular meaning on its own, gains its significance through recurrence within the narrative framework. A theme—an abstract idea or value—often emerges through its association with a motif.²⁴ In a modern

---

20. Evans, "Luke's Use of the Elijah-Elisha Narratives," 82.

21. Evans's short article mentions, but does not expand on, the latter category ("Luke's Use of the Elijah-Elisha Narratives," 83).

22. Evans, "Luke's Use of the Elijah-Elisha Narratives," 83.

23. Alter, *Art of Biblical Narrative*, 120.

24. There is some confusion in that these terms are often used interchangeably (cf. Jost, "Introduction," 1:xv–xxiii). However, contemporary consensus is that a motif is concrete, while a theme is abstract and often made manifest by its association with a motif (Baldick, *Oxford Dictionary of Literary Terms*, 215–16, 333–34; Harmon, *Handbook to Literature*, 323, 508).

example, James Joyce's *Ulysses* utilizes a Hamlet motif through recurring references to Shakespeare's tragic prince and connected characters (e.g., Ophelia) in order to evoke the theme of paternity, especially in regards to Stephen Dedalus's conflicted feelings toward his parents.[25] Within biblical literature, the Joseph narratives employ a dream motif in connection with the theme of knowledge that drives the plot.[26] The Lukan narrative is already known to employ such literary devices, such as the meal motif used in conjunction with the theme of inclusion within the kingdom of heaven (cf. esp. Luke 1:53; 5:30–32; 13:29; 14:15, 21–24).[27]

We will be arguing that Luke, in drawing on a common association between Elijah and the OT concept of remnant, employs an Elijah motif at key points in his narrative in order to develop a theme of remnant theology.[28] As we shall see, the presence of this association in OT Scripture as well as later Jewish and Christian texts (see esp. 1 Kgs 18:22; 19:10, 14; Sir 48:10; Rom 11:1–5), would have made the connection a natural one for Luke and his readers. Through frequent allusions to the Elijah-Elisha narratives throughout Luke-Acts, the narrator develops a theme of remnant that serves to explain and affirm his readers' experiences within the context of salvation history.[29] Specifically, it creates a framework within which the gospel can be seen as the consummation of Israel's hopes for salvation even when it is rejected by many in Israel, the newness of God's salvation in Christ can stand in accordance with his ancient promises to the patriarchs, and the mission to the gentiles can be legitimized alongside an enduring hope for the redemption of Israel.

---

25. See, e.g., Edwards, "Hamlet Motif in Joyce's Ulysses," 5–13; Levin, *James Joyce*, 117–18.

26. Alter, *Art of Biblical Narrative*, 120.

27. Smith, "Table Fellowship," 613–38. See also Moessner, *Lord of the Banquet*; Weatherly, "Eating and Drinking in the Kingdom of God," 18–32; Pao, "Waiters or Preachers," 127–44; Poon, "Superabundant Table Fellowship," 224–30.

28. There is the potential for confusion in that "remnant" can function as a motif in some contexts, such as OT prophetic literature where concrete imagery or technical vocabulary are used (see, e.g., Graham, "Remnant Motif in Isaiah," 217–28], or as a theme in other contexts, such as the present, where the abstract theological concept is in view.

29. Because of the close connection between Elijah and his successor in the Kings narratives and in later tradition (2 Kgs 2:15; cf. Sir 48:12), and because the two figures are explicitly linked and given the same theological significance in the Lukan narrative (Luke 4:25–27), we will be considering allusions to Elisha as included within the "Elijah" motif.

To this end, the first section of this study will establish a definition for the remnant concept and demonstrate the common association between Elijah and the remnant in Jewish and Christian literature.[30] Chapter 2 will examine contemporary research on the remnant concept as well as relevant OT texts in order to establish our criteria for identifying remnant in terms of (1) the *removal* of some, (2) the *remainder* of a representative portion, and (3) the hope of *renewal* for the whole, often tied to a further *reaching out* to the nations. Chapter 3 will then discuss key passages that establish Elijah's function as a remnant figure within the OT (1 Kings 17–19; Mal 3:1, 23–24). Chapter 4 will look at later Jewish texts referring to Elijah (Sir 48:1–10; 4Q521; 4Q558; 4 Ezra 6:24–26), as well as non-Lukan NT texts (Rom 11:1–6; Heb 11:32–38; Jas 5:17–18; Rev 11:1–13). Though these texts appeal to Elijah in various ways, there is a steady stream of tradition that connects the OT prophet with the remnant concept.

The remaining portion of this study will examine the key passages in Luke-Acts that appeal to Elijah, tracing the development of the remnant theme. Though not denying an aspect of typological fulfillment in John's role, ch. 4 will show that in connection with John the Baptist, the Elijah motif highlights the removal of the wicked from within Israel so that a remnant may be revealed (Luke 1:17, 76; 3:1–20; 7:27). In ch. 5, the connection between Jesus and Elijah will be shown to highlight the nature of Israel's righteous remnant: the humble and repentant who can accept the purposes of God (Luke 4:25–27; 7:1–17; 9:1–62; Acts 1:2–9). Chapter 6 will show that, in connection with the disciples, especially in Acts, the Elijah motif shows this remnant experiencing the beginnings of renewal that come with the outpouring of the Holy Spirit so that they are able to take on Israel's mission as a light to the nations, even as they hope for a full restoration of the kingdom (Luke 9:52; 10:1; Acts 8:26–40; 9:36–43; 10:1–48; 20:7–16).[31]

---

30. We will not be arguing that Luke was necessarily aware of or had access to all of these texts, but rather seeking to demonstrate that this perception of Elijah was one already familiar within Luke's religio-cultural milieu.

31. This division of chapters, focusing on John, Jesus, and the disciples, respectively, enables us to interact more directly with secondary literature on the topic while, with few exceptions, still following the order of the Lukan narrative. One must resist the impulse, however, to see in this arrangement a tacit acceptance of the models of one-to-one correlation addressed above.

Israel and the Remnant in Luke-Acts

In addressing the Elijah question, this study will also seek to answer the perplexing question of Luke's presentation of the nation of Israel. How can we understand the tension between nationalistic expectation, especially at the beginning of both books, and the widespread Jewish rejection of the gospel, especially in the face of a successful mission to the gentiles? Put another way, "How can [Luke] hold to a universalism and maintain an openness to Jewish particularity at the same time?"[32] Scholarship tends to offer one of two basic proposals, with attempts at a third, mediating view as well. The first, which until the last few decades has been considered the standard view, is best represented by Ernst Haenchen and, more recently, Jack T. Sanders.[33] By this view, Luke considers the mission to the Jews to have failed. Because of wholesale Jewish rejection of the gospel, the promises to Israel, so critical especially in the opening chapters of Luke, remain unfulfilled. Sanders in particular resolves the tensions in the narrative by prioritizing the speeches in Acts, which are consistently negative towards the Jews, over against the actions within the narrative itself, which are often ambiguous.[34] Furthermore, he emphasizes a corporate view of Israel, which, though conceding that some individual Jews do embrace the gospel, sees the nation as a whole as having rejected the gospel and thus forfeiting their primacy of place within salvation history.[35] Thus the primary reason for the mission to the gentiles is seen to be this Jewish rejection of the gospel. The church, if not the true Israel, is the true successor of Judaism, and Paul's potentially

---

32. Marguerat, "Jews and Christians in Conflict," 1151.

33. Haenchen, "Judentum und Christentum," 155-87; Haenchen, *Acts of the Apostles*; Sanders, "Jewish People in Luke-Acts," 51-75; Sanders, *Jews in Luke-Acts*. See also Räisänen, "Redemption of Israel," 61-84; Tyson, "Problem of Jewish Rejection," 124-37.

34. "Thus Jesus, Peter, Stephen, and Paul present in Luke-Acts, *in what they say on the subject*, an entirely, completely, wholly, uniformly consistent attitude toward the Jewish people as a whole" (Sanders, "Jewish People in Luke-Acts," 58, emphasis original). Sanders explains contradictory details in the narrative, such as Paul's continued preaching to the Jews, in terms of literary or other reasons (73). See also Cook, "Mission to the Jews," 106-9.

35. "[Luke] can only speak of a a partial Jewish acceptance—and that is not enough. Thus, even the part finally becomes irrelevant" (Tyson, "Problem of Jewish Rejection," 137). See also Räisänen, "Redemption of Israel," 74.

ambiguous words in Acts 28:25–28 are seen as a final judgment against the nation: "Luke has written the Jews off."[36]

This view was directly challenged by Jacob Jervell, who argued that rather than a failure, the Jewish mission is presented as a success, at least in part.[37] He supports this by a focus on cues from the narrative, especially pointing to the thousands of Jews said to embrace the gospel, particularly at the beginning of Acts (2:41, 47; 4:4; cf. 21:20).[38] In place of Sanders's corporate perspective, Jervell sees a "divided" Israel. Thus God's irrevocable promises are fulfilled in and for the many believing Jews, while those Jews who reject the gospel are in effect apostate and have forfeited their place within Israel (see esp. Acts 3:23). This position is insistent that the gentile mission is warranted theologically on the basis of large-scale Jewish acceptance of the gospel, even if Jewish rejection of the gospel serves as the historical occasion for it.[39] Regarding the final scene of Acts, Jervell himself agrees with Sanders that the Jewish mission has come to a close, for with Paul's preaching in Rome, Jews all over the known world have had the opportunity either to repent or to be cut off.[40] Numerous proponents of his view, however, disagree, pointing to hints in the narrative of a future conversion of the nation as a whole.[41]

Though even the scholars mentioned above generally acknowledge that the evidence points in both directions, a few scholars attempt to preserve the ambivalence in the text, arguing that Luke is either unable or unwilling to resolve the tension between the promises to Israel and their apparent lack of fulfillment.[42] For Daniel Marguerat, Luke's purpose was

---

36. Haenchen, *Acts of the Apostles*, 53–54, quoted in Sanders, "Jewish People in Luke-Acts," 66.

37. Jervell, "Divided People of God," 41–74; Jervell, "Church of Jews," 11–20; Jervell, "God's Faithfulness," 29–36. See also Lohfink, *Die Sammlung Israels*, 60–62; Brawley, *Luke-Acts and the Jews*; Tiede, *Prophecy and History*.

38. Jervell, "Divided People of God," 42–43. Though Tannehill's view differs slightly from Jervell's (see below), they agree on the importance of interpreting the speeches in light of the narrative (Tannehill, "Rejection by Jews," 83–84).

39. "Jervell, "Divided People of God," 41–43; cf. Barrett, *Acts*, 657.

40. Jervell, "Divided People of God," 63–64.

41. E.g., Tiede, *Prophecy and History*, 96; Tiede, "'Glory to Thy People Israel,'" 33–34. See also Marshall, "'Israel' and the Story of Salvation," 356–57; Moessner, "Ironic Fulfillment," 49–50; Fusco, "Luke-Acts," 1–17.

42. Marguerat, "Enigma," 284–304; Marguerat, "Jews and Christians," 129–54; Tannehill, "Israel in Luke-Acts," 69–85; Tannehill, "Rejection by Jews," 83–101; Moessner, "Ironic Fulfillment," 35–50; Moessner, *Historian*. See also Pervo, "Israel's Heritage," 137–38.

to force his readers to grapple with this difficult question as the church advances in mission.[43] Robert Tannehill sees a "tragic" storyline for Israel, meant to engender sympathy and perhaps hope, while David Moessner suggests that the tension is "ironic," prompting the reader to reevaluate the expectations for Israel as a nation in terms of Jesus and his followers.[44] Whether or not "irony" is the best term, Moessner's appeals to the Deuteronomistic pattern and the Isaianic Servant Songs demonstrate a pattern in which God's purposes for Israel are accomplished through a faithful portion of the nation, despite wholesale national rebellion.[45] These OT precedents enable him to navigate the various tensions in the Lukan narrative: the corporate as well as the individual perspective on Israel, and the failure as well as the success of the Jewish mission. Moessner rightly notes that, in the OT passages in question, this believing portion of Israel is understood as the "remnant," suggesting that the situation in Luke-Acts is functionally the same, though also acknowledging that Luke never appeals to any of the classic OT remnant texts (cf. Paul's use of Isa 1:9; 10:22–23 in Rom 9:27–29).[46] Other scholars agree that "remnant" may provide the best framework within which to understand Luke's perspective on Israel, but the suggestion has never gained widespread acceptance.[47] The lack of traction appears to be due not only to the absence of appeals to classic remnant texts, but also the absence of any technical remnant vocabulary in Luke-Acts.[48] However, these objections stem in turn from an overall lack of clarity regarding appropriate criteria for identifying the remnant concept. This study will seek to address these concerns, not only by providing clarity regarding the characteristics of

---

43. Marguerat, "Enigma," 301.

44. "Part of the function of the birth story is to awaken a lively sense of great expectations so that readers will feel the tragic loss more vividly" (Tannehill, *Narrative Unity*, 1:37; Moessner, "Ironic Fulfillment," 38–40).

45. Moessner, "Ironic Fulfillment," 47–50.

46. "Luke does *not* seem to draw specifically on 'remnant' scriptural passages to represent the *ecclesia* that is forming *out of* repentant Israel and believing Gentiles, though the image of a smaller group emerging in the 'end time' as an obedient Israel is reminiscent of and functions more or less like a 'remnant'" (Moessner, *Historian*, 290, emphasis original). See also Moessner, "Ironic Fulfillment," 49–50; Moessner, "Paul in Acts," 101.

47. Esp. Keener, *Acts*, 1:475; Strauss, *Davidic Messiah*, 246–47; Butticaz, "Salvation of Israel," 148–64.

48. Pao's review of Keener's commentary may be representative and highlights all three of these concerns ("Israel and Israel's Scriptures," 50–56).

the remnant concept, but also by demonstrating that through use of a literary Elijah motif, Luke is able to evoke the remnant theme without the need of recourse to technical vocabulary. At the conclusion of this study, we shall see first of all that Luke does indeed understand the Israel of his day in terms of the OT concept of remnant—a concept that he develops primarily through literary motif and allusion. Second, we shall see that this concept provides the best explanation for Luke's ambivalent presentation of Israel: how the mission to Israel can be seen as both a success and a failure; how the salvation-historical primacy of Israel can be preserved alongside the universality of the gospel; how the mission to the gentiles can be justified by the restoration of Israel in the form of the remnant, even as it is occasioned by the refusal of many Jews to embrace the hope of Israel.

Method

Given the literary nature of our thesis, this study will utilize narrative criticism, though in conjunction with more traditional historical-critical methods, including redaction criticism.[49] In presupposing the literary unity of Luke-Acts, we shall assume not only the possibility of certain themes and motifs occurring throughout the Lukan narrative, but also that a given motif will build on itself so that earlier instances of the Elijah motif set the reader's expectations for subsequent occurrences, which will bring further development to its significance as the narrative unfolds.[50] We will find that, when available, insights from Luke's redactional decisions will shed light on his purposes or emphases in a given narrative. In these cases, we shall assume Lukan access to Mark. Though our findings will not be significantly affected by whether Luke had direct access to Matthew or knew the Double Tradition material from another source

---

49. See Powell, *Narrative Criticism*, 1–22. On narrative-critical approaches to Luke-Acts in particular, see Tannehill, *Narrative Unity*, 1:1–9; Green, *Luke*, 9–16.

50. While the theological and literary unity of Luke-Acts has long been assumed (cf. Cadbury, *Making of Luke-Acts*), this has been questioned based on both internal evidence (Parsons and Pervo, *Rethinking*) and reception history (Rowe, "Literary Unity," 449–57; cf. Gregory, "Reception of Luke and Acts," 459–72). See the discussion and summary in Bird, "Unity of Luke-Acts," 425–48. A majority of scholars still favor the unified view (see esp. Verheyden, "Unity of Luke-Acts," 3–56; Marguerat, "Luc-Actes," 57–81; Alexander, "Back to Front," 207–30; Marshall, "Acts and the 'Former Treatise,'" 163–82; Marshall, "Story of Salvation," 340–57).

(i.e., Q), we shall refer to Matthean parallels for the purpose of comparison only, without assuming dependence.[51]

The procedure of this study will be to examine a given passage within its context in Luke-Acts before establishing the presence of the Elijah motif through quotations and direct references, allusions, and echoes.[52] Once the Elijah motif is established, the pericope will be examined for developments in remnant theology, using the subthemes of removal, remainder, and renewal as the criteria for identification. Though in general we will not explicitly list them through the course of the study, we will be using Richard B. Hays's seven criteria for identifying echoes and allusions.[53] Modified slightly, they are as follows:

1. *Availability.* Was the proposed source of the echo available to the author and/or original readers?[54]

2. *Volume.* The volume of an echo is determined primarily by the degree of explicit repetition of words or syntactical patterns, but other facts may also be relevant: how distinctive, prominent, or familiar is

---

51. On the question of Luke's sources, see esp. Fitzmyer, *Luke*, 1:63–106; Marshall, *Gospel of Luke*, 30–33. It must be stressed that even where he is dependent upon other sources, the final product is Luke's own, for he is no "scissors and paste editor," but is involved in the process of creating a literary piece in its own right (Fitzmyer, *Luke*, 1:92).

52. The distinction between "allusion" and "echo" is difficult to pinpoint, and Hays chooses to "make no systematic distinction between the terms," saying only that, in general, "*allusion* is used of obvious intertextual references, *echo* of subtler ones" (*Echoes of Scripture*, 29). To this we will add that allusions tend to be in some way necessary for a full understanding of the alluding text, while this is not required of echoes. On these and further distinctions, see esp. Beetham, *Echoes of Scripture*, 15–24; Beale, *Handbook*, 29–40; Allison, *Intertextual Jesus*, 1–13. We shall use the term "reference" in its broadest sense, to refer to any quotation, direct appeal, allusion, or echo.

53. Hays, *Echoes of Scripture*, 29–32. See also Hays, *Conversion of the Imagination*, 34–44; Beale, *Handbook*, 33–34; Beetham, *Echoes of Scripture*, 15–24. On critiques of Hays, see Porter, "Allusions and Echoes," 29–40; Porter, "Use of the Old Testament," 79–96; Green, "Doing the Text's Work," 58–63; Beker, "Echoes and Intertextuality," 64–69; cf. Lucas, "Assessing," 93–111; Shaw, "Converted Imaginations," 234–45; Emadi, "Intertextuality," 8–23. These critiques notwithstanding, Hays's method is still widely regarded as definitive, though of course, even through rigorous application of these criteria, this method cannot escape some measure of subjectivity (see esp. Allison, *Intertextual Jesus*, 13).

54. The identification of what is now known as the Alexandrian text type of the LXX as Luke's probable source is still generally accepted (Holtz, *Untersuchungen*, 166–70; cf. Clarke, "Use of the Septuagint," 2:66–105; Rese, *Alttestamentliche Motive*; Bovon, *Luke the Theologian*, 115).

the precursor text within Scripture, and how much rhetorical stress does the echo receive in the author's discourse?[55]

3. *Recurrence.* How often does the author cite or allude to the same scriptural passage in this context or elsewhere?[56]

4. *Thematic Coherence.* How well does the alleged echo fit into the line of argument that the author is developing?

5. *Historical Plausibility.* Could the author have intended the alleged meaning effect? Could readers have understood it?[57]

6. *History of Interpretation.* Have other readers, both critical and pre-critical, heard the same echoes?

7. *Satisfaction.* With or without clear confirmation from the other criteria listed here, does the proposed reading make sense? Does it illuminate the surrounding discourse?

Certainly, some of the echoes proposed in this study will be more convincing than others. We will find, however, that even those proposed echoes that may seem weak in isolation are often strengthened considerably by their proximity to other echoes ("recurrence") and their place within the unfolding Elijah motif ("thematic coherence"). The criterion of recurrence will be of particular importance for this study, for Luke frequently refers back to a given passage after having appealed to it more explicitly.[58] We shall argue, for example, that Luke alludes to the account of the Zarephathite widow twice in Acts (Acts 9:32–43; 20:7–12; cf. 1 Kgs 17:8–24). Even though verbal parallels there are limited at best, Luke's interest in the OT episode has already been demonstrated through Jesus's direct reference to it at a key point in the narrative (Luke 4:25–26), as well as in a more explicit allusion shortly after (7:11–17), making subsequent echoes more likely.[59] Similarly, we shall suggest that the more explicit

---

55. Beetham uses the more specific phrase "rare concept similarity" to describe what Hays refers to as "distinctiveness" (Beetham, *Echoes of Scriptures*, 29).

56. Beale, *Handbook*, 33, helpfully focuses first on recurrence within the immediate context before looking more broadly.

57. Chapters 2 and 3 are in large part meant to lay a foundation of historical plausibility for our overall argument.

58. "*When we find repeated [Lukan] quotations of a particular passage, additional possible allusions to the same passage become more compelling*" (Hays, *Conversion of the Imagination*, 37, emphasis original).

59. The same is true for echoes of Naaman's healing, which is more clearly referenced early on (Luke 4:27; cf. 7:1–10), allowing for recurrence in more subtle echoes (Acts 8:26–40; 10:1–48).

quotations of Mal 3:1 toward the beginning of the Lukan narrative (1:17, 76; 7:27) lend credence to later, more subtle echoes (9:52; 10:1).

Summary

The Third Gospel has the highest concentration of references to Elijah in the NT, yet there is still no scholarly consensus or satisfactory explanation for the phenomenon. By establishing an Elijah motif in connection with John, Jesus, and the disciples, we hope to push the discussion past the either/or mentality of one-to-one correspondence in order to recognize the richer literary aspects at play in the Lukan narrative. This in turn will give further insight into Luke's use of the OT more generally, demonstrating an interest that extends beyond mere prophecy fulfillment to entail the application of Scripture to other theological issues as well. More significantly, the link between Elijah and remnant theology provides key insight into Luke's perception of the nation of Israel and its place within salvation history. This one concept encompasses election and rebellion, renewal and apostasy, the Jewishness of the gospel and the global mission of the church.

2

A Theology of Remnant

THE CONCEPT OF A remnant occurs throughout the entire span of the biblical account of Israel's history, from the prehistoric flood account to the postexilic prophets. It can be variously applied to present the hope of survival, the threat of destruction, or the promise of eschatological renewal. Despite the prevalence of the concept, however, there is very little scholarly consensus regarding its origin or meaning. Most studies of remnant in the OT use as their starting point four Hebrew roots with their derivatives: שאר, the broadest in scope, can refer to anything left remaining, from leftover wood (Isa 44:17, 19) to the surviving members of a defeated army (Deut 3:11); יתר adds the idea of excess or being left over (Num 33:55; 2 Kgs 4:43); פלט focuses on escape or deliverance (Ezek 7:16); and שרד deals with the idea of survival or being left behind (Jer 44:14).[1] However, vocabulary by itself is not sufficient for identifying the concept, since all of the terms have mundane usages in addition to their technical or semi-technical sense (e.g., שאר in 1 Sam 9:24; Isa 44:17, 19), and, more significantly, like all theological concepts, this one is broader than its vocabulary (e.g., Amos 3:12; 9:8).[2] Especially as we move into the NT, where technical vocabulary of remnant is rare—occurring a handful

---

1. On the vocabulary of remnant, see Hausmann, *Israels Rest*, 199–201; Hasel, *Remnant*, 386–87; Hasel, "Semantic Values," 152–69; Gerleman, "Rest und Überschuss," 71–74; Herntrich and Schrenk, "*leimma*," 4:194–214.

2. *Pace* Gerleman, "Rest und Überschuss," 71–74. On the so-called "word-concept fallacy," see Barr, *Semantics of Biblical Language*, 206–19; Silva, *Biblical Words*, 22–28.

of times, if not only twice—it will be essential to identify the concept by other criteria.³

History of Research

Werner E. Müller's seminal monograph argues that the origins of the remnant concept are found historically in the Assyrian practice of total annihilation in warfare. He therefore defines remnant as the group remaining out of a larger body of people in the wake of a political catastrophe.⁴ This remainder then provides the hope of continued existence for the whole.⁵ His study is rightly recognized as the definitive work on the subject, yet even so, despite his sensitivity to theological developments within the OT, his focus remains largely political, and so fails to account for the more abstract or spiritual understandings of remnant that develop. Building off of Müller, Gerhard Hasel broadens the scope of research, examining not only Assyrian war texts, but other ANE texts of various genres, especially flood narratives. His work shows a deeper appreciation for the theological and psychological significances of the concept, and he helpfully recognizes the category of an ethical/religious remnant—that is, one that is recognized in the face of spiritual diminution through apostasy rather than merely physical destruction through war or judgment—which he sees coming to fore especially in the Elijah cycle.⁶ For Hasel, the remnant represents the hope of continued survival: its absence implies annihilation, while its existence carries within itself the potentialities of renewal, life, and continued existence.⁷ At the same time, however, his focus on the religious or existential experience of the remnant at the expense of historical factors makes his criteria for identifying the concept in a given text too broad to be helpful.⁸ Omar Carena's work builds on Müller's

3. Rom 9:27 and 11:5 are universally recognized. Some instances of λοιπός in Revelation (esp. Rev 2:24 and 12:17) may also be technical (see further in ch. 4).

4. "Wir verstehen unter dem Rest den im Verfolg einer politischen Katastrophe übrigbleibenden Bestand einer aus zahlreichen Einzelgliedern zusammengesetzten Einheit von Menschen, sei es eine Familie, ein Stammverband, eine Stadt, ein Volk oder das Heer als die bewaffnete Mannschaft dieser Größen" (Müller, *Die Vorstellung vom Rest*, 13).

5. Müller, *Die Vorstellung vom Rest*, 46.

6. Hasel, *Remnant*, 164.

7. Hasel, *Remnant*, 46–47.

8. In particular, Hasel's idea that the remnant concept is grounded in "the

definition while also drawing from Hasel's sensitivity to theological and psychological dimensions.[9] He argues that the biblical remnant concept arose when the pre-exilic prophets (esp. Amos, Isaiah, and Micah) began to invert the concept as it was found in Assyrian war propaganda, making it instead an emblem of hope for renewal. By contrast, Jutta Hausmann, along with several other scholars, argues for a postexilic emergence of the biblical concept, as the community of Israel sought to recreate its self-understanding. Rather than merely the survivors of a catastrophe, they came to see themselves as the divinely-preserved kernel of the nation.[10] Hausmann sees a particular emphasis on the eschatological dimension of the remnant, as the struggling postexilic community anticipated ethical and political rebirth into a new Israel, which would in turn be sent on mission to the nations.[11]

The lack of consensus regarding the dating of texts, the origin of the concept, and the breadth of its scope indicates that further research on remnant is needed. Nevertheless, this brief survey shows a general agreement on the key concepts involved. Building in large part off of Müller's original definition, we can define remnant as the representative portion of a people or group that remains after a (generally greater) portion has been removed through judgment, catastrophe, or apostasy. The existence of this remainder carries with it at least implicitly the hope of renewal or rebirth, including the potential impact that this will have on other peoples or groups. More simply put, we can speak of the *removal* of many, the *remainder* of some, the hope of *renewal*, often accompanied by a *reaching out* to other nations. A brief overview of key OT remnant passages will illustrate these key concepts.

---

death-and-life tension in connection with the existential concern of man's survival" is so broad that nearly any passage in the OT could conceivably be considered a remnant text (Hasel, *Remnant*, 146n33; cf. 141). See critique by Gerleman, "Rest und Überschuss," 72.

9. Carena, *Il resto*.

10. Hausmann, *Israels Rest*, 1–5. See also Stegemann, "Restgedanke bei Isaias," 161–86; Japhet, "'Remnant' in the Restoration Period," 432–49. It is disappointing that none of these studies interact substantially with Carena's work which, whatever its shortcomings, presents a substantial challenge to the late dating of certain key remnant texts.

11. Hausmann, *Israels Rest*, 205, 208, 215–17.

The Remnant Concept in the Old Testament

The first identifiable occurrence of this concept in the OT canon is in the flood narrative, in which we read that Yahweh "blotted out every living thing that was on the face of the ground, man and animals and creeping things and birds of the heavens. They were blotted out from the earth. Only Noah was left [יִשָּׁאֶר], and those who were with him in the ark" (Gen 7:23).[12] Through Noah and his family, humanity was spared, and the earth repopulated (cf. Gen 9:1). As Genesis unfolds, Lot, Joseph, and others are presented similarly, as figures saved from destruction and thus preserving their respective family groups.[13]

In Exodus, after the golden calf incident, Moses emerges as a remnant figure when Yahweh threatens to wipe out all the Israelites for their apostasy, leaving only Moses alive, and to rebuild "a great nation" from him (Exod 32:10; cf. Deut 9:14). Moses intercedes for the people and they are spared, but the threat of being reduced to a remnant hangs over the people of God, and the situation is essentially repeated with the Israelites' rebellion in Numbers 14 (esp. v. 12). Yahweh's allusion to Gen 12:2 in both passages implies that with only a remnant—even a remnant of one—he is nevertheless able to fulfill his promises to Israel and the patriarchs. Through the rest of the Pentateuch, this threat is raised as a potential consequence of covenant unfaithfulness (Lev 26:36, 39; Deut 4:27; 28:62). Alongside these warnings, however, are the promises that Yahweh will destroy even the remnant of Israel's enemies (Deut 7:20). This military emphasis of the concept predominates in the conquest, and Israel is said to leave enemy nations with no survivors (Deut 2:34; Josh 8:17, 22), or only a few (Deut 3:11; 1 Sam 11:11), as a sign of total defeat.

Elijah, like Moses, appears before God on Mount Horeb and is distinguished from the people of Israel as the only one faithful, and thus the remnant (1 Kgs 19:10, 14; cf. 18:22). Unlike his predecessor, however, Elijah does not intercede for the Israelites, though neither does Yahweh wipe them all out. Instead, he promises a remnant of seven thousand who will emerge and join the prophet (1 Kgs 19:18). Many scholars see a

---

12. Unless otherwise indicated, Scripture quotations are from the New Revised Standard Version Bible, copyright 1989, Division of Christian Education of the National Council of the Churches of Christ in the United States of America. Scripture references follow the versification in the NRSV unless alternate versification is indicated.

13. See Hasel, *Remnant*, 154–59, on the intriguing application of remnant terminology with respect to a hypothetical or future calamity in the Joseph narrative (cf. Gen 45:7).

marked development in the remnant theme here, for the remnant and the apostate alike are marked out in advance of any actual judgment, with the result that the remnant is characterized by covenant faithfulness, while the nation as a whole, as apostate, is removed from view.[14] Furthermore, Elijah can be seen to be "against" Israel, in that he is her accuser, but also in a much greater sense "for" Israel, in that he facilitates her renewal and restoration to the covenant. Such themes will be further developed in the Prophets.

Within the book of Isaiah, remnant theology comprises a major theme in the book as it now stands, serving as a bridge between a theology of judgment for covenant unfaithfulness and sin on the one hand, and of national election and promises of salvation on the other.[15] In the opening oracle, the only thing distinguishing Zion's fate from the utter desolation of Sodom and Gomorrah is the presence of "a few survivors" (1:8-9). Though there are hints even here that the coming judgment will be a refining process (vv. 22-26), the emphasis is on the otherwise total destruction.[16] Isaiah's commissioning likewise anticipates that his preaching will effect thorough destruction in which "the cities lie waste ... and the land is utterly desolate" (6:11). Any remnant that does remain will be burned again (v. 13a-b).[17] While there is hope of a "holy seed," the focus is on the otherwise total destruction of the land.[18] This ambivalence

---

14. Müller, *Die Vorstellung vom Rest*, 55; Hasel, *Remnant*, 164-73; Jeremias, "Der Gedanke," 184; von Rad, *Old Testament Theology*, 2:19-22.

15. Oswalt suggests that the term "remnant" is "perhaps the most apt summary of the entire book, since it captures the interwoven themes of redemption and judgment that prevail from beginning to end" (*Isaiah*, 1:269). See also Stegemann, "Restgedanke bei Isaias," 162, 167; Hasel, *Remnant*, 223; Pfaff, *Entwicklung*, 180. It is therefore unfortunate that so few attempts at a synchronic study have been made.

16. Cf. Hasel, *Remnant*, 253.

17. The idea of a tenth part remaining is familiar to the remnant concept (cf. esp. Amos 5:3), as is the image of a "stump." See Hasel, *Remnant*, 238. With the majority of commentators, we shall render מַצֶּבֶת as "stump," seeing a reference to the remnant, which is further purged (Childs, *Isaiah*, 57-58; Wildberger, *Isaiah*, 1:251, 274-75; Oswalt, *Isaiah*, 1:187n4; Blenkinsopp, *Isaiah*, 1:223-24). Cf. Beale, who renders it "sacred pillar," arguing for a polemic against idolatry, in which an unfaithful remnant suffers judgment until the cause of idolatry is completely destroyed (Beale, "Isaiah 6:9-13," 257-78; Iwry, "*Maṣṣēbāh* and *Bāmāh*," 225-32). In this case, the passage would focus entirely on the thorough eradication of idolatry, with any hope for a holy remnant suspended until later in the book.

18. The last line of Isa 6:13 is commonly thought to be a much later addition, especially given its omission in most versions of the LXX (though it is present in other ancient versions). Even if this is the case, it need not rule out the ray of hope for

of the remnant concept is perhaps best captured through the name Shear-Jashub (10:12; cf. 7:3), for it entails both the certainty of decimation from a nation as numerous as "the sand of the sea" to a mere remnant (10:22; cf. Gen 32:12), but also the promise of a remnant as surety against annihilation.[19] Nor would this remnant consist merely of the stragglers left over, but it would be made up of those who return in faith "to the mighty God" and "lean on the Lord, the Holy one of Israel, in truth" (10:20–21).[20] Therefore, in contrast to Israel's oppressors, who would face annihilation in death, the prophet anticipates Israel's restoration through a raising of the dead (Isa 26:14–19), introducing another key metaphor for the remnant theme.[21] As this remnant underwent the process of refinement through God's judgment on the nation, they could look forward to a day in which they would be considered holy, the land restored to its former fruitfulness, and Yahweh himself would be their crown of glory (28:5–6; cf. 4:2–6).[22]

With such a vision, the prophecies concerning the remnant turn increasingly towards the hope of renewal. The remnant would be established and fruitful (37:30–32), and survivors scattered among the nations

---

the preservation of a remnant in this passage, which is not only consistent with the prophetic message throughout the book, but also likely implied by the image of the stump that remains (Childs, *Isaiah*, 58). See also Oswalt, *Isaiah*, 1:187, 190–91; Evans, "Isa 6:9–13," 139–46; Graham, "Remnant Motif," 218–19; Gosse, "Isaïe VI," 340–49; Metzger, "Horizont der Gnade," 281–84; cf. Stegemann, "Restgedanke bei Isaias," 169; Pfaff, *Entwicklung*, 57–59. Cf. Beale, "Isaiah 6:9–13," 270, who understands "holy seed" negatively as the "unfaithful remnant" (cf. Ezra 9:1–2).

19. See esp. Hasel, *Remnant*, 287; Graham, "Remnant Motif," 219; Rice, "Interpretation of Isaiah 7:15–17," 366; Stegemann, "Restgedanke bei Isaias," 175; Day, "Shear-jashub," 77; Clements, "'Remnant Chosen by Grace,'" 114.

20. "The remnant of Israel is not just what is left over (v. 19), but the people of God defined by its faith" (Childs, *Isaiah*, 94).

21. On whether the resurrection in view here is only metaphorical of national restoration (cf. Ezek 37:1–14), or also entails an eschatological raising of the dead (cf. Isa 25:8), see esp. Wildberger, *Isaiah*, 2:567–70; Watts, *Isaiah*, 342–45; Roberts, *First Isaiah*, 332–33; Oswalt, *Isaiah*, 485–87; Kleger, "Die Struktur," 526–46; Kline, "Death, Leviathan, and Martyrs," 229–49; Blenkinsopp, *Isaiah*, 1:370–71; Childs, *Isaiah*, 191–92. Cf. Hasel, "Resurrection," 267–83; Smith, *Isaiah*, 451–55.

22. Oswalt, *Isaiah*, 2:570–71, notes that the hope intrinsic to the remnant concept is the critical difference between Isaiah's oracles concerning Israel and those concerning the nations. While Israel's oppressors will be destroyed never to be rebuilt, for Jerusalem and Judah, "no matter how long the ruins may have existed, they will be rebuilt, and no matter how terrible the desolation, new life for Israel will spring up again (cf. 35:1–2)."

would be gathered back (49:22; cf. 11:11).²³ The ruined cities of the nation would be rebuilt to their former splendor (61:4), and the nation—blind, lame, and oppressed—would experience Yahweh's healing and favor (61:1–3; cf. 35:5–10; 43:8–13). As the remnant experienced restoration, she would be like a bereaved woman who suddenly finds her home repopulated beyond capacity (49:20–21). This restoration to former glory, however, is "too light a thing" in Yahweh's eyes; instead the restoration of the remnant through "my servant" would lead to God's salvation reaching "the end of the earth" (49:6; cf. 56:3–8).²⁴ The final oracle of the book anticipates not only the ingathering of the exiles of Israel, but also the sending out of the remnant on a mission to "declare my glory among the nations" (66:19).²⁵ Thus, the book of Isaiah applies the remnant concept to provide theological insight into the crises befalling Israel: what is, politically speaking, a devastating blow, is in fact an opportunity for covenantal renewal, as a holy and purified remnant emerges from the nation's ashes, able to again enjoy God's favor, and even become a conduit of his salvation to the nations.²⁶

The prophets Jeremiah and Ezekiel, faced with the reality of the deportation, explore the question of who or what defines the remnant, and in so doing bring both withering judgments and profound promises of hope to their people. For Jeremiah, the remnant left in Jerusalem, far from a holy remnant, was compared to "figs that are so bad they cannot

---

23. The connection between the remnant and the "branch" or "shoot" of Jesse (11:1; cf. 4:2) is a fascinating one. Intrinsic to the hope of national renewal is the hope for a renewed Davidic dynasty, and the image of a branch is itself evocative of a remnant. However, eventually the idea of a "branch" would come to take on a more overtly messianic meaning (cf. Jer 23:5; 33:15; Zech 3:8; 6:12), by which the Branch is himself the one who restores the remnant of Israel. See esp. Oswalt, *Isaiah*, 1:278–79; Wildberger, *Isaiah*, 1:470–71; cf. Blenkinsopp, *Isaiah*, 1:263–64, 266–67.

24. See Goldingay and Payne, *Isaiah 40–55*, 2:165–66. The overlap between the servant and the remnant in this particular song (Isa 49:1–6) is frequently noted (see esp. Rowley, "Servant of the Lord," 53–56; Haag, *Gottesknecht*, 27, 156; Beers, *Followers of Jesus*, 38, 55–60; Knight, *Deutero-Isaiah*, 184; Pao, *Isaianic New Exodus*, 57–58). Numerous scholars have attempted to identify Isaiah's servant with the remnant in every instance, though this equation is not without difficulties (see discussion in North, *Suffering Servant*, 202–4; cf. 9–10, 35–36, 62–64; Haag, *Gottesknecht*, 115–20, 138–55).

25. Westermann, *Isaiah 40–66*, 425; Childs, *Isaiah*, 542; Oswalt, *Isaiah*, 2:688–89; cf. Blenkinsopp, *Isaiah*, 3:314; cf. Preuss, *Old Testament Theology*, 2:301–3.

26. "The coming fires of the Exile will only serve to make his people more what God has always wanted them to be.... They will not lose their royal priesthood (Exod. 19:6) because of the coming judgment. In truth, they will find it (cf. Mal. 3:3, 4)" (Oswalt, *Isaiah*, 1:145; cf. 146n12).

be eaten" (24:8–10; 29:17). They would need to be pared further, like a vine gleaned a second time (6:9).²⁷ Ironically, though this group appears to have based their identity as the remnant solely on their physical presence in Jerusalem (Jer 40:11, 15; 42:10–12; cf. Ezek 11:15), their decision to ignore Jeremiah's warnings and flee to Egypt not only deprived them of this claim, but also placed them under judgment that would leave them "with no remnant or survivor" (Jer 42:17; cf. 44:7). By contrast, the exiles will find favor and "grace in the wilderness" (31:2–6; cf. 24:5–7), eventually returning to Judah pardoned and purified (50:20; cf. 23:3; 31:7–9). Likewise, Ezekiel witnessed the destruction of "the remnant of Israel" in his visions of divine judgment on the Jerusalem community, including the death of Pelatiah, whose name means "remnant" (11:13; cf. 9:1–8). Those who did survive the judgment on Jerusalem would be no holier than those who perished, and their deeds would only serve as evidence that the judgment was not without cause (14:22–23).²⁸ Yet among the exiles would be some who were "tucked away" for preservation (5:3) and who would repent of their sin (6:8–10; 12:15–16). It is from this group that a true remnant would be gathered, given a new heart, and eventually restored to the land in a restoration that can be described best as a raising of the dead (37:1–14; cf. 11:14–19). Thus, while both prophets hold presence in the land as an ultimate goal, they hold repentance and faith as the true characteristics of the remnant.

The Book of the Twelve highlights the contrasting extremes of the remnant concept, such that the divine judgment that devastates the nation is also the cleansing fire that reveals a purified core through which the nation is saved.²⁹ The earlier books tend to highlight the extent of divine judgment: the remnant is merely what is left over after successive waves of locusts (Joel 1:4), or the bloodied scraps of a carcass useful only as proof of the death of a sheep (Amos 3:12; cf. Exod 22:13), so that it is small consolation that anything is left at all (Amos 5:3; 6:9; 9:1, 10).³⁰

27. See esp. Hausmann, *Israels Rest*, 95, 137; Brueggemann, *Theology of Jeremiah*, 129–31; cf. Japhet, "'Remnant' in the Restoration Period," 432–49.

28. "This 'unspiritual remnant' will provide evidence of Yahweh's justice in annihilating the nation" in a manner similar to the "two legs or a piece of an ear" in Amos 3:12 (Block, *Ezekiel*, 1:451).

29. House, "Dramatic Coherence," 204. On the unity of the Twelve, as well as the ordering of the books within the MT and LXX, see Lim, "Which Version," 21–36; Sweeney, "Sequence and Interpretation," 49–64; House, *Unity of the Twelve*; Jones, *Formation of the Twelve*.

30. Hasel, *Remnant*, 190; Müller, *Die Vorstellung vom Rest*, 58–59.

Nevertheless, these prophets also hold out the offer of repentance in the hopes that some will be graciously spared: "hate evil and love good, and establish justice in the gate; it may be that the Lord, the God of hosts, will be gracious to the remnant [שְׁאֵרִית] of Joseph" (Amos 5:15).³¹ A remnant of those who call on Yahweh and are given his spirit will be preserved in Jerusalem (Joel 2:32) so that the ruins of the nation will be rebuilt (Amos 9:11; cf. Obad. 17, 21). Like a dead man raised to life, the remnant would be raised up from destruction (Hos 6:1–3). Thus, Micah expresses confidence that Yahweh will gather the remnant as a shepherd gathers his sheep (Mic 2:12), pardoning them and showing his love (7:8). More dramatic still, in an inversion of Amos's image, Micah portrays the remnant as a lion among the sheep (Mic 5:8; cf. Amos 3:12), although, paradoxically, it will also be a source of blessing for the nations (Mic 5:7).³² The postexilic community, though it served as a sign of renewal (Hag 1:12, 14; 2:2; cf. Ezra 9:8–9), was at the same time still corrupt (Hag 2:14; cf. Ezra 9:10–15), and a radical revival was necessary for the nation to avoid total destruction (Mal 3:24).³³ Nevertheless, the prophets were able to direct their expectations towards a purified eschatological remnant, "a people humble and lowly" who "do no injustice and speak no lies" (Zeph 3:12–13). Intriguingly, even the remnants of other nations would share in the blessing and restoration of Israel, coming to Jerusalem to worship Yahweh (Zech 14:16).³⁴

---

31. On the theologically weighty combination of divine grace with an ethical call to repentance in this verse, see esp. Müller, *Die Vorstellung vom Rest*, 62; Hasel, *Remnant*, 203–4; cf. Carena, *Il resto*, 63.

32. The two images together portray the remnant "neither dependent upon nor vulnerable to mere human strength" (Mays, *Micah*, 123; cf. Wolff, *Micha*, 130). Like dew, it owes its existence to God, and like a lion, it cannot be stopped by any human being. Although some commentators suggest that the dew represents judgment on the nations (cf. 2 Sam 17:12), the comparison here to "showers on the grass" strongly suggests a source of blessing (cf. esp. Ps 72:5) (see discussion in Smith, *Micah–Malachi*, 46–47).

33. On the ambiguity and likely double entendre of שְׁאֵרִית in Haggai (1:12, 14; 2:2; cf. Neh 7:71; 10:29; 11:1, 20), see Japhet, "'Remnant' in the Restoration Period," 433–36, 444–49.

34. "God's ultimate purpose in rescuing and reestablishing the people in Zion is that the rest of the world will join in the acknowledgement of Yahweh's sovereignty" (Meyers and Meyers, *Zechariah 9–14*, 492; cf. 463–64).

The Question of Remnant Theology in Second Temple Jewish Literature

Although specific texts from STJ literature will be examined in ch. 4, it is important to comment briefly on the appropriation of the remnant concept in the time leading into the NT era. In recent times several scholars, most notably E. P. Sanders, have challenged the presence of any proper remnant theology in post-biblical Jewish literature, appealing primarily to the irrevocable national election of Israel as a pillar of Judaism. In particular, Sanders argues first that the Qumran sectarians are not willing to apply the term "Israel" exclusively to themselves, even when they are able to describe non-sectarian Jews as "wicked" or "condemned."[35] Second, he asserts that the Qumran community "never applies [the title 'remnant'] to itself during its own historical existence."[36] Third, Sanders believes that the expectation of an eschatological remnant gave way to an expectation of restoration.[37] The rest of Israel would either join with the sectarians or perish, making any talk of a remnant irrelevant, since all Israel would become the "remnant."[38]

Many of Sanders's objections appear to stem from an overly rigid definition of the remnant concept, in which the term can only refer to the physical survivors of a past calamity (the "historical" remnant), or the future, purified core of renewed Israel (the "eschatological" remnant).[39] This overly binary categorization leaves no room for the well-attested concept of a righteous remnant in a time of apostasy, such as Moses or Elijah. Once this middle category is opened, it becomes plain that the Qumran sectarians did in fact see themselves as such a remnant. Sanders's student Robert Huebsch uses the phrase "proleptic representatives of the eschatological remnant" to describe the sect's self-identity, a phrase

---

35. "Even those who thought that they were the only true followers of Moses, or the only ones who knew the correct interpretation of the covenant and its laws, nevertheless did not think of God's reducing Israel to coincide with their group, but rather of the reassembly of Israel under the covenant rightly understood" (Sanders, *Jesus and Judaism*, 96). See also Sanders, *Paul, the Law, and the Jewish People*, 175–76; Sanders, *Paul and Palestinian Judaism*, 245–47; Huebsch, "'Remnant' in Qumran Literature," 349; Watts, "Remnant Theme," 112.

36. Sanders, *Jesus and Judaism*, 96.

37. Sanders, *Jesus and Judaism*, 113.

38. Sanders, *Paul and Palestinian Judaism*, 250.

39. See Watts, "Remnant Theme," 112. The prevalence of this polarization is primarily due to Hasel's influence (cf. *Remnant*, 397–402).

which, though cumbersome, is quite close to the mark.[40] The community saw themselves as members of the remnant, for they expected to be saved from the coming judgment, but not coterminous with the remnant, for they hoped that many, if not all, of their fellow Israelites would join them.[41]

In response to Sanders's specific objections, we may remark first of all that the exclusive appropriation of the title "Israel" is not necessary to identify the remnant concept.[42] In their discourse on the topic, the Qumran community seemed quite comfortable with the concept of a "'remnant' that was *not* equivalent to 'Israel.'"[43] In the interim before the final judgment, it appears that the sect still held out hope that their kinsfolk would repent, and thus they were not yet willing to deny them the title "Israel."[44]

Second, as argued above, the explicit application of terminology is not necessary for the concept to be present. It is enough to say that this group had a "sense of continuing, or conserving, the true Israelite religion" when the nation as a whole had departed from it, and hoped to be saved from the coming judgment while those who remained outside would not.[45] Furthermore, there appear to be instances in which the group does in fact apply remnant vocabulary to itself, indirectly if not directly.[46] "The protest of Sanders that these groups did not actually call themselves a remnant (which, by the way, is certainly not even correct, as far as it goes) is to look for the wrong kind of evidence," for the concept is present, even where technical vocabulary is not uniformly applied.[47]

---

40. Huebsch, "'Remnant' in Qumran Literature," 156, 460, 462. Similarly, Bryan, *Jesus and Israel's Traditions*, 117, describes the Qumran group's self-application of the remnant concept as part of a "partially realized eschatology."

41. Huebsch recognizes this category within the OT Prophets ("'Remnant' in Qumran Literature," 155).

42. To the contrary, Elijah, in his accusation that the Israelites had utterly abandoned the covenant with Yahweh, nevertheless refers to them as "the Israelites" (1 Kgs 19:10, 14). Cf. also Rom 9:6.

43. Elliott, *Survivors of Israel*, 628, emphasis original.

44. Huebsch, "'Remnant' in Qumran Literature," 463–64 writes that at the final judgment, "those Jews who have not joined the sectarian covenant [will have] renounced their place within Israel and are now counted amongst the Gentiles."

45. Elliott, *Survivors of Israel*, 242.

46. Elliott suggests in particular CD 1.4–5; 2.11–12; 3.12–15 and 4Q390 (*Survivors of Israel*, 626–29).

47. Elliott, *Survivors of Israel*, 626.

Sanders's third objection touches on a real ambiguity present in the remnant concept. By definition, remnant entails not only the removal of the majority and the remainder of a representative portion, but also at least the hope of renewal and rebirth. The greatest hope of the remnant is that it will no longer be a remnant, but rather a nation reborn. The Hebrew Scriptures contain numerous examples both of texts that focus on how few will survive (Isa 10:22; Amos 5:3) as well as those that focus on how great the nation restored from that group will be (Isa 37:31–32; 49:19–21; Mic 4:6–7). Sanders is correct that the hope of eschatological restoration eventually overshadows the concept of remnant as such. It may even be true that the Qumran documents focus more on the former than the latter. However, that is different from saying that remnant theology is irrelevant to their beliefs. Thus, while the Qumran community placed a high value on national election, they also had a deep sense of Israel's unfaithfulness to the covenant. One way in which these ideas were synthesized was in the concept of the remnant. Although this appropriation entailed an understanding that they as faithful Israelites would be the recipients of salvation while their fellow Jews were liable to judgment, there is also a sense of hope that, through them, the nation as a whole would be restored.

Summary

We have defined the OT remnant concept in terms of the *removal* of a large portion of the people, usually through divine judgment, and the gracious provision of a *remainder* as a representative portion, which holds with it the hope of *renewal* of the whole. This renewal generally has international ramifications, and in the Prophetic Books is often accompanied by a *reaching out* to the nations. This complex concept allows OT authors to explore in various ways the realities of sin, apostasy, and judgment, along with election, promise, repentance, and eschatological hope. Although OT remnant discourse may be polarizing, identifying one portion of the population with the righteous remnant and others with the apostate (e.g., Jer 24:1–10), at the same time, it always keeps in view the ultimate good (and hopeful renewal) of the whole, and in so doing avoids becoming elitist or sectarian. In other words, remnant discourse can be simultaneously "against" Israel (as she presently is) and "for" Israel (as she ought to be, will be, and presently is, at least in part). Though various

OT figures exemplify the remnant concept, from Noah to Moses and even Isaiah, it is Elijah who best epitomizes the notion of a holy remnant. Not only does he remain faithful to Yahweh during one of the nation's worst times of apostasy, but his prophetic call to repentance guarantees a purified core that will emerge after divine judgment on Israel.

3

Elijah and the Remnant in the Old Testament

THE FIGURE OF ELIJAH has captivated the imaginations of Jewish and Christian readers of Scripture for thousands of years. He is the fiery prophet, zealous for the Lord of Hosts; he is the revealer of mysteries, the mysterious guest at the Seder, and the last great prophet of the apocalypse. Elijah is associated with Phinehas for his zeal, with Enoch for his dramatic escape from death, with Moses for his prophetic boldness. Over the centuries, tradition has connected him with the resurrection of the dead, the final judgment, the opposition of the faithful against the antichrist, and the resolution of all impossible questions. With so many dramatic roles throughout the ages, it is easy to overlook one of the earliest and most notable significances attributed to him: that of the remnant. However, as we shall see, the OT depiction of Elijah portrays him as the paradigm of one who remains faithful during his earthly life, as well as the prophetic patron of the remnant in his eschatological return. The present chapter will examine this connection as it exists in three key OT texts. The Mount Carmel narrative (1 Kgs 18:16–46) shows Elijah as the last faithful prophet in an apostate nation. The Mount Horeb account (1 Kgs 19:1–18) anticipates a faithful remnant that will be gathered around the lone prophet. Finally, the conclusion of Malachi (Mal 3:23–24) speaks of Elijah's return to restore the remnant of Israel.

Elijah in 1–2 Kings: A Model Remnant Figure

The remnant theme permeates the Elijah-Elisha narratives, serving as a crucial backdrop to the life-and-death struggle between the prophets of Yahweh and those of Baal.[1] Neither system can tolerate the other; thus, Jezebel murders all of Yahweh's prophets but one (1 Kgs 18:4, 13, 22), and Elijah in turn leaves no survivors from among the prophets of Baal after the showdown at Mount Carmel (18:40; 19:1). Jezebel's subsequent threat to Elijah's life (1 Kgs 19:1) is no mere act of revenge, but functions as an attempt to remove the last living representative of Yahweh's prophets (19:10, 14). Yahweh's solution, on the one hand, is to cut down the house of Ahab and the cult of Baal with no one remaining, and, on the other, to provide a remnant of faithful Israel (19:15–18; cf. 21:21–22). As the ensuing narrative recounts Jehu's bloody coup against the house of Ahab, each episode is punctuated with the phrase "not one."[2] It is against this background of annihilation or survival that, in the two mountaintop scenes of his career—Mount Carmel and Mount Horeb—Elijah stands out as the remnant of Israel.[3] Yet more dire even than the physical annihilation he faces is the rampant apostasy and covenant infidelity that leaves him as the only faithful Israelite.

Mount Carmel (1 Kings 18:20–46)

During the years of drought, while Israel was closed off to his message and Ahab was seeking his life (1 Kgs 18:10), Elijah sojourned outside of Israel, bringing the word of the Lord instead to a foreign widow in Zarephath (17:8–24). Ironically, the Sidonian widow was more receptive to the prophet's words than his own people were. But after three years, with his characteristic abruptness (cf. v. 1), Elijah reappeared, demanding an audience with Ahab and all of Israel (18:19). In his famous contest

---

1. Müller, *Die Vorstellung vom Rest*, 55.

2. "Let no one slip out" (2 Kgs 9:15); "he left him no survivor" (10:11); "he spared none of them" (10:14); "he killed all who were left" (10:17); "let no one be missing" (10:19); "there was no one left" (10:21); "let no one escape" (10:25).

3. Although the remnant theme is woven throughout much of the Elijah-Elisha narratives, it is not our aim here to establish its explicit presence in every episode, but merely to demonstrate that these two episodes at the beginning of the prophet's career so dramatically link Elijah with the remnant concept that later allusions to the prophet—even allusions to different episodes—can, by virtue of this association, also evoke the remnant concept.

on Mount Carmel, Elijah challenged the 450 prophets of Baal (and with them, the four hundred prophets of Asherah) (vv. 19, 22) to call down fire from heaven in the presence of all Israel. We shall see that Elijah is not only a remnant of the prophets—the only prophet to survive Jezebel's massacre—but also a remnant of Israel—the only Israelite to remain faithful to Yahweh and his covenant.

Elijah's statement introducing the showdown on Mount Carmel is the first explicit identification of the prophet with the remnant: "Then Elijah said to the people, 'I, even I only, am left a prophet of the Lord [אֲנִי נוֹתַרְתִּי נָבִיא לַיהוָה לְבַדִּי]; but Baal's prophets number four hundred fifty'" (1 Kgs 18:22). The wording is dramatic, and emphatic almost to the point of redundancy, with "I" (אֲנִי) at the beginning for emphasis, and "alone" (לְבַדִּי) at the end to underscore the point.[4] He is the only surviving member of a group (the prophets of the Lord), and the majority has been killed or driven underground. While, on the one hand, it is true that Jezebel has been systematically murdering the prophets of Yahweh and Elijah has survived, numerous commentators have noted on the other hand that the prophet's statement here is not technically correct.[5] What of Obadiah's hundred, hidden away in caves? It is for this reason that Hasel argues that "it is obvious that the remnant motif appears here in connection with a religio-cultural threat and not with a politico-military one."[6] This may be an overstatement, for Jezebel's threat is certainly military (1 Kgs 18:4, 13; 19:10, 14), but Hasel is right that Elijah's isolation is seen here primarily in that he is the only remaining player on the field in the arena of religious dispute. Though Obadiah's one hundred prophets are still alive, they are nevertheless out of play. Elijah's voice alone remains.[7]

Yet Elijah is not merely the only remaining prophet; the narrative also presents him as the only remaining Israelite still faithful to Yahweh. The distinction between Elijah and the nation as a whole can be seen from the very beginning of the contest, which, properly speaking, is between

4. The LXX translates the already emphatic לְבַדִּי with the superlative μονώτατος, bringing out the emphasis on Elijah's aloneness. This also occurs in 1 Kgs 19:10, 14. See Dharamraj, *Prophet like Moses*, 67.

5. Wray Beal, *1 and 2 Kings*, 253; Cogan, *1 Kings*, 440; Glover, "Elijah versus the Narrative," 459; Gregory, "Irony," 105; Nelson, *First and Second Kings*, 126; Walsh, *1 Kings*, 273; Garsiel, *From Earth to Heaven*, 72.

6. Hasel, *Remnant*, 164; cf. Müller, *Die Vorstellung vom Rest*, 55–56.

7. In this respect, Obadiah's primary role within the narrative is to illustrate the extent of Jezebel's killings and thus underscore the danger that Elijah faces as the lone opponent of Ahab and Jezebel (Sweeney, *I and II Kings*, 222).

Elijah and the pagan prophets, with the people of Israel as spectators or referees. Yet from the beginning the true contest appears to be directed against a different set of opponents, for in his initial charge Elijah pays no heed to his actual adversaries, aiming his accusations at the Israelites instead: "How long will you go limping between two different opinions?" (v. 21). As Elijah sets the terms of the contest, the lines are drawn even more sharply, for he tells the people of Israel: "*You* call upon the name of *your* god, and I will call upon the name of the Lord" (v. 24, emphasis added). Elijah sets up the distinction between the "you" whose god is Baal and the "I" who alone stands for Yahweh. The speech is addressed to "the people" (v. 22), and the prophets of Baal are clearly identified in the third person (v. 23), so "the subject can only be the people whom Elijah was addressing."[8] Furthermore, the assembly is described as "all the people of Israel" (v. 20), so the reader is meant to envision Elijah addressing the entire nation, not just a deviant group of idolators within it. The lines of conflict are drawn: the apostate nation as a whole and Elijah alone as the remnant of the faithful.[9] The people's silence in the face of his accusation is telling: Elijah's is the only voice for Yahweh (v. 21b).[10] Though the people may have come as spectators, they find themselves brought into the contest, and in Elijah's estimation, so long as they are even open to Baal as an option, they have closed themselves off from Yahweh on the terms he requires.[11]

The most dramatic clue to Israel's condition is the altar to Yahweh, which had been "thrown down" (v. 30), apparently in a deliberate act of destruction by the Israelites (19:10, 14).[12] Stalling the action to describe the state of the altar, it is as if the narrator "slows down the pace to note its state of disrepair and describe Elijah's rebuilding of it."[13] The careful observation that he "took twelve stones, according to the number of the tribes of the sons of Jacob, to whom the word of the Lord came, saying, 'Israel shall be your name'" (18:31) connects the stone structure itself to

---

8. Cogan, *1 Kings*, 440. Contra Garsiel's suggestion that "Elijah makes a slip of the tongue" (Garsiel, *From Earth to Heaven*, 73).

9. "What is new here [within the remnant concept] is that Elijah represents . . . a remnant of one loyal to Yahweh within an apostate Israel" (Hasel, *Remnant*, 165).

10. Cf. von Rad, *Old Testament Theology*, 2:17.

11. See Fretheim, *First and Second Kings*, 102–3; Dharamraj, *Prophet like Moses*, 27.

12. Sweeney, *I and II King*, 229; Cogan, *1 Kings*, 442.

13. Dharamraj, *Prophet like Moses*, 37.

the nation of Israel and their covenant relationship with Yahweh.[14] This act of covenant renewal has strong parallels with Moses and the initial establishment of the covenant in Exodus 24.[15] Elijah's reconstruction of the altar depicts him, as the remnant and therefore Israel's true representative, restoring the covenant with Yahweh that the nation as a whole had utterly broken.[16]

Finally, Elijah's prayer serves to remind the readers of Israel's condition: "Answer me, O Lord, answer me, that this people may know that you, O Lord, are God, and that you have turned their hearts back" (1 Kgs 18:37). The final phrase "and you have turned their hearts back" (וְאַתָּה הֲסִבֹּתָ אֶת־לִבָּם אֲחֹרַנִּית) poses some difficulty but is probably best understood as saying that Israel's repentance is effected by Yahweh himself (as with the NIV's "you are turning their hearts back again").[17] Thus the prophet's verdict regarding Israel is clear: they are so far gone that only an act of God is able to bring them back. It is this task of "turning hearts" that epitomizes Elijah's role vis-à-vis a backsliding nation, both in the present narrative and in his return (cf. Mal 3:24).[18] Yahweh answers with fire from heaven (v. 38), and the people appear to have a turn of heart, proclaiming that the Lord is God (v. 39) and seizing the prophets

---

14. Dharamraj, *Prophet like Moses*, 37; Cogan, *1 Kings*, 442; Roberts, "God, Prophet, and King," 637. Garsiel, *From Earth to Heaven*, 78, suggests further that in stressing the unity of the twelve tribes, Elijah could be encouraging Ahab's alliance with Jehoshaphat, and thus with Yahweh, over against his alliance with Ethbaal and Baal.

15. Parallels include the erection of an altar and the mention of twelve stones (v. 31; cf. Exod 24:4), the prophet's address to "all the people" (v. 21; cf. Exod 24:3), the sacrifice of bulls (v. 23; cf. Exod 24:5), and eating and drinking before God on the mountaintop (v. 41; cf. Exod 24:11) (see Dharamraj, *Prophet like Moses*, 27–43). Sadly, just as the account of the golden calf (Exod 32:1–6) comes right on the heels of the covenant's ratification (Exod 24:7–8), this reestablishment under Elijah will prove to be equally short-lived.

16. See below for further elements of covenant renewal in this passage, including the sending of rain (Roberts, "God, Prophet, and King," 632–44).

17. Leithart, *1 and 2 Kings*, 136; Wray Beal, *1 and 2 Kings*, 245; cf. DeVries, *1 Kings*, 230. It is also possible that Elijah is saying that Yahweh had turned Israel's hearts away in the first place, in which case he "does not even credit Baal with enough reality to be an effective rival to Yahweh" (Walsh, *1 Kings*, 253). However, even in this case, the prophet's point would still be that only an act of Yahweh could now restore Israel's hearts again (Cogan, *1 Kings*, 443).

18. Garsiel, *From Earth to Heaven*, 26, suggests that even the title "the Tishbite" (תִּשְׁבִּי) may be intended to evoke wordplay with the Hebrew word for repentance (תְּשׁוּבָה). The proposal is intriguing, though the absence of תְּשׁוּבָה within the Elijah-Elisha narratives lessens the likelihood of deliberate wordplay.

of Baal (v. 40). This episode concludes with a covenant renewal feast on the mountaintop (v. 41; cf. Exod 24:9–11), the restoration of rain (vv. 41–45; cf. Deut 11:13–17), and Elijah miraculously running before the king like a royal herald (v. 46; cf. 1 Kgs 1:5).[19] With the covenant restored, king and prophet, heaven and earth, and the people and their God are all in right relationship. At this point, it appears that Elijah's role as the remnant has come to an end, with the hearts of the apostate nation restored. Unfortunately, this happy state is short-lived.

Mount Horeb (1 Kings 19:1–18)

Immediately after the high note at the end of ch. 18, Ahab reports everything to Jezebel, and Elijah is again in danger for his life. He flees, alone and discouraged, into the wilderness, even asking God to take his life (19:1–4). He then appears before Yahweh on Mount Horeb, expressing his grievance that the Israelites have abandoned the covenant and that he alone is faithful—the remnant of Israel (vv. 10, 14). Yet in a theophanic vision, Yahweh answers Elijah's complaint with the promise to judge Israel as a whole while sparing seven thousand faithful Israelites. This passage, then, portrays Elijah at his most isolated before speaking of the remnant that will be gathered around him. We shall first examine Elijah's claim to be the remnant of Israel (vv. 10, 14), discussing parallels with Moses and addressing potential objections to his claim. Next we will examine the divine response (vv. 15–18) and the promise of a greater remnant.

Elijah's Claim: "I Alone Am Left"

"Then the word of the Lord came to him, saying, 'What are you doing [מַה־לְּךָ֥] here, Elijah?' He answered, 'I have been very zealous for the Lord, the God of hosts; for the Israelites have forsaken [עָזְב֤וּ] your covenant, thrown down your altars, and killed your prophets with the sword. I alone am left [וָאִוָּתֵ֥ר אֲנִ֖י לְבַדִּ֑י], and they are seeking my life, to take it away'" (1 Kgs 19:9–10). The divine question in v. 9, repeated in v. 11, is frequently interpreted as a rebuke: Elijah should not be "here" but back in Israel.[20] However, more likely, the question is meant as an invitation

---

19. See Roberts, "God, Prophet, and King," 632–44; DeVries, *1 Kings*, 219; Wray Beal, *1 and 2 Kings*, 253. This anticipates his role as forerunner in Malachi.

20. Walsh, *1 Kings*, 272–73, 276–77; DeVries, *1 Kings*, 237; Fretheim, *First and*

for Elijah to state his purpose. The question מַה־לְּךָ is frequently used by kings when addressing petitioners (2 Sam 14:5; 1 Kgs 1:16; 2 Kgs 6:28; Esth 5:3), and, in each instance, the question marks the audience of the king, inviting those petitioning to state their case.[21] This fits well with the setting at Horeb, a divine courtroom of sorts where the law was first given and where the first case against Israel was tried (cf. Exod 32:7–14). "Elijah is not at Sinai to vent, but to exercise the privilege of the prophet" as a member of Yahweh's divine council.[22] Like Moses before him, Elijah stands before the Lord on the mountain of God to represent the people of Israel, only this time, he presents "evidence for the prosecution."[23] The case as Elijah presents it consists of two related complaints: Israel's apostasy and his unique position as the remnant.

Israel's national apostasy is highlighted first by Elijah's statement of his zeal: "I have been very zealous [קַנֹּא קִנֵּאתִי] for the Lord, the God of Hosts; for [כִּי] the Israelites have forsaken your covenant . . ." (vv. 10, 14). This is not a boast, but rather a complaint about the service that has been required of him because of (note the causal use of כִּי) Israel's threefold sin.[24] Throughout the OT, the zeal of God and his prophets is incited when the nation abandons Yahweh for other gods (Exod 20:5; 34:14; cf. Deut 32:16, 21; Ps 78:58), to the effect that to speak of zeal is almost to imply apostasy.[25] The specific sins that prompted the prophet's zeal are then rehearsed in rapid succession: "The Israelites have forsaken your covenant, thrown down your altars, and killed your prophets with the sword" (vv. 10, 14). The choice of these three is revealing, for though Elijah might well have

---

Second Kings, 109; Garsiel, *From Earth to Heaven*, 93; Reiss, "Elijah the Zealot," 174–80; Nelson, *First and Second Kings*, 128; Cogan, *1 Kings*, 456–57; Childs, "Elijah Narratives," 135; Gregory, "Irony," 146.

21. Dharamraj, *Prophet like Moses*, 53. See also Gen 21:17; Josh 15:18; Judg 1:14; though cf. Judg 18:3.

22. Leithart, *1 and 2 Kings*, 141. See also Thiel, "'Es ist genug,'" 202–3. Garsiel, *From Earth to Heaven*, 93, 96, though he misses the judicial implications of the divine question, notes that Elijah chose Horeb rather than the Jerusalem temple because the former was the appropriate place to present his case against the Israelites.

23. Leithart, *1 and 2 Kings*, 141.

24. See Dharamraj, *Prophet like Moses*, 62–65. This causal use of כִּי is further confirmed by the use of ὅτι in the LXX.

25. Elijah is frequently associated with Phinehas in later Jewish tradition, since the latter was also known for zeal (קִנְאָה) prompted by Israel's widespread sin and idolatry (cf. Num 25:1–9, 11, 13). See esp. Poirier, "Endtime Return of Elijah," 23–35; Öhler, *Elia im Neuen Testament*, 21–25; Dharamraj, *Prophet like Moses*, 57–60.

listed such equally serious sins as worshiping Jeroboam's golden calves, pursuing unlawful foreign alliances, building a temple and altar for Baal worship, and erecting Asherah poles (1 Kgs 16:31–33), none of these are included. For him, the most serious concern is not idolatry per se, but the issue that lay at the root of it: Israel's utter abandonment of Yahweh. All three items listed—the covenant, the altars, and the prophets—represent links between Yahweh and his people that Israel has systematically broken. With the covenant broken through idolatry, the cult abolished, and the prophetic guild all but annihilated, Elijah stands as the last remaining link between Yahweh and an apostate Israel, a link which they are now attempting to sever.[26] "Elijah's most grievous plaint was his conviction that the cause of Jahwism was utterly lost in Israel."[27]

It is against this backdrop of Israel's apostasy that Elijah stands out in stark relief as the remnant: "I alone am left [וָאִוָּתֵר אֲנִי לְבַדִּי], and they are seeking my life, to take it away" (vv. 10, 14). As in 18:22, the positioning of the pronoun (אֲנִי) is emphatic, as is the use of "alone" (לְבַדִּי). Furthermore, his verbatim repetition of the claim in v. 14 gives it still greater emphasis.[28] The verb (יתר) refers particularly to what remains after a removal: after the nation as a whole has turned away from Yahweh, Elijah remains as the only Israelite still faithful to the covenant. The national scope of Elijah's complaint—that he is not merely the last of the prophets but the last faithful Israelite—is further substantiated by the divine response in v. 18, in which Elijah's complaint of isolation is answered by the promise of seven thousand faithful Israelites.[29]

Parallels with Exodus 24–34

As we have already noted briefly, Moses's own dialogue with Yahweh on Mount Horeb presents him as a remnant figure (Exod 32:10), and at this point it will be helpful to note the many parallels between our

---

26. Cf. Thiel, "Es ist genug," 207–8.

27. Von Rad, *Old Testament Theology*, 2:21.

28. It is best to understand v. 14 as a repetition for dramatic emphasis, a literary device frequently employed in the Elijah-Elisha cycles (Carlson, "Élie à l'Horeb," 421; DeVries, *1 Kings*, 236; cf. Sweeney, *I and II Kings*, 232), rather than as obstinacy on Elijah's part, as is often asserted (*pace* Cogan, *1 Kings*, 457; Gregory, "Irony," 134; Walsh, *1 Kings*, 277; Nelson, *First and Second Kings*, 125; Robinson, "Elijah at Horeb," 522).

29. Leithart, *1 and 2 Kings*, 142; Hasel, *Remnant*, 168; Thiel, "Es ist genug," 203; *pace* Cogan, *1 Kings*, 453.

present passage and Exodus 24–34.[30] The general progression of events is similar in both passages: a covenant feast (1 Kgs 18:41–42; cf. Exod 24:1–11) followed by apostasy (1 Kgs 19:1, 10; cf. Exod 32:1–6), then prophetic dialogue (1 Kgs 19:10–18; cf. Exod 32:7–14; 33:12–16), and finally a mountaintop theophany (1 Kgs 19:11–13; cf. Exod 33:18–34:9). The setting is particularly striking, for 1 Kings 19 is the only OT narrative outside of the Pentateuch to occur at Horeb. Additional parallel elements include the wilderness (1 Kgs 19:4; cf. Exod 19:2), miraculous provision of bread (1 Kgs 19:5–7; cf. Exod 16:1–36), a forty-day fast (1 Kgs 19:8; cf. Exod 24:18; 34:28), and a request for death (1 Kgs 19:4; cf. Exod 32:32). Even the two theophanic accounts are connected by such details as their occurring early in the morning (1 Kgs 19:9; cf. Exod 34:4), the prophets' hiding in a cave or crag (1 Kgs 19:9, 13; cf. Exod 33:22), covering their faces (1 Kgs 19:13; cf. Exod 34:8), and dialoguing with Yahweh about Israel's sinful state (1 Kgs 19:10, 14; cf. Exod 34:8). Clearly, 1 Kings 19 is meant to be read in light of Moses's Sinai experience.

Most significantly, Moses also stands out as a remnant figure when on the mountain Yahweh tells him, "Now let me alone, so that my wrath may burn hot against them and I may consume them; and of you I will make a great nation" (Exod 32:10; cf. Deut 9:14).[31] Generations before Elijah's day, Moses too stood before God as the only person faithful to him while the rest of the nation fell under his wrath because of outright apostasy and idolatry. Though threatening to wipe out Israel as a whole, Yahweh offered to preserve Moses as the representative through which the nation would be reborn into "a great nation" (Exod 32:10), thus maintaining his promise to the patriarchs and extending the hope of renewal. Even with a remnant of one man, God can still make Abraham into "a great nation" (Gen 12:2).[32] Happily, Moses is only temporarily cast in the role of remnant, for Yahweh relents and has mercy after he appeals not

---

30. See Niehaus, *God at Sinai*, 245–47; Dharamraj, *Prophet like Moses*, 42; Carlson, "Élie à l'Horeb," 430–37; Cogan, *1 Kings*, 456–57; Walsh, *1 Kings*, 286; Childs, "Elijah Narratives," 135; cf. Garsiel, *From Earth to Heaven*, 178–83; Thiel, "Es ist genug," 209–10.

31. Huebsch, "'Remnant' in Qumran Literature," 61. See also Propp, *Exodus 19–40*, 554; Dozeman, *Exodus*, 705–6; Childs, *Exodus*, 567–68.

32. Gen 22:17 appears throughout the OT in connection to the remnant, as an appeal for the preservation of at least a remnant (Gen 32:12; cf. vv. 8, 11), a warning that Israel could be reduced to a remnant (Isa 10:22–23), and a word of hope for the restoration of the remnant (Isa 51:1–3; Hos 1:10). See also Gen 15:5 in Exod 32:13.

only to the promises to the patriarchs, but also to Yahweh's glory among the nations (Exod 32:12–13).[33]

In light of this parallel, Elijah's role as Israel's remnant becomes clearer. Like Moses before him, Elijah fills the role of the faithful remnant of Israel. Like Moses, he stands alone before God on Mount Horeb, the divine courtroom. However, the situation is far more precarious now. When Elijah returns to this same mountain under the same circumstances, it is not as their advocate but as their prosecutor, as if to say that in all these centuries the situation has only gotten worse. It is no longer the nation of Israel that is under threat of immediate annihilation, but Elijah himself, and with him the last vestige of faithful Israel.[34] The question is not whether or not Israel will be spared physically, but whether or not they can ever be brought back to the Lord. What Yahweh once delayed in his mercy must now finally come about. Yahweh's solution exemplifies that same mix of judgment and mercy by which he identified himself earlier to Moses (Exod 34:6–7). Elijah will initiate a complex series of international upheavals by which Yahweh will send devastating judgment on Israel for their sins. But in so doing, he will bring about the renewal of Israel.[35]

Possible Objections: Elijah as a Reliable Figure[36]

Modern commentaries raise several objections to our claim that Elijah is presented on Mount Horeb as the remnant of faithful Israel. Most of

---

33. This connection between the remnant and the faithfulness of God—and the remnant and the nations—will reemerge when we examine Romans 11 in the next chapter.

34. In fact, the situation is so dire that some question whether Elijah can rightly be called a remnant at all, since at this point he is "by no means safe" (Dharamraj, *Prophet like Moses*, 131). However, the remnant is never guaranteed preservation from danger or persecution, only survival (cf. Gen 32:8; Ezra 9:13–15; Isa 1:9, 19–20; Jer 21:7; Amos 6:9; 9:1). Though discussing the concept as it is found in Qumran rather than the OT, Elliott notes that the remnant "will certainly not be removed from the scene of battle, or avoid all suffering . . . yet they shall be saved from slaughter" (*Survivors of Israel*, 629).

35. Dharamraj remarks aptly that it is "the very penalty that awaits Israel that performs as the instrument by which true Israel will be saved" (*Prophet like Moses*, 134).

36. A reliable character is one whose views represent those of the implied author. Put simply, a reader can trust that what reliable characters say is an accurate portrayal of the narrative world (see Tannehill, *Narrative Unity*, 1:7–8). This does not necessarily mean that the character is infallible, as in the case of Zechariah (Luke 1:18–20) (cf.

these objections are related to the prophet's reliability at this point in the narrative. Contemporary scholarship tends to portray the events of ch. 19 in predominantly unsympathetic terms, portraying Elijah as sulking in the wilderness, manic-depressive, and egotistical. Many see his claim in 19:10 to be the only faithful Israelite to be inaccurate and self-centered, pointing either to Obadiah (18:3–4) or to Israel's apparent repentance (18:39) in the previous chapter. Furthermore, his repetition of the claim verbatim in v. 14 is seen as stubborn and rebellious.[37] If Elijah's claim is fallacious, or if he himself has fallen out of God's favor by his actions, this would seriously undermine his role as a remnant figure. However, we will argue for a sympathetic reading of the text which, though not denying the human weakness and emotions that the prophet surely experienced, still sees him as a faithful and reliable figure in the narrative.

First of all, Elijah, and in particular Elijah's words, have been portrayed as reliable in every respect up until this point. He is called "a man of God," in whose mouth is "the word of the Lord" and "truth" (1 Kgs 17:24), and so we are given every reason to trust what he says. This impression is further confirmed in the subsequent narratives, in which it is reiterated that his words are still reliable (2 Kgs 9:36; 10:10, 17).[38] Given the particular emphasis on the truth and power of Elijah's word throughout his life, we ought to expect that, when he says, "I alone am left," this is true in at least some sense. Furthermore, we must observe that Elijah's complaints regarding Israel's apostasy and his own state of isolation are more justified than most contemporary scholars give him credit for. Israel had in fact done everything of which he accused them (1 Kgs 19:10, 14). That there was apparently some measure of repentance after the fact

---

1:22). See also Booth, *Rhetoric of Fiction*, 169–210.

37. Nelson's comments are illustrative: "Elijah forgets Obadiah's prophets; he ignores the great conversion on Carmel. Jezebel disappears as a villain and the whole people take her place. The burned-out prophet can see only the darkest side of the situation as he voices his ego-centered complaint to God (cf. the grammatical emphasis on 'I' in vv. 10, 14)" (Nelson, *First and Second Kings*, 126). See also Reiss, "Elijah the Zealot," 174–80; Hauser, "Yahweh versus Death," 67–69; Gregory, "Irony," 105; Walsh, *1 Kings*, 273, 289; Cogan, *1 Kings*, 453; Wray Beal, *1 and 2 Kings*, 253; Glover, "Elijah versus the Narrative," 457–60; Garsiel, *From Earth to Heaven*, 95–102.

38. Throughout the Elijah narratives, there is a special emphasis on the word of the Lord through Elijah. See esp. 1 Kgs 17:1, 2, 5, 8, 16, 24; 18:1, 31; 19:9; 21:17, 28; 2 Kgs 1:17; 9:36; 10:10, 17.

may make the timing of the prophet's complaint surprising, but it does not change the essence of it.[39]

Second, Elijah is never rebuked or corrected for his repeated claim of being alone (1 Kgs 19:10, 14).[40] Far from being rebuked, the prophet is answered: the divine response in 1 Kgs 19:15–18 addresses point for point Elijah's complaint. Due to the abandoned covenant, Yahweh would abandon Israel to foreign enemies (cf. 2 Kgs 8:12; 10:32; 13:3); because they tore down Yahweh's altars, he would send Jehu to tear down the altars of Baal (2 Kgs 10:26–28); in place of the slain prophets, God would send Elisha, who would in turn mentor the prophetic guild (cf. 2 Kgs 2:15); and because Elijah has served zealously alone, he would be joined by seven thousand.[41] The mention of the seven thousand is not a rebuke, for neither Elijah nor the readers have any prior knowledge of them, but rather a promise.[42] Were a rebuke intended, an appeal to Obadiah and his hundred prophets would be a much more logical choice. Furthermore, that Yahweh would offer to send such severe judgment on the nation seems to indicate that, even if Elijah has used some hyperbole in stating his case, his basic complaint still stands: he is the only one left opposing a wicked king and an apostate nation. "Even if commentators do not, Yahweh agrees with Elijah's assessment of Israel's condition."[43]

Third, the parallels in this passage between Elijah and Moses, outlined above, do not give any indication of a negative portrayal of the prophet.[44] To the contrary, Elijah is presented as a prophet like Moses, who must be listened to (Deut 18:15). Although there are points of difference between the two mountaintop scenes, the contrast is not strong enough to present Elijah as a negative foil to Moses. Elijah's complaint about the people's apostasy and his own aloneness, for example, need not be seen as a sign of the prophet's vindictiveness in contrast to Moses's

---

39. Leithart, *1 and 2 Kings*, 142; DeVries, *1 Kings*, 237.

40. Leithart, *1 and 2 Kings*, 142.

41. Niehaus, *God at Sinai*, 246.

42. "The alignment of opposites is not Elijah's 'I alone' with the 'seven thousand,' as most commentators suggest. In the context of covenant, so crucial to this passage, the contrast is between the covenant-breakers and the seven thousand covenant-keepers" (Dharamraj, *Prophet like Moses*, 135). Pace Childs, "Elijah Narratives," 135.

43. Leithart, *1 and 2 Kings*, 142.

44. Dharamraj, *Prophet like Moses*, 67–68; Sweeney, *I and II Kings*, 232; Niehaus, *God at Sinai*, 245–49.

compassion as their advocate.[45] Rather, his complaints are modeled after Moses's own complaints regarding those same two issues (cf. Exod 32:31; 33:12), and his despair is more likely an indication of the depths to which Israel had fallen in his day.[46] Exodus 32–34 paints Moses in particularly glowing terms, and the comparison cannot help but be flattering for Elijah.[47]

Fourth, there are hints that the apparent repentance of ch. 18 was only temporary.[48] The climax of the present narrative, in which "the Lord was not in the fire" but chose instead to reveal himself through a "voice" (1 Kgs 19:11–13), suggests that a conversion based on heavenly fire alone, with no real accompaniment of the prophetic word, cannot last.[49] Throughout the Elijah narratives, miraculous acts are meant to point to the *word* of the Lord through his prophet (see esp. 1 Kgs 17:23–24). Conversion based on miracles alone, unsupported by the prophetic word, die out with the last embers of the heavenly fire. It may even be that the parallel structure with Exodus 24–32, in which Israel's apostasy after the covenant feast is plainly dramatized, may be sufficient grounds to infer a similar progression in this case as well.[50] Dramatic as the contest at Carmel was, Elijah's victory—and Israel's profession—was short-lived and superficial.[51]

---

45. Contra Garsiel, *From Earth to Heaven*, 182; Gregory, "Irony," 146.

46. Dharamraj, *Prophet like Moses*, 69–70; Niehaus, *God at Sinai*, 245–46; von Rad, *Old Testament Theology*, 2:21. Cf. Wray Beal, *1 and 2 Kings*, 252–53. Nor is the fact that Yahweh appeared to Elijah in a whisper rather than in fire make him less worthy a prophet than Moses (cf. Exod 33:22) (*pace* Childs, "Elijah Narratives," 135; Cogan, *1 Kings*, 456–57).

47. Dharamraj, *Prophet like Moses*, 68.

48. See esp. Fretheim, *First and Second Kings*, 108, Rice, *Nations under God*, 154.

49. Thus von Rad, *Old Testament Theology*, 2:19, aptly states regarding this passage: "With an Old Testament theophany, everything depends on the pronouncement: the phenomena which accompany it are always merely accessories." See also Leithart, *1 and 2 Kings*, 142; House, *1, 2 Kings*, 223–24; Cross, *Canaanite Myth*, 193–94.

50. Dharamraj, *Prophet like Moses*, 68.

51. Walsh, *1 Kings*, 286–87, makes the appealing suggestion that the conversion was limited in scope, rather than duration. Pointing to parallels with the Levites in Exodus 24, he argues that the Israelites on Carmel represent a small portion of the nation, while Israel as a whole was still in rebellion. Certainly only a portion of the nation could be present on the mountain at one time. However, the narrator's repeated use of "all Israel" and "all the people" (1 Kgs 18:19, 20, 21, 30, 39) indicates that this group was meant to represent the entire nation.

Finally, the role of Ahab is often overlooked in the matter of Israel's return to apostasy in ch. 19. Throughout the book of Kings, a key principle at work is that the king represents the people. The monarch is uniquely the "representative of the people before God," so that it can be said that "the sins of the king . . . are the sins of the people."[52] We have already seen this connection presented in the previous scene, in which we stated that Ahab's ascending Mount Carmel to "eat and drink" (18:41–46) serves as a covenant renewal feast in which the king, representing the people, renews Israel's covenant with Yahweh.[53] If Ahab is seen so clearly to represent Israel at the end of ch. 18, is it any wonder that the representation should continue in the very next verse? The king's regression to Jezebel and thus to Baal is also the regression of the people (1 Kgs 19:1). Ahab is consistently a weak and wavering character, fluctuating between Elijah and Jezebel, wickedness and repentance (1 Kgs 18:19–20, 41–46; 21:27–29; cf. 1 Kgs 19:1; 21:5–7).[54] This same ambivalence that characterizes their head is also the chief fault of the people, for Elijah accuses them first and foremost of "limping with two different opinions" (1 Kgs 18:21). Whether the people's repentance crumbles at the same time as Ahab's, or whether their return to apostasy is more gradual, they share in the failure of their king. Thus when Jezebel, under royal authority, threatens Elijah's life, he can rightly say that *Israel* seeks his life, to take it away (1 Kgs 19:10, 14).

In conclusion, the text of 1 Kings 19 presents Elijah as a reliable character. This is the presentation of Elijah in the passages before and after this scene, and as we shall see in the next chapter, this is the reception he has received from Jewish and Christian interpreters for centuries. Perhaps he was weak and discouraged in the wilderness, certainly he was lonely and scared, but he was faithful, and his despair was rooted not in egotism or misguided perfectionism but in sorrow for his people. Elijah recognizes the fact that he has failed to bring about lasting change in an apostate people, that he is the last remaining link between Yahweh and Israel, and that their attempt to take his life is tantamount to severing that last tie.

---

52. Gray, *I and II Kings*, 38.

53. Roberts, "God, Prophet, and King."

54. Walsh, *1 Kings*, 363. Interestingly, this ambivalence is even more pronounced in the LXX. See esp. LXX 1 Kgs 20:16, in which he tears his clothes before claiming Naboth's vineyard, and LXX 1 Kgs 20:25, which calls him "foolishly" (ματαίως) deceived by Jezebel (cf. MT 1 Kgs 21:25).

The Divine Response (1 Kings 19:15–18)

Elijah has presented his evidence for the prosecution and rested his case. He has not proposed a judgment but leaves it for the Judge of heaven and earth to decide what to do about Israel. The divine decision shows the paradoxical blend of judgment and mercy characteristic of the remnant theme: Israel will be destroyed for apostasy, yet in spite of, or even through that judgment, Israel will also be spared by means of a remnant.[55] "Whoever escapes from the sword of Hazael, Jehu shall kill; and whoever escapes from the sword of Jehu, Elisha shall kill. Yet I will leave [הִשְׁאַרְתִּי] seven thousand in Israel, all the knees that have not bowed to Baal, and every mouth that has not kissed him" (1 Kgs 19:17–18).[56] The remnant theme is undeniably present in this verse: the removal of the apostate whole is clear in the threefold swords of divine judgment, the remainder of the few is likewise explicit in the seven thousand, and the hope of renewal is implicit in the cultic fidelity of the remnant as well as in the ordination of Elisha as a prophetic successor.[57] Furthermore, the divine use of שאר approaches technical usage.[58] Yahweh would preserve a portion from his fierce judgment on Israel—a remnant chosen by his grace, yet characterized by their covenant faithfulness to him.

Implications

This passage, famously called "the *locus classicus* for the promise of the remnant," connects Elijah with a future, righteous remnant of Israel, thereby creating several noteworthy developments within the remnant

---

55. Moberly's comments on Exodus 34 are equally apropos here: "that same factor, the sin of Israel, which causes Yahweh's wrath, also brings about mercy" (Moberly, *Mountain of God*, 89; see also Carlson, "Élie à l'Horeb," 437).

56. LXX has "you will leave [καταλείψεις]," giving Elijah direct agency in the creation of this future remnant. While it is true that Elijah is ultimately responsible for this remnant, this reading is most likely a later corruption (Stanley, "Significance of Romans 11:3–4," 43–54). On similarities between Elijah's seven thousand and the Levites who gather around Moses (Exod 32:26–29) see esp. Childs, *Exodus*, 563, 569; Moberly, *Mountain of God*, 55.

57. Note again the recurring motif of refining the remnant through three successive waves of judgment (cf. Ezek 5:1–4; 12:16; Zech 13:8–9).

58. With Yahweh as the subject, this verb in the Hiphil stem almost always indicates a technical application of the remnant concept (Hausmann, *Israels Rest*, 206).

concept in the OT.⁵⁹ First of all, Elijah, as the central remnant figure, has a polarizing effect on Israel. After his emergence, Israel is no longer able to waver (cf. 1 Kgs 18:21) but must choose between Yahweh and Baal. This drawing of lines enables the prophet to stand against his kinsfolk as their accuser while at the same time to be working for the good of his nation and its renewal through the establishment of the remnant. Second, as was the case with Moses, the remnant concept can be narrowed to a single person, but it is now also seen to be by its nature dynamic. Elijah is identified personally and uniquely with the remnant, which is why later tradition associates him with the gathering of the eschatological remnant, yet a remnant of one cannot exist for long, and so first he is joined by Elisha, who is heir to his spirit (2 Kgs 2:9, 15; cf. Sir 48:12) and carries out his calling as "the extended arm of Elijah."⁶⁰ Around this nucleus would eventually be gathered seven thousand yet-unidentified Israelites, faithful to Yahweh, who would form the core of a renewed nation, which would in turn have international implications. Finally, this passage speaks of a future, righteous remnant, to be spared from judgment that is yet to come.⁶¹ This anticipates further development in the prophetic writings as well as in later tradition, in which the remnant can be identified more clearly along ethical or cultic lines than in terms of mere survival.⁶² The hope for a future, righteous group would come to take shape as the eschatological remnant, and it is with good reason that the figure who would come to represent this group was none other than Elijah (Mal 3:23–24).

---

59. Jeremias, "Der Gedanke,'" 184.

60. Carlson, "Élie à l'Horeb," 438–39 (my translation). See also Fretheim, *First and Second Kings*, 110–11. On the close identification of Elisha with his master, note that Jehu recognized that the message he had received from Elisha via a messenger was ultimately attributable to Elijah (2 Kgs 9:36; 10:10, 17; cf. 9:6–10). So too, in later tradition they were recognized as "two facets of a composite prophetic mission" (Danker, *Jesus and the New Age*, 161).

61. The development in "Elijah's use of the concept is that he refers it to preservation from calamities which are still to come and which Jahweh himself is to bring about" (von Rad, *Old Testament Theology*, 2:22; see also Hasel, *Remnant*, 171).

62. See esp. Hasel, *Remnant*, viii.

Turning the Hearts of Israel (Malachi 3:23–24)

Outside of the Historical Books, the Hebrew Scriptures mention Elijah only at the end of Malachi (Mal 3:23–24).[63] These two seemingly obscure verses, however, reverberate through later Jewish and Christian writings, establishing the expectation for Elijah's eschatological return. In his characteristic abruptness (cf. esp. 1 Kgs 17:1), Elijah appears on the scene as the zealous reformer, radically opposing sin and corruption, demanding covenant faithfulness, and staying divine judgment: "Lo, I will send [הִנֵּה אָנֹכִי שֹׁלֵחַ] you the prophet Elijah before the great and terrible day of the Lord comes. He will turn [הֵשִׁיב] the hearts of parents to their children [אָבוֹת עַל־בָּנִים] and the hearts of children to their parents, so that I will not come and strike the land with a curse [חֵרֶם]" (Mal 3:22–24).[64]

Malachi 3:23–24 in Context

In the present form of the book, the introduction of Elijah in 3:23 is clearly meant to be a further identification of the "messenger" in 3:1, as indicated by the repetition of the introductory formula.[65] "Behold, I am sending [הִנְנִי שֹׁלֵחַ] my messenger [מַלְאָכִי] to prepare the way before me. And the Lord [הָאָדוֹן] whom you seek will suddenly come [יָבוֹא] to his temple. And the angel of the covenant [מַלְאַךְ הַבְּרִית] in whom you

---

63. On the placement and function of these verses within Malachi and within the Minor Prophets, see esp. Hill, *Malachi*, 363–66; Assis, "Moses, Elijah and the Messianic Hope," 207–9; Kessler, *Maleachi*, 303–4; Meinhold, *Maleachi*, 403–5; Glazier-McDonald, *Malachi*, 241–45; Sweeney, *Twelve Prophets*, 2:713–14, 746–50; Sweeney, "Sequence and Interpretation," 49–64. Regardless of their origin, these verses in their present form are woven thematically and verbally into the rest of Malachi, so that they are clearly meant to be read within the context of that book, which is certainly the way the Luke read them (Luke 1:17, 76; cf. Mal 3:1, 23) (cf. Childs, *Old Testament as Scripture*, 498).

64. Unless otherwise specified, versification in this section will follow the MT, as found in BHS. The EVV notate the last six verses of Malachi as a fourth chapter, while the LXX transposes Mal 3:22 MT to the end (v. 24), presumably to end the book with an invitation to Torah rather than a threat of the *herem*. Thus Mal 3:23–24 MT corresponds to Mal 4:5–6 EV and Mal 3:22–23 LXX. See Kessler, *Maleachi*, 302; Petersen, *Malachi*, 227–28; cf. Jones, *Formation of the Twelve*, 122–23.

65. Hill, *Malachi*, 383; Kessler, *Maleachi*, 308; Childs, *Old Testament as Scripture*, 495–98; Assis, "Moses, Elijah, and the Messianic Hope," 214–15; Malchow, "Messenger of the Covenant," 252–55; Glazier-McDonald, *Malachi*, 135; Petterson, *Malachi*, 362; Smith, *Micah–Malachi*, 342; cf. Snyman, "Once Again," 1042.

delight—indeed, he is coming [בָּא], says Yahweh of hosts" (3:1).⁶⁶ The identification of the three figures named in 3:1 is a notorious interpretive crux for this book.⁶⁷ However, when connected to v. 23, it is safe to identify "my messenger [מַלְאָכִי]" who is sent (שֹׁלֵחַ) as Elijah or an Elijianic figure—a prophetic forerunner of the "Lord."⁶⁸ The "Lord [הָאָדוֹן]" who "will come [יָבוֹא]" is almost unanimously understood to be Yahweh, with the "angel of the covenant [מַלְאַךְ הַבְּרִית]" who "is coming [בָּא]" likely the angel of Yahweh or a similar figure.⁶⁹ The Elijianic messenger's task of preparing the way entails "removing the 'obstacles' of self-interest, spiritual lethargy, and evil behavior embedded in the people of God" (cf. v. 5).⁷⁰ In this way, the prophet draws on wording and imagery from Isa 40:3, though inverting its optimism.⁷¹ In its Isaianic context, "preparing the way" for Yahweh is primarily an image of hope, anticipating a new exodus, but here it will first of all mean removing the wicked from among God's people.⁷² This verse is also commonly seen to be a reworking of Exod 23:20, in which Yahweh promises to send an angel ahead of the Israelites into Canaan who will assist in driving out the inhabitants and their idolatry (Exod 23:22–24; cf. 33:2).⁷³ On the one hand, this connection offers hope to the Israelite community: as in the days of the Exodus, Yahweh's presence, mediated through his messenger, will be with his

---

66. My translation. Because later echoes of this verse often depend not only on the figures named but also on the verbs used of them (esp. 4Q558; Luke 3:16; 7:20, 27), we will include the verbs in our discussion here and throughout.

67. See esp. the history of interpretation in Snyman, "Once Again," 1033–37; cf. Hill, *Malachi*, 286–89.

68. Meinhold, *Maleachi*, 417; Kessler, *Maleachi*, 309.

69. Glazier-McDonald, *Malachi*, 133; Kessler, *Maleachi*, 230–31; Smith, *Micah-Malachi*, 328; Hill, *Malachi*, 268–69; Verhoef, *Haggai and Malachi*, 288–89; Snyman, "Once Again," 1037; Malchow, "Messenger of the Covenant," 253. The "angel/messenger of the covenant" is by far the most difficult of the three titles to establish, but the case is strongest to make the identification with the "angel of the Lord" who will accompany and act for Yahweh in the day of his appearance (cf. Zech 3:11–12).

70. Hill, *Malachi*, 267.

71. "And he will prepare the way before me [וּפִנָּה־דֶרֶךְ לְפָנָי]" (Mal 3:1) // "Prepare the way of the Lord [פַּנּוּ דֶּרֶךְ יְהוָה]" (Isa 40:3).

72. Juncker, "Angel of the Lord," 171. See also Petersen, *Malachi*, 209–10; Bascom, "Preparing the Way, 227; Pao, *Isaianic New Exodus*, 42.

73. Smith, *Micah–Malachi*, 328; Petterson, *Malachi*, 362; Kessler, *Maleachi*, 228; Hill, *Malachi*, 265. *Pace* Snyman, "Once Again," 1042, who holds that the context of Exod 23:20 is too different to be of relevance.

people.⁷⁴ On the other hand, this "coming" will be scarcely sufferable, for it will be one of refining fire (v. 2). This time it is not the Canaanites, whom Yahweh had originally promised to blot out without a remnant (cf. Exod 23:23; Deut 7:20), but the post-exilic Judahites themselves whose moral corruption has placed them in danger of total annihilation. As we shall see below, the Elijianic messenger will embody this tension between hope and judgment by preparing a righteous remnant to be saved before the great and terrible day of Yahweh.⁷⁵

The Remnant Theme in Malachi 3:23-24

Elijah's task in preparing the remnant is seen most clearly in what he comes to avoid. The alternative to his return is *herem* (חֵרֶם), a decree of "total destruction" (Mal 3:24). By its very definition, the "total destruction" of the ban implies the absence of a remnant (cf. Deut 2:34; Josh 10:28, 37, 39, 40). As with Moses and Elijah on Mount Horeb (cf. Exod 32:10; 1 Kgs 19:14), the postexilic prophet saw his community as in imminent danger of total destruction. The only hope for avoiding *herem*— and thus the only hope for a remnant—is Elijah's return "before the great and terrible day of the Lord [יוֹם יְהוָה]" (Mal 3:23).

The reference to "day of the Lord" also captures this tension between judgment and salvation inherent in the remnant concept. A recurring theme, especially in the Book of the Twelve, the phrase is used both to describe judgment against Israel (e.g., Amos 5:18-20; Joel 1:15) and vindication of Israel (Joel 3:14 [MT 4:14]; Obad 15).⁷⁶ Earlier in Malachi "the day" is described as one in which the wicked of the land will be burned up, with "neither root nor branch" left to them (3:19)—that is, without a remnant. Nevertheless, this day is not one of indiscriminate judgment against Israel, but rather a day of cleansing fire (3:1-2, 19), in which clear distinction will be made between the righteous and the wicked (3:18), and a righteous remnant of those who fear Yahweh will arise, preserved from the judgment of the wicked majority (vv. 20-21).⁷⁷ As the appendix

---

74. Kessler, *Maleachi*, 228.
75. See esp. House, *Unity of the Twelve*, 159.
76. See House, *Unity of the Twelve*, 208-9; Nogalski, "Recurring Themes," 125-36. See also Nogalski, "Day(s) of YHWH," 192-213; Hoffmann, "Day of the Lord," 37-50; Ishai-Rosenboim, "YOM H," 395-401; Everson, "Days of Yahweh," 329-37; Bakon, "Day of the Lord," 149-56.
77. This shift in focus to the righteous remnant rather than the nation as a whole

to the book makes clear, the only hope for Israel to be preserved from total destruction on this "great and terrible day" is for Elijah to precede it and gather this righteous remnant.[78]

The manner in which Elijah is to gather such a remnant is broadly one of repentance and reconciliation (v. 24), though its precise nature is variously understood.[79] Some commentators see Elijah's task as one of resolving intergenerational strife, perhaps the familial strife described in Mic 7:6, although this theme is not taken up anywhere else in the book of Malachi.[80] Others see the "fathers" as metonymic for the covenant relationship that the previous generation enjoyed with Yahweh, although 3:7 indicates that even they had not kept the covenant.[81] Finally, it is possible that "parents" and "children" form a merism to represent a cross-section of society, in which case what is in view is the return of "all manner of people" to Yahweh (cf. Joel 2:28).[82] By this line of interpretation, the preposition על is best rendered not as "to" but as "with" or "in addition to."[83] This last interpretation best aligns with the themes of the book as

---

is considered Malachi's unique contribution to the Day of Yahweh theme (Nogalski, "Recurring Themes," 127; see also Hill, *Malachi*, 290–91).

78. See esp. Glazier-McDonald, *Malachi*, 260.

79. Even ancient interpretations of this verse are varied, as evidenced by the several different renderings of the second line (cf. Meinhold, *Maleachi*, 423–27; Kessler, *Maleachi*, 311). Though most ancient versions follow the MT, the LXX has "and the heart of a person to his neighbor" (NETS) for the second line. Alluding to this verse, Sirach agrees with the first line, but reads "and to restore the tribes of Jacob" (Sir 48:10) in the second. The allusion in Luke 1:17 has "and the disobedient to the wisdom of the righteous." The MT reading is likely original, as the reading that best accounts for the others (though cf. Jones, *Formation of the Twelve*, 120–25). Nevertheless, the later interpretations give us helpful insight into what Elijah's ministry would be thought to entail, an issue we shall discuss in the next chapter.

80. Kessler, *Maleachi*, 310–11; Smith, *Micah–Malachi*, 341; Koet, "Elijah as Reconciler," 173–90; cf. Glazier-McDonald, *Malachi*, 254–55; Sweeney, *Twelve Prophets*, 749–50.

81. Verhoef, *Malachi*, 342. See also Hill, *Malachi*, 387–88. Petersen, *Malachi*, 231, presents the converse of this view, in which the present generation is no longer suffering for the sins of their fathers and is thus able to relate to their ancestors in a more positive way.

82. Glazier-McDonald, *Malachi*, 256–57; Stuart, "Malachi," 3:1395. In a similar vein, Petterson, *Malachi*, 386, understands this verse as describing the return to Yahweh of the present generation, and the resultant unity with future generations.

83. See *HALOT*, s.v. "על" (6b–d). See esp. Gen 32:12 (EV 32:11) "he may come and kill us all, the mothers with the children [אֵם עַל־בָּנִים]." See also Exod 35:22; Num 31:8; Hos 10:14; Amos 3:15.

a whole, and it is, of course, this vision of national repentance that lies at the heart of all three views, for "the restoration of human relationships is but the by-product of the act or process of reconciliation" and is "contingent upon personal repentance."[84] This spiritual restoration of the nation was precisely Elijah's task during his earthly ministry as well. His prayer on Mount Carmel was that Yahweh would answer him with fire so that "the people may know that you, O Lord, are God, and that *you have turned their hearts back*" (1 Kgs 18:37, emphasis added).[85] Elijah of old had set out to effect national repentance that encompassed young and old, rich and poor. Once again a nationwide revival was needed to produce a repentant remnant.[86]

The mention of Moses and Mount Horeb in the preceding verse (3:22) may also have the effect of drawing out Elijah's connection with the hope of a remnant. Although the prophet specifically speaks of Mount Horeb in the context of the giving of the Law, at the same time, "the place name 'Horeb' yokes the two appendixes by connecting the ideal figures of Moses and Elijah with the site they had in common—the 'mountain of God' (cf. Deut 5:2; 29:1; 1 Kgs 8:9; 19:8)."[87] To speak of Moses on Mount Horeb and then immediately to speak of Elijah has the effect of recalling to the reader's mind that prophet's dramatic experience on the same mountain, where he, like Moses before him, stood before Yahweh as the remnant of Israel and furthermore was commissioned to initiate a purging throughout Israel that would reveal the faithful remnant (1 Kgs 19:18). It is this portrait of the Tishbite from his earthly career that best captures the role that is anticipated for Elijah in his return: to gather the faithful remnant before the day of judgment. This righteous remnant will be preserved while the wicked in the land will be utterly destroyed, as in the *herem*.

---

84. Hill, *Malachi*, 387. See also Verhoef, *Malachi*, 343. For a detailed list of the various interpretative options, see Meinhold, *Maleachi*, 426–28.

85. The verbal connection with this passage, while clear in the MT, is somewhat obscured in the LXX by the use of ἀποκαθίστημι in Malachi, rather than the more common ἐπιστρέφω. Nevertheless, the conceptual link is clearly identifiable. See Glazier-McDonald, *Malachi*, 255–56.

86. Childs, *Old Testament as Scripture*, 496.

87. Hill, *Malachi*, 372. See also Glazier-McDonald, *Malachi*, 246–47; Kessler, *Maleachi*, 306; Meinhold, *Maleachi*, 406; Sweeney, *Twelve Prophets*, 749; Assis, "Moses, Elijah, and Messianic Hope," 211.

Conclusion

Elijah is a fiery prophet, zealous for Yahweh of Hosts, and when he appears, judgment is never far behind, be it famine, fire, sword, or the *herem*. Yet despite all this, he is no "troubler of Israel" (cf. 1 Kgs 18:17). His zeal is reflective of deep sorrow for her infidelities, and though he precedes judgment, he comes to forestall annihilation. For in his earthly ministry, this lone faithful Israelite was the kernel of purified Israel around whom Yahweh began to gather a remnant. And in his eschatological return, he was expected to effect the turning of the hearts of the remnant back to Yahweh so that the great and terrible day of the Lord would result, not in destruction, but in the rising up of a purified people of God.

4

Elijah and the Remnant in Later Jewish and Christian Literature

IN THE PREVIOUS CHAPTER, we argued that the OT Elijah narratives present him as the remnant of Israel (1 Kgs 19:10, 14), sent to proclaim repentance to an apostate nation. Likewise, Mal 3:23–24 anticipates his return to gather and prepare a repentant remnant before the day of Yahweh. We shall see that this portrait of Elijah, though variously applied and developed, remained largely consistent in the decades leading into the NT era, with very little of the speculation and legendary embellishment that would emerge in later centuries. Though the prophet came to represent many things, there is a steady stream in both Jewish and Christian writings that saw Elijah as the quintessential remnant figure and the nucleus around which the righteous remnant was to be gathered

Second Temple Jewish Literature

Sirach 48:1–11[1]

Ben Sira's *Laus Patrum* (Sir 44:1–50:24) rehearses the major turning points in Israel's history in a "patchwork of allusions to scriptural texts and concepts."[2] Though all of the heroes named are commended as "godly men" (44:10), often in contrast to idolatrous generations, the

---

1. Unless otherwise noted, all references to Sirach refer to the NRSV translation and versification.
2. Koet, "Elijah as Reconciler," 182.

Elijah section in particular is strategically placed so that as the threat of judgment reaches its climax, so does the hope of preservation for a faithful few.[3] This is highlighted especially through an inclusio in which the section on Elijah is framed on either end by a reference to God's faithful preservation of a remnant, despite judgment brought about by Israel's sin. Just before mentioning Elijah, the sage says of the divided monarchy that, despite the exile, the Lord "gave a remnant [κατάλειμμα] to Jacob and to David a root [ῥίζαν] from his own family" (47:22). Likewise, after the ministry of Elijah and his successor Elisha, it is said that "Despite all this the people did not repent, nor did they forsake their sins, until they were carried off as plunder from their land, and were scattered over all the earth. The people were left [κατελείφθη] very few in number, but with a ruler from the house of David" (48:15).[4] Lévêque insightfully notes that vv. 15–16 reveal the theological message of the entire passage: "Two centuries of history in the Northern Kingdom of Israel are shrouded in sin, and *all Yahwistic fidelity is concentrated in the person and work of Elijah and his successor.*"[5] Thus, in the progression of Israel's history as Ben Sira presents it, Elijah stands out as a solitary light in a time of utter darkness: the remnant of Israel.

> 1 Then Elijah arose, a prophet like fire,
>   and his word burned like an oven [תַּנּוּר; LXX λαμπάς].
> 2 He brought a famine upon them,
>   and by his zeal [ζήλῳ] he made them few in number [ὠλιγοποίησεν].
> 3 By the word of the Lord he shut up the heavens,
>   and also three times brought down fire.
> 4 How glorious you were, Elijah, in your wondrous deeds!
>   Whose glory is equal to yours?
> 5 You raised a corpse from death
>   and from Hades, by the word of the Most High.
> 6 You sent kings down to destruction,
>   and famous men, from their sickbeds.
> 7 You heard rebuke [ἐλεγμόν] at Sinai
>   and judgments of vengeance at Horeb.
> 8 You anointed kings to inflict retribution,

---

3. Wright, "'Put the Nations in Fear of You,'" 137.

4. Wright, "'Put the Nations in Fear of You,'" 141; Beentjes, "In Search of Parallels," 194, esp. n. 31.

5. Lévêque, "Le Portrait d'Élie," 217 (my translation here and throughout, emphasis added).

and prophets to succeed you.
9 You were taken up by a whirlwind of fire,
   in a chariot with horses of fire.
10 At the appointed time, it is written, you are destined
   to calm the wrath of God before it breaks out in fury,
 to turn [ἐπιστρέψαι] the hearts of parents to their children,
   and to restore the tribes of Jacob.
11 Happy are those who saw you
   and were adorned with your love!
 For we also shall surely live.[6]

Portrayal of Elijah in Sirach 48:1-11

Elijah is first introduced as "a prophet like fire," whose words "burned like an oven [תַּנּוּר]" (v. 1), an allusion to Mal 3:19, in which the day of the Yahweh is said to come "burning like an oven [תַּנּוּר]" to consume the wicked of the land, leaving only a purified remnant.[7] Thus, from the very start, Elijah's ministry is characterized by a refining of Israel to create a remnant. The sage then enumerates his many dramatic exploits, including summoning heavenly fire (v. 3), raising the widow's son (v. 5), anointing Elisha, and with him Hazael and Jehu (v. 6), and of course his ascension in a whirlwind (v. 9). Most significantly for our purposes, though, it is said that "in his zeal [ζήλῳ] he made them few in number [ὠλιγοποίησεν]" (48:2), a likely reference to the Horeb account (ζηλῶν ἐζήλωκα; 1 Kgs 19:10, 14) and the promise of a remnant emerging from devastating judgment (1 Kgs 19:17).[8]

The passage climaxes with the expectation of Elijah's eschatological return, using a direct appeal to Mal 3:23-24.[9] "At the appointed time, it is written, you are destined to calm the wrath of God before it breaks out

---

6. Modified slightly to correspond to the Hebrew. For translation and text critical issues in this passage, see Skehan and Di Leila, *Ben Sira*, 529-35; Lévêque, "Le Portrait d'Élie," 215-29.

7. NRSV, following the LXX, has Elijah's words burning like "a torch" (λαμπάς), which obscures the parallel. See Skehan and Di Leila, *Ben Sira*, 533; Lévêque, "Le Portrait d'Élie," 218; Beentjes, "In Search of Parallels," 194; Miller, "Messenger," 8, esp. n27.

8. Lévêque, "Le Portrait d'Élie," 219, 221. Note also the mention of judgment and vengeance pronounced at Horeb in v. 7.

9. Though the *Laus Patrum* is replete with Scripture references, the allusion to Mal 3:24 (4:6 EV) in 48:10 is highlighted by the unusual use of a formal introduction ("it is written"), showing its significance to the author (Koet, "Elijah as Reconciler," 181-82).

in fury, to turn the hearts of parents to their children, and to restore the tribes of Jacob" (Sir 48:10). Elijah's eschatological role in calming or turning back the wrath of God stands in contrast to the fiery descriptions of his earthly ministry (vv. 3, 6–7). However, it matches perfectly with Mal 3:24, in which Elijah's coming is the only thing that can prevent a curse on the land.[10] He will accomplish this task by turning "the hearts of parents to their children" and restoring "the tribes of Jacob" (v. 10). The first line comes from Mal 3:24. As we argued in the previous chapter, this task is best understood as a cross-generational revival across Israel: the hearts of parents as well as children will be restored to Yahweh. This emphasis on national revival is strengthened by the next line which, in place of "and the hearts of children to their parents," has "and to restore the tribes of Israel," taken from Isa 49:6. In this passage from Isaiah, Yahweh commissions the Servant not only to restore Israel's remnant, but to bring salvation to the nations as well.[11] Ben Sira, it seems, is attributing to Elijah this task associated with the Isaianic Servant.[12] Whatever specific parallels the sage may have intended between the figures of Elijah and the Servant, the conceptual parallels between the two passages are clear enough. Isaiah 49 speaks of a prophetic figure who is both identified as Israel and sent on mission to a rebellious Israel (Isa 49:3–5).[13] Furthermore, this lonely figure is tasked with restoring the "survivors [נְצִירֵי] of Israel."[14] More importantly, the remnant concept is plainly present throughout Isaiah 49.[15]

10. Lévêque, "Le Portrait d'Élie," 224.

11. "It is too light a thing that you should be my servant to raise up the tribes of Jacob and to restore [לְהָשִׁיב; ἐπιστρέψαι] the survivors [נְצִירֵי; διασπορά] of Israel; I will give you as a light to the nations, that my salvation may reach to the end of the earth" (Isa 49:6). LXX translates the first line as "It is a great thing," apparently in an attempt to avoid downplaying the importance of national repentance. Even so, the general sense of the verse is kept: as great as the restoration of Israel is, the Lord will do something greater still among the nations. See esp. Bauckham, "Restoration of Israel," 440–41; Lévêque, "Le Portrait d'Élie," 225.

12. Skehan and Di Leila, Ben Sira, 534; Martin, "Ben Sira's Hymn," 112. See also Puech, "Ben Sira 48:11," 82; Lévêque, "Le Portrait d'Élie," 225; Öhler, Elia im Neuen Testament, 7. Cf. Bauckham, "Restoration of Israel," 441. On the links between Elijah and the anointed prophet in Isaiah 61, see below on 4Q521.

13. See esp. Childs, Isaiah, 383–86; Motyer, Isaiah, 388; Wilcox and Paton-Williams, "Servant Songs," 79–102.

14. The root נצר, meaning "to preserve," can be used to refer to the remnant, especially when in parallel with more common remnant terms, such as שאר (cf. Ezek 6:12) (see HALOT 2:718; cf. Motyer, Isaiah, 388n1).

15. Note especially Zion's response to Yahweh in Isa 49:21, with its emphatic use of

Thus, whether Ben Sira intended further connections between Elijah and the Isaianic Servant, the portrayal of Elijah as a lone representative of faithful Israel, prophetically commissioned to gather a greater remnant, makes this passage from Isaiah a natural choice. Finally, it is intriguing that Isa 49:6 anticipates not just the restoration of Israel's remnant, but also connects this restoration to light and salvation for foreign nations as well, a connection we shall see further developed elsewhere.[16]

Summary

In its broader context within the *Laus Patrum* as well as in the specific exploits mentioned, Sir 48:1–11 clearly identifies Elijah as a central figure for the remnant, both in his earthly ministry and in his eschatological return. As in the canonical accounts, the sage sees Elijah as bringing wrath on the wicked in Israel and gathering the purified remnant. Ultimately he represents the hope that, through these survivors, Israel would be restored. It would also seem from his incorporation of Isa 49:6 that the sage connects this restoration with a reaching out to the nations.

Qumran Literature

Considering the wealth of texts discovered at Qumran, as well as the relatively prominent place that Elijah holds in later Jewish thought, it is somewhat surprising how few extant manuscripts include references to the ancient prophet. Furthermore, they show little indication of the legendary embellishments that would later develop, instead fitting well within the trajectory we have already seen stemming from the OT portrayal of the prophet.

4Q521 [4QMessianicApocalypse]

The manuscript 4Q521, though fragmentary, contains a clear allusion to Mal 3:24: "it is su[re:] The fathers will return towards the sons. [. . .]" (נכ[?]) באים אבות על בנים) (2 III 2).[17] Although the size of the fragments

---

both אֲנִי and לְבַדִּי (cf. 1 Kgs 18:22; 19:10, 14).

16. Pfaff, *Entwicklung*, 187, 195; Motyer, *Isaiah*, 388–89; cf. Lévêque, "Le Portrait d'Élie," 225.

17. All quotations and versification are taken from Garcia, Martínez and Tigchelaar,

makes certainty impossible, several other links to Malachi 3 have been proposed or identified on the strength of this allusion, including one to 3:18 ("between the righteous and the wicked," 14 I 2).[18] The identity of the eschatological figure in view as Elijah is further confirmed by additional links to the prophet, such as the ability to control the heavens (2 II 1; cf. Sir 48:3) and to "make the dead live" (2 II 12; cf. 1 Kgs 17:17–24).[19] The latter is particularly interesting in that it is added to a paraphrase of Isa 61:1–2 (cf. Isa 26:19; 35:5–6) and so aligns with a stream of tradition connecting Elijah with the anointed prophet/priest of Isaiah 61.[20] The document addresses a remnant of Israel that is "poor" and "badly wounded" but also "pious" and "righteous" (2 II 5, 12).[21] They are promised the hope of life and preservation from the condemnation and destruction of the wicked (7 I 4–6, 12–13).[22] Intriguingly, one of the immediate results of Elijah's anticipated restoration appears to be that, as Israel enjoys restoration, her joy and blessing will spill outwards to all places on earth (2 III 4).[23] Thus 4Q521 presents a picture of Elijah as an eschatological prophet

---

Dead Sea Scrolls. The participle באים ("coming"), rather than הֵשִׁיב ("will return") as found in the MT of Mal 3:24, may imply spatial rather than metaphorical movement, causing some to see here a return from Sheol and thus resurrection (cf. 2 II 12), perhaps symbolic of the restoration of Israel. See esp. Bauckham, "Restoration of Israel," 443n20; Kvalbein, "Die Wunder der Endzeit," 120. If this is the case, this is the second time in which Elijah's coming is connected with resurrection (see above on Sir 48:11).

18. Émile Puech, "Une apocalypse messianique," 475–522; see summary in Miller, "Messenger," 8–10.

19. Collins, *Scepter and the Star*, 117–20; Kvalbein, "Die Wunder der Endzeit," 111–25; Puech, "Une apocalypse messianque," 475–522; Wold, "Raising the Dead," 1–19; Xeravits, *King, Priest, Prophet*, 110; Duhaime, "Le messie et les saints," 269.

20. This view of Elijah as priest stems from his authority to offer sacrifices (1 Kgs 18:31–38) and anoint a successor (1 Kgs 19:15), his connection with the Levites as a covenant messenger (Mal 2:4–8; cf. 3:1, 23), as well as a popular identification of the prophet with Phinehas (Num 25:6–13), and can be found throughout rabbinic literature (e.g., Tg. Ps.-J. at Exod 6:18; 40:10; Deut 30:4). See Poirier, "Endtime Return of Elijah," 228–36; Clark, "Elijah as Eschatological High Priest," 120; Collins, *Scepter and the Star*, 118–19; Dharamraj, *Prophet like Moses*, 56–60. On Elijah as the figure in Isa 61:1, see Poirier, "Jesus as an Elijianic Figure," 353–59. As we shall see in subsequent chapters, Jesus makes the same addition of the raising of the dead to a paraphrase of Isaiah 61, also in the context of Elijah (Luke 7:22//Matt 11:5).

21. See description in Kvalbein, "Die Wunder der Endzeit," 113–14.

22. Puech, "Une apocalypse messianique," 502–4, 507.

23. "May the [ea]rth rejoice in all the pla[ces . . .]." See Xeravits, "King, Priest, Prophet," 118; cf. Puech, "Une apocalypse messianique," 498.

who preserves the righteous remnant through divine judgment and, despite their pitiful state, offers a promise of blessing that overflows to all the world.

4Q558 [4Visionb ar or 4QarP]

Though 4Q558 comes to us in 146 "extremely small, damaged fragments," the allusion to Mal 3:24 is clear enough: "to you I will send Eliyah, befo[re ...]" (4Q558 1 II 4).[24] It is likely that, following Malachi, the line ends with "the day of the Lord" or something similar.[25] The imperfect verb אשלח ("I will send") brings out the future aspect more clearly than does the participle in the MT (שֹׁלֵחַ), perhaps emphasizing the eschatological expectation.[26] Reference to "lighting and meteors" (1 II 5) and the cutting down of trees, apparently in judgment (3 II 3) point to the apocalyptic nature of this text, giving further credence to the idea that the author is essentially reflecting Malachi's expectation for Elijah's eschatological return to gather the remnant of Israel before the final judgment. Thus we can conclude that the Qumran documents, in the few places where they do refer to Elijah, portray him as the eschatological reformer who will gather the repentant remnant of Israel, with further hints of the universal implications of Israel's restoration.[27]

---

24. Xeravits, "King, Priest, Prophet," 120.

25. Although possible references to a Davidic messiah have been considered in this text, it is unlikely that Elijah here is said to precede the Messiah. See discussion in Öhler, *Elia im Neuen Testament*, 17; Fitzmyer, "'Elect of God' Text," 355; Xeravits, "King, Priest, Prophet," 187; Faierstein, "Why Do the Scribes Say," 80.

26. Xeravits, "King, Priest, Prophet," 187.

27. Elijah's name appears in two other documents that both appear to paraphrase events from the Book of Kings (4Q382, 4Q481a). Neither of these differs from the text of Kings in ways that would shed further light on the perception of the prophet or his expected return. The document 4Q382 does also contain fragments that mention a "remnant" and "survivors" (frags. 43, 45), but the document is too fragmentary to confirm what connection, if any, these have with Elijah (see Feldman, *Rewriting Samuel and Kings*, 54-150). Several other Qumran texts deal with an eschatological prophet, but the figure either is not or cannot be identified with Elijah (cf. Xeravits, "King, Priest, Prophet," 186, 191).

First Enoch 89:51–52; 90:31

The Animal Apocalypse of 1 Enoch (1 En. 85–90) (cir. 165–161 BC) uses animals to depict Israel's history from Adam to the Maccabean revolt and the eschatological new age.[28] Elijah appears once in Israel's history (89:51–52) and once with Enoch at the end of the age (90:31). In his earthly life he is a lone righteous figure, crying out to a sinful nation to repent until, when they try to kill him (89:52), he is taken away to safety. In his return at the end of time, he is placed among the remnant (90:31) and, it seems, is instrumental in preserving the remnant through the final judgment until they are joined, first by the rest of Israel, and then by all nations (90:37–38).

In his depiction of the divided kingdom, Enoch describes Israel (the sheep) going astray and abandoning the Lord's house (89:50):

> Then the Lord of the sheep called some from among the sheep and sent them to the sheep, but the sheep began to slay them. However, one of them was not killed but escaped alive and fled away; he cried aloud to the sheep, and they wanted to kill him, but the Lord of the sheep rescued him from the sheep and caused him to ascend to me and settle down (89:51–52).[29]

The "one" sheep who survives the slaughter is unanimously recognized as Elijah, portrayed as the only faithful Israelite in "a time of unmitigated apostasy and rejection of the prophetic call to repentance."[30] It is striking that, of the many aspects of his life that could be emphasized, the seer highlights this function as a remnant figure.[31] Elijah is said to ascend to Enoch, and remains there during the duration of Israel's history, including the exile, the Hellenistic period, and the Maccabean revolt.[32] Eventually the "Lord of the sheep" intervenes on behalf of Judas and the sheep, bringing about a great judgment on the enemy nations as well as

---

28. Charlesworth, *OTP*, 1:5, 67–71; Nickelsburg, *1 Enoch*, 384–407; Tiller, *Animal Apocalypse*, 317–80; Olson, *Animal Apocalypse*, 183–230.

29. Translation and versification taken from *OTP*, 67.

30. Nickelsburg, *1 Enoch 1*, 384. See also Olson, *Animal Apocalypse*, 58–59.

31. It is further striking that, unlike in the 2 Kings narrative, Elijah's ascent is depicted as a rescue (v. 52)—the sheep are so far astray that the remnant cannot remain among them.

32. Although the ram in 90:9–15 is almost definitely Judas Maccabeus, his similarities with Elijah are noteworthy, including his prophetic call to some of the sheep while the majority remain blind (90:7). See Tiller, *Animal Apocalypse*, 9, 62.

the fallen angels (90:24–27). It is at this point that the seer mentions seeing the remnant ("all the sheep that had survived," v. 30). Angelic figures come to take Enoch and Elijah ("that ram") and set them down "in the midst of those sheep prior to the occurrence of this judgment" (v. 31).[33] The question of chronology is difficult, since Enoch and Elijah's descent is depicted after the full description of the final judgment but said to have occurred "prior to the occurrence of this judgment" (v. 30). Whether a scribal gloss or original to the text, the temporal indicator is presumably included to ensure that Elijah's return is seen to be in fulfillment of Mal 3:23–24, where it plainly precedes the final judgment.[34] In a final development, the snow-white sheep (i.e., the purified remnant) are joined by the other sheep who had been "destroyed and dispersed" (i.e., straying and apostate Israelites) but also by "the beasts of the field and the birds of the sky" (i.e., gentile nations). At this point, in a surprising conclusion, a "snow-white bull," a messianic figure, transforms all creatures — sheep and beasts alike — into snow-white bulls like himself.[35] We have already seen hints in other STJ texts that the restoration of Israel through Elijah's remnant would bring light to gentile nations as well, but this is the most explicit depiction of this theme, and may mark a growing interest in the missional or global aspect of the remnant concept.[36]

Other Texts (1 Enoch 93:8; 4 Ezra 6:26; Tg. Ps.-J. Deut 33:11)

Several other Jewish texts from this period make mention of Elijah and so merit brief comment. The Apocalypse of Weeks (1 En. 93:1–10; 91:12–17) is a short apocalyptic schematization of Israel's history from the antidiluvian era to the final judgment and the new creation.[37] The sixth week, summarizing the divided kingdom, notes that "Therein, a (certain) man

---

33. Even though Judas Maccabeus is the most recently mentioned ram, the ram in v. 31 must logically be Elijah, since he is already described as ascending up to the heavens to join Enoch. Tiller, *Animal Apocalypse*, 377; Olson, *Animal Apocalypse*, 253; contra Öhler, *Elia im Neuen Testament*, 15.

34. Cf. Olson, *Animal Apocalypse*, 227, 253; Horsley, "'Prophets of Old,'" 440; Faierstein, "Why Do the Scribes Say," 78. On the textual difficulties, see Tiller, *Animal Apocalypse*, 379.

35. See esp. discussion in Nicklesburg, *1 Enoch*, 405–7.

36. Nickelsburg, *1 Enoch*, 407; Tiller, *Animal Apocalypse*, 383–89. The inclusion of gentiles after the restoration of the remnant can also be seen in 1 En. 10:17–22.

37. VanderKam, "Apocalypse of Weeks," 511–23; Nickelsburg, *1 Enoch*, 438–39.

shall ascend" (93:8).³⁸ This man is unanimously recognized as Elijah, and it is noteworthy that, as in Sirach and the Animal Apocalypse, he is the only figure deemed worthy of mentioning in such a long span of history. No further comment is made, but Elijah, with Noah (v. 4), sets a paradigm for faithful ones who are spared despite the wickedness of their generations—a paradigm that the final weeks depend upon for their portrayal of the last judgment and the vindication of the remnant.

Fourth Ezra 6:25-26 states that "whoever remains" and is saved through the final woes (i.e., the remnant) "shall see those who were taken up" and "have not tasted death."³⁹ This is generally understood to refer to Elijah and Enoch, and possibly others as well.⁴⁰ Subsequent to this, "the heart of the earth's inhabitants shall be changed and converted to a different spirit." The wording here is reminiscent of Elijah's task of turning the hearts of the people (Mal 3:24).⁴¹ Here again is a pattern in which Elijah comes to the eschatological remnant, and their salvation is linked to a transformation of the nations.⁴²

Although Targum Pseudo-Jonathan makes several mentions of Elijah and his eschatological return (Tg. Ps.-J. on Exod 6:18; 40:10; Deut 30:4; 33:11; 34:3), most of the material is thought to postdate the NT. One reference, however, is thought to date back to the Maccabean revolt.⁴³ The passage identifies Elijah as a Levitical priest and prays for judgment

---

38. *OTP*, 74.

39. *OTP*, 535. Fourth Ezra is dated c. AD 100, yet despite its late dating it is worth including because of the significance of this emerging pattern of Elijah appearing to the remnant before their restoration and the subsequent conversion of the nations. See Stone, *Fourth Ezra*, 9-10; Myers, *I and II Esdras*; Knibb, "2 Esdras," 147-53; Öhler, *Elia im Neuen Testament*, 14.

40. Stone, *Fourth Ezra*, 172; Myers, *I and II Esdras*, 198; and Knibb, "2 Esdras," 152; Elliott, *Survivors of Israel*, 465-66. This passage is another instance of the expectation of Elijah's return with Enoch, first attested in 1 En. 90:31 and further developed in later Jewish and Christian literature (Rev 11:1-12; Apoc. El. 4:7-19; 5:30-32). See Tiller, *Animal Apocalypse*, 377-78; Charlesworth, *OTP*, 721-22; Frankfurter, *Elijah in Upper Egypt*, 76-77.

41. Stone, *Fourth Ezra*, 172; Myers, *I and II Esdras*, 199; Öhler, *Elia im Neuen Testament*, 14. See also Longenecker, *Eschatology and the Covenant*, 116-17; Elliott, *Survivors of Israel*, 632.

42. On the idea of gentiles joining the remnant in 4 Ezra, see also 13:13 (Stone, *Fourth Ezra*, 387).

43. Syrèn, *Blessings in the Targums*, 179-82; Meyer, "'Elia' und 'Ahab,'" 356-68; York, "Dating of Targumic Literature," 49-62; Öhler, *Elia im Neuen Testament*, 22-25; though cf. Flesher and Chilton, *Targums*, 160-66.

against "Ahab" and "the false prophets," who are "enemies of Johanan the high priest."[44] Johanan is generally understood to be John Hyrcanus, and the association with Elijah as one who will drive out falsehood and restore right worship is understandable. Though there is no explicit mention of a remnant here, as we have seen, these functions of Elijah's are tied to his role vis-à-vis Israel's remnant. Of further interest in this passage is the association of Elijah with the priesthood, a connection which we have already seen, and which develops significantly in later Jewish thought.[45] In later tradition, Elijah would be seen as a sort of eschatological high priest who would gather the scattered Israelites and so restore the nation.[46]

Summary and Conclusions

Markus Öhler concludes his survey of early Jewish Elijah traditions by suggesting that "the expectation of Elijah did not essentially change between Malachi, Sirach, and the first century CE."[47] Though we have tracked some developments in the tradition, such as the increased association with Enoch and an increased interest in the fate of the nations, we agree that Second Temple Jewish literature is fairly consistent in portraying Elijah as a remnant figure himself in his earthly life and as the champion of the eschatological remnant of Israel. We will find that these connections, and especially the interest in the salvation and spiritual transformation of the gentiles, will continue in the NT literature as well.

New Testament Literature

Outside of the Gospels, the NT contains only two direct references to Elijah (Rom 11:3; Jas 5:17), as well as two possible indirect references (Heb 11:35–38; Rev 11:1–11). Nevertheless, these texts give important insight into Christian appropriation of the remnant theme. They show a faithful prophet confronting wickedness and calling on the people of

44. All references and quotations are taken from Clarke, *Targum Pseudo-Jonathan*.

45. See Syrèn, *Blessings in the Targums*, 171; Öhler, *Elia im Neuen Testament*, 24–25; and above discussion on 4Q521.

46. Esp. Tg. Ps.-J. on Deut 30:4: "Even though your dispersal will be to the ends of the heavens, from there will the Memra [Word] of the Lord gather you through the mediation of Elijah, the great priest, and from there he will bring you near through the mediation of the King Messiah."

47. Öhler, "Expectation of Elijah," 463.

God to repent. More significantly, they see in Elijah's story an explanation for Israel's general rejection of the gospel, justification for the inclusion of gentiles into the people of God, and hope for a renewed Israel.

Romans 11:1–6

Not only does Romans 9–11 give the clearest articulation of remnant theology in the NT, but it also climaxes in an appeal to Elijah as the primary example of a faithful remnant (Rom 11:2–5), making it a crucial text for our present line of investigation.[48] Paul seeks a delicate balance between God's faithfulness to his covenant promises and the reality of Israel's widespread rejection of Christ, and the fulcrum balancing these two ideas is his appropriation of the OT concept of remnant. For Paul, Elijah is the key figure attached to this theme (11:2–5), and he uses the OT prophet as evidence that not only is the reduction of Israel to a mere remnant no threat to God's faithfulness, but also the presence of this remnant is the source of hope for future blessing for both Israel and the gentiles.

Beginning with an expression of deep personal desire for his fellow Israelites to be saved (9:1–5), Paul addresses the question of God's faithfulness to his covenant promises to Israel despite Israel's apparent unresponsiveness to the gospel. Appealing to a robust theology of election, Paul argues that God's authority to elect some but not others even from among the patriarchs (vv. 7–13) indicates that he can surely do the same in the present day (cf. v. 16).[49] He establishes this point with a string of OT quotations that argue essentially that, although God has promised to make Abraham's descendants as numerous as the sand, this does not rule out their reduction to a tiny remnant. So long as at least a remnant remains, there is hope of restoration and these promises can still stand (vv. 25–29; cf. Hos 2:23; 1:10; Isa 10:22–23; 1:9). Hosea 2:23 and 1:10 reflect the hope of restoration no matter how harsh the judgment, while, conversely, Isa 10:22–23 describes the reduction of Israel to a remnant

---

48. Jewett, *Romans*, 650–66; Moo, *Romans*, 670–83; Dunn, *Romans 9–16*, 632–50; Hafemann, "Salvation of Israel," 38–58; Johnson, "Romans 9–11," 91–103; Käseman, *Romans*, 298–302; Munck, *Christ and Israel*.

49. Paul's reference to the gentiles here (v. 24) comes as something of a surprise (though cf. v. 6), but it functions as a "proleptic hint" of what he will cover in more depth in Romans 11 (Wright, *Paul and the Faithfulness of God*, 1187).

despite the patriarchal promises.[50] Finally, Isa 1:9 discusses the existence of a remainder or "seed [σπέρμα]," which separates Israel's experience from the annihilation experienced by other nations.[51] So long as there is a remnant, there is hope for Israel.

After a discussion in 9:30—10:21 of Israel's failure to submit to or attain God's righteousness, as well as his heartfelt longing for their salvation, Paul resumes his discussion of the remnant in 11:1, insisting that God cannot have been unfaithful to his people, if for no other reason than that he himself is by lineage an Israelite. Yet he is not satisfied with the remnant functioning merely as a token; it must be a pledge of something greater.[52] For this reason he quickly introduces the figure of Elijah (vv. 2–4). Though he shortens and paraphrases the quotation somewhat, Paul is clearly dependent on 1 Kgs 19:10, 14 in presenting Elijah as the quintessential remnant figure: "Lord, they have killed your prophets, they have demolished your altars; I alone am left [κἀγὼ ὑπελείφθην μόνος], and they are seeking my life" (v. 3). Although Paul does not make the analogy between himself and the prophet explicit, the similarities are evident: both deeply lamented Israel's condition, both had a prophetic role within Israel as well as to gentiles, and both suffered isolation, persecution, and threat of death from their fellow Israelites.[53] More significantly to Paul's point, both were eventually joined by others who were also faithful. Thus, in the next verse, he cites the divine response: "I have kept [κατέλιπον] for myself [ἐμαυτῷ] seven thousand who have not bowed the knee to Baal" (v. 4).[54] Rounding off his argument, Paul draws the link between

---

50. Both Hos 1:10 and Isa 10:22 allude to Gen 22:17, which is likely why Paul links them together here (Moo, *Romans*, 614n20). This brilliant juxtaposition allows him to appeal to multiple aspects of the remnant concept simultaneously—both the hope of renewal and the threat of removal in judgment—basing them both in faithfulness of God to his word.

51. Paul follows the LXX, which has σπέρμα ("seed") in place of the more explicit שְׁאָר ("remnant") (although σπέρμα too is often used of the remnant in Isaiah [6:13; 14:22, 30; 15:9 LXX]). This allows him again to connect the present situation (i.e., the existence of a remnant) to God's conduct in the past with respect to the patriarchal promises (cf. v. 8).

52. Campbell, *Creation of Christian Identity*, 128; Hafemann, "Salvation of Israel," 49–51; Moo, *Romans*, 677.

53. Moo, *Romans*, 677; Munck, *Christ and Israel*, 108–9; Fitzmyer, *Romans*, 605; Dunn, *Romans 9–16*, 645; Öhler, *Elia im Neuen Testament*, 257; Jewett, *Romans*, 657.

54. As in the LXX, the verbs ὑπολείπω and καταλείπω serve to underscore the remnant theme. The shift from future to aorist tense in this verse likely reflects Paul's historical perspective on the event (Moo, *Romans*, 676n26; Jewett, *Romans*, 657). The

the seven thousand in Elijah's day and the Jewish believers of his own day, especially, it would seem, those who professed faith as a result of his own ministry: "So too at the present time there is a remnant [λεῖμμα], chosen by grace" (v. 5).

Although Paul appears confident that this remnant of believing Jews will grow, he also introduces universal dimensions to his remnant theology at this point, for the existence of a Jewish remnant of believers in Jesus provides a theological apologetic for the mission to the gentiles. First, the present existence of this remnant serves as surety of God's continued faithfulness to Israel in a way that is neither threatened by the hardening of so many Jews to the gospel nor by the receptivity of so many gentiles (vv. 1, 11–12). Second, it is Israel's partial "hardening" (cf. v. 25) and resultant reduction to a remnant that is the historical phenomenon opening the door for evangelistic outreach among the gentiles (v. 11; cf. Acts 13:46). Finally, because the presence of a remnant implies at least the hope of future restoration, it follows logically that the present gentile mission is no threat to Israel's future. To the contrary, Paul sees the conversion of gentiles as facilitating this future revival (vv. 11, 13–14).[55] Though the relationship between Israel's remnant and the conversion of the nations can be found in several key OT texts (esp. Isa 11:10; 49:6; 66:19), Paul chooses instead to add a further dimension, drawing on the OT concept of jealousy (vv. 11, 14; cf. Deut 32:21).[56] It is not the full restoration of Israel that leads to gentile conversion, but rather the salvation of gentiles that prompts Israelite jealousy, thereby leading to their conversion.[57]

---

addition of ἐμαυτῷ suits Paul's theological purposes, pointing to God as the one ultimately responsible for creating the remnant (cf. vv. 5–6).

55. Though the interpretation of v. 26 is strongly debated, it is best understood as referring to a large-scale future conversion of ethnic Israelites. See esp. Moo, *Romans*, 724; Hafemann, "Salvation of Israel," 52–53; Dunn, *Romans 9–16*, 682; Baker, "Salvation of Israel," 480–84; Johnson, "Romans 9–11," 91–103. Cf. Zoccali, "'All Israel Will Be Saved,'" 289–318; Barth, "One People," 17, 22; Stendahl, *Paul among Jews and Gentiles*, 4; Chilton, "Romans 9–11," 33; Horne, "All Israel Will Be Saved," 329–34; Ridderbos, *Paul*, 358, 433, 511.

56. Moo, *Romans*, 692; Dunn *Romans 9–16*, 631, 669–70; Munck, *Christ and Israel*, 125; cf. Bell, *Provoked to Jealousy*, 7–43. Though cf. Baker, "Salvation of Israel," 469–84.

57. Paul further elaborates on these concepts in vv. 16–32, still drawing from the concept of the remnant, which may be depicted in v. 16 in the first fruits and the tree root, as well as in the branches remaining on the olive tree (vv. 17–24) (Hafemann, "Salvation of Israel," 51; Johnson, "Romans 9–11," 99; Gorman, *Apostle of the Crucified Lord*, 387–88; Chilton, "Romans 9–11," 33; though cf. Moo, *Romans*, 699–700;

Paul's appeal to Elijah as a remnant figure—faithful to Yahweh despite widespread apostasy and persecution—is consistent with the OT texts as well as the presentations of the prophet in contemporary literature. Although Paul shows no interest here in eschatological views of Elijah as other Jewish writings do, he does share and expand on their interest in the conversion of gentiles. However, in an apparent variation from the progression in STJ literature, once the remnant is established in God's blessing, salvation is extended to gentiles *before* the full restoration of Israel (cf. esp. 1 En. 90:31–38). Thus, the hardening of a large portion of Israel to the gospel, in combination with the preservation of Israel in the form of a believing remnant, has opened the way for a gentile mission, though in the hope of a future Israelite restoration. These same issues of Israelite hardening and gentile mission will prove significant in Luke's portrayal of Elijah and the remnant as well.

General Epistles

Elijah is mentioned twice in the General Epistles, once explicitly (Jas 5:17–18) and once, apparently, by allusion (Heb 11:32–38). In both instances, the author exhorts Christians to consider the prophet as a model of perseverance and faith. Aspects of the remnant concept are certainly present in these passages, though neither author has an explicit interest in remnant theology, either in these passages or elsewhere.

Hebrews 11:32–38

Among the dozens of passing references to OT heroes, several vignettes may appeal to the Elijah narratives.[58] Most notable is the mention of women who "received their dead by resurrection" (v. 35; cf. 1 Kgs 17:17–24; 2 Kgs 4:18–37). The reference to wearing "skins of sheep [μηλωταῖς] and goats" (v. 37) is also traditionally understood as referring to Elijah

---

Campbell, *Creation of Christian Identity*, 129; Barth, "One People," 16–17). Though the precise meaning of these images is debated, they nevertheless depict an organic relationship between the inclusion of gentiles and the gathering of the remnant in Paul's mind.

58. On allusions to Elijah in Heb 11:34–37, see, e.g., Lane, *Hebrews 9–13*, 386–91; Bruce, *Hebrews*, 324–28; Attridge, *Hebrews*, 348–51; Öhler, *Elia im Neuen Testament*, 260–62.

(1 Clem. 17:1) (cf. μηλωτή in 3 Kgdms 19:13, 19; 4 Kgdms 2:8, 13–14).[59] The heroes commended here are praised for their unswerving faithfulness, even in the face of death and persecution—certainly a characteristic of the remnant—but no appeals to other aspects of the remnant concept are made.[60]

James 5:17–18

James mentions Elijah at the end of his epistle as an example of a man who, though he was a "human being like us," was able, through fervent prayer, to stop the rain for "three years and six months" and then, again through prayer, to cause the heavens to give rain (Jas 5:17–18).[61] The primary context of these verses revolves around faithful prayer especially in times of suffering, with particular attention to sickness (vv. 13–14) and sin (vv. 15–16). The focus of the passage is on the restoration that comes through confession and prayer (v. 16; cf. vv. 19–20).[62] Most commentators understand James's appeal to the drought story as an example of fervent and persistent prayer during times of difficulty and sickness.[63] It may even be that James is presenting sickness, like the drought in Elijah's day, as an opportunity for self-examination and repentance.[64] This theme of the restoration of the repentant is in keeping with Elijah's role vis-à-vis the remnant, but the other aspects of the remnant concept are less pertinent to James's goals in this exhortation.

---

59. The references to escaping "the edge of the sword" (vv. 34, 37; cf. 1 Kgs 19:10, 14) and to wandering "in caves" (v. 38; cf. 1Kgs 18:4, 13; 1 Kgs 19:8–9) are too broad to be included with any certainty (Öhler, *Elia im Neuen Testament*, 261–62).

60. In particular, there is no mention of removal of the wicked in judgment, and any hope of renewal is deferred until the resurrection (cf. v. 35).

61. Moo, *Letter of James*, 248–49; Johnson, *Letter of James*, 344–45; Davids, *Epistle of James*, 197–98; Dibelius, *James*, 256–57; Öhler, *Elia im Neuen Testament*, 257–59.

62. It is therefore likely that James is dependent here on Jewish tradition, which does directly speak of the prophet's intercessory role (2 Esd 7:109; cf. Sir 48:2–3). See esp. Davids, *Epistle of James*, 197.

63. Johnson, *Letter of James*, 344; McCartney, *James*, 259; Moo, *Letter of James*, 248; Hartin, *James*, 271. Hence the reference to "three years and six months" of drought (v. 18; cf. Luke 4:25; Rev 11:3–6) in contrast to the OT's "in the third year" (1 Kgs 18:1) (cf. Dan 7:25 and 12:7).

64. Cf. Johnson, *Letter of James*, 342. This would account for why James mentions Elijah praying fervently *for* the drought (v. 17), rather than the sevenfold prayer at the end of the drought (cf. 1 Kgs 18:42–44).

Revelation 11:1-13

Although the vision of the two witnesses in Rev 11:1-13 presents numerous interpretative difficulties, ancient and modern commentators alike are consistent in recognizing parallels with Elijah.[65] Parallels include their ability to call down fire on their enemies (v. 5; cf. 2 Kgs 1:10, 12),[66] the ability to "shut the sky" for three and a half years (v. 6; cf. 1 Kgs 18:1; Luke 4:25; Jas 5:17); and possibly their sackcloth clothing (v. 3; cf. 2 Kgs 1:8).[67] Other possible parallels may include their bold confrontation of corrupt powers (v. 7)[68] and their ability to cheat death (though this time after first experiencing it) and ascend into heaven on a cloud (vv. 7-12; cf. 2 Kgs 2:11).[69] Modern commentators tend to associate the second figure with Moses (cf. Mal 4:4-6; Deut 18:15), although Enoch cannot be ruled out (cf. 1 En. 90:31).[70] Since the two figures are called "lampstands," they are likely meant to represent the experiences of the church during the time of persecution (v. 4; cf. 1:20).[71]

---

65. Koester, *Revelation*, 1:474-511; Aune, *Revelation*, 2:585-631; Bauckham, "Martyrdom of Enoch and Elijah," 447-58; Bauckham, *Climax of Prophecy*, 283-387; Beale, *Revelation*, 558-607; Osborne, *Revelation*, 408-37; Mounce, *Revelation*, 211-24; Watts, "Remnant Theme," 109-29.

66. That the fire emerges from their mouths may parallel Sir 48:1, which describes Elijah's words as burning.

67. Beale, *Revelation*, 576; Osborne, *Revelation*, 420. Though אִישׁ בַּעַל שֵׂעָר in 2 Kgs 1:8 is best translated as "a hairy man," rather than that he had "a garment of hair," the fact that Elijah was known for wearing a mantle (1 Kgs 19:13, 19; 2 Kgs 2:8, 13, 14), possibly one made of hair or sackcloth (cf. Zech 13:4), probably accounts for the later Jewish and Christian tradition connecting this garment with Elijah (cf. Matt 3:4; Mark 1:6) (Cogan and Tadmor, *II Kings*, 26). Sackcloth is certainly also symbolic of a prophetic call to repentance, which was also characteristic of Elijah's life.

68. Cf. Rev 2:20-24. Pollard, "ΛΟΙΠΟΣ," 50. Mounce, *Revelation*, 222, adds that, like Ahab calling Elijah "troubler of Israel" (1 Kgs 18:17), the inhabitants of the earth blame the witnesses for the calamities they have brought upon themselves (v. 10).

69. Beale and McDonough, "Revelation," 1121; cf. Öhler, *Elia im Neuen Testament*, 277-78.

70. See Bauckham, "Martyrdom of Enoch and Elijah," 452. For other proposed identifications, see Aune, *Revelation*, 2:599-603; Wong, "Two Witnesses," 344-47.

71. See esp. Bauckham, *Climax of Prophecy*, 274; Aune, *Revelation*, 2:631; Beale, *Revelation*, 547-75; Mounce, *Revelation*, 217. Even if they are understood as two literal individuals identified with Moses and Elijah, their experiences are shared by the church more broadly, so that there is no need "to choose between a literal and a symbolic meaning" (Osborne, *Revelation*, 417-18).

That these visions portray the church as the eschatological remnant is seen first of all in the vision of the temple (vv. 1–2). The inner court (and the worshipers inside) is measured as a mark of protection (v.1; cf. esp. Ezek 40:1–6; 42:20; Zech 2:5) and so represents "the divinely protected remnant," while the outer court is "thrown out" (ἔκβαλε ἔξωθεν, v. 2; cf. John 9:34, 35; 12:31) to be trampled, indicating the apostate.[72] More significantly, the pattern of death and resurrection that the witnesses embody—a pattern already broadly familiar from prophetic remnant discourse (cf. Hos 6:1–2; Isa 26:19)—is drawn specifically from Ezek 37:1–14, in which Yahweh promises to restore life to the dry bones of Israel's remnant.[73]

The most interesting development of the remnant theme occurs in v. 13, in which a great earthquake destroys one tenth of the great city and kills seven thousand people while the "rest [οἱ λοιποί] were terrified and gave glory to the God of heaven" (v. 13). Although the term λοιπός is more general in meaning than its more technical cognate λεῖμμα, it can be used indicate a remnant (e.g., LXX Isa 17:3), and in the context of a group surviving a calamity, this certainly appears to be the case.[74] The same is true for the figures one-tenth (Isa 6:13; Amos 5:3) and seven thousand (cf. 1 Kgs 19:18; Rom 11:4). However, in a surprising series of inversions, it is the seven thousand (i.e., the smaller portion) that is destroyed, while the greater portion remains. Furthermore, this "remnant," rather than being spared because of their faith, are only converted after the disaster.[75] "In a characteristically subtle use of these Old Testament

---

72. Aune, *Revelation*, 2:597–98; Kiddle, *Revelation of St. John*, 189; cf. Ladd, *Revelation*, 152–53; McNicol, "Revelation 11:1–14," 199–201, who see the outer court as referring specifically to Israelites who reject Jesus as the Messiah. Other commentators see the two courts as representing the inner and outer realities of the church, respectively, so that the church is spiritually protected but physically trampled, though this need not exclude an identification of the church with the eschatological remnant. See esp. Koester, *Revelation*, 484–85; Bauckham, *Climax of Prophecy*, 270–72; Mounce, *Revelation*, 214; Osborne, *Revelation*, 410; Beale, *Revelation*, 558.

73. πνεῦμα ζωῆς ἐκ τοῦ θεοῦ εἰσῆλθεν ἐν αὐτοῖς, καὶ ἔστησαν ἐπὶ τοὺς πόδας αὐτῶν (v.11) // εἰσῆλθεν εἰς αὐτοὺς τὸ πνεῦμα, καὶ ἔζησανκαὶ ἔστησαν ἐπὶ τῶν ποδῶν αὐτῶν]" (LXX Ezek 37:10); cf. πνεῦμα ζωῆς (LXX Ezek 37:5).

74. A case can be made for a technical use of λοιπός in Rev 2:24 and 12:17 (see esp. Pollard, "ΛΟΙΠΟΣ," 45–63). The other instances in the book are probably non-technical (3:2; 8:13; 9:20; 19:21; 20:5).

75. That the survivors were "terrified [ἔμφοβοι ἐγένοντο]" and "gave glory to the God of heaven [ἔδωκαν δόξαν τῷ θεῷ τοῦ οὐρανοῦ]" (v. 13) indicates a response of repentance and genuine conversion (cf. 14:7; 15:4; 16:9). See Aune, *Revelation*, 2:628;

allusions, Revelation reverses the arithmetic. Only a tenth, only seven thousand suffer the judgment, while the remnant (οἱ λοιποί) who are spared are the nine-tenths. Not the faithful minority, but the faithless majority are spared, so that they may come to repentance and faith."[76]

The book of Revelation appears to play with the remnant theme—on the one hand, the witnesses are not survivors at all but are only saved after tasting death, and on the other hand, the future restoration is so great that the repentant remnant far outweighs the portion destroyed in judgment. Nevertheless, it is consistent in portraying Elijah (along with Moses) as the figure who embodies the experiences of the remnant, and as the nucleus around which the future repentant remnant is gathered.

Summary and Conclusion

Paul appeals to Elijah as a salvation-historical precedent explaining the present state of the church with respect to Jews and gentiles. Those Jews who have embraced Jesus as the Messiah are "the remnant chosen by grace" (Rom 11:5), while the rest who are hardened to the gospel are the apostate. Furthermore, the universal mission of the remnant, already present in the Prophets (Isa 66:19; Mic 5:7) and dramatically adumbrated in Elijah's encounter with the gentile widow, is now brought to the fore in Romans, as Paul makes it a critical piece of his strategy for the restoration of Israel as a whole.[77] Hebrews and James both appeal to Elijah as a model of faith/faithfulness during difficult times. Neither author appears to have an explicit interest in remnant theology, yet their portrayals of Elijah draw on the themes often related to the concept, such as faithfulness, persecution, and repentance. Finally, the book of Revelation draws on Elijah tradition to depict witnesses fulfilling Elijah's apocalyptic function of gathering a repentant remnant before the final judgment. Though the seer plays with stock remnant imagery—inverting numbers and key concepts—the vision clearly connects Elijah with the remnant theme. By

---

Bauckham, *Climax of Prophecy*, 278–79; Öhler, *Elia im Neuen Testament*, 279; Osborne, *Revelation*, 433–34; Koester, *Revelation*, 511–12.

76. Bauckham, *Climax of Prophecy*, 283.

77. Although the particular progression of Paul's remnant theology (in which the full restoration of Israel comes only *after* the gentile mission) appears to be Paul's own contribution, it may have a parallel in Acts 1:6–8, in which the question of the restoration of Israel is deferred in favor of the spirit-empowered mission to Jerusalem, Judea, and the ends of the earth.

virtue of their faithful testimony despite dreadful persecution, this eschatological remnant is joined by converts from every nation.

Though not every NT passage clearly connects Elijah with the remnant theme, the connection is explicit in Romans, and very strong in Revelation. In both of these passages, Elijah's experience as the remnant of Israel helps early Christians make sense of the rejection of the gospel, whether by Jews or by the world at large, and his experiences give them hope for vindication in the form of a future large-scale repentance and conversion not only of Israelites but of many from all nations. As we shall see in the next section, it is precisely these characteristic aspects of Elijah's experience that capture Luke's attention.

5

Elijah and John the Baptist in Luke

IN THE PREVIOUS CHAPTERS, we saw that Elijah's establishment of the remnant is characterized by invoking judgment against the wicked within Israel (removal), issuing a call to repentance to all who will listen (remainder), and regathering the people of God to include all who are receptive (renewal). In the present chapter, we shall see that, from the very first mention of him (1:17) wherever Luke connects John to the figure of Elijah, it is precisely in relation to these three ideas.[1] The opening chapters of Luke's Gospel are thick with anticipation of the fulfillment of God's ancient promises to Israel, and it is in this context that John's coming ministry is announced. Yet the Elijianic nature of John's ministry, while placing it in continuity with these expectations, also serves to set expectations of judgment. The nation becomes polarized in response to his preaching: some are marked out for the coming salvation, while others are in danger of the coming wrath.

The Spirit and Power of Elijah (Luke 1:5-17)

Set in Jerusalem—with a Levitical priest offering incense in the holy sanctuary of the temple—the opening scene of Luke's Gospel draws not

---

1. On the theological and narrative significance of John the Baptist for Luke, see esp. Müller, *Mehr als ein Prophet*, 77; Rindoš, *He of Whom It Is Written*, 231-33; Bock, *Luke*, 1:901-2; Marshall, *Gospel of Luke*, 59-60, 295-96; Marshall, *Historian and Theologian*, 120-25, 145-47; Miller, "Elijah, John, and Jesus," 611-22; Conzelmann, *Theology of St. Luke*, 20-27; Fitzmyer, *Luke*, 1:181-86, 213-15; Wink, *John the Baptist*, 42-84; Ernst, *Johannes der Täufer*.

only on familiar OT imagery (cf. esp. Isa 6:1-2), but also on national icons, thus setting the stage for the hope for national restoration expressed in the ensuing scenes (cf. esp. vv. 68-79).² At the center of these anticipations are the expectations for the yet unborn John: "With the spirit and power of Elijah he will go before [ἐνώπιον] him, to turn the hearts of the parents to their children [ἐπιστρέψαι καρδίας πατέρων ἐπὶ τέκνον], and the disobedient to the wisdom of the righteous, to make ready [ἑτοιμάσαι] a people prepared [κατεσκευασμένον] for the Lord" (Luke 1:13-17).

John and the Elijah Motif

Following the typical pattern of OT birth announcements (Gen 16:10-12; 17:15-22; 25:21-23; Judg 13:3-5; cf. Luke 1:26-38), the angel's message gives prophetic insight into the life and career of the one to be born, with the result that this first mention of John at the very beginning of the book establishes the reader's expectations for him as one who will carry out his ministry "in the spirit and power" of Elijah (v. 17). To have Elijah's "spirit [πνεύματι]" indicates a close identification and spiritual succession (cf. 2 Kgs 2:9, 15).³ "Power [δυνάμει]" here refers to Elijah's charisma.⁴ Thus, the angelic annunciation establishes John as one who will fulfill expectations for Elijah's return through his prophetic call to repentance.

This prophetic role is then outlined with allusions to Malachi (esp. 3:1, 22-23 LXX [3:1; 4:5-6 EV]), probably with an eye towards Isa 40:3 as well. The angel's prediction that "he will go before [ἐνώπιον] him [the Lord] in the spirit and power of Elijah" (v. 17; cf. v. 76) recalls Mal 3:1, which predicts an Elijianic messenger who will "prepare the way before

---

2. On OT themes in Luke 1, see esp. Green, "Problem of a Beginning," 61-86. The suggestion that even Luke's grammar and syntax are deliberately evocative of the LXX is particularly intriguing (see Jung, *Original Language*, 33-44; Wifstrand, "Luke and the Septuagint," 28-45; Öhler, *Elia im Neuen Testament*, 79; Fitzmyer, *Luke*, 1:312).

3. Fitzmyer, *Luke*, 1:319; Green, *Luke*, 78; Marshall, *Historian and Theologian*, 147; Müller, *Mehr als ein Prophet*, 104-5; Carlson, "Élie à l'Horeb," 439; Öhler, *Elia im Neuen Testament*, 81-82, though cf. 79, 86. Contra Wink, *John the Baptist*, 43, who sees the phrase "spirit and power of Elijah," as a deliberate distancing of the two figures.

4. Green, *Luke*, 77-78. Fitzmyer, *Luke*, 1:319-20, expects "power" to indicate miracles, and, noting that John is never attributed with miraculous feats, suggests that Luke disagrees with his source regarding John's Elijianic identity (though cf. 9:7-9). It is more likely, however, that Luke uses δύναμις in reference to charismatic preaching, as in his other uses of the term (Luke 4:14-15; Acts 1:8; 4:33).

[πρὸ προσώπου]" the Lord.⁵ Despite the difference in wording, the concept is plainly analogous, and the volume of the echo is amplified not only by the explicit mention of Elijah in the same line, but also by the stronger allusion to Mal 3:23 LXX (4:6 EV) in this verse (see below).⁶ The verb κατασκευάζω at the end of the verse ("a people prepared [κατεσκευασμένον] for the Lord") is used elsewhere in the Gospels only in quotations of Mal 3:1 (esp. 7:27; cf. Matt 11:10; Mark 1:2), raising the possibility that its appearance here likewise has this verse in view.⁷ That John would prepare the Lord's way by preparing the Lord's people is consistent with the role of Elijah we have seen in Malachi 3.

In going before the Lord, John will "turn [ἐπιστρέψαι] the hearts of parents [πατέρων] to their children [τέκνα]" (Luke 1:17b; cf. Mal 3:23 LXX). This reference too is a somewhat free paraphrase of the LXX (ἀποκαταστήσει καρδίαν πατρὸς πρὸς υἱόν), with ἐπιστρέφω ("to turn") as in Sir 48:10 in place of ἀποκαθίστημι ("to restore"), and τέκνον ("child") rather than υἱός ("son").⁸ Like Sirach and the LXX, Luke retains only the first half of Malachi's couplet, replacing "and the hearts of children to their parents" with "and the disobedient to the wisdom of the righteous [καὶ ἀπειθεῖς ἐν φρονήσει δικαίων]," a possible allusion to Mal 2:6 and 3:18 (cf. v. 16).⁹ The parallelism suggests that the restoration of

---

5. Nolland, *Luke*, 1:31. See also Bovon, *Luke*, 1:37; Bock, *Luke*, 1:88; Fitzmyer, *Luke*, 1:326-27; Green, *Luke*, 77; Marshall, *Gospel of Luke*, 58; Miller, "Elijah, John, and Jesus," 616-17. On the identification of the "Lord" with the God of Israel in the immediate context (v. 16) as well as, more broadly, with Jesus, see Rowe, *Early Narrative Christology*, 56-59.

6. See also the numerous proposed links between these verses and Malachi 3 in Wink, *John the Baptist*, 75-76.

7. Snodgrass, "Streams of Tradition," 37; Fitzmyer, *Luke*, 1:327; Nolland, *Luke*, 1:32.

8. Marshall, *Gospel of Luke*, 59, suggests that the latter may be to avoid confusion with the use of υἱός in 1:16. Luke's agreement with Sirach against LXX Malachi is striking, and it is not inconceivable that he was familiar with this tradition, though the many echoes of the book of Malachi as a whole demonstrate his familiarity with the canonical text as well (cf. Kurz, "Use of Sirach 48.1-16," 308-24; Burnett, "Eschatological Prophet," 7). Cf. Rindoš, *He of Whom It Is Written*, 53-54, who suggests that Sirach's conflation of Isa 49:6 with Mal 3:24 is in the background, and with it, the adumbration of universal salvation.

9. See esp. Green, *Luke*, 77; Pao and Schnabel, "Luke," 258. Malachi 2:6 speaks of the priest who, as God's "messenger [ἄγγελος]" (cf. 2:7), "turned many from sin [πολλοὺς ἐπέστρεψεν ἀπὸ ἀδικίας]." John's priestly lineage, which is in view in this passage, makes such an echo very plausible. Malachi 3:18 anticipates a distinguishing between the "righteous [δίκαιος]" and the "wicked [ἄνομος]" on the day of Yahweh (3:17).

the disobedient to the wisdom of the righteous is a further explanation of what the restoration of fathers and sons looks like—namely, repentance and renewed obedience across generations.[10] The nature of this repentance is described in v. 16: "He will turn [ἐπιστρέψει] many [πολλούς] of the children of Israel to the Lord their God." Turning the hearts of the children of Israel was, of course, Elijah's task both in his earthly life and his eschatological return (cf. 1 Kgs 18:36–37; Mal 3:24 [4:6 EV]). In this way, John the Baptist is expected to "make ready [ἑτοιμάσαι] a people prepared for the Lord" (v. 17) by calling them to repentance in advance of the Lord's visitation and the day of judgment.[11]

Thus, both in explicitly naming the OT prophet as well as in drawing from Malachi's expectation of Elijah's return, Gabriel's introduction of the yet-unborn John portrays him as clearly as possible after the figure of Elijah—a depiction which will color every subsequent appearance of John in Luke. Like the Elijianic messenger of Malachi 3, he will go before the Lord, preparing the way by preparing a righteous and repentant remnant.

John and the Remnant Theme

Luke's association of John with Elijah is no mere perfunctory fulfillment of prophecy but serves to flag a key theme, also introduced in this opening passage: the in-gathering of the remnant of Israel. Although there are hints of the removal of the wicked and the remainder of the righteous, this passage, consistent with the major themes of the opening chapters of Luke, is charged with the hope of the renewal of Israel in fulfillment of God's promises to Abraham and the patriarchs (vv. 55, 72–73). This is seen first of all in the parallels drawn between Zechariah and Elizabeth and Abraham and Sarah: they are referred to as "blameless" (ἄμεμπτοι; 1:6; cf. Gen 17:1); they are "advanced in age" (προβεβηκότες ἐν ταῖς ἡμέραις αὐτῶν; 1:17) and elderly (πρεσβύτεροι; 1:18) (cf. Gen 18:11; πρεσβύτεροι προβεβηκότες ἡμερῶν); they are without children (1:7; cf. Gen 11:30; 18:11–12); they are promised a child by an angelic visitor

---

10. See discussion in ch. 2 on Mal 3:24 [4:6 EV] as a reference to cross-generational revival. Though some aspect of interpersonal reconciliation is likely also in view, most commentators see a nation-wide call to repentance at the heart of the message.

11. The use of ἑτοιμάζω here is likely an echo of Isa 40:3, which is frequently used in conjunction with Mal 3:1 and the Elijah expectation (cf. 1:76; Mark 1:2–3) (see esp. Snodgrass, "Streams of Tradition," 37; Bock, *Luke*, 1:90). See below on Luke 3:4–6.

(1:13; cf. Gen 18:10); they respond initially in unbelief (1:18; cf. Gen 15:8; 17:17); and the child's name is divinely appointed (1:13; Gen 17:19).[12] The link between Isaac, through whom God built a great nation, and the remnant, through which he would rebuild it, had already been made by the prophets (Isa 51:1-2; cf. Hos 1:10), and by casting John in the light of this child of promise, Luke sets expectations for his role in the renewal of Israel.

Zechariah's prayer, with its links to Daniel 9-10, further highlights the focus on the redemption of Israel. Parallels include a prayer at the time of the evening sacrifice (1:9-10; cf. Dan 9:20-21); the appearance of Gabriel, who is named in the canonical texts only there and in Luke 1 (vv. 19, 26; cf. Dan 8:16; 9:21); and the announcement that his prayer had been answered (εἰσηκούσθη ἡ δέησις; v. 13; cf. Dan 9:20, 23; 10:12).[13] Daniel's prayer was specifically for Israel's redemption (9:20), and this was likely the content of Zechariah's priestly prayer as well.[14] Nevertheless, Zechariah's prayer for the redemption of Israel is answered in the form of an answer to his own apparently long-abandoned prayer for a child (cf. v. 18). Just as the Lord granted Abraham's personal desire for a son by making him the father of Israel, Zechariah's prayer for the reestablishment of Israel is answered by the granting of a son.[15]

Despite the dominant optimism for national renewal in this passage, there are also hints of the division that will later characterize John's ministry. John's work of effecting repentance or "turning" hearts (vv. 16-17), so central to the angel's description, indicates that, as in Elijah's day, Israel was much in need of repentance. Furthermore, that "many [πολλούς]" (v. 16) would turn implies that others—perhaps many more—would not.[16] In this way, John/Elijah's ministry serves a double function: removing the disobedient and revealing the righteous who will remain. Only with this accomplished can there be hope for a renewed Israel.

---

12. On Luke's utilization of the Abraham narratives throughout Luke 1-2, see esp. Green, *Luke*, 52-58; Green, "Problem of a Beginning," 61-86.

13. Marshall, *Gospel of Luke*, 56; Rindoš, *He of Whom It Is Written*, 48-49; Plummer, *Gospel according to S. Luke*, 13. Note also the parallel use of μὴ φοβοῦ (v. 13; cf. Dan 10:12).

14. On this significance of the evening sacrifice prayer, see Marshall, *Gospel of Luke*, 54; Green, *Luke*, 71; Fitzmyer, *Luke*, 1:324.

15. Fitzmyer, *Luke*, 1:325; Bovon, *Luke*, 1:35; Green, *Luke*, 73-74; Bock, *Luke*, 1:82-83.

16. Bovon, *Luke*, 1:37; Green, *Luke*, 76; Bock, *Luke*, 1:91.

Echoes in this passage of Isaiah 6, which also appears notably in the final scene of the Lukan narrative to describe the unresponsiveness to the gospel on the part of many Jews (Acts 28:26–27; cf. Luke 8:10), also point towards an eventual hardening to the prophetic message by all but a remnant in Israel (Isa 6:9–13).[17] Parallels include an angelic appearance in the temple—an event occurring only in these two passages in canonical Scripture (Luke 1:11; cf. Isa 6:2); a chronological reference to a king of Israel (1:5; cf. Isa 6:1); a response in fear (1:11–12; cf. Isa 6:5); smoke of incense (1:9–10; cf. Isa 6:4); unclean or unbelieving lips (1:18, 20; cf. Isa 6:5); and a divine commission to prophetic ministry (1:15–17; cf. Isa 6:8–13).[18] As the rest of the narrative confirms, many in Israel would hear John's message with deaf ears, effectively removing themselves from the covenant people (Isa 6:9–10). Yet from the "stump" that remains, a holy remnant would emerge like the shoot of a tree being reborn (Isa 6:13).[19]

In this first reference to Elijah in the opening scene of Luke's Gospel, John's Elijianic role is not merely one of typological fulfillment but is closely tied to the gathering of the remnant. Not only will he come in the "spirit and power" of the prophet of old, but, in keeping with Mal 3:23–24 (4:5–6 EV), he will "go before the Lord" in order to facilitate widespread national repentance, gathering a righteous portion before the day of judgment.

A Prophet of the Most High (Luke 1:67–79)

Zechariah's *Benedictus* (1:67–79) concludes John's birth narrative, looking back to the angel's words and anticipating his future career as a prophet like Elijah.[20] The allusion to Mal 3:1 in 1:76 stands out especially in light of the earlier echo of this reference in 1:17. "And you, child, will be called the prophet of the Most High; for you will go before the Lord to prepare his ways [προπορεύσῃ γὰρ ἐνώπιον κυρίου ἑτοιμάσαι ὁδοὺς αὐτοῦ]" (1:76).[21] John's identification as a "prophet" may in itself be sufficient to

---

17. On Isa 6:9–13 in Luke-Acts, see esp. Pao, *Isaianic New Exodus*, 101–9; cf. Tannehill, "Israel in Luke-Acts," 69–85.

18. See Bovon, *Luke*, 1:32; Marshall, *Gospel of Luke*, 55; cf. Bock, *Luke*; 1:81. Commentators also note the similarities with John Hyrcanus's vision described in Josephus (*Ant.* 13.282–83).

19. See discussion on Isa 6:13 in ch. 2.

20. Müller, *Mehr als ein Prophet*, 133.

21. Given this allusion, several other possible allusions to Malachi in this passage

evoke the Elijah motif (cf. 7:16), but when we consider that the reason (γάρ) for this identification is his mission to go before the Lord, the connection with the prophetic messenger of Mal 3:1 is clear, especially in the light of the earlier echo in v. 17. As there, Mal 3:1 (καὶ ἐπιβλέψεται ὁδὸν πρὸ προσώπου μου) is likely conflated with Isa 40:3 (ἑτοιμάσατε τὴν ὁδὸν κυρίου), for while Luke's use of ἑτοιμάζω ("prepare") creates stronger verbal links with the latter, the conceptual parallel of an emissary sent before the Lord derives more clearly from the former.[22] What John will accomplish in his prophetic ministry is exactly what was foretold of Elijah: he will proclaim salvation from divine wrath through a message of repentance and forgiveness (1:77; cf. Mal 3:23-24 [4:5-6 EV]).

As with the annunciation scene (1:5-23), the remnant theme is present particularly in the hope of national restoration and redemption, which is especially prominent in Zechariah's prayer (vv. 67-79). The reference to "those who sit in darkness" (τοῖς ἐν σκότει . . . καθημένοις) (v. 79) draws on OT imagery describing the condition of remnant Israel in exile (Isa 9:1 LXX [9:2 EV]; Ps 106:10 LXX [107:10 EV]), as does the mention of oppression by enemies (vv. 71, 74).[23] Yet rather than focusing on Israel's current condition as a beleaguered remnant, Zechariah draws from OT images of salvation, including the Exodus (v. 68; cf. Exod 4:31; 6:6), the patriarchal promises (vv. 72-73), and the Davidic dynasty (v. 69), proclaiming that God has "visited" (ἐπεσκέψατο) his people, and "redeemed" (ἐποίησεν λύτρωσιν) them. As in the OT prophetic remnant texts, Zechariah links national restoration inextricably with a restoration

---

arise (see esp. Wink, *John the Baptist*, 76). In particular, the idiom for "pondered" (ἔθεντο . . . ἐν τῇ καρδίᾳ αὐτῶν) (v. 66; cf. 2:19, 51) is used twice in the LXX of Malachi to describe the ideal response of the prophet's audience (Mal 1:1 LXX; 2:2), and the "dawn [ἀνατολή]" in v. 78 may echo LXX Mal 3:20 (4:2 EV), which speaks of the "sun of righteousness" that will "rise [ἀνατελεῖ] with healing in its wings" on those who revere the Lord (see Wink, *John the Baptist*, 76; Bock, *Luke*, 1:191-92; Bovon, *Luke*, 1:76; Carroll, *Luke*, 61; Marshall, *Gospel of Luke*, 94-95; Gathercole, "Heavenly *Anatole*," 471-88). See also the LXX's use of ἀνατολή in Jer 23:5; Zech 3:8; 6:12.

22. Bock, *Luke*, 1:188; Marshall, *Gospel of Luke*, 93; Pao and Schnabel, "Luke," 265; Green, *Luke*, 118; Wink, *John the Baptist*, 66, 69. Cf. Rindoš, *He of Whom It Is Written*, 85, who notes that Theodotion also has ἑτοιμάζω in Mal 3:1. On the conflation of Isa 40:3 and Mal 3:1 in the Gospel tradition, see discussion below (cf. esp. Snodgrass, "Streams of Tradition," 37; Juncker, "Jesus and the Angel of the Lord," 296-301).

23. See esp. Bauckham, "Restoration of Israel," 455-56. Though the concept of "forgiveness of sins" (v. 77) takes on particular significance as the Lukan narrative develops, it too draws on imagery for Israel's beleaguered condition (cf. esp. Isa 40:2; 55:7).

to right worship (v. 74; cf. esp. Amos 5:14-15; Zeph 2:3; cf. Isa 10:20). John's Elijianic proclamation of repentance and the forgiveness of sins grounds the hope of salvation that the divine visitation will bring. Apart from this return to God, Israel would remain oppressed and in darkness (v. 79), but through John's ministry, many would return to the Lord and thus experience the hope of renewal (v. 17).

The Prophet Preparing the Way (Luke 3:1-20)

The significance that Luke attaches to John's preaching and baptism is seen not only in the added space he devotes to it (cf. Mark 1:1-8; Matt 3:1-12), but also in his subsequent references back to this moment (Acts 1:22; 10:37; cf. 13:24). This scene is presented as a programmatic indicator of the Baptist's life and ministry, and it confirms what has been foreshadowed: that John appears like Elijah of old, calling the nation to repentance, and gathering the remnant of Israel.[24] We will examine the connections with Elijah in this passage, looking first at clues within the narrative frame (3:1-6, 18-20), then within the content of his teaching, before examining the presence of the remnant theme throughout this pericope.

John's Elijianic Ministry

Parallels between John and Elijah in this passage have been called into question, especially by Conzelmann, because of Luke's omission of the description of John's clothing (Matt 3:4 // Mark 1:6; cf. 2 Kgs 1:8).[25] However, not only does this miss the significance of the birth narratives (1:17, 76), which set our expectations for this passage, but it also misses several nuanced references to the Elijah narrative, which Luke retains or even adds. These include the prophetic formula (v. 2), John's denunciation of Herod (Luke 3:1, 19-20), the location of his ministry (vv. 2-3), the application of the quotation from Isaiah 40, and the dependence upon Malachi 3.

---

24. Müller, *Mehr als ein Prophet*, 166; Bovon, *Luke*, 1:166. See next ch. on parallels with Luke 4:16-30 as the programmatic introduction to Jesus's ministry.

25. Conzelmann, *Theology of St. Luke*, 22. See also Wink, *John the Baptist*, 42n1; cf. Fitzmyer, *Luke*, 1:215, 469.

Luke's unique introductory formula—"the word of God came to John [ἐγένετο ῥῆμα θεοῦ ἐπὶ Ἰωάννην] son of Zechariah in the wilderness" (Luke 3:2)—does not merely establish John's credentials as a prophet, but, with its use of the less common noun ῥῆμα (cf. λόγος in Hos 1:1; Joel 1:1; Jonah 1:1; Mic 1:1), most closely matches the refrain that marks each major development in the Elijah cycle: "The word of the Lord came to Elijah [ἐγένετο ῥῆμα κυρίου πρὸς Ηλιου]" (1 Kgs 17:2, 8; 18:1; 19:9; 21:28 [20:28 LXX]).[26] Furthermore, Luke 3:2 follows the distinct pattern of 1 Kgs 17:2 in that the formula comes uncharacteristically after the synchronism or "time stamp" (1 Kgs 16:29-30), rather than the typical placement before (cf. Jer 1:2). In both cases, this arrangement may have the effect of highlighting the royal antagonist as the one against whom the prophet is commissioned.[27] Thus, with the simple addition of this formula, Luke can reaffirm the reader's expectations for John as an Elijianic figure.

Herod Antipas, whose reign is characterized as "evil," and whose wicked deeds culminate in the imprisonment of John (vv. 19-20; cf. 1 Kgs 16:30-34), is easily cast in the role of the "wicked king of Israel" and antagonist of the prophet—a role epitomized by Ahab (2 Kgs 8:18, 27).[28] Furthermore, his illegitimate marriage tightens the link with Ahab specifically (v. 19; cf. 1 Kgs 16:31).[29] Throughout the Lukan narrative, Herod's prominence as an Ahab-like antagonist is greatly increased in the Lukan narrative as compared to the other Gospels, not least in the addition of his participation in Jesus's trial (23:6-12).[30] Thus, in his pro-

---

26. Fitzmyer, *Luke*, 1:458-59; Marshall, *Gospel of Luke*, 134; Bock, *Luke*, 1:284-86; Danker, *Jesus and the New Age*, 83. Outside of 1 Kings there is also a close verbal parallel to LXX Jer 1:1 (Τὸ ῥῆμα τοῦ θεοῦ, ὃ ἐγένετο ἐπὶ Ιερεμιαν), though there is little other evidence of a deliberate parallel between these two figures (contra Nolland, *Luke*, 1:140).

27. Rindoš, *He of Whom It Is Written*, 105-9.

28. Darr, *Herod the Fox*, 131-36, 157-58; Rindoš, *He of Whom It Is Written*, 149-50; Schürmann, *Das Lukasevangelium*, 184.

29. Darr, *Herod the Fox*, 158; Bock, *Luke*, 1:329. Though Luke's omission of Herodias's role in the execution of John (cf. Mark 6:14-29) does somewhat diminish her parallel with Jezebel, the essential elements are still present for the basic analogy to exist (Janes, "Daughter of Herodias," 455-57). See also Rindoš, *He of Whom It Is Written*, 104; Burnett, "Eschatological Prophet," 4-5. Note also Herod's ties to pagan powers, suggested by his placement in vv. 1-2 (Darr, *Herod the Fox*, 139-40; Carroll, *Luke*, 90-91; Green, *Luke*, 166-69; Webb, *John the Baptizer*, 356-57; cf. Josephus, *Ant.* 18.2.3).

30. In fact, while Matthew and Mark allow the tetrarch to fade from view with the death of John, Herod (or one of the Herods) appears as an antagonist "in every major

phetic confrontation with him in this opening scene, John appears as an Elijianic figure.[31]

The setting of John's ministry also evokes the Elijah motif. References to "the wilderness [ἐρήμῳ]" (v. 2; cf. 1:80) and "the Jordan" (v. 3) are highly significant for the Elijah narratives. It was in the wilderness that "the word of the Lord came to Elijah" repeatedly (1 Kgs 19:4, 15; cf. 17:3–9).[32] Likewise, Elijah began his ministry by crossing the Jordan (cf. 1 Kgs 17:3) and was taken up into heaven after recapitulating the miraculous Jordan crossing (cf. 2 Kgs 2:6–14). For John—already expected to come in the spirit of Elijah—to begin his prophetic ministry in the same setting where the prophet concluded his strongly suggests that the ministry to follow will in some way fulfill Elijianic expectations.[33] It was across the Jordan that Elisha received the departing Elijah's spirit (2 Kgs 2:9–15), and it is here that John emerges in that same spirit and power (cf. 1:17).[34]

Finally, John's role as the Elijianic messenger before the Lord is confirmed by his sermon itself, which is significantly influenced by Malachi 3.[35] He situates himself just before the day of the Lord's coming and offers his baptism of repentance as a means by which one may be saved

---

section of Luke's double work" (cf. Darr, *Herod the Fox*, 12). Antipas is mentioned in Luke 3:19; 8:3; 9:7, 9; 13:31; 23:7–15; Acts 4:27; 13:1, his father Herod the Great in 1:5, and his great-nephew, Herod Agrippa II, fills the role in the latter part of Acts (Acts 25:13—26:32).

31. Herod's role opposite both John and Jesus continues throughout the Gospel as he demonstrates an ambivalence similar to that of Ahab with Elijah, in which he is both drawn to the prophet, but also responsible for seeking his death (see esp. 9:9; 13:31; 23:8) (cf. Darr, *Herod the Fox*, 158, 191).

32. Burnett, "Eschatological Prophet," 9–10; cf. Green, *Luke*, 163, 169–70. Of course, the link is found in the desert setting, not the geographic location (cf. 1 Kgs 19:3–4, 8).

33. Öhler, *Elia im Neuen Testament*, 105; see also Trumblower, "Role of Malachi," 36–37; Rindoš, *He of Whom It Is Written*, 113).

34. It is also intriguing to consider whether Luke's surprising inclusion of soldiers present to be baptized (v. 14) echoes the account of Naaman, who "immersed himself [ἐβαπτίσατο]" in the Jordan (2 Kgs 5:14), especially in light of the importance of the Naaman account for Luke's Elijah motif (Luke 4:27; cf. 7:1–10; Acts 10:1–48). See Danker, *Jesus and the New Age*, 83; Trumblower, "Role of Malachi," 37.

35. See Trumblower, "Role of Malachi," 28–41; Öhler, *Elia im Neuen Testament*, 62–65; Miller, "Messenger," 11–16. On OT allusions more broadly in this pericope, see Dunn, "Use of Scripture," 42–54.

from "the wrath to come" (v. 7; cf. Mal 3:23–24; Sir 48:10).[36] More significantly, he speaks of one who "is coming [ἔρχεται]" after him (v. 16). The emphatic positioning of ἔρχεται at the beginning of the sentence, along with later uses of the verb by Luke (cf. 7:19, 20; Acts 13:24–25) leads numerous scholars to see a reference to Mal 3:1 ("Behold, he is coming [ἰδοὺ ἔρχεται]").[37] In this case John, as the Elijianic messenger, anticipates the "Lord," who "is coming" after him.[38] In light of this parallel, John's depiction of the coming wrath likely echoes parts of Malachi's description of the day of Yahweh. In particular, scholars point to the emphasis on fire as both a cleansing agent and a form of judgment (vv. 16–17; cf. Mal 3:1, 19); the burning of the wicked like chaff or stubble (v. 17; cf. Mal 3:19); and the cutting of a tree at its roots for burning (v. 9; cf. Mal 3:19).[39] In this way, John's role is characterized as "a prophet before the day of Yahweh, who restrains the wrath of God with his call to repentance and the prophetic sign of baptism. This is nothing other than what the returning Elijah shall do."[40]

Although Isa 40:3–5 does not itself mention Elijah, we have already seen that there is a long stream of tradition that connects this passage with Mal 3:1.[41] To begin with, the parallel imagery and vocabulary strongly

36. On the precise meaning of John's question "Who warned you to flee from the wrath to come," see esp. Marshall, *Gospel of Luke*, 139; Bock, *Luke*, 1:304.

37. See esp. Fitzmyer, *Luke*, 1:472; Miller, "Messenger," 12–14; Green, *Luke*, 180; Rindoš, *He of Whom It Is Written*, 130–32; Trumblower, "Role of Malachi," 36; Pao and Schnabel, "Luke," 279; Miller, "Messenger," 14–15; Robinson, "Elijah, John and Jesus," 263–81; Miller, "Elijah, John, and Jesus," 315; Dunn, "Use of Scripture," 50. On further implications of the phrase ὁ ἐρχόμενος in Luke, including echoes of Ps 118:26, see esp. Bock, *Proclamation*, 118; Rowe, *Early Narrative Christology*, 163; Turner, *Power from on High*, 179–80.

38. Several commentators see the line "Behold, he is coming" in Mal 3:1 as referring to Elijah rather than the one he precedes, concluding that John is rejecting the title of Elijah for himself and applying it instead to Jesus (Robinson, "Elijah, John and Jesus," 263–81; Fitzmyer, *Luke*, 1:472; Miller, "Elijah, John, and Jesus," 315). However, as discussed in ch. 2, it is best to understand the final form of Mal 3:1 as referring to a "messenger" (Elijah) who is "sent" (LXX ἀποστέλλω) and the "Lord" who "is coming" (ἔρχεται) (see Petterson, *Malachi*, 363; Glazier-McDonald, *Malachi*, 132; cf. Hill, *Malachi*, 265, 270–71). This makes the best sense of Luke's use of Mal 3:1 throughout Luke-Acts (1:17, 76; 7:19–29; Acts 13:24–25). See discussion in Miller, "Messenger," 12–15.

39. See Trumblower, "Role of Malachi," 35–40; Dunn, "Use of Scripture," 49–50; Öhler, *Elia im Neuen Testament*, 62–65; Pao and Schnabel, "Luke," 278–79.

40. Öhler, *Elia im Neuen Testament*, 64–65.

41. See Snodgrass, "Streams of Tradition," 24–45; cf. Bascom, "Preparing the Way,"

suggest that Mal 3:1 is drawing from Isa 40:3.[42] In fact, the concept of someone preparing the way for Yahweh ahead of him is found only in these two passages, prompting later Jewish writings to link the two passages (esp. Deut. Rab. 4:11; cf. Num. Rab. 4:11).[43] These two texts (along with Exod 23:20) are famously conflated in the opening quotation of Mark's Gospel (Mark 1:2), with the result that the "messenger" is identified as "the voice crying out in the wilderness."[44] As we have already seen, Luke makes the same conflation in multiple places (1:17, 76; cf. 9:52).[45] In his lengthy quotation of Isa 40:3–5 (vv. 4–6), Luke effectively reminds the reader of these allusions from the birth narratives. Though of course the primary function of the quotation is to illustrate the type of role that John will have in the restoration of Israel's remnant, the quotation also serves to remind us that he will fulfill this role as the Elijianic messenger.[46]

225–27; DeYoung, "Malachi 3.1 in Matthew 11.10," 66–91; Juncker, "Jesus and the Angel of the Lord," 296–328; Watts, *New Exodus in Mark*, 53–90; Pao, *Isaianic New Exodus*, 40–45; Marcus, *Way of the Lord*, 12–13.

42. In particular the use of פנה in the piel with דרך is found elsewhere only three times in the OT, all of them in the latter part of Isaiah (Isa 40:3; 57:14; 62:10). Kessler, *Maleachi*, 229; Hill, *Malachi*, 86, 266; Petterson, *Malachi*, 362; Snodgrass, "Streams of Tradition," 25.

43. Snodgrass, "Streams of Tradition," 43n35; Marshall, *Gospel of Luke*, 295. The LXX of Isa 40:2 addresses this passage to the "priests" (ἱερεῖς), which Snodgrass believes could show a connection by the translators with the priestly messenger of Mal 3:1; cf. 2:7 (Snodgrass, "Streams of Tradition," 26). Exodus 23:20, the other passage influencing Mal 3:1, presents the inverse image—Yahweh or his angel preparing the way for his people (cf. also Isa 57:14; 62:10). On the intertextual links between Mal 3:1 and Exod 23:20, see esp. Glazier-McDonald, *Malachi*, 129–32; Watts, *New Exodus in Mark*, 71–72, 74–76.

44. See Juncker, "Angel of the Lord," 316–28; Watts, *New Exodus in Mark*, 53–90; Bascom, "Preparing the Way," 230–35; Snodgrass, "Streams of Tradition," 34–36. The NT citations of Isa 40:3 follow the LXX in connecting ἐν τῇ ἐρήμῳ ("in the wilderness") with φωνὴ βοῶντος ("a voice of one calling") rather than with ἑτοιμάσατε τὴν ὁδὸν κυρίου ("prepare the way of the Lord") as in the MT. There is, however, some evidence of a competing Hebrew *Vorlage* behind the LXX. See esp. Watts, *New Exodus in Mark*, 63; Bock, *Luke*, 1:290; Oswalt, *Isaiah*, 2:51; Westermann, *Isaiah*, 2:37–38; Snodgrass, "Streams of Tradition," 26–27. Luke does not follow Mark here in including Mal 3:1 in his quotation of Isa 40:3–5 (cf. Mark 1:2), yet this is likely due to the awkwardness in apparently attributing to "Isaiah" words from Malachi, rather than a desire to downplay John's connection with Elijah (cf. 7:27).

45. The "distinct attestation [of this pairing] in a variety of Gospels shows it to be a strongly held tradition" already (Bock, *Luke*, 1:90). On possible echoes of Mal 3:1 and Isa 40:3 in Luke 9:52, see Snodgrass, "Streams of Tradition," 39–40.

46. Fitzmyer, *Luke*, 1:452; Miller, "Elijah, John, and Jesus," 317–18; Öhler, *Elia im*

John and the Remnant of Israel

As it unfolds in Luke 3, John's Elijianic ministry is brimming with both hope and dread—the promise of renewal and the threat of burning judgment. These two poles are characteristic of the remnant theme, which we will trace out by examining (1) his removal of the wicked through judgment, (2) the gathering of a righteous remainder, and (3) the hope of renewal for the people of God.

Removal through Judgment

John's fiery sermon announces the coming wrath of God (v. 7) and the removal of all wickedness and evildoers from Israel (vv. 9, 17, 19). In keeping with the Lukan theme of power reversals (see esp. 1:52), John's invectives are directed especially at the powerbrokers of his day, with Herod in particular called out for his unlawful marriage (vv. 19-20).[47] There appears also to be at least implicit judgment on Israel's religious leaders, for proclaiming the forgiveness of sins in the wilderness rather than at the temple would surely be seen as a critique of the temple cult.[48] At the very least, his warning of wrath and call for repentance suggests that the religious leadership is ineffective.[49] The narrator may also hint

---

Neuen Testament, 86-87; contra Danker, *Jesus and the New Age*, 84-85; Conzelmann, *Theology of St. Luke*, 22. On Luke's possible sources in this section, see esp. Fitzmyer, *Luke*, 1:451-52; Marshall, *Gospel of Luke*, 132.

47. It may be that the narrative pits John against Roman authorities as well, for he is certainly aware of extortion by the military (v. 14), and the opening reference to Tiberius Caesar and Pontius Pilate must be read in light of the expectation that the unfolding events will bring "down the powerful from their thrones" (1:52). Darr, *Herod the Fox*, 139-40; Green, *Luke*, 167-69; Webb, *John the Baptizer*, 373. On the complex portrayal of the Roman Empire in Luke-Acts more broadly, see esp. Rowe, *World Upside Down*.

48. Müller, *Mehr als ein Prophet*, 165-66; Trumblower, "Role of Malachi," 39; Webb, *John the Baptizer*, 370-72; Green, *Luke*, 166-67; Carroll, *Luke*, 91. A similar move is made in Stephen's speech in Acts 7:1-53 (esp. vv. 48-50). Though Luke lacks Matthew's mention of the Pharisees and Sadducees (Matt 3:7; though cf. Luke 7:29-30), this is likely a Matthean addition rather than a Lukan omission (Luz, *Matthew*, 1:169-70; Marshall, *Gospel of Luke*, 139).

49. Webb, *John the Baptizer*, 371; Green, *Luke*, 170. Given John's priestly lineage and the positive portrayal of the temple in chs. 1-2, for him to now act independently of the temple cult comes as a surprise to the reader (Müller, *Mehr als ein Prophet*, 165-66; Darr, *Herod the Fox*, 141). It may be, given the influence of Malachi on the presentation of John's ministry, that the removal and disgrace of the priesthood

at this in naming Annas and Caiaphas together and listing them among other Roman-sanctioned authorities (vv. 1–2), drawing attention to the power held by this elite family—power given by Caesar rather than God.[50] Conflict with the priestly elite will continue to unfold throughout Luke-Acts, yet even here, John's words of judgment present them as liable to condemnation.

Yet John is no mere revolutionary, for his fiery words are addressed to the nation as a whole (vv. 7, 10, 15, 18, 21).[51] That soldiers (v. 14) and "even tax collectors" (v. 12) were present—another Lukan addition—further suggests a broad cross-section of the nation, in which people from all walks of life are confronted with imminent judgment.[52] In his opening diatribe, John divides the people into two groups: those who repent and turn to righteousness are like fruitful trees that will be spared (v. 7), while the rest— those who rely on their physical descent from Abraham—are fruitless trees that will be cut down at the root and burned (v. 8).[53] They are warned that their evil deeds have made them effectively a "brood of vipers" (v. 7)—not children of Israel, but children of the devil![54] God could wipe them all out in judgment and still be faithful to his patriarchal promises, for he is able to "raise up children to Abraham" from the rocks in the wilderness (v. 8).[55] The hyperbolic language points to

---

prophesied in Mal 2:1–4 is in view here (Trumblower, "Role of Malachi," 39; Webb, *John the Baptizer*, 371n47).

50. Webb, *John the Baptizer*, 371–72; Rindoš, *He of Whom It Is Written*, 104–51; Green, *Luke*, 169; Marshall, *Gospel of Luke*, 134; Bock, *Luke*, 1:283–84; Fitzmyer, *Luke*, 1:458. Taylor, *Immerser*, 106–11, rejects the idea that John would have been "anti-temple," though she does appear to place him within the prophetic tradition that denounced cultic corruption and elevated inner repentance above the sacrificial system.

51. Nolland, *Luke*, 1:147; Bovon, *Luke*, 1:132; Bock, *Luke*, 1:302–3; Fitzmyer, 1:464, 467; cf. Marshall, *Gospel of Luke*, 138–39.

52. It is likely that the "soldiers" were Jewish conscripts rather than gentiles (Nolland, *Luke*, 1:150). See further below.

53. Taylor, *Immerser*, 127–30, suggests that it was not physical descent per se that the people were relying upon, but rather the accumulated merit of Abraham (*zekhut*). Nevertheless, the effect is that the people were depending upon inherited favor rather than true obedience.

54. Marshall, *Gospel of Luke*, 139; Fitzmyer, *Luke*, 1:465, 467; Green, *Luke*, 175; Bock, *Luke*, 1:303–5.

55. Many commentators see an echo of Isa 51:1–2, for only here in the OT is the imagery of stone used to describe Abraham's descendants. Likewise, in both passages, the concept is of rebuilding Israel from little or nothing (Rindoš, *He of Whom It Is Written*, 119–20; Fitzmyer, *Luke*, 1:468; Bovon, *Luke*, 1:123; Green, *Luke*, 176–77;

God's ability to fulfill his plans with even a meager remnant, and thus the folly of presuming upon Israelite descent.[56] In his closing remarks, John applies another agricultural image, stating that the one who is coming has his "winnowing fork" in hand (v. 17). The images of threshing and winnowing are common metaphors in the OT for the separation of the righteous (grain) from the wicked (chaff) (esp. Isa 41:15–16; Ps 1:4; cf. Amos 9:9). The emphasis here is on the chaff, which will be burned "with unquenchable fire" (v. 17).[57] Thus, John describes his ministry as a nationwide sifting in which all the wicked of the land either repent or are marked for judgment, so that only a righteous remnant remains.

Remainder by Grace

Although John's sermon is filled with withering words of judgment, at the same time, it is in some way "good news" (v. 18)—the wicked are removed from among Israel, but a righteous remainder is preserved. His location, use of Scripture, and baptism of repentance all present him as acting to gather the remnant of Israel. The wilderness was associated with Israel's return from exile, as the setting of the highway through which the remnant would return in a new exodus (esp. Isa 35:1–10; 40:3–5; 43:16–21; Jer 31:2–3), as well as the place where Yahweh dealt with Israel's sin and renewed his covenant with her (Ezek 20:33–38; Hos 2:14–23).[58] Likewise, the Jordan River was a national symbol of entrance into the promised land, and served as a physical reminder of Yahweh's fulfillment of his promises to the patriarchs (Josh 3:1–17).[59] Since even the first Jordan crossing was linked with covenant renewal in the form of circumcision

---

Bock, *Luke*, 1:305). See discussion below.

56. See esp. Dunn, "Use of Scripture," 49.

57. The winnowing shovel was used to "clear the threshing floor" (v. 17) after the grain and chaff had been separated in the threshing process. The pile of wheat would then be shoveled into the granary, and the chaff into the fire. John's ministry, then, is one of separating the righteous from the wicked in advance of the judgment, while Jesus, the greater one, will enact the judgment itself with his winnowing shovel. See, Webb, *John the Baptizer*, 295–300, 305; Green, *Luke*, 182; Turner, *Power from on High*, 171; cf. Nolland, *Luke*, 1:153–54.

58. Müller, *Mehr als ein Prophet*, 163; Green, *Luke*, 169–71; Brown, "John the Baptist," 48–49; Burnett, "Eschatological Prophet," 9–10.

59. Burnett, "Eschatological Prophet," 12–13; Müller, *Mehr als ein Prophet*, 163; Rindoš, *He of Whom It Is Written*, 113; Webb, *John the Baptizer*, 363–64.

and reconsecration of the people (Josh 5:2–7), entrance into the river here would suggest a purified core of Israel.[60]

The significance of the Baptist's movement is elaborated in Luke's lengthy application of Isa 40:3–5. According to Luke, John's proclamation in the wilderness is itself a fulfillment of this OT passage: "as it is written in the book of the words of the prophet Isaiah" (v. 4).[61] The correspondence is found not merely in the fact that John's voice was heard in the wilderness, but in that he raised his voice to "prepare the way [τὴν ὁδὸν] of the Lord" (v. 4).[62] This application highlights John's preparatory work as forerunner for the coming of Jesus in a way similar to the application of Mal 3:1 that we have already seen (cf. 1:17, 76).[63] However, the use of this text in addition to Mal 3:1 emphasizes that the nature of this work involves the gathering of a particular people (cf. 1:16, 17)—the remnant of Israel. "Way-terminology," drawn from Isa 40:3, was often evoked in Jewish circles to identify true Israel, often to the exclusion of others, in anticipation of God's renewal of his people.[64] For John to prepare a "people" (cf. 1:17) by preparing "the way" (3:4) is tantamount to preparing the remnant.

Finally, John's administration of baptism suggests that his ministry consisted of the gathering of a remnant.[65] The Lukan narrative depicts

60. The "people, now constituting the true, remnant Israel, were re-entering their land in a symbolic act of 'possessing it'" (Webb, *John the Baptizer*, 364; see also Brown, "John the Baptist," 44–47). John's was certainly not the only movement to recall Joshua's conquest in order symbolically to inaugurate a renewed Israel. See esp. Josephus's account of Theudas, who promised to part the Jordan and cross it (*Ant.* 20.97–98) (cf. Webb, *John the Baptizer*, 333–39; Horsley, "'Prophets of Old,'" 435–63; Trumblower, "Role of Malachi," 29–32; Öhler, *Elia im Neuen Testament*, 99–101).

61. Marshall, *Gospel of Luke*, 136; Fuller, *Restoration of Israel*, 220–22; Bock, *Luke*, 1:290.

62. See above on the use of the LXX reading here.

63. Luke's shift to "make straight his paths [εὐθείας ποιεῖτε τὰς τρίβους αὐτοῦ]" from "make straight the paths of our God [εὐθείας ποιεῖτε τὰς τρίβους τοῦ θεοῦ ἡμῶν]" (Isa 40:3 LXX), apparently following Mark (cf. Mark 1:2), allows for the identification of the "Lord" with Jesus (Bovon, *Luke*, 1:121; Green, *Luke*, 171; Nolland, *Luke*, 1:143; Pao, *Isaianic New Exodus*, 38; Rindoš, *He of Whom It Is Written*, 116–17; cf. Rowe, *Early Narrative Christology*, 71–72).

64. Pao, *Isaianic New Exodus*, 59–68. See also usage in Acts (9:2; 19:9, 23; 22:4; 24:4, 22). On the similar uses of "way" terminology in Qumran literature, see also Dunn, "Use of Scripture," 45–46; Pao and Schnabel, "Luke," 276–77; Fitzmyer, *Luke*, 1:460–61. This would be true whether one understands "the way" primarily ethically or apocalyptically (cf. Marcus, *The Way*, 29–31).

65. Parallels to John's baptism may be found especially within the Qumran

John's baptism above all as a "baptism of repentance" (3:3; cf. Acts 13:24; 19:4), and those who express their repentance through baptism are expected to demonstrate their change of heart through appropriate good works or "fruits" (v. 8).[66] As we have seen, John's preaching denounces his audience, from the leadership to "the people" (vv. 13, 21; cf. v. 7), as covenant-breakers and therefore outside the bounds of Israel. Yet if wickedness removes one from the covenant community, repentance leads to the forgiveness of sins and thus to readmission into the people of God.[67] Because of this emphasis on repentance, "even tax collectors" and "soldiers" (vv. 12, 14)—those who had estranged themselves from Israel—may be considered children of Abraham again.[68] Repentance is frequently a defining characteristic of the remnant in the Prophets (e.g., Isa 10:20-21; Ezek 6:8-10; Amos 5:14-15; Zeph 2:3), and particularly in the Elijah narratives (1 Kgs 18:37; Mal 3:24 [4:6]), making it the ideal characteristic by which John's ministry, expressed by baptism and manifested by good works, marks out the community gathered around him as the remnant of Israel.[69]

community and, though only arising later in Judaism, in the initiation rite for gentile proselytes, so that "each element of John's baptism is quite understandable within his Jewish milieu. Yet, John's baptism manifests distinctive features which indicate that he was a creative and innovative person who was able to formulate from within his heritage and milieu a coherent response to the problems he perceived among his people" (Webb, *John the Baptizer*, 216. See also Taylor, *Immerser*, 49-100; Bock, *Luke*, 1:287-89; Fitzmyer, *Luke*, 1:459-60; Green, *Luke*, 164-65; Nolland, *Luke*, 1:141-42; cf. Brown, "John the Baptist," 37-49).

66. On interpretative options for the genitive construction βάπτισμα μετανοίας, see esp. Porter, "Baptism and Translation," 81-98; Green, "Significance of Baptism," 157-72; Webb, *John the Baptizer*, 186-87. Whether one sees a descriptive, subjective, or objective genitive, the important point is the close connection between John's baptism and repentance.

67. Green, *Luke*, 170-71. A similar pattern is found in Isa 40. Although repentance is not explicitly mentioned in that passage, there again the people can only be gathered into a new community through the new exodus (Isa 40:3) after their sins are appropriately dealt with (Isa 40:2) (cf. Pao, *Isaianic New Exodus*, 45-50).

68. The soldiers were likely Jews working as military police who enforced the collection of tolls, hence their presence with the tax collectors and John's instructions regarding money (v. 14). See Danker, *Jesus and the New Age*, 89-90; Fitzmyer, *Luke*, 1:470; Marshall, *Gospel of Luke*, 143-44; cf. Brink, *Soldiers in Luke-Acts*, 100-101; Müller, *Mehr als ein Prophet*, 179-80. It is striking that neither group is required to leave their profession, but merely to practice them uprightly (see Danker, *Jesus and the New Age*, 87-88; Green, *Luke*, 179-80).

69. "By means of this baptism he 'gathered together' his group (*Ant*. 18.117), which became the true, remnant Israel" (Webb, *John the Baptizer*, 360; cf. 215).

Hope of Renewal

For all his withering words of judgment, John's ministry was still profoundly one of hope, with the people "filled with expectation" and wondering whether he could be the Messiah, who would restore Israel (v. 15). As mentioned above, the new exodus imagery in this passage—the Jordan River, the wilderness, and the appeal to Isaiah 40—gives rise to the expectation that a renewed Israel will arise from the repentant core that John gathers.[70] Another aspect of this renewal is found in the image of the "stones" from which God is able to raise up true descendants of Abraham (v. 8). Though there are no explicit verbal links, many commentators see an echo of Isa 51:1–3, the only passage in the OT that uses stone imagery to speak of Abraham's descendants.[71] In its original context, it communicates God's ability to restore Israel in miraculous ways despite its reduction to a mere remnant.[72] Although John's use of this imagery within the narrative inverts the message of hope to a word of warning—one ought not presume upon one's lineage, for God can fulfill his promises to Abraham even with stones—at the same time, the element

---

70. "From Luke's account of John the Baptist in chapter 3, it is clear the restoration programme announced in chapters 1–2 has unambiguously begun" (Bauckham, "Restoration of Israel," 466).

71. "Listen to me, you that pursue righteousness, you that seek the Lord. Look to the rock [LXX, πέτραν] from which you were hewn, and to the quarry from which you were dug. Look to Abraham your father and to Sarah who bore you; for he was one when I called him, but I blessed him and made him many. For the Lord will comfort [παρακαλέσω] Zion; he will comfort [παρεκάλεσα] all her waste places [ἔρημα], and will make her wilderness [ἔρημα] like Eden, her desert like the garden of the Lord; joy and gladness will be found in her, thanksgiving and the voice of song" (Isa 51:1–3). See Jeremias, "λίθος," 4:269–71; Rindoš, *He of Whom It Is Written*, 119–20; Fitzmyer, *Luke*, 1:468; Green, *Luke*, 176–77; Bock, *Luke*, 1:305; Pao and Schnabel, "Luke," 278–79; Marshall, *Gospel of Luke*, 141; cf. Bovon, *Luke*, 1:123; Dunn, "Use of Scripture," 49. This passage points back to Isa 40:1–9, not only thematically with the hope of national restoration, but also in their shared vocabulary: "comfort" (נחם, LXX περικαλέω; Isa 40:1; cf. Isa 51:3), "Zion" (Isa 40:9; cf. Isa 51:3), and "wilderness" (מִדְבָּר, LXX ἔρημος; Isa 40:3; cf. Isa 51:3) (cf. Childs, *Isaiah*, 402; Oswalt, *Isaiah*, 2:335; Pao, *Isaianic New Exodus*, 46). The extended quotation of Isa 40:3–5 in vv. 4–6 may increase the volume of an echo here. On possible wordplay in the Aramaic behind this verse, see esp. Bovon, *Luke*, 1:123; though cf. Jeremias, "λίθος," 171.

72. "As God [at the birth of Isaac] caused the children of Abraham to spring up miraculously out of the rock Abraham, so He can now in the same way call children of Abraham back to life" (Jeremias, "λίθος," 271).

of hope remains—God can and will restore Israel from just a few faithful ones into a great nation.⁷³

The culmination of John's ministry, characterized by Isa 40:3-5, would be that "all flesh shall see the salvation of God" (v. 6). Luke has likely extended the quotation from Isaiah 40 precisely in order to end on this universalist vision (cf. Mark 1:3; Matt 3:3).⁷⁴ It will take the rest of the Lukan narrative to draw out how precisely "the salvation of God [τὸ σωτήριον τοῦ θεοῦ]" would be sent to the nations (Acts 28:28).⁷⁵ Yet even here, with the focus of John's ministry so clearly on the renewal of Israel, one cannot help but note the universal impact this renewal will have.

Summary

Introducing the main body of the Lukan narrative, John's bold prophetic rebukes match Malachi's expectations for Elijah, who will come to lead a nationwide call to repentance. In this way, John serves to remove wickedness from the land in preparation for "the coming one," who will burn the "chaff" but gather up the "grain"—the righteous and repentant remnant. Even so, there remains an electric expectation that the renewal of Israel is on the way, and beyond that, salvation to "all flesh."

The One about Whom It Is Written (Luke 7:18–35)

After seeing John's Elijianic identity attested in the angelic pronouncement (1:17), in his father's prophetic oracle (1:76), and from his own mouth (3:1–17), we turn to a final pericope, which records Jesus's testimony regarding the Baptist. Jesus's testimony emphasizes the polarizing nature of John's ministry (as well as his own)—many will miss what the Baptist's coming represents, and only a few will respond in wisdom. This task of gathering the remnant of Israel from a corrupt generation is again presented in terms of Malachi's Elijianic messenger.

---

73. The image of life from stone also carries the concept of spiritual revival necessary for Israel's renewal (cf. Ezek 36:26). See Bovon, *Luke*, 1:122–23.

74. Marshall, *Gospel of Luke*, 137; Bock, *Luke*, 1:295–96; Fitzmyer, *Luke*, 1:461.

75. In each of the three occurrences of neuter σωτήριον in Luke-Acts, Isa 40:5 appears to be in view. The only other instance in the NT (Eph 6:17) is drawn from Isa 56:17. On the likely intertextual link between Acts 28:28 and Luke 2:30; 3:6, see esp. Tannehill, *Narrative Unity*, 1:40–42.

The Elijah Motif

The volume of Elijah allusions in this pericope is significantly increased by its immediate context, for the preceding two pericopae (7:1–10, 11–17) are among the best attested allusions to Elijah in Luke-Acts. As we shall see in the next chapter, Jesus performs actions reminiscent of the healing of Naaman (7:1–10; cf. 2 Kgs 5:1–14) and Elijah's raising of the widow's son (7:11–17; cf. 1 Kgs 17:17–24; 2 Kgs 4:32–37). The transition in v. 18, which refers to "all these things"—presumably Jesus's miracles in 7:1–17—"ties this pericope directly into the antecedent material." Thus, the reader's expectations are primed for similar themes and motifs here.[76] That Jesus is the subject of these preceding actions does not diminish the John-Elijah connection in the present passage.[77] Rather, with the recurrence of such strong Elijah allusions, the reader's ear is particularly well attuned to catch the several references to Mal 3:1 as well as other clues that point to the Tishbite.[78] Given the parallelism Luke develops between the ministries of John and Jesus—a parallelism that becomes explicit in this passage (vv. 33–34)—it should be no surprise that the same motif is attached to both figures, especially since both figures, in their respective roles, contribute to the hope that Luke attaches to Elijah.[79] Thus, while Luke appears to have taken this pericope largely unchanged from his source (though with the addition of vv. 29–30), his placement of the text in connection with other Elijah material serves to heighten the John-Elijah connections already present in this material.[80]

The first section of this pericope (vv. 18–27) is bookended by references to Mal 3:1 (vv. 18–19, 27), and frames the narrative argument in terms of the sent messenger and the coming Lord.[81] If John is recognized as the Elijianic messenger, and Jesus, who is now performing deeds of

---

76. Green, *Luke*, 294.

77. Contra Danker, *Jesus and the New Age*, 163; Wink, *John the Baptist*, 44–45; cf. Brown, "Jesus and Elisha," 85–104.

78. See Beale, *Handbook*, 33, who defines the criterion of "recurrence," as whether or not there are "references in the immediate context . . . to the same OT context from which the purported allusion derives" (cf. Hays, *Echoes of Scripture*, 30).

79. Nolland, *Luke*, 1:327, calls this juxtaposition "the controlling motif of 7:1–50."

80. On the question of sources, see Fitzmyer, *Luke*, 1:662–65, 670–73; Marshall, *Gospel of Luke*, 287–89, 292–93.

81. Carroll, *Luke*, 171, notes further that "the dismissal of the messengers from John (v. 24; only Luke calls them ἄγγελοι, messengers) prepares the way for a quotation from Mal 3:1." Note also the use of "sent" (ἀπέστειλεν) in v. 20.

power, has come after him, is he to conclude that Jesus is the "coming one"? The Baptist's opening question, "Are you the one who is to come?" (v. 19), repeated in Luke's account for emphasis (v. 20; cf. Matt 11:2-3), directs the reader back to his prediction of the "coming one" in 3:16.[82] As we saw there, the reference was to "the Lord," whose coming, as anticipated in Mal 3:1, was preceded by a "messenger," who is identified as Elijah.[83] The Lukan identification of Jesus as "the Lord [ὁ κύριος]" at precisely this point (v. 19; cf. v. 13) further indicates that this is the figure he has in mind.[84] John's questioning of Jesus's identity stems most likely from a disparity between his expectations for the coming Lord and Jesus's deeds to this point.[85] Interestingly, it is assumed that John fills the role of Elijah, especially given the appeal to Mal 3:1 (v. 27); the only question is whether Jesus is "the Lord."[86] That is to say, it is Jesus's relationship to John and his ministry that is temporarily in question, not John's connection to Elijah. Jesus's quotation of Mal 3:1 with reference to John's identity (v. 27) is one of the strongest attestations of the Baptist's Elijianic role.[87] This is now the third and clearest application of Mal 3:1 to John the Baptist—a final confirmation of his role as Malachi's Elijianic messenger (1:17, 76).[88]

82. Green, *Luke*, 295; Fitzmyer, *Luke*, 1:666; Nolland, *Luke*, 1:329; Rindoš, *He of Whom It Is Written*, 171; Müller, *Mehr als ein Prophet*, 238.

83. Contra Fitzmyer, *Luke*, 1:666, who identifies ὁ ἐρχόμενος as Elijah. See discussion above.

84. Rindoš, *He of Whom It Is Written*, 171; cf. Bock, *Luke*, 1:665. On this and other Lukan additions of κύριος to his shared material, see Rowe, *Early Narrative Christology*, 120, 130. On the text-critical question, see Metzger, *Textual Commentary*, 119.

85. "Apparently, John's interest lies on the fault line between his eschatological expectations and the realities of Jesus' performance" (Green, *Luke*, 295). For other common interpretations of John's question, see Fitzmyer, *Luke*, 1:664-65; Bock, *Luke*, 1:664-65.

86. It is best to understand Jesus's reply as an affirmative, if indirect, answer to John's question (see esp. Nolland, *Luke*, 1:232; Marshall, *Gospel of Luke*, 292; Green, *Luke*, 297; Bock, *Luke*, 1:667-69. Contra Fitzmyer, *Luke*, 1:666-68, who sees Jesus as rejecting John's characterization of him as an eschatological judge or fiery Elijianic reformer).

87. See Fitzmyer, *Luke*, 1:672-73; Bock, *Luke*, 1:674-75; Green, *Luke*, 298. Contra Wink, *John the Baptist*, 43, who argues that Luke retains from his sources the concept of John as the "forerunner" of Mal 3:1, but nevertheless "divests John of the role of Elijah *redivivus.*" Luke already recognizes the connection between Mal 3:1 and Elijah in 1:17—a fact which Wink himself acknowledges—and it is highly unlikely that he would quote this text here in such a prominent position and not intend the same connection with Elijah.

88. With the use of the second person (σου), the language is slightly closer to that

Jesus's testimony concerning John (vv. 24–26) points back to Luke 3, emphasizing his role as a "prophet" in the "wilderness." Jesus's identification of him as not merely a prophet, but "more than a prophet" (v. 26), followed as it is by his quotation of Mal 3:1 in the next verse, suggests that John's greatness as a prophet is directly linked to his position within salvation history, and in particular, his privileged position as the one who "goes before the Lord" (cf. 1:76).[89] In the Matthean parallel, Jesus's testimony also includes the pronouncement, "if you are willing to accept it, he is Elijah who is to come" (Matt 11:14), yet this is almost certainly a Matthean addition, and Luke, having already stated the John-Elijah connection explicitly in 1:17, has no need of such explanations here.[90] In contrast to Matthew, Luke's interests do not lie primarily in showing John as the fulfillment of Malachi's Elijah expectations but in showing that, as the returned Elijah, John gathers the remnant of Israel.[91]

John's doubt and confusion at this point in the narrative bears some striking resemblances to Elijah's own state of despair in the wilderness (1 Kgs 19:4). Like Elijah, he is in danger for his life from the king, on account of the queen (3:19–20; 9:7–9; cf. 1 Kgs 19:1–2). This threat similarly arose after he had just completed a dramatic and successful renewal movement in the presence of "all the people" (3:21; 7:24–26; cf. 1 Kgs 18:21). In the midst of his doubts regarding the lack of judgment on Israel, he too is able to have an audience with "the Lord" (v. 19; cf. 1 Kgs 19:10).[92] Finally,

---

of Exod 23:20, though the surrounding context makes clear that Mal 3:1 is the primary text in view. See Fitzmyer, *Luke*, 1:674; Nolland, *Luke*, 1:337; Pao and Schnabel, "Luke," 301; cf. Marshall, *Gospel of Luke*, 296. It is likely that the "you" here refers to Jesus as the "Lord" (Fitzmyer, *Luke*, 1:674; Nolland, *Luke*, 1:336–37; Marshall, *Gospel of Luke*, 296); though cf. Bock, *Luke*, 1:673–74; Danker, *Jesus and the New Age*, 97.

89. Marshall, *Gospel of Luke*, 294–95; Bock, *Luke*, 1:672; Fitzmyer, *Luke*, 1:674–75; Nolland, *Luke*, 1:338; Green, *Luke*, 299; Wink, *John the Baptist*, 53–54. Even Conzelmann, who sees John as the last of the prophets of the old era, still acknowledges his privileged place within salvation history (*Theology of St. Luke*, 25).

90. Miller, "Elijah, John, and Jesus," 618; Green, *Luke*, 298–99; cf. Fitzmyer, *Luke*, 1:672. It is generally agreed that Matt 11:14–15 are a Matthean addition (see Luz, *Matthew*, 1:136–37). It is therefore unreasonable to ask why Luke does not include such a statement here (cf. Wink, *John the Baptist*, 43).

91. See esp. Öhler, *Elia im Neuen Testament*, 76, 88–89 on the contrast between Matthew's and Luke's theological purposes with respect to the Elijah motif. It may be that Luke omits the discussion about Elijah after the transfiguration narrative (cf. Mark 9:10–13//Matt 17:10–13) for similar reasons.

92. "John the Baptist may have been perplexed by the ministry of Jesus [because] the action of bringing about final judgment is conspicuously absent" (Marshall, *Gospel*

like Elijah on Mount Horeb, he is given a pronouncement that entails both judgment and salvation (v. 23; cf. 1 Kgs 19:15–18). John's ministry, like Elijah's before him and like Jesus's after him, has a polarizing effect on Israel.

The Remnant Theme

The polarizing aspects of John's ministry established in Luke 3 are further developed in this passage, as Jesus's words make clear that those who do not respond favorably in the time of salvation are in danger of being removed from among the saved (vv. 23, 31–35). Jesus's macarism—directed at John but addressed to "all" (v. 23)—offers both warning and exhortation. Many will fall away, but there is blessing to those few who remain in faith.[93] This division is illustrated more explicitly in Luke's unique addition of vv. 29–30. The "Pharisees and lawyers"—the powerbrokers of society—refused John's message of baptism and repentance, and in so doing "rejected God's purpose [βουλήν] for themselves" (v. 30). Their rejection is a rejection both of God's call to repentance as well as the salvation he offers to the repentant.[94] By contrast, "all the people," having received John's baptism of repentance, were able to rejoice and "acknowledged the justice of God [ἐδικαίωσαν τὸν θεόν]" (v. 29).[95] Many are removed from among the people of God for their stubborn refusal to repent, while the repentant remnant remain in God's salvation.

This division is brought to its climax in Jesus's parable of the children in the marketplace (vv. 31–35). While the particulars of this parable are notoriously difficult to interpret, Jesus's explanation in vv. 33–35 enables us to understand the basic point as one of condemnation on the generation as a whole for their recalcitrance with regards to the ministries

---

of Luke, 292). See also, Bock, Luke, 1:669; Nolland, Luke, 1:328; Green, Luke, 295. It is not necessary, however, to speak of Jesus's rejection of the role of judge altogether (contra Fitzmyer, Luke, 1:664, 667–68; Bovon, Luke, 1:282).

93. Marshall, Gospel of Luke, 292; Bock, Luke, 1:669–70; Nolland, Luke, 1:331.

94. The term βουλή is a favorite of Luke's to describe the will of God for salvation through the gospel (esp. Acts 2:23; 4:28). See Bock, Luke, 1:677–78; Fitzmyer, Luke, 1:179; Bovon, Luke, 1:285; Green, Luke, 300–301.

95. To speak of the "justice of God" refers to the joyful acknowledgment of God's righteous acts in bringing about salvation as well as, perhaps, the humble acknowledgment of their need for repentance in light of God's justice (see Bock, Luke, 1:677; Fitzmyer, Luke, 1:676; Marshall, Gospel of Luke, 298–99; Green, Luke, 301).

of John and Jesus.[96] John's ascetic lifestyle and harsh call to repentance were rejected by most for upsetting the status quo (v. 33)—"troubling Israel," as it were (cf. 1 Kgs 18:17).[97] By contrast, Jesus's proclamation of salvation to the repentant was rejected because of the background of the people who received it (v. 34).[98] In both cases, the failure of "the people of this generation" lies in their rejection of repentance: with John, they deny their need for it, and with Jesus, its efficacy for those who do embrace it. Interestingly, while the narrator sets up the contrast between "all the people" and "the Pharisees and the lawyers" in vv. 29–30, Jesus sets up the division in starker terms: the generation as a whole has rejected God's plan and so stands condemned.[99] Additionally, Luke's shift to second person in vv. 33–34 (cf. "they say" in Matt 11:18–19) increases the sense of the widespread nature of the generation's obstinacy—even those present are rejected.[100] Nevertheless, despite the overwhelming odds, there will be some "children of wisdom" who remain (v. 35)—those who

---

96. For interpretive options, see esp. Zeller, "Die Bildlogik," 252–57; Cotter, "Parable of the Children," 289–304; Luz, *Matthew*, 2:146–48; Fitzmyer, *Luke*, 1:678–79. The context of the parable makes it most likely that "this generation" are the children playing, while John, Jesus, and presumably the remnant who follow them, are those who fail to play by their rules (Bock, *Luke*, 1:680–82; Green, *Luke*, 302–4; Marshall, *Gospel of Luke*, 300–301; Cotter, "Children in the Market-Place," 302–4), though others see the generation as the "spoilsports" who refuse or fail to play along with the messengers of God (Fitzmyer, *Luke*, 1:678–79; Bovon, *Luke*, 1:286–88; Nolland, *Luke*, 1:348; Zeller, "Die Bildlogik," 255–56). In either case, the parable serves to condemn the generation for their failure to respond rightly.

97. "John's ascetic self-denial was a sign of the pressing need to prepare in repentance for the eschatological intervention of God, but his strangeness was dismissed as the deranged behavior of a demoniac" (Nolland, *Luke*, 1:345).

98. The concept of eating and drinking has a particular significance as a metaphor for salvation and the kingdom of God throughout the Lukan narrative (cf. 22:30). As elsewhere in Luke, Jesus's eating with "sinners" is a mark of their salvation born of repentance, while those on the outside reject it as license (cf. Luke 19:1–10).

99. The phrase "this generation [ἡ γενεὰ αὕτη]" is used throughout the Synoptics to describe the faithless or apostate majority within Israel (e.g., Luke 9:41; cf. esp. Deut 32:5, 20; Ps 78:8) (Marshall, *Gospel of Luke*, 299; Bock, *Luke*, 1:679; Fitzmyer, *Luke*, 1:679). On the possibility that the phrase is used synchronically, to refer to the group of unbelievers throughout time, see esp. Nelson, "'This Generation,'" 369–85.

100. Nolland, *Luke*, 1:345; Marshall, *Gospel of Luke*, 301–2; Bock, *Luke*, 1:682. The shift is generally agreed to be Luke's own (Fitzmyer, *Luke*, 1:678). A similar effect may be accomplished with Luke's reference to "the people of this generation [τοὺς ἀνθρώπους τῆς γενεᾶς ταύτης]" (cf. "this generation" in Matt 11:16), which seems to suggest that the majority of people fall into this category (Bock, *Luke*, 1:679).

"acknowledged the justice [ἐδικαίωσαν]" of God through repentance (v. 29).[101] Thus, Jesus attests that John's ministry as the Elijianic messenger served to place the "many"—especially the elite—under judgment for their failure to repent, while the unlikely few—the repentant remnant—were allowed to remain in God's blessing. "The obedient and contrite remnant of Israel has justified [ἐδικαιώθη] God."[102]

Though much of this passage deals with the polarization of the rejected whole and the repentant remnant, at the center lies a word of hope for renewal. Jesus's response to John's messengers characterizes his ministry as one of renewal and eschatological salvation (v. 22). His "symphony of Isaianic echoes" serves to show the "expansive scope of salvation."[103] Whatever ailments were crippling remnant Israel, their time has now passed, as indicated by the many healings Jesus had accomplished "in that very hour" (ἐν ἐκείνῃ τῇ ὥρᾳ) (v. 21). Isaiah 61 anticipates a day in which ruined Israel will be built up (Isa 61:4), and the people, once reduced to a few, will be known and honored among all nations as the people of God (Isa 61:9; cf. 60:22).[104] If John's ministry gathered the remnant through a call to repentance, Jesus completes the work by inaugurating national renewal through that remnant.

Summary and Conclusions

Luke-Acts makes an undeniable connection between John the Baptist and the figure of Elijah. Even before his birth, the very first references to him anticipate a prophetic forerunner who will be the Tishbite's spiritual successor and the fulfillment of Malachi's expectations for Elijah's return (1:17, 76). In his actual appearance and public ministry, John is seen to follow Elijah's footsteps in his opposition to Herod, whom Luke sets up as a new Ahab (3:18–20). His preaching parallels Malachi's apocalyptic imagery, especially in his anticipation of a "coming one" (3:16), and thus establishes him as Malachi's Elijianic messenger. Finally, Jesus's own testimony concerning the Baptist removes all doubt concerning the

---

101. Moessner, "'Leaven of the Pharisees,'" 30. Note the use of ἐδικαιώθη in v. 35, pointing back to v. 29 (Marshall, *Gospel of Luke*, 303; cf. Bovon, *Luke*, 1:285).

102. Bovon, *Luke*, 1:285.

103. Green, *Luke*, 297.

104. See the discussion on Isa 61 in the next chapter.

connection: John functions as Elijah, the messenger sent to prepare the way for the coming Lord (7:27).

While there is certainly an element of prophecy fulfillment in Luke's account of John as Elijah (esp. 7:27), Luke makes clear that he has other theological goals in mind. In each instance of the Elijah motif, we have also seen a correlating development of the remnant theme—John's ministry entails the removal of the wicked, the remainder of the repentant, and the renewal of the people of God through this remnant. Though expectations surrounding his birth focus heavily on national restoration, John's actual ministry revolves primarily around the preparatory work of removing wickedness through his proclamation of a baptism of repentance. The corrupt and unrepentant are denounced as children of the devil, while those who do repent form the remnant—the core from which a renewed Israel will arise. However, as we shall see in the next chapter, it is with Jesus, whose way John prepared, that the nature of this remnant is more fully developed.

6

Elijah and Jesus in Luke-Acts

THE LUKAN JESUS IS introduced from the start as one who will cause "the fall and rising of many in Israel" (Luke 2:33).[1] Indeed, as his ministry begins, he is seen to pronounce the fulfillment of Israel's eschatological hopes and, in the same breath, judgment and condemnation on his kinspeople (4:21–25), to show compassion to a Roman soldier while rebuking all of Israel for their faithlessness (7:9). Within this complex of contradictory images, Luke is consistent in presenting Jesus after the pattern of Elijah, not only in the broad framework of a miracle-working prophet who ascends to heaven, leaving his spirit upon his disciples, but in specific acts, such as raising a widow's dead son (7:11–17).[2] In this chapter we shall see that Luke employs the Elijah motif in connection with Jesus to illustrate the kind of remnant that he gathers: the humble, poor and faithful, in contrast to those who reject the will of God for themselves (cf. 7:30). Ultimately, the remnant theme will narrow down to Jesus alone as the only one who truly understands and is faithful to God's plan. Like Elijah, Jesus becomes the nucleus of the remnant, gathering around himself the humble and repentant who not only become witnesses to the rest of Israel but will take up Israel's mission as a light to the nations.

---

1. See esp. Tiede, "Glory to Thy People Israel," 21–34.
2. See esp. Brodie, *Crucial Bridge*, 83; Brodie, "Luke's Use of the Elijah-Elisha Narrative," 6.

A Prophet without Honor (Luke 4:16–30)

The importance of Luke 4:16–30 to the interpretation of the Third Gospel—and to Luke-Acts as a whole—cannot be overstated. It is a commonplace to observe that this passage is "programmatic" for Jesus's ministry.[3] This is the inaugural speech of the hero in a work that, along with its sequel, places utmost importance on speeches.[4] Not only so, but the Evangelist has deliberately rearranged his material so as to introduce Jesus's ministry with this scene (cf. Mark 6:1–6).[5] The episode introduces key themes that will be developed throughout the rest of the double work, such as the Holy Spirit (v. 18), the proclamation of good news to the poor (vv. 18–19), and the forgiveness of sins (cf. v. 18).[6] More significantly, it contains *in nuce* the plot of the whole Gospel: a Spirit-empowered ministry that fulfills OT prophetic expectation, the initially positive response of his own people, followed by violent rejection, and a miraculous deliverance from death, as well as hints of gentile inclusion.[7] For our present study, it is noteworthy that in the middle of this integral passage Jesus should make an explicit connection between his own ministry and that of Elijah/Elisha (vv. 25–27). The connections made in this programmatic passage should set our expectations for Jesus's ministry as a whole, such that we can see his entire mission as in some sense Elijianic.[8]

---

3. Sanders, *Jews in Luke-Acts*, 165; Nolland, *Luke*, 1:195; Marshall, *Gospel of Luke*, 177–78; Green, *Luke*, 204; Pao, *Isaianic New Exodus*, 71.

4. Tannehill, *Narrative Unity*, 52, notes that Luke uses programmatic speeches with lengthy Scripture quotations to introduce not only John (3:4–14) and Jesus (4:16–27), but also Peter (Acts 2:14–36) and Paul (Acts 13:16–41). Numerous other factors in this passage also indicate its central importance, including a statement of commissioning, disclosures by a reliable character, and lengthy OT quotations (see Tannehill, *Narrative Unity*, 61; Green, *Luke*, 207).

5. This is seen not only in the fact that the apparent parallel (Mark 6:1–6) occurs later in the Markan narrative, but also in Jesus's reference to Capernaum (Luke 4:23) before the narration of his ministry there (4:31–41). For a discussion on these and other redactional decisions, see Marshall, *Gospel of Luke*, 177–80; Bock, *Luke*, 1:394–98; Stein, *Luke*, 154; Fitzmyer, *Luke*, 1:526–30; Bovon, *Luke*, 1:150–51; Nolland, *Luke*, 1:191–94.

6. See Green, *Luke*, 210–12.

7. Fitzmyer, *Luke*, 1:529; Marshall, *Gospel of Luke*, 178; Ringe, *Luke*, 71; Tannehill, *Narrative Unity*, 1:61, 73.

8. Evans, "Luke's Use of the Elijah-Elisha Narratives," 79.

The Elijah Motif in Luke 4:16-30

As Jesus, the Spirit-empowered prophet (3:22; 4:1 [x2], 14, 18; cf. 1 Kgs 18:12, 46; 2 Kgs 2:11, 16), emerges from the wilderness after a forty-day fast (4:2; cf. 1 Kgs 19:8), it is no coincidence that he chooses to compare his ministry with that of Elijah (4:25-27).[9] Though there are several points of comparison, such as miraculous aid to the poor (vv. 18, 26), the primary parallel made has to do with reception by one's own people. Elijah sought to restore his people to Yahweh, yet he was accused as a "troubler of Israel" (1 Kgs 18:17). Likewise, while his kinspeople ought to have eagerly claimed the eschatological blessings that Jesus proclaimed (vv. 18-19), he too found that no prophet is acceptable in his hometown (v. 24).[10] Yet even if his own people would not receive him, the prophet was sent to unlikely places—even to gentiles.[11]

In light of this appeal to Elijah as paradigmatic, Jesus's selection of Isa 61:1-3 to describe his ministry is also significant.[12] This is the first of two quotations Jesus makes of this passage (cf. 7:22)—both times in order to characterize his ministry, and both times in the context of parallels to Elijah (cf. 4:25-27; 7:1-17, 21). Because of these connections, the two passages will be considered together here. While the Isaianic text does not explicitly mention the prophet, the figure it describes has some parallels with Malachi's Elijah (cf. Mal 3:1, 23-24). Both are eschatological messengers who are sent by God before the day of his judgment to bring a message of both judgment and salvation. Additionally, a prophetic anointing (Isa 61:1) is paralleled only in the Elijah narratives (cf. 1 Kgs 19:17).[13]

---

9. See esp. Poirier, "Jesus as an Elijianic Figure," 359-61. Note that Elisha's ministry is seen as parallel to and a continuation of Elijah's, so that episodes such as Naaman's healing may be rightly considered under the "Elijah" motif. See discussion in ch. 2; Carlson, "Élie à l'Horeb" 438-39; Danker, *Jesus and the New Age*, 161.

10. See below on the question of the crowd's rejection of Jesus.

11. Evans, "Luke's Use of the Elijah-Elisha Narratives," 79. This is not an instance of Elijah *redivivus* or a returning Elijah (*pace* Fitzmyer, *Luke*, 1:214). However, Öhler, *Elia im Neuen Testament*, 184, in his attempt to deny the Elijah *redivivus* theme, goes too far, denying any identification of Jesus with Elijah here.

12. This particular passage was chosen by Jesus, as indicated through the use of εὗρεν ("to find," v. 17). See discussion in Marshall, *Gospel of Luke*, 181-82. On Luke's additions and emendations of the LXX of this passage, see esp. Bock, *Luke*, 1:404-5; Pao, *Isaianic New Exodus*, 71-74; Pao and Schnabel, "Luke," 289; Nolland, *Luke*, 1:198.

13. Blenkinsopp sees the charismatic anointing in Isa 61:1 as a sign of prophetic succession modeled specifically after the Elijah-Elisha narratives (cf. 1 Kgs 19:16) (Blenkinsopp, *Isaiah*, 3:222; see also Collins, *Scepter and Star*, 117-22). By contrast,

"Since there was an undeniable similarity between the restoration work described in this passage and that attributed to Elijah in Mal. 3:23-24 . . . it was only natural that Isa. 61:1-5 would come to be identified with Elijah's endtime return."[14] As we saw in ch. 2, at least one line of ancient interpretation did make this very connection (4Q521 2 II), apparently attributing a list of wonders from Isa 61:1-5 to the eschatological Elijah, with the addition of the raising of the dead and the cleansing of lepers—two miracles performed in the OT only in the Elijah narratives, and the very two Jesus mentions in vv. 25-27.[15] Jesus's second lengthy allusion to Isaiah 61 (7:22), this time in response to John the Baptist's question concerning his identity (7:18-20), shows striking similarities to 4Q521, especially in the addition of these two characteristically Elijianic miracles to Isaiah's list of restoration.[16] That Jesus mentions these two miracles in connection with Elijah and Elisha in 4:25-27, and then reenacts them in 7:1-17 just before this quotation, strengthens the possibility that such an Elijianic interpretation of Isaiah 61 is intended here too. While there is no evidence that Luke (or Jesus) had direct access to 4Q521, the parallels are remarkable. If Jesus's contemporaries were interpreting Isaiah 61 as referring to an Elijah figure, then his appeal to Elijah and Elisha after reading this text (4:25-27) would be a deliberate and logical choice for interpretation.[17]

Remnant in Luke 4:16-30

On the surface, it might seem that any one of the OT prophets might serve equally well to prove Jesus's point about the rejection of prophets

---

Poirier points to a line of tradition that saw Elijah as an eschatological priest and identified him with the speaker of Isaiah 61 (Poirier, "Endtime Return of Elijah," 227-36; Poirier, "Jesus as an Elijianic Figure," 353-59).

14. Poirier, "Endtime Return of Elijah," 229.

15. See discussion on 4Q521 in ch. 3 (cf. esp. Collins, "Herald of Good Tidings," 235-36; Poirier, "Jesus as an Elijianic Figure," 353-59; Puech, "Une apocalypse messianique," 475-522). The raising of the dead is mentioned in Isa 26:19, but the cleansing of lepers is not found in Isaiah. A similar connection appears to be made in Tg. Ps-J. Num 25:12, which connects the redemption of Isa 61:1 with the messenger of Mal 3:1.

16. Collins, "Herald of Good Tidings," 238. The parallel in Matt 11:5 is not preceded by the Elijianic miracles that Luke's account contains (7:1-17). However, it does still allude to Isa 61:1-2 in connection with Mal 3:1 (Matt 11:10; cf Luke 7:27). On the question of Luke's sources, see esp. Marshall, *Luke*, 291-92.

17. See Poirier, "Jesus as an Elijianic Figure," 361.

by their own people (cf. Luke 6:26; 13:33–34; Acts 7:52). However, the example of the Elijah narratives was not chosen arbitrarily. Elijah is chosen specifically because he is uniquely suited to represent an even more important theological theme: the remnant.

Removal

The events at the Nazareth synagogue presage the removal of a substantial portion of Israel from the eschatological blessings just proclaimed in Jesus's reading from the Prophets.[18] In Luke's placement of the episode, Jesus's kinspeople in Nazareth stand *pars pro toto* for his kinsfolk more broadly—the nation of Israel.[19] In an ironic reversal, those who ought to have been most eligible to receive these blessings have, as a group, been disqualified from them. The reason for the Nazarene rejection is a matter of considerable debate.[20] Whatever the precise reason, the episode hinges on Jesus's shocking statement that prophets are not acceptable in their own hometowns (v. 24). Prophets are rarely acceptable (δεκτός) among their own, for they are charged with the unwelcome task of confronting sin and calling for repentance.[21] Though the Nazarenes ought to have

---

18. However, Jack T. Sanders goes too far in arguing that this passage shows the total rejection of the Jewish people (Sanders, "Jewish People in Luke-Acts," 65). It is essential to note that "Luke has carefully avoided setting up a simple reversal of roles—privileging Gentiles to the exclusion of Jews" (Ringe, *Luke*, 71; see also Green, *Luke*, 218). This is seen not least in that the narrative depicts Jesus departing, not for a gentile city, but for Capernaum, where he is well received (4:31) (see Tannehill, *Luke*, 94; Tannehill, *Narrative Unity*, 82–83).

19. See, e.g., Fitzmyer, *Luke*, 1:528–29; Tannehill, *Narrative Unity*, 71; Marshall, *Gospel of Luke*, 177–78; Sanders, "Jewish People in Luke-Acts," 63.

20. For a summary of positions, see Cuany, "'Physician, Heal Yourself!'" 347–68. Common views involve the crowd's offense at Jesus's claims regarding his person (Nolland, *Luke*, 1:199; Stein, *Luke*, 158; Danker, *Jesus and the New Age*, 108; Marshall, *Gospel of Luke*, 186; Sloan, *Favorable Year*, 85); their offense at the scope of his ministry (esp. the inclusion of gentiles) (Green, *Luke*, 216; Tannehill, *Narrative Unity*, 69; Fitzmyer, *Luke*, 1:538; Ringe, *Luke*, 70–71; Evans, *Luke*, 72; cf. Sanders, "From Isaiah 61 to Luke 4," 103); or their unreceptiveness to the prophetic challenge (Cuany, "'Physician, Heal Yourself,'" 347–68; cf. Sanders, "From Isaiah 61 to Luke 4," 99; Ringe, *Biblical Jubilee*, 39, 42–44). See also Nolland, "Classical and Rabbinic Parallels," 193–209. The third position not only fits the context best, but also matches Elijah's own experiences, thus making the best sense of the parallel (see further below).

21. "No prophet, that is, no true prophet of the Elijah, Amos, Isaiah, Jeremiah type is *dektos* by his own countrymen precisely because his message always must bear in it a divine challenge to Israel's covenantal self-understanding in any generation" (Sanders,

flocked to him like sick people to the local physician, they failed to see themselves as "sick" or "poor," and so responded with the same unbelief by which their ancestors rejected the prophets of old (cf. Acts 7:52). Just as John "roughly rejects any claim on God based on the assertion that 'we have Abraham as father (πατέρα),'" so Jesus also "abruptly rejects a claim to benefits on the basis of sharing a common 'fatherland (πατρίς).'"[22] Like the apostate in Elijah's day, the unbelieving and unrepentant are removed from the covenant blessings that are promised to their nation and are worse off, in fact, than even those few gentiles who will respond favorably.[23]

Though this passage does anticipate the theme of gentile mission that will be taken up in Acts, the emphasis here is not on the foreigners helped but on the "many in Israel" who were not helped.[24] Especially in light of the proverb in the preceding verse (v. 23), the point of the comparison is that "unbelief has created a situation where . . . benefits do not flow, a situation parallel to the occasions when the prophetic ministry of Elijah and Elisha (prophets raised up in Israel and for Israel) brought no blessing to Israel."[25] Why was Elijah sent to no one in Israel? Because they had turned to false gods and, in their refusal to believe the prophet of God, had fallen under God's judgment (1 Kgs 17:1; cf. Deut 11:16–17; 28:24).[26] Why were no Israelite lepers cleansed? Because even the king

---

"Isaiah 61 to Luke 4," 99).

22. Tannehill, *Narrative Unity*, 69–70. The parallels between Jesus's and John's inaugural sermons are illuminating. Both prophets emerge from the wilderness (4:14; cf. 3:2) teaching or preaching, so that word spreads to all the region (περίχωρος) (4:14; cf. 3:3); both ministries are introduced with lengthy quotations from Isaiah (4:18–19; cf. 3:4–6), and in both cases, the initial response is favorable (4:22; cf. 3:7). Moreover, in both cases, the prophets respond harshly, rebuking their audience for relying on lineage rather than true repentance (4:24; cf. 3:7).

23. It may be that Jesus's appeal to the Elijah parallel provides helpful insight into the question of the Nazarene rejection (see common interpretations listed above). Elijah was not rejected because he claimed to be a prophet or because he went to foreigners—to the contrary, even his opponents acknowledged his status (cf. 2 Kgs 1:9), and Ahab himself had a foreign wife. Rather, he was rejected because of his unpopular message of repentance (cf. esp. 1 Kgs 18:17–18).

24. Nolland, *Luke*, 1:201. That the gentile mission is anticipated but not developed here, see esp. Tannehill, *Narrative Unity*, 71, 94.

25. Nolland, *Luke*, 1:201.

26. Jesus's use of the phrase "three years and six months" (4:25) (cf. "in the third year" in 1 Kgs 18:1), draws on apocalyptic imagery of "divine retribution" (Dan 7:25; 12:7; cf. Jas 5:17) (Marshall, *Gospel of Luke*, 188). It is even possible that Jesus's

had forgotten that there was a prophet of God in Israel (2 Kgs 5:8). That foreigners received aid that ought to have gone to Israelites is not the point of the analogy, but rather serves to highlight the severity of the problem—that many Israelites, through unbelief, have failed to obtain what ought to be theirs. Nevertheless, that some gentiles do benefit from Israel's unbelief is an important issue that will be addressed below.

Remainder

Although this episode foreshadows Israel's substantial removal from the covenant blessings of God, it does not speak of the removal of Israel *in principle*.[27] Jesus's message from Isaiah is thoroughly one of hope, at least for those who will receive it, and while the broader context of Isaiah 61 speaks of Israel as "ruined," she is clearly not destroyed.[28] "Ancient ruins" and "ruined cities" (v. 4) are not so far gone that they cannot be rebuilt. The "poor" are in fact a "shoot" preserved by God and with the potential to grow into a "mighty nation" (60:21–22; cf. 11:1). The prophet indicates that there is hope for Israel so long as there is a remnant.

As with the account of John's baptism, Luke 4:18–30 does not explicitly mention any who respond favorably at the time, but rather sets up our expectations for what such people will look like in the rest of Jesus's ministry to Israel: "the poor," "the broken hearted," and "those who mourn" (Isa 61:1–2).[29] The "poor" (πτωχοί) are of particular interest in Lukan studies (cf. 4:18; 6:20; 7:22; 14:13; 14:21; 16:20, 22).[30] Though often used with reference to economic impoverishment (18:22), πτωχοί, along with its Hebrew counterpart (עֲנָוִים) has more to do with social standing or a posture of humility.[31] In prophetic literature, the remnant is described as עָנִי ("humble" or "poor") (esp. Zeph 3:12; cf. 2:3), an association that was

---

statement that "there were many widows in Israel" further hints at God's judgment on the nation (cf. Exod 22:24).

27. Contra Sanders, "Jewish People in Luke-Acts," 65.

28. Oswalt, *Isaiah*, 2:571, makes the contrast with Israel's enemies, who are destroyed never to be rebuilt (i.e., without a remnant) (cf. 13:19–22; 34:8–17).

29. Nevertheless, the role of Jesus's brother James in the book of Acts shows that Luke is aware of some at least from Nazareth who do eventually repent (cf. Acts 12:17; 15:13; 21:18).

30. See Green, "Good News to Whom," 59–74; Albertz, "Die 'Antrittspredigt' Jesu," 182–206; Hays, "'Give to the Poor,'" 43–63.

31. Moisés Silva, "πτωχός," 181–87; Hauck and Bammel, "πτωχός," 885–915.

taken up especially in the Qumran community as a self-designation (esp. CD XIX 9–10; 4Q521 2 II).[32] While the proud and haughty are removed from the land (cf. Zeph 3:11–12), the "poor" are the recipients of divine favor because, having nowhere else to turn, they have adopted a posture of humility and utter reliance upon God.[33] In such a posture, they are ready to receive the good news of renewal. Though it would be claiming too much to suggest that "poor" is synonymous with "remnant" in the OT or in Luke-Acts, they are certainly overlapping concepts.

Renewal

Jesus's proclamation of Isaiah 61 is a proclamation of renewal. The prophet employs a series of images to depict the restoration of Israel's remnant: Israel's ruins will be rebuilt (v. 4), the captives released (v. 3), and the tiny "shoot" (Isa 60:21) will grow into a mighty "oak of righteousness" (Isa 61:3). The controlling image, however, indicated in v. 1 through the use of דְּרוֹר ("liberty"), is that of an eschatological Jubilee (cf. Lev. 25:10).[34] Every fiftieth year, the people were to proclaim liberty (דְּרוֹר) throughout the land: Israelite slaves were to be released (vv. 35–55), property restored to family allotments (vv. 23–34), and all Israelites were to return to their family territory (vv. 9–10).[35] There is also an element of covenant renewal

---

32. Note in particular the dependence on Isaiah 61, as noted above. See Meyer, "Jesus and the Remnant," 130; Jeremias, "Der Gedanke," 184; Kvalbein, "Die Wunder der Endzeit," 112–13; Jacob, *Theology of the Old Testament*, 324–25. See also Carena, *Il resto*, 77; Müller, *Die Vorstullung vom Rest*, 71–75, 95; Silva, "πτωχός," 183; Bammel, "πτωχός," 896–99.

33. Thus, while Jesus's ministry in Luke is one of "good news to the poor," many of those to whom he brings good news are people of means (7:1–10; 19:1–10) (Green, "Good News to Whom," 60; Albertz, "Die 'Antrittspredigt' Jesu," 199–200).

34. Wolf, "דרר," 198; Bruno, "'Jesus Is Our Jubilee,'" 85–86; Motyer, *Isaiah*, 500; Westermann, *Isaiah 40–66*, 367; Childs, *Isaiah*, 505; Oswalt, *Isaiah*, 2:565n19. The term דְּרוֹר is used also of Jubilee in Ezek 46:17. In Jer 34:8, 15, 17 the reference appears to be the seventh-year release of slaves commanded in Deuteronomy 15, rather than the Jubilee specifically. See also Collins, "Herald of Good Tidings," 230, who does not see evidence that Isaiah 61 has Leviticus 25 in view, though he does acknowledge that the two passages are connected in Qumran writings (11QMelch). Nevertheless, he agrees that the prophet has applied the concept of release of slaves to restoration from exile. Beyond the lexical connection, themes of restoration, aid for the poor, and redemption/vengeance serve to connect these two passages (see esp. Gregory, "Postexilic Exile," 484).

35. Bovon, *Luke*, 1:156, notes that it is therefore particularly appropriate that Jesus

in these laws, indicated by the fact that the restoration is predicated on the redemption of the exodus (vv. 38, 42; cf. vv. 23–24), and that the Jubilee was proclaimed not at the beginning of the year but on the Day of Atonement.[36] The liberty of the Jubilee was thus meant to bring "the restoration of the proper order among the covenant people, the covenant land, and the covenant God."[37] It is no surprise, therefore, that the Isaianic prophet would appropriate the Jubilee concept to depict the renewal anticipated in the return from exile. What Levitical law prescribed on the household level, Isaiah 61 reapplies on a much broader scale, predicting the restoration of the land as a whole to the Israelites returning from exile.[38] Under a renewed and everlasting covenant (cf. Isa 61:8), the people's time of slavery and exile was over, and they were to return to their ancestral land. The beleaguered remnant, weak and few in number, would again be a mighty nation (cf. 60:22).

The narrative does not make clear at this point exactly how or in what way Jesus brings about eschatological Jubilee—presumably this is the reason for the people's amazement and rapt attention (Luke 4:22). However, the double use of ἄφεσις ("release") in v. 18 may offer a clue.[39] Although ἄφεσις is the LXX translation of דְּרוֹר in both Lev 25:10 and Isa 61:1, and must be understood primarily in that context in the present passage, its greater significance throughout Luke-Acts cannot be ignored.[40] In every other instance of the term, it is not so much release from

---

pronounces the Jubilee after first returning to his hometown (πατρίς) of Nazareth.

36. Sloan, *Favorable Year*, 14; Ringe, *Jesus, Liberation, and Biblical Jubilee*, 32.

37. Bruno, "'Jesus Is Our Jubilee,'" 89. See also Sloan, *Favorable Year*, 12–17, who notes the cultic and social elements of Jubilee restoration.

38. Brueggemann, *Isaiah 40–66*, 214–15; Bruno, "'Jesus Is Our Jubilee,'" 93–94; Gregory, "Postexilic Exile," 484–87; Sloan, *Favorable Year*, 1. It could be for this reason that the Lukan Jesus adds "to let the oppressed go free [ἄφεσιν]" from Isa 58:6 (cf. 4:18e). Though not quite in keeping with a literal Jubilee, the release of captives was precisely what the post-exilic "Jubilee" would entail.

39. The second instance of ἄφεσις—imported from Isa 58:6—serves to reemphasize the theme Jubilary release. Although ἄφεσις is a more common word than its counterpart דְּרוֹר, it is consistently applied in the translation of Leviticus 25 and would be sufficient to recall the Jubilee theme for those familiar with the LXX. See Bruno, "'Jesus Is Our Jubilee,'" 96–97; Nolland, *Luke*, 1:197; Pao and Schnabel, "Luke," 289.

40. For a discussion of Luke's use of the double meaning of the word, see Tannehill, *Narrative Unity*, 65–66. See also Fitzmyer, *Luke*, 1:533; Green, *Luke*, 211–12; Bruno, "'Jesus Is Our Jubilee,'" 97–98. In a similar way, ευαγγελίζομαι (4:18b) has specific implications for Luke, which his narrative will flesh out.

captivity, but the forgiveness of sins that is in view.⁴¹ This understanding is not foreign to the context of Isaiah 61, for the concept of release from captivity was intrinsically interwoven with the notion of forgiveness of sins—it was the one that caused the other (see esp. Isa 40:1).⁴² As with John's ministry, Jesus's Nazareth sermon announces (εὐαγγελίζομαι, 4:18; cf. 3:18) the forgiveness of sins (ἄφεσις, 4:18; cf. 3:3) that makes possible a renewed Israel, restored in their covenant to the Lord, in keeping with the covenant renewal implied in the Levitical Jubilee. Yet not only this, but this renewed people will be "priests" and "ministers" among the nations (Isa 61:6), bringing God's blessings to all peoples.

At this point we must examine Jesus's statements concerning gentiles (vv. 25-27). This episode anticipates questions not only about the gentile mission, but about the relationship of gentiles to the remnant—questions that are largely left suspended throughout Luke's Gospel, and only addressed explicitly in the narrative of Acts. However, it is noteworthy that Jesus's references to the widow "of Zarephath in Sidon" (v. 25) and to Naaman "the Syrian" (v. 27) emphasize that these two individuals received God's blessing as gentiles. This dynamic is present within the narrative of Kings as well, for the widow confesses faith in Yahweh's word and his prophet (1 Kgs 17:24), but there is no indication that she leaves her pagan land to assimilate into the people of Israel. More explicitly, Naaman converts to exclusive Yahwism, yet he is permitted to return to a pagan land, serve a pagan master, and even kneel in a pagan temple (2 Kgs 5:17-18). In other words, he converts to the God of Israel, but does so as a gentile.⁴³ The two cartloads of dirt (2 Kgs 5:17) appear to symbolize what Naaman's confession states explicitly: that the true God is "in Israel," but he is the one God "in all the earth" (2 Kgs 5:15). "Naaman's confession is remarkably sophisticated in its understanding of God in both particular and universal terms."⁴⁴ Thus, the request for Israelite soil to bring back to Aram particularizes God but does not localize him.

---

41. Luke 1:77; 3:3; 24:47; Acts 2:38; 5:31; 10:43; 13:38; 26:18 all use ἄφεσις, and always in the phrase "forgiveness of sins" (ἄφεσις ἁμαρτιῶν).

42. This nuance is brought out further in 11QMelchizedek which, in an allusion to Isa 61:1 states that "liberty [דרור] will be proclaimed for them, to free them from [the debt of] all their iniquities" (11Q13 II, 6) (Collins, "Herald of Good Tidings," 229-30; Bruno, "'Jesus Is Our Jubilee,'" 94-95; Gregory, "Postexilic Exile," 496; cf. de Jonge and van der Woude, "11Q Melchizedek," 302, 306).

43. See esp. Schöpflin, "Naaman," 41. Brueggemann, "One-Person Remnant," 53-59, takes this idea in an intriguing direction.

44. Fretheim, *First and Second Kings*, 155. See also Hobbs, *2 Kings*, 66.

A similar clue is given within the context of Isaiah 61, which predicts that the remnant of Israel would become priests and ministers of Yahweh among the nations (Isa 61:6; cf. 49:6; 66:19).[45] In announcing the words of Isaiah "fulfilled," Jesus is not merely proclaiming that the good news of restoration is now brought to the "poor," but that this remnant who receive it are appointed as "priests" to the world. As the Lukan narrative develops, and especially as the gentile mission unfolds in Acts, Jesus and his followers are presented as the remnant of Israel who are able to draw gentiles as gentiles into worship of Israel's God.

Conclusion

Luke's strategic placement of the Nazareth episode establishes Elijah as the paradigm for Jesus's ministry, and the Tishbite's task of restoring the tribes of Jacob casts its shadow over all the subsequent instances of the Elijah motif. Jesus, like Elijah, is the nucleus of the remnant, gathering the repentant remnant around him while those who fail to receive the prophetic rebuke are cut off. At the same time, this scene foreshadows another development, which was also anticipated in the Elijah narratives: as the remnant is entrusted with Israel's mission to the world, gentiles and other outsiders who repent may also receive the same forgiveness and blessing.

The Widow and the Gentile Officer (Luke 7:1–17)

Building off of Jesus's inaugural sermon (4:25–27), the next two instances of the Elijah-Jesus connection show Jesus reenacting the very two miracles to which he has just appealed, namely, the healing of Naaman (7:1–10; cf. 2 Kgs 5:1–14) and the raising of the widow of Zarephath's son (7:11–17; cf. 1 Kgs 17:17–24).[46] Since these two episodes are already linked for us in 4:25–27 and appear to make the same point about Jesus and his connection to Elijah, we will treat them together.[47] As we shall

---

45. Oswalt, *Isaiah*, 2:571–72, notes that, even with a reversal of fortunes in which the nations now serve Israel (v. 5), the prophet carefully "avoids the other extreme," for the restored Israel "is not ruler of the world but priest of the world, just as Exod 19:6 and Deut 33:10 had earlier stated."

46. Note also the appeal to Isaiah 61 in 7:22 (cf. 4:18–19) (Shelton, "Healing of Naaman," 68–69).

47. This passage falls into a familiar pattern within Luke's Gospel in which passages

see, both narratives not only connect the Elijah motif with Jesus, but in so doing, they also develop our understanding of the remnant of Israel and its role among the nations.

Elijah in Luke 7:1–17

Especially in its Lukan form, the healing of the centurion's servant is strongly reminiscent of Elisha's healing of Naaman (vv. 1–10; cf. 2 Kgs 5:1–16).[48] Parallels between the two passages include a respected gentile military officer as the central figure who seeks healing (vv. 2, 4–5; cf. 2 Kgs 5:1);[49] commendation on his behalf by Jews and those of high rank (vv. 3–5; cf. 2 Kgs 5:3–6);[50] a second delegation that prevents a direct meeting with the prophet (vv. 6–9; cf. 2 Kgs 5:5–10); and a healing from a distance (v. 10; cf. 2 Kgs 5:14).[51] Though a similar version of this narrative exists in Matthew (Matt 8:5–10), Luke's version increases the parallels with the Naaman account, not only in its placement next to another Elijah

---

are paired by the presentation of a man and a woman in sequence (e.g., Zechariah and Mary in 1:5–25, 26–38; Simeon and Anna in 2:25–35, 36–38; etc.). This doubling "not only reinforces the message, since it is presented twice, but also suggests an inclusive application" since women as well as men can identify with the characters (Tannehill, *Narrative Unity*, 132–33).

48. Ringe, *Luke*, 98, 100; Tannehill, *Luke*, 123–24; Green, *Luke*, 283; Pao and Schnabel, "Luke," 298–99; Brink, *Soldiers in Luke-Acts*, 130. Joseph Verheyden, though he rightly criticizes many aspects of Shelton's argument for literary dependence, is perhaps too quick to dismiss any influence from 2 Kgs 5:1–14 in Luke's redactional process (see Verheyden, "In Response to John Shelton," 153–60; Shelton, "Healing of Naaman," 65–87). Cf. Brodie, who rather surprisingly argues instead for parallels with Elijah's miraculous provision for the widow and her son in 1 Kgs 17:7–16 (see Brodie, *Birthing of the New Testament*, 291; Brodie, "Luke's Use of the Elijah-Elisha Narrative," 7).

49. Although the centurion himself is not sick, but rather his highly valued slave (δοῦλος) (v. 2), at the same time, it is clear that the centurion is the central figure, not the slave, who never appears in the narrative. Furthermore, it is noteworthy that Naaman is referred to by the king as "my servant" (δοῦλος) (2 Kgs 5:6) and is highly valued by him (2 Kgs 5:1).

50. The suggestion from Naaman's slave girl (2 Kgs 5:3) is probably more analogous to the centurion's hearing about Jesus (v. 3), while the king of Aram's letter to the Israelite king (who ought in turn to have recommended Naaman to the prophet) is a better parallel to the delegation of Jewish elders (vv. 4–5).

51. See esp. Green, *Luke*, 284. Cf. Gagnon, "Luke's Motives for Redaction," 128n16, who lists several differences.

allusion (vv. 11–17), but also in the addition of the two delegations.[52] This Lukan addition creates a parallel structure with 2 Kings 5 and, as in the OT narrative, draws attention to the issue of humility.[53]

The second episode, depicting Jesus's raising of a widow's dead son (vv. 11–17) is even more clearly linked to Elijah's similar action in 1 Kgs 17:8–24.[54] This uniquely Lukan account has numerous points of connection, including meeting a widow at the gates of the town (v. 12; cf. 1 Kgs 17:10);[55] the death of the widow's only son (v. 12; cf. 1 Kgs 17:17);[56] the raising of the dead son and returning him to his mother (v. 15; cf. 1 Kgs 17:19–23);[57] and the ensuing recognition of "a great prophet" of the Lord (v. 16; cf. 1 Kgs 17:24).[58] The phrase "and he gave him to his mother [καὶ

---

52. Though the question of source is difficult, these are likely Lukan expansions. See Bock, *Luke*, 1:630–33; Fitzmyer, *Luke*, 1:645–50; Marshall, *Gospel of Luke*, 277–78; Gagnon, "Statistical Analysis," 709–31; Gagnon, "Luke's Motives for Redaction," 122–45.

53. Although the purpose in the OT narrative is to humble Naaman, while the purpose in Luke is to show the centurion's humility.

54. Bovon, *Luke*, 1:268; Marshall, *Gospel of Luke*, 283; Müller, *Mehr als ein Prophet*, 239; Fitzmyer, *Luke*, 1:656; Tannehill, *Luke*, 127; Green, *Luke*, 290; Pao and Schnabel, "Luke," 299; Evans, "Luke's Use of the Elijah-Elisha Narratives," 79–80; Evans, *Luke*, 115; Dabeck, "Moses und Elias," 180; Nolland, *Luke*, 1:321–23; Bock, *Luke*, 1:652. There are also some similarities to Elisha's miracle at Shunem (2 Kgs 4:18–37), yet even Brown, who argues for a connection between Jesus and Elisha (rather than Elijah) throughout Luke's Gospel, acknowledges that style, verbal links, and the reference to Zarephath in 4:25–26 make the connection with 1 Kings 17 the stronger of the two (Brown, "Jesus and Elisha," 91).

55. Nolland, *Luke*, 1:322, notes the verbal similarity between vv. 11–12 (ἐπορεύθη εἰς πόλιν καλουμένην Ναΐν . . . ὡς δὲ ἤγγισεν τῇ πύλῃ τῆς πόλεως, καὶ ἰδοὺ . . . ἦν χήρα) and 1 Kgs 17:10 (καὶ ἐπορεύθη εἰς Σαρέπτα εἰς τὸν πυλῶνα τῆς πόλεως, καὶ ἰδοὺ ἐκεῖ γυνὴ χήρα).

56. In the LXX account, the widow appears to have other children as well (1 Kgs 17:12, 13, 16), possibly suggesting that Luke is drawing from an earlier narrative tradition that was dependent upon the Hebrew text (Nolland, *Luke*, 1:321; cf. Cogan, *1 Kings*, 428). The verbal links with the LXX narrative would then be the result of Lukan redaction. It is, of course, also possible that Luke had access to a Greek translation that more closely followed the Hebrew in this particular.

57. Luke's inclusion of the detail that the boy sat up "and began to speak" (v. 15) may correspond to LXX 1 Kgs 17:22, "and the boy cried out" (see Nolland, *Luke*, 1:323).

58. Some commentators also point to a possible link between Nain (v. 11) and Shunem (2 Kgs 4:8), which may have been connected in the reader's mind due to their geographic proximity and similarity of names (see esp. Bovon, *Luke 1*, 268; Fitzmyer, *Luke*, 656; Evans, "Luke's Use of the Elijah-Elisha Narratives," 79n22).

ἔδωκεν αὐτὸν τῇ μητρὶ αὐτοῦ]" is an exact quotation of LXX 1 Kgs 17:23. The acclamation of Jesus as "a great prophet [προφήτης μέγας]" (v. 16), though incomplete in its understanding of Jesus's full identity (cf. 9:8, 19), is an appropriate response to the Elijianic miracles they have seen him perform.[59]

The Remnant Theme in Luke 7:1–17

The transition statement in v. 1 connects these two episodes with Jesus's preceding sermon (6:20–49), in which he has just pronounced woes on the "rich" who presume upon their own resources rather than trusting in God (6:24–26), and blessing on the "poor" (πτωχοί) and those who mourn (6:20–23).[60] The remnant that Jesus gathers to himself has already been described in terms of the "poor" in 4:18 (cf. Isa 61:1), and now this concept forms the backdrop by which the remnant theme can be seen in the present section as well.

Removal of the Faithless in Israel

Given the proximity to Jesus's direct appeal to Naaman and the Zarephathite widow in 4:25–27, the allusions to them here evoke the same "many in Israel ... but none of them" pattern by which Israelite unbelief is contrasted with gentile professions of faith. Thus, just as Naaman's faith stands in stark relief against the king of Israel's unbelief (2 Kgs 5:7–8) and Gehazi's greed (2 Kgs 5:25–27), it is the Roman centurion who is commended for his faith (7:9). By contrast, the Jewish leaders appeal to worthiness (ἄξιος), honor, and social indebtedness (vv. 5–6), demonstrating an adherence to patronal ethics typical of Roman society but soundly rejected by Jesus in the preceding sermon (6:32–36; cf. 14:12–14).[61] It is

---

59. Tannehill, *Narrative Unity*, 96–97; Holtz, "Zur christologischen Relevanz," 493–94; Green, *Luke*, 293; Dabeck, "Moses und Elias," 180; cf. Rowe, *Early Narrative Christology*, 119); Bock, *Luke*, 1:653–54; Green, *Luke*, 292–93; Fitzmyer, *Luke*, 1:660; Nolland, *Luke*, 1:323.

60. See esp. Nolland, *Luke*, 1:287. On the connection between the Beatitudes (esp. 6:20) and Isa 61:1, see esp. Marshall, *Gospel of Luke*, 249; Tannehill, *Narrative Unity*, 64; Pao and Schnabel, "Luke," 295. See previous section on the connection between πτωχοί and the remnant.

61. Green, *Luke*, 284–85, mentions especially their appeal to honor language (ἄξιος) as well as the centurion's role as patron/benefactor, building the Jewish

this reliance on worldly position that causes some of these leaders to "reject God's purpose for themselves" in the next episode (7:30). Ironically, the centurion rejects this worldly mind-set, pointing instead to his unworthiness (vv. 6–7) and Jesus's power and authority (v. 8). "In effect, this episode presents these Jewish elders as captive to a world system that has been nullified by the dawning of salvation," while the centurion possesses "remarkable insight into the character of Jesus' mission."[62] Jesus's concluding statement, "I tell you, not even in Israel have I found such faith" (v. 9), though certainly intended to commend the centurion, nevertheless has the effect of chastising Israel's faithlessness.[63]

Remainder of the Faithful

The climax of the centurion narrative is Jesus's implicit call to faith.[64] In turning to his followers to commend him to them (v. 9), Jesus urges the same posture of trust, which forgoes any claim to worthiness on his own merit, and instead relies entirely on the authority of the one before him. Although a centurion with the resources to fund a synagogue could hardly be considered "poor" in economic terms, his faith and humility (vv. 6–8) are, in contrast to the Jewish leaders, an example of what the humble remnant ought to look like.[65] It is, however, the next figure to appear, the widow of Nain, who best exemplifies that posture. She is the very picture of the remnant concept, for having lost her husband and now her only child, she is quite literally left alone. She has no need of denying her worthiness or rejecting social currency—she has none. With no one left to provide social or economic security, she is the epitome of the "poor" who most need good news.[66] Yet it is on such a remnant that the Lord will have compassion (v. 13) and bring renewed life.

---

synagogue and thus placing the Jewish leaders under obligation to him.

62. Green, *Luke*, 285.

63. Green, *Luke*, 288, even sees a parallel with John's words, which negate "the special status of Israel (3:7–9)." See also Fitzmyer, *Luke*, 1:653; Bovon, *Luke*, 1:263; Green, *Luke*, 288; contra Nolland, *Luke*, 1:318, who sees no criticism of Israel.

64. Bock, *Luke*, 1:642–43 notes that, while many have taken note of Jesus's miraculous power (cf. 4:40–41), the centurion is unique in expressing faith in the person and authority of which that power is an indicator.

65. See esp. Green, "Good News to Whom," 59–74. With regards to a centurion's material means, see Bock, *Luke*, 1:635–36; cf. Nolland, *Luke*, 1:317.

66. See Green, *Luke*, 290; Nolland, *Luke*, 1:324; Fitzmyer, *Luke*, 1:658.

Renewal of Life

Both episodes together share in common a theme of restoration to life, already a familiar OT metaphor for Israel's reversal of fortunes and her rebirth as a great nation from a remnant (esp. Ezek 37:1-14; Hos 6:1-2). The centurion's servant was sick and "at the point of death [ἤμελλεν τελευτᾶν]" (v. 2) but was miraculously found in good health (ὑγιαίνοντα) (v. 10). The widow's son had already died (τεθνηκώς) (v. 12), is called a "corpse [νεκρός]" (v. 15), and was carried out in a coffin (v. 14), yet he was fully restored to life, able to sit up and speak (v. 15).[67] In the close conceptual parallel, Isa 49:20-21 describes Israel's restoration from a remnant in terms of a bereaved widow, whose reversal of fortunes is depicted in terms of the return to life of the dead children whom she had lost.[68] Additionally, as we saw in the previous section, a contemporary interpretation of Isaiah 61 included the raising of the dead as an image of divine restoration of Israel's remnant (4Q521 2 II 12). It is striking that the very next pericope in the Lukan narrative will allude to Isaiah 61, with the inclusion of the raising of the dead (7:22). The new era of salvation inaugurated with the Lord's coming is not merely one of miraculous deeds, such as the restoration of an only son to a bereaved widow. Rather, such wonders point to a divine visitation in which the fortunes of his people are restored (v. 16).

The crowd's attestation that "God has visited his people [ἐπεσκέψατο ὁ θεὸς τὸν λαὸν αὐτοῦ]" (v. 16) must be read in light of the Lukan narrative, in which ἐπισκέπτομαι along with its cognates refers specifically to divine intervention on behalf of Israel (esp. Luke 1:68, 78).[69] Luke's use of the term draws from a distinctly septuagintal application, in which it is linked to exodus/new exodus imagery (esp. Exod 3:16; 4:31; Ps 106:4 [LXX 105:4]), and can be used to speak of God's restoration of Israel from

---

67. The resuscitation is all the more noteworthy in that, though Elijah must stretch out on top of the boy and pray to God for a miracle, Jesus has within himself the authority to raise the young man, and does so merely by the power of his own word (v. 14) (Fitzmyer, *Luke*, 1:656; Green, *Luke*, 292; Pao and Schnabel, "Luke," 299; Bock, *Luke*, 1:652).

68. The connection is particularly clear in v. 21 in the LXX, which reads "childless and a widow" (ἄτεκνος καὶ χήρα) (cf. "bereaved and barren" [שְׁכוּלָה וְגַלְמוּדָה] in the MT).

69. Tannehill, *Narrative Unity*, 87; Holtz, "Zur christologischen Relevanz," 494; Bock, *Luke*, 1:654; Fitzmyer, *Luke*, 1:660; Pao and Schnabel, "Luke," 263.

a remnant (esp. Ps 80:14 [LXX 79:15]; Zeph 2:7).[70] That God has visited his "people [λαός]" (v. 16; cf. 1:68) further establishes that the salvation in view is that which God has promised to Israel.[71] Not only has a divine visitation occurred in the person of Jesus, but he has brought the restoration which Israel awaited.[72]

Though Jesus's visitation represents the fulfillment of Israel's hopes for restoration, once again, one of the beneficiaries is a gentile. Whether the centurion is of Roman birth or another ethnicity, he is clearly a non-Jew (v. 9), possibly a "God-fearer," (φοβούμενος/σεβόμενος τὸν θεόν; cf. Acts 10:2, 22; 18:7).[73] It is far less likely that he is a proselyte, both because he appears sensitive to Jewish sensibilities regarding entering his house (v. 6) and because the Jewish envoy describes him as one who "loves our nation" (v. 5), a phrase that implies an outsider, albeit a sympathetic one.[74] Like his OT counterpart Naaman, the centurion receives the blessing of restoration as a gentile alongside the remnant, while many in Israel miss it entirely.

Conclusion

Jesus's reenactment of the accounts of Naaman and the Zarephathite widow underscores his connection with Elijah, already delineated in his inaugural sermon at Nazareth. By this point in the Lukan narrative, it can be seen that Jesus's similarities with the Tishbite do not merely serve to show his prophetic authority or his power to do miracles but serve Luke's theological purpose in revealing the nature of the true people of God. As in Elijah's day, Jesus's ministry reveals the unbelief of many in Israel, effectively removing them from the covenant blessings. Yet, also like Elijah, he forms the head or nucleus of the remnant, gathering to himself the humble and faithful of the nation, to whom hope of renewal is extended. On top of this, gentiles who attach themselves to this remnant,

---

70. See esp. Silva, "ἐπίσκοπος," 250–51. On this usage as distinctly septuagintal, see Beyer, "ἐπισκέπτομαι, κτλ.," 602.

71. On Luke's use of λαός, see esp. Tannehill, *Narrative Unity*, 143–44; cf. Silva, "λαός," 88–93.

72. Cf. Bovon, *Luke*, 1:274. Note also the focus on the nation of Israel even in the centurion episode (vv. 5, 9; cf. vv. 6–7).

73. See Green, *Luke*, 287, esp. n13; cf. Nolland, *Luke*, 1:316.

74. Bock, *Luke*, 1:637–38.

demonstrating the same faith and humility, are given the same hope of blessing and renewal originally promised to Israel.

Some Say Elijah (Luke 9:1–62)

The Elijah motif reaches a crescendo in Luke 9, with every major episode containing some kind of allusion to the Elijah-Elisha narratives, and the prophet himself appearing at the very center of this section, on the Mount of Transfiguration (v. 30).[75] Luke's redactional hand is evident throughout this chapter, not least in the so-called "great omission" (vv. 17, 18; cf. Mark 6:45–8:26), but also in several notable additions (esp. vv. 51–56, 61–62).[76] The resultant unit consists of a series of brief episodes, often linked by transition statements (cf. vv. 10, 28, 37, 43, 57), and bracketed by the missions of the twelve and the seventy-two, respectively (vv. 1–6, 10; 10:1–12).[77] These redactions also have the effect of consolidating, both through addition and omission, a large concentration of material connecting Jesus to Elijah. While this material shows points of contrast between Jesus and Elijah (in particular, that Jesus is greater than the OT prophet), we shall argue that the passage as a whole nevertheless makes a positive comparison, and one that identifies Jesus as the true remnant. Because of the unity of this passage, we shall consider it all together.

75. On the unity of Luke 9, see Fitzmyer, "Composition," 139–52; Green, *Luke*, 351–55; Moessner, "Luke 9:1–50," 575–605; O'Toole, "Luke 9:1–50," 74–89. The passage as a whole functions as a hinge between the Galilean ministry and the Travel Narrative, with v. 51 marking a major structural shift. However, the thematic continuity of vv. 51–62 with the rest of the chapter (esp. the nature of true discipleship, on which, see below) justifies the inclusion of the clear appeals to Elijah in these verses with those in the passage preceding them.

76. Fitzmyer, *Luke*, 1:771, is right that "the reasons for the omission of the Marcan material are not nearly as important as the resultant shape of this part of the Lucan Gospel." One significant part of this resultant shape is the repeated emphasis on Elijah. On various proposed reasons for the omission, see Fitzmyer, *Luke*, 1:770–71; Marshall, *Gospel of Luke*, 364; Bovon, *Luke 1*, 361–62; Conzelmann, *Theology of St. Luke*, 52–55; Danker, *Jesus and the New Age*, 192–93.

77. Luke has also repeatedly linked episodes using participles where Mark has a new section, giving the section further unity (see esp. v. 22; cf. Mark 8:31; v. 43; cf. Mark 9:30; v. 49; cf. Mark 9:38). On the thematic unity of this passage, especially the interconnected themes of discipleship and Christology, see Green, *Luke*, 351–57. Arguably, the twofold mission of the twelve (vv. 1–6, 10) and the seventy-two (10:1–12) that brackets this passage is also part of the Elijah motif, showing Jesus as possessing Elijah's unique authority to call disciples to himself and grant them his own spiritual power (see Öhler, *Elia im Neuen Testament*, 158, 248).

The Elijah Motif in Luke 9:1–62

This section begins with Herod's response to popular speculation that, in light of the miraculous healings taking place, Jesus might be Elijah or one of the prophets (vv. 7–9), making the question of Jesus's identity—including his identity vis-à-vis Elijah—a major theme for this chapter of Luke's Gospel.[78] The Lukan account shows Herod's puzzlement to be in response to "all these things [τὰ γινόμενα πάντα]" (v. 7), drawing attention to Jesus's healing miracles as particularly reminiscent of Elijah (vv. 1, 6; cf. esp. 8:49–56).[79] Luke's omission of nearly two chapters of Markan material (Mark 6:45–8:26) puts this episode in close proximity with the second report of the crowd's speculations about Jesus's identity (v. 19), this time from the lips of the disciples, thus highlighting the question of Jesus's relationship to Elijah. It is important to note that while the crowds are, strictly speaking, wrong—Jesus is not Elijah, just as he is not the resurrected John or one of the prophets of old—their speculations were not entirely baseless. Jesus was thought to be Elijah because he was in many ways *like* Elijah.[80] The crowd had good reasons for their mistake.

The feeding of the five thousand (vv. 10–17) is present in all four canonical Gospels, and in each case the basic facts of the story—a miraculous feeding of many people with only a little food—recalls Elisha's feeding of one hundred men with twenty loaves (2 Kgs 4:42–44).[81] Even

---

78. Fitzmyer, "Composition," 140–43; Darr, *Herod the Fox*, 169. Edwards notes further that the very wording of the question places emphasis on Jesus's identity, for "people normally ask what others *do*, not who they *are*" (Edwards, *Gospel according to Luke*, 268).

79. See Fitzmyer, "Composition," 142–43; Green, *Luke*, 361; Stein, *Luke*, 270. The raising of Jairus's daughter, which Luke places immediately before this (8:40–42, 49–56) may echo 1 Kgs 17:17–24, not only in its portrayal of the resuscitation of an only child, but in Luke's addition of καὶ ἐπέστρεψεν τὸ πνεῦμα αὐτῆς (v. 55), which appears to echo 1 Kgs 17:21 (ἐπιστραφήτω δὴ ἡ ψυχὴ τοῦ παιδαρίου τούτου εἰς αὐτόν). See esp. Edwards, *Gospel according to Luke*, 258–59; Marshall, *Gospel of Luke*, 348; Schürmann, *Lukasevangelium*, 495n173.

80. Öhler, *Elia im Neuen Testament*, 230, is right that Luke presents all three options as unsatisfactory, both to the reader and to Herod and Peter. However, it does not therefore follow that these verses are a "negative link" between Elijah and Jesus. As in 7:16, the crowd's speculations are imprecise, yet they nevertheless express something true about Jesus. See Stein, *Luke*, 277; Tannehill, *Narrative Unity*, 97. Bock, *Luke*, 840, notes insightfully that "even [Peter's] correct view needs additional definition," for Christology must be understood in terms of the cross (cf. v. 20).

81. See esp. Pao and Schnabel, "Luke," 310; Schürmann, *Lukasevangelium*, 517; Bock, *Luke*, 825; Marshall, *Gospel of Luke*, 357, 363; Bovon, *Luke*, 1:358. There are also

the style of the story in the Synoptics—short and terse, with no comment as to how the food was actually multiplied—echoes the simplicity of Elijah's and Elisha's multiplication miracles (2 Kgs 4:44; cf. 1 Kgs 17:8–16; 2 Kgs 4:1–7). In addition, the Lukan version is framed by the two accounts of the crowd's speculative identification of Jesus with Elijah (vv. 7–9, 19), effectively highlighting the parallels within this narrative. Further Lukan redactions include abbreviated dialogue between Jesus and the disciples (vv. 13–14; cf. Mark 6:37–38) and mention of the number of people earlier in the narrative (v. 14; cf. Mark 6:44). These changes more closely align this version with the structure of the 2 Kings 4 account: the command to the disciples to feed the crowd (v. 13; cf. 2 Kgs 4:42), the disciples' dubious response (v. 13; cf. 2 Kgs 4:43), reference to the number of people (v. 14; cf. 2 Kgs 4:43), the reissuing of the command (v. 14; cf. 2 Kgs 4:44), the distribution of bread (v. 16; cf. 2 Kgs 4:44), and mention of surplus (v. 17; cf. 2 Kgs 4:44).[82] It is even possible that Luke's unique mention of the nearby town of Bethsaida (Βηθσαϊδά) (v. 10) is a play on the LXX rendering of Baal-shalisha (Βαιθσαρισα) (2 Kgs 4:42).[83] Jesus's miracle is greater than that of Elisha, feeding more people with less food, and doing so of his own authority, rather than by a word from the Lord (2 Kgs 4:43), yet it is plain that this messianic banquet should be seen through an Elijianic lens.

At the heart of this section, the appearance of Elijah in person at the transfiguration (vv. 28–36) is a high point for the Elijah motif, even if the significance of Moses and Elijah together is not made clear.[84] Certainly, their appearance recalls Mal 3:22–24 (4:4–6 EV), the only OT passage to mention both figures together, and one that mentions them in the context of Horeb, the mountain of theophany.[85] It is true that Elijah's

---

similarities to Elijah's and Elisha's multiplications of oil (1 Kgs 17:8–16; 2 Kgs 4:1–7). Parallels with Moses and manna in the wilderness are developed in John 6:31–34, but are less obvious in the Synoptics (Nolland, *Luke*, 1:442; see also Fitzmyer, *Luke*, 1:767).

82. Nolland, *Luke*, 1:437; Danker, *Jesus and the New Age*, 191–92; Fitzmyer, *Luke*, 1:766; Marshall, *Gospel of Luke*, 360–63.

83. See above on similar possible wordplay with Nain and Shunem (7:11; cf. 2 Kgs 4:8).

84. For common views, see Nolland, *Luke*, 1:498–99; Bock, *Luke*, 1:868–69; Edwards, *Gospel according to Luke*, 281–82; Heil, *Transfiguration of Jesus*, 95–113; Schürmann, *Lukasevangelium*, 557–58.

85. Nolland, *Luke*, 1:499, suggests that in light of this connection, in which Moses represents the past and Elijah the eschaton, the two figures here represent "the sweep of the unfolding of God's purposes leading on to the role of Jesus." Bock, *Luke*,

physical presence alongside Jesus rules out any possibility of Jesus as a literal Elijah *redivivus*, but it does not follow that this shows an attempt on the part of the narrator to distance the two figures.[86] To the contrary, the Tishbite's appearance next to Jesus at this point in the narrative allows for greater points of connection between the two figures.[87] Jesus is not Elijah, and he is in fact more glorious than Elijah, yet Elijah's presence at such a critical juncture in the narrative draws out the undeniable Elijianic elements of Jesus's ministry. Luke's omission of the disciples' discussion about Elijah during their descent from the mountain (cf. Mark 9:11–13) is somewhat surprising given the confluence of so many Elijah references in this chapter. It may be that Luke desired to avoid the strict typology implied in this episode (cf. Matt 17:13) in order to be free to develop Elijah's theological significance in connection to the remnant. Regardless of the reason, the "positive effect" of this omission is to more closely link the Transfiguration narrative with the episodes to follow, keeping the focus on the identity of Jesus himself, rather than on John the Baptist.[88]

After their descent from the mountain, the Elijah motif continues with another miraculous healing. The Lukan account of Jesus's healing of the demon possessed boy (vv. 37–43) bears unmistakable similarities to Elijah and Elisha's healing miracles (1 Kgs 17:17–24; cf. 2 Kgs 4:25–37), especially with the raising of the widow's son still fresh in the readers' minds (cf. 7:11–17).[89] Luke adds verbal links with the addition of a near quotation of 1 Kgs 17:23 ("and [he] gave him back to his father [καὶ ἀπέδωκεν αὐτὸν τῷ πατρὶ αὐτοῦ]," v. 42), as well as the description of the boy as an "only child [μονογενής]" (v. 38; cf. 7:12; 1 Kgs 17:17; 2 Kgs 4:14–17).[90] In light of these parallels, several commentators also connect the disciples' inability to cast out the demon with Gehazi's inability

---

1:868–69, similarly suggests that "Moses looks back to the exodus and Elijah looks forward to the fulfillment of promise in the eschaton."

86. *Pace* Rowe, *Early Narrative Christology*, 124; Green, *Luke*, 381.

87. In the same way, the presence of Moses, while eliminating the possibility of Jesus as Moses *redivivus*, at the same time draws out Mosaic and new exodus elements in this scene and in Jesus's ministry (esp. v. 31).

88. Marshall, *Gospel of Luke*, 389. See also Fitzmyer "Composition," 147; Nolland, *Luke*, 2:506; cf. Bock, *Luke*, 1:879.

89. On the links between this passage and 7:11–17, see Nolland, *Luke*, 1:506; Tannehill, *Narrative Unity*, 94; Green, *Luke*, 388.

90. *Pace* Öhler, *Elia im Neuen Testament*, 201, who suggests that Luke simply "liked to use this LXX phrase."

to raise the Shunammite boy apart from Elisha (v. 40; cf. 2 Kgs 4:31).[91] Finally, as in 1 Kings 17, Luke's version of the healing results in praise to God (v. 43; cf. 1 Kgs 17:24).[92]

Jesus's journey to Jerusalem is introduced in v. 51 with a somewhat abrupt reference to his "ascension" (ἀναλήμψεως)—a term frequently used in the LXX for Elijah's ascension (cf. 2 Kgs 2:9, 10, 11; 1 Macc 2:58; Sir 48:9).[93] The wording of this verse also recalls the introduction to the story of Elijah's assumption: "When the days drew near [Ἐγένετο δὲ ἐν τῷ συμπληροῦσθαι] for him to be taken up [ἀναλήμψεως], he set his face to go [πορεύεσθαι] to Jerusalem" (v. 51).[94] Both verses introduce the imminent ascension of the hero as if it were already known and as the fulfillment of a divine plan, and both speak of a journey with multiple stops that culminates in the place of destiny, whether Jerusalem or the Jordan valley.[95] Jesus's ascension bears unparalleled weight in the Lukan portrait of Jesus, being narrated twice (Luke 24:50–53; Acts 1:6–11) and referenced multiple times (Luke 9:51; Acts 1:2, 22; 3:21; cf. Luke 22:69). As we shall see, it will play a climactic part in the Elijah motif, and the foreshadowing of it here sets an Elijianic tone to the fateful journey to Jerusalem.[96]

---

91. Marshall, *Gospel of Luke*, 391; Fitzmyer, *Luke*, 1:809; Nolland, *Luke*, 1:509.

92. See esp. Marshall, *Gospel of Luke*, 389–90, on Luke's abbreviations and additions in this episode.

93. On ἀνάλημψις as "ascension" here, see esp. Edwards, *Gospel according to Luke*, 296; Zwiep, *Ascension of the Messiah*, 80–86; Stein, *Luke*, 298; Wolter, *Das Lukasevangelium*, 369; cf. Fitzmyer, *Luke*, 1:827–28. Contra Öhler, *Elia im Neuen Testament*, 207, who sees a reference only to Jesus's death (cf. Pss. Sol. 4:18). It is likely that Luke is using the term metonymically for the whole sequence of events in Jerusalem, beginning with his arrest and reaching its culmination in his ascension (Nolland, *Luke*, 2:535; Marshall, *Gospel of Luke*, 405; Bock, *Luke*, 2:967–68; Tannehill, *Luke*, 168; Bovon, *Luke*, 2:6; cf. Evans, "Central Section," 37–54, who includes the whole central section as well). Though the nominal form is a *hapax legomenon* in the NT, the verbal form (ἀναλαμβάνω) is used several times by Luke to refer to Jesus's ascension (Acts 1:2, 11, 22).

94. "Now when the Lord was about to take Elijah up [Καὶ ἐγένετο ἐν τῷ ἀνάγειν κύριον] by a whirlwind, Elijah and Elisha were on their way [ἐπορεύθη] from Gilgal" (2 Kgs 2:1).

95. See esp. Brodie, "Departure for Jerusalem," 103, 107; cf. Dabeck, "Moses und Elias," 182.

96. Note also the connection between vv. 31 and 51. The events to be fulfilled in Jerusalem are first referred to as his ἔξοδυς (v. 31), drawing from the Moses tradition, and then as his ἀνάλημψις (v. 51), drawing from Elijah tradition. "The choice of these *termini* is not coincidental, of course" (Zwiep, *Ascension of the Messiah*, 86).

Jesus's interaction with the Samaritan village (vv. 52–56) bears obvious allusions to Elijah's encounter with the Samarian soldiers in 2 Kgs 1:9–16 (cf. esp. 2 Kgs 1:10, 12), especially in the disciples' offer to call "fire to come down from heaven to consume them" (πῦρ καταβῆναι ἀπὸ τοῦ οὐρανοῦ καὶ ἀναλῶσαι αὐτούς) (v. 54; cf. 2 Kgs 1:10, 12, 14).[97] This is further indicated in the narrative gloss "as also Elijah did," found in many MSS in v. 54.[98] Other parallels include the location in Samaria (v. 52; cf. 2 Kgs 1:2, 3) as well as a dispute concerning the legitimacy of the Jerusalem temple (v. 53; cf. 2 Kgs 1:3, 6, 16).[99] The fact that Jesus never summons heavenly fire, and in fact rebukes his disciples for the very suggestion (v. 55), has led some scholars to see a deliberate negation, or at least a downplaying, of the Elijah-Jesus connection.[100] However, a careful observation of the text reveals the opposite. First, the climax of the OT narrative is not fire coming down from heaven, but Elijah coming down (κατέβη) to the soldiers, having compassion on them despite their impious errand (2 Kgs 1:15), a compassion reflected in Jesus's forbearance here. Second, the

97. Καὶ κατέβη πῦρ ἐκ τοῦ οὐρανοῦ καὶ κατέφαγεν αὐτόν (2 Kgs 1:10, 12, 14). On these and other parallels, see esp. Brodie, "Departure for Jerusalem," 104–7; Dochhorn, "Die Verschonung," 362; Evans, "Elijah-Elisha Narratives," 80–81; Pao and Schnabel, "Luke," 315–16. The phrase "he sent messengers ahead of him" (ἀπέστειλεν ἀγγέλους πρὸ προσώπου αὐτοῦ) (v. 52) echoes Mal 3:1, which Luke has already appealed to multiple times in reference to an Elijianic messenger/messengers (esp. 7:27; cf. 1:17, 76; 10:1) (see esp. Nolland, *Luke*, 2:535, 537; Tannehill, *Luke*, 168–69). Verse 52 will be addressed in the next chapter.

98. ὡς καὶ Ἐλίας ἐποίησεν is missing from the earliest mss. (esp. 𝔓45, 𝔓75, ℵ, and B), though otherwise widely attested (esp. A, C, D, W, Θ, and 𝔐). On text critical issues, see esp. Fitzmyer, *Luke*, 1:830; though cf. Bovon, *Luke*, 2:5.

99. Structurally within Luke, this passage bears many similarities to 4:16–30 in that both episodes introduce a new phase of Jesus's ministry while using rejection by a village to foreshadow his ultimate rejection in Jerusalem (Tannehill, *Narrative Unity*, 230; Fitzmyer, *Luke*, 1:827; Öhler, *Elia im Neuen Testament*, 198; Bovon, *Luke*, 2:5). It is no surprise, then, to see a similar appeal to Elijah in the characterization of Jesus and his ministry here.

100. Many see the image of Elijah as fiery reformer and judge as incompatible with the Lukan Jesus (esp. Fitzmyer, *Luke*, 1:664, 830; Allison, "Rejecting Violent Judgment," 476–77; Öhler, *Elia im Neuen Testament*, 231; Rowe, *Early Narrative Christology*, 124; cf. Danker, *Jesus and the New Age*, 209). This seems also to be the view of the textual addition in v. 56 ("For the Son of Man has not come to destroy the lives of people, but to save them"), which is probably a gloss based on Luke 19:10 (see Bovon, *Luke*, 2:5; Marshall, *Gospel of Luke*, 407–8; Fitzmyer, *Luke*, 1:830; cf. Dochhorn, "Die Verschonung," 371). Others see eschatological concerns (Wink, *John the Baptist*, 45; cf. Miller, "Elijah, John, and Jesus," 620–21) or a desire to preserve the John-Elijah typology (cf. Marshall, *Historian and Theologian*, 147).

contrast is more properly with James and John, who, in offering to summon heavenly fire, attempt to set themselves up as Elijah-figures yet are found in every way unlike him. They lack the authority Elijah had to act on his own accord (vv. 54-55; cf. 2 Kgs 1:10, 12), they are rebuked by the Lord rather than given encouragement (v. 55; cf. 2 Kgs 1:15), and unlike Elijah they never succeed in gaining an audience (v. 56; cf. 2 Kgs 1:16).[101] The disciples have already been given instructions on how to respond to rejection (9:5; cf. 10:10-12), but apparently assume a harsher response is warranted when Samaritans are involved.[102] In portraying James and John as lacking Elijah's power and authority, the narrative is implicitly criticizing their failure to live up to Elijah's example of compassion towards outsiders (cf. 4:25-27).[103] By contrast, Jesus, in demonstrating this quality, is, at least in the Lukan conception of the prophet, most truly like Elijah. While James and John attempt (and fail) to emulate Elijah's actions, Jesus embodies his mission.

In the Lukan account of the would-be disciples (vv. 57-62), the two exchanges familiar from the double tradition (cf. Matt 8:18-22) are supplemented with a third, which is strongly reminiscent of Elijah's call to Elisha (1 Kgs 19:19-21).[104] The disciple's words to Jesus, "I will follow [ἀκολουθήσω] you, Lord; but let me first say farewell to those at my home" (v. 61), are a clear echo of Elisha's words to Elijah (1 Kgs 19:20), especially in light of Jesus's warning against putting one's hand to the plow [ἄροτρον] and looking back (v. 62; cf. 1 Kgs 19:19, 21).[105] This episode

---

101. Other reversals include the destination (Elijah rebukes the king and his men for going to a pagan shrine [2 Kgs 1:3], while Jesus and his disciples are rejected for going to the Jerusalem temple [v. 53]) and the direction of motion (Elijah sits on a hilltop as the soldiers approach [2 Kgs 1:9], while in Luke 9 it is James and John who go up to the Samaritan village [v. 52]). See Otten, "Bad Samaritans," 375-89.

102. Danker, *Jesus and the New Age*, 209; Bovon, *Luke*, 2:7; Bock, *Luke*, 2:970; Marshall, *Gospel of Luke*, 406-7.

103. See Green, *Luke*, 385-87, 406. Note that this passage falls within a series of failures by the disciples, most of which are related to disdain for outsiders (cf. vv. 40, 45, 46, 49, 57-62).

104. On questions of source, see Marshall, *Gospel of Luke*, 408-9; Bock, *Luke*, 2:974-76; cf. Fitzmyer, *Luke*, 1:833-34.

105. "Let me kiss my father [πατέρα] and my mother, and then I will follow [ἀκολουθήσω] you." See Bovon, *Luke*, 2:14; Pao and Schnabel, "Luke," 316; Fitzmyer, *Luke*, 1:837; Bock, *Luke*, 2:983; Marshall, *Gospel of Luke*, 412; cf. Brodie, "Luke 9:57-62," 237-45. The use of ἀκολουθήσω (v. 57) and πατέρα (v. 59) in the first two episodes also serve as echoes of 1 Kgs 19:20 (Bock, *Luke*, 2:980; Marshall, *Gospel of Luke*, 411; Pao and Schnabel, "Luke," 316).

certainly shows the urgency of Jesus's call, which surpasses even that of Elijah, yet it is an oversimplification to say that Jesus denies what Elijah permits.[106] First, Elijah's response in 1 Kgs 19:20 ("Go back again, for what have I done to you?"; לֵךְ שׁוּב כִּי מֶה־עָשִׂיתִי לָךְ) is ambiguous, and many commentators interpret it not as permission but as a dismissal (cf. 1 Kgs 19:15), meant to challenge Elisha's resolve or reproach him for vacillating.[107] Second, even if we are to understand Elijah's response as granting permission, it is a permission that places a strong emphasis on "the uncompromising nature of the call," exemplified in Elisha's slaughtering of his oxen and roasting them over the broken plow (1 Kgs 19:21).[108] In a similar way, "Jesus' reply here is not so much a refusal as it is a warning."[109] Certainly his words imply a tacit denial, but, as with the Elisha pericope, the point of the narrative is not a matter of kissing of one's parents or not, but of an irreversible break with the past: true disciples cannot look back.[110] Especially in light of the series of discipleship failures in this passage, this episode is not meant to highlight how different from Elijah Jesus is, but rather how discipleship with Jesus requires at least the level of commitment that Elisha showed his master.

Luke 9 presents an impressive series of Elijah allusions that consistently connect Jesus with the OT prophet. The links are not free from contrast, for it is clear, especially at the transfiguration, that Jesus is set apart from and exalted over both Elijah and Moses. Similarly, the text makes plain that Jesus is not in any literal sense Elijah *redivivus* or a returned Elijah: even Herod finds this identification lacking. However, the rapid succession of so many episodes casting Jesus in an Elijianic light

---

106. *Pace* Öhler, *Elia im Neuen Testament*, 231, who sees in this episode a radical distancing of Jesus from Elijah. Cf. Fitzmyer, *Luke* 1:214; Tannehill, *Narrative Unity*, 230; Danker, *Jesus and the New Age*, 211.

107. See esp. Cogan, *1 Kings*, 455; DeVries, *I Kings*, 239–40; Fretheim, *First and Second Kings*, 111. The LXX rendering (Ἀνάστρεφε, ὅτι πεποίηκά σοι) is even more obscure, but appears to support a dismissal of Elisha's request. Thus NETS translates "Go back again, for I am done with you."

108. Wray Beale, *1 and 2 Kings*, 255; cf. Gray, *I and II Kings*, 413.

109. Bock, *Luke*, 2:983.

110. Blair, "Hand to the Plough," 342–43, suggests that the phrase "put a hand to" in v. 62 refers to breaking apart the plow as Elisha did. Thus he paraphrases Jesus's response to be "You have made the same request as Elisha made; you must be prepared for the same ruthless break with the past as he made." While the interpretation of the idiom is unlikely (cf. Bovon, *Luke*, 2:14n33), his paraphrase still captures the sentiment of v. 62.

serves to establish once again that there is something strongly reminiscent of the Tishbite in Jesus's ministry.

The Remnant in Luke 9

Luke's remnant theology reaches a highpoint in ch. 9, as Jesus's person and his mission begin to gain focus and significance. Those unable to accept either his identity as Christ or his mission to the cross begin to fall from view, so that soon Jesus alone is left as the only one truly faithful to God's purposes. The cross, with its journey through rejection and isolation, death, and ultimate resurrection, epitomizes Jesus's experience as the remnant *par excellence*, and it becomes the touchstone for all who would participate in the remnant he gathers. Those who would experience the renewal he offers must follow him in taking up their cross as well.

Removal

In the pattern we have already seen, what removes "many in Israel" from the blessings of God's salvation is a failure to appreciate God's purposes and God's appointed agent (cf. esp. 4:23–27; 7:30). At this juncture of the narrative, that failure is shown to be all-pervasive at every level of society within the nation. This failure also begins to take on a particular shape, as God's purposes are increasingly defined by the cross (esp. vv. 22–27). First and foremost, it is the powerful and elite who fail to understand Jesus's mission—though ironically it is they who will bring it about (cf. vv. 22, 44). The tension that has been developing with the religious leaders erupts to the surface when Jesus predicts that the "elders, the chief priests and the teachers of the law" will be responsible for his death (v. 22; cf. 44).[111] Although the reason for their antagonism is not expanded on here, Luke's earlier statement that they had "rejected God's purpose for themselves" (7:30) places them in opposition to the divine plan of salvation now unfolding.[112] Likewise, Herod's eagerness to see

---

111. Though at other points Luke differentiates the various factions of religious leadership, in his use of a single article here (cf. Mark 8:31), he lumps them together as a single group representing the "religious elite." See Wolter, *Lukasevangelium*, 345; cf. Nolland, *Luke*, 1:464; Green *Luke*, 371.

112. See esp. Marshall, *Gospel of Luke*, 299; Bock, *Luke*, 1:678; Green, *Luke*,

Jesus takes an ominous tone after his admission to beheading John (v. 9), and foreshadows his role in Jesus's death (cf. 13:31–32; 23:6–12).[113] Even the statement that Jesus "set his face [τὸ πρόσωπον ἐστήρισεν] to go to Jerusalem" is an implicit judgment on the religious establishment (v. 51), for not only does it foreshadow his death at their hands (cf. vv. 22, 31), but the phrase also echoes OT prophetic acts of judgment, especially Ezekiel's oracle against Jerusalem for her corruption (see Ezek 21:2–6).[114] Thus, many who would have been thought of as exemplars in Israel are now seen to be outside the bounds of the people of God.

Yet what we encounter in this series of narratives is not a simplistic reversal in which the kings and priests give way to the common folk, for, surprisingly, the crowds are equally culpable in their faithlessness.[115] The crowds take a great interest in Jesus, but it is the interest of ignorant bystanders, their attempts to identify him being so unsatisfying as to be rejected even by Herod (vv. 7–9).[116] They are part of a "faithless and perverse generation [γενεὰ ἄπιστος καὶ διεστραμμένη]" (v. 41; cf. 7:31; 11:29–32, 50–51) that, like the wilderness generation in Moses's day, had entirely rejected God and his salvation (Deut 32:5, 20).[117] Even those from among the crowd who do express interest in following Jesus quickly become examples of a lack of resolve (vv. 57–62). Nor do the social outcasts fare any better — with the sensitivity towards ethnic and social outsiders that we have already seen cultivated in Luke's Gospel (esp. 4:18–19, 25–27), we might well expect the Samaritans to be the heroes in this passage, yet they too are ignorant of Jesus's identity and the significance of his mission (vv. 51–56). Had the Samaritans been able to see past their own ethno-religious biases and truly understand what it

---

300–301.

113. Darr, *Herod the Fox*, 170–73.

114. See esp. Evans, "Luke 9:51 Once Again," 80–84.

115. At this point in the Lukan narrative, the crowds appear as mere spectators, possibly not even aware of the miracles occurring in their midst (see Nolland, *Luke*, 1:444; Marshall, *Gospel of Luke*, 357; Green, *Luke*, 387).

116. Schürmann, *Lukasevangelium*, 508. See also Green, *Luke*, 353.

117. Though it is the disciples' faithlessness demonstrated in their inability to perform the exorcism that prompts Jesus's rebuke (see below), the language indicates that the whole crowd is in view as well. See esp. Bock, *Luke*, 1:883; Marshall, *Gospel of Luke*, 391; Danker, *Jesus and the New Age*, 203; Fitzmyer, *Luke*, 1:809; *pace* Schürmann, *Lukasevangelium*, 570; Green, *Luke*, 389; Tannehill, *Luke*, 163. On the allusions to Deuteronomy 32, see esp. Nolland, *Luke*, 2:510; Pao and Schnabel, "Luke," 303–4, 312.

meant for Jesus to "set his face towards Jerusalem," they would presumably have been quick to receive him (v. 51).[118]

The disciples do not fare much better at this point in the narrative. Up until now they have been portrayed in a largely positive light, and even within this chapter, they are given special access to Jesus and special insight into his identity and mission that the crowds are not permitted to have (vv. 20–22, 43–44).[119] However, at the same time they fail to grasp Jesus's ability to feed the multitudes with a little (v. 13), though they had just returned from experiencing provision while carrying nothing (vv. 3, 10).[120] They fail to drive out a demon though they had already been granted the authority to do so (v. 40, cf. v. 1), and as a result, they are the chief representatives of the "faithless and perverse generation" (v. 41).[121] They squabble over rank (v. 46), and they even attempt to stop an exorcist from successfully doing what they were unable to do (v. 49).[122] Even Peter, James, and John are named more for their failures than their successes (vv. 33, 49, 54).[123] Though this inner circle is permitted to accompany Jesus to the Mount of Transfiguration while the other nine are not (v. 28; cf. 8:51), Peter is ignorant of what is happening, and they all tremble with fear (vv. 33–34).[124] Likewise, James and John are named for their

---

118. On the ethnic tensions, see Josephus, *J.W.* 2.12.3; *Ant.* 20.6.1, though cf. Böhm, *Samarien und die Samaritai*, 213, 218; Pummer, *Samaritans in Flavius Josephus*, 222–62.

119. On the theme of discipleship throughout Luke 9, see esp. Green, *Luke*, 352, 354–55.

120. Green, *Luke*, 363–64; Bock, *Luke*, 1:830–31; Edwards, *Gospel according to Luke*, 265–66.

121. Green, *Luke*, 387; Nolland, *Luke*, 2:509; Tannehill, *Luke*, 163.

122. Green, *Luke*, 392. Tannehill, *Narrative Unity*, 213, notes further that the use of ἐπιστάτης in this verse "may be a further indication of their inadequacy, for, when used by the disciples, this title always appears in situations in which the disciples fail to understand Jesus' power or purpose." See also Rowe, *Early Narrative Christology*, 84.

123. It is true that Luke's account of Peter's confession omits his failure and rebuke from Jesus (vv. 18–20; cf. Mark 8:32–33; Matt 16:22–23), but this likely has more to do with focusing the episode on Jesus's true identity and the resultant call to imitate him (vv. 23–27) than it does with presenting Peter in a better light. See Marshall, *Luke*, 367; Fitzmyer, "Composition," 145–46; cf. Fitzmyer, *Luke*, 1:777.

124. The text does not explain in what way Peter "did not understand what he was saying." However, the use of ἐπιστάτης again here (see above note), as well as the reference to three tents, suggests that his error was in failing to understand Jesus's identity, perhaps putting him on the same level as Moses and Elijah. This also accounts for the divine response from the cloud, which distinguishes Jesus from his companions (vv. 34–35). See esp. Bock, *Luke*, 1:872; Stein, *Luke*, 285; cf. Schürmann, *Lukasevangelium*,

prejudicial response to the Samaritans and subsequent rebuke from Jesus (vv. 54–55). Though the Twelve will step into their apostolic calling by the end of the Lukan narrative, at this point they are as lost as the crowd, and for the same reason: they fail to grasp the significance of the cross. They are privy to Jesus's mission, yet they lack the ability to understand it (v. 45).[125] Although those readers familiar with the end of the narrative rightly associate the Twelve with the remnant, at this point they are better aligned with the wicked generation around them—thankfully, this situation is not permanent. In contrast to those who "look back" and so are not fit for the kingdom (v. 62), Jesus alone "sets his face for Jerusalem," remaining resolute in his mission.

Remainder

Luke 9 sets Jesus apart as the true remnant, and most clearly so at the climax of this section, the transfiguration (vv. 28–36). The presence of Moses and Elijah atop a mountain before the blazing glory of God recalls their parallel experiences on Mount Horeb. As we have already seen, both figures stood before God in theophanic visions on Mount Horeb and were distinguished from within Israel as remnant figures (Exod 32:10; 1 Kgs 19:14).[126] Thus, when Jesus is portrayed in a similar setting—on a mountain before God in blazing glory—and accompanied by just these two figures, it logically follows that he too is being identified as a remnant figure, and in fact, as the remnant *par excellence*. Just as Moses and Elijah were distinguished from Israel as a remnant because of their zealous faithfulness even in the face of death (1 Kgs 19:10, 14; cf. Exod 32:10, 32), Jesus's faithfulness becomes plain in his unique mission to the cross, by which he too will accomplish both salvation and judgment for Israel (cf. vv. 24–26).[127] Yet even these two figures—who have proven faithful

---

560; Heil, *Transfiguration of Jesus*, 127. Green, *Luke*, 383, also notes that the disciples' drowsiness is "likely a figurative allusion to their spiritual dullness."

125. Schürmann, *Lukasevangelium*, 573, suggests this may be willful ignorance, for fear of the implications Jesus's mission will have on their lives (cf. Marshall, *Gospel of Luke*, 394; Bock, *Luke*, 1:890). Whatever the cause, this ignorance would not be fully dispelled until the end of the narrative (cf. 24:26).

126. On the numerous links between this passage and Moses's and Elijah's theophanic experiences on Horeb, see esp. Pao and Schnabel, "Luke," 311–12.

127. Luke's reference to Jesus's "exodus" (ἔξοδος) in Jerusalem infuses this scene of glory with an ominous note (see esp. Nolland, *Luke*, 2:499–500; Pao and Schnabel,

in the past and are even knowledgeable of Jesus's mission (v. 31)—fade in comparison to Jesus, who alone is identified as God's chosen servant and the one to whom to listen (v. 35).[128] After they disappear, he is left alone (μόνος) in "an aloneness that is divinely orchestrated and used to underline" Jesus's unique identity.[129]

It is ultimately Jesus's unique mission—his death and resurrection—that sets him apart as the true remnant. Jesus's passion, which has only been hinted at until now (cf. 2:25–26; 4:28–30; 6:11, 16), suddenly becomes explicit (vv. 22, 44), and the cross looms ominously over the coming journey to the holy city. His first passion prediction, that the Son of Man "must undergo great suffering, and be rejected by the elders, chief priests, and scribes, and be killed, and on the third day [τῇ τρίτῃ ἡμέρᾳ] be raised" (v. 22) appears to have Hos 6:1–2 in view.[130] There the remnant of Israel is compared to the remains of a man mauled by a lion (Hos 5:14; 6:5) who, though slain, will experience a "resurrection" (on which, see below).[131] It is worth noting again the use of death imagery to describe the experiences of the remnant in the prophets (cf. Ezek 37:11; Isa 59:10; Amos 3:12).[132] It is this brush with death that makes Elijah's appeal so

---

"Luke," 311–12; Marshall, *Gospel of Luke*, 384–85; Fitzmyer, *Luke*, 1:800; cf. Schürmann, *Lukasevangelium*, 558).

128. On the influence of Isaiah 42 on this passage, see esp. Fitzmyer, "Composition," 146–47; Marshall, *Historian and Theologian*, 169–75.

129. Nolland, *Luke*, 2:502.

130. The use of Hos 6:1–2 in this and other NT passages (esp. 1 Cor 15:3–4) has been the topic of endless debate, though a majority allow this as the only possible OT text that could be pointed to as a prediction of a third-day resurrection (Dempster, "From Slight Peg," 371–409; Dupont, "Ressuscité 'le troisième jour,'" 742–61; Proctor, "After Three Days," 131–50; Russell, "On the Third Day," 1–17; see also Delling, "Τρεῖς, κτλ.," 220, who calls this link "fairly obvious"). Luke's insistence of a scriptural basis for Jesus's resurrection after three days strongly suggests that he was aware of this text (19:31–33; 24:44–46; cf. 24:6–7), and his use of τῇ τρίτῃ ἡμέρᾳ is closer to Hos 6:2 (cf. μετὰ τρεῖς ἡμέρας in Mark 8:32), though he uses ἐγερθῆναι rather than Mark's ἀναστῆναι (cf. ἀναστησόμεθα in Hos 6:2). Dupont, "Ressuscité 'le troisième jour,'" 758–59, rightly argues that it is expecting too much to require exact verbal correspondence, here or elsewhere in the NT (*pace* Bock, *Luke*, 1:848n7; Nolland, *Luke*, 1:467; Schürmann, *Lukasevangelium*, 535).

131. This interpretation is to be preferred over the view that the prophet is quoting an inadequate or insincere prayer of the people. See Macintosh, *Hosea*, 216–19; Andersen and Freedman, *Hosea*, 417–26; cf. Dearman, *Book of Hosea*, 191. *Pace* Wolff, *Hosea*, 116–17.

132. It is also worth noting that the "death" in Hosea 6, though inflicted at the hand of Israel's enemies, is ultimately attributed to Yahweh (cf. esp. Hos 5:14). A similar

poignant (1 Kgs 19:10, 14), and it is this element that serves to distinguish the remnant theme from other common OT patterns of suffering and vindication (e.g., Psalm 22).[133] Yet what the prophets said of Israel metaphorically would now be enacted literally in the person of Jesus, so that at the cross (and with it, the empty tomb), Jesus is most truly set apart as Israel's remnant.

Though Jesus's unique identity and mission set him apart as the true remnant, those who come to appreciate the significance of the cross and follow his example are able to join him. If the cross best epitomizes Jesus's role as remnant, it is little wonder that all those who wish to be part of the remnant must lead similarly cruciform lives (v. 23), for they too will find themselves opposed by the wickedness of the world at large.[134] It is only because they embrace this radical calling that "some" will be able to see the kingdom of God (v. 27). It is when they fail to understand the cross and its implications that the disciples are seen most to fail in this chapter (esp. vv. 45, 46–48, 49–50), and it is the cost of denying oneself—poverty and isolation—that causes otherwise eager disciples to turn back (vv. 57–62). Only those who, like Elisha, are willing to turn their backs on their former lives and follow their master all the way to his departure can expect to share in his spirit or participate in the remnant he gathers. However, the remnant does not expect to share in his sufferings only, but also in his restoration to new life.

Renewal

Although Jesus's rejection and sufferings receive the bulk of the attention in ch. 9, the expectation of resurrection serves to foreshadow the renewal for which the remnant hopes. As we saw above, Jesus's likely reference to Hos 6:2 in v. 22 appeals to a familiar pattern in the prophets in which Israel's remnant, reduced to the point of death, is raised up.[135] Just as the

---

effect is produced through Luke's use of δεῖ, indicating divine will and purpose while discussing suffering "at the hands of" the Jewish leaders (cf. Bovon, *Luke*, 1:363).

133. Although he overstates the case, Hasel is right to see the question of "continued existence" as fundamental to the remnant concept (*Remnant*, 383).

134. Here Green, *Luke*, 372, is helpful in reminding us that the Lukan narrative has already shown that even among those who "want to become" Jesus's disciples (v. 23), only some will persist in their faith to do so (cf. 6:16; 8:13).

135. Luke's use of the passive ἐγερθῆναι in place of ἀναστῆναι (Mark 8:31; cf. Hos 6:2) is likely meant to preserve God's role in Jesus's resurrection/vindication, which is

dry bones would be revived (Ezek 37:1-14) and the dead nation would be raised up (Isa 26:19), the Son of Man would "be raised," an embodiment of Israel's hope. And so too, those who follow him in losing their lives could look forward to newness of life as well (v. 24). As we saw already in Luke 7, Jesus's power to heal and raise to life is indicative of the time of restoration that he brings (7:16, 21-22; cf. Isa 61:1-2). So too, the numerous healing miracles in the present passage (vv. 1, 2, 6, 11, 37-43; 10:9), including one patterned after a resuscitation (vv. 37-43; cf. 1 Kgs 17:23), serve as further indicators of the renewal of the kingdom that Jesus brings, flowing out of his own resurrected life (cf. Acts 3:15-16; 4:10).

Renewal is seen also in the proclamation of the kingdom (cf. vv. 1-2, 11), another major emphasis in this section (vv. 2, 11, 27, 60, 62), and the sending of the "twelve" to preach the kingdom surely indicates restoration to Israel (9:1).[136] Not only are the healing miracles signs of the kingdom (vv. 1-2, 6, 11), but Luke's account of the feeding miracle (vv. 11-17) makes it a part of Jesus's kingdom teaching rather than an interruption to his retreat with the disciples (v. 11; cf. Mark 6:30-34). The crowds, rather than being a nuisance or an object of pity (cf. Mark 6:30-34; Matt 14:14) are welcomed as honored guests (v. 11).[137] This miraculous meal in the wilderness (cf. v. 12), with its adumbrations of manna and a new exodus, becomes an "antepast of the heavenly banquet"—a foretaste of the kingdom (cf. esp. Isa 25:6).[138] The restoration of the kingdom of God, joyfully anticipated in the birth narratives (esp. 1:33), and proclaimed by Jesus and his disciples, is now seen to be present, at least in part.

The transfiguration narrative (vv. 28-36) shows an even greater anticipation of the kingdom. The temporal modifier (v. 28) connecting this pericope with Jesus's words that "some" would not die before seeing the kingdom (v. 27) shows this event to be at least a partial fulfillment of that

---

of major theological import for Luke (cf. Acts 2:23), and thus need not call into question the echo of Hos 6:2 (*pace* Nolland, *Luke*, 1:466).

136. Not only does Luke bookend this section with accounts of Jesus's sending the twelve and the seventy-two "to proclaim the kingdom of God" (9:2; cf. 10:9), but of the five references to the kingdom in ch. 9 (vv. 2, 11, 27, 60, 62), all but one is a Lukan addition (cf. v. 27 // Mark 9:1). On the theme of kingdom restoration in Luke-Acts, see esp. Tannehill, "What Kind of King?," 17-21; Bauckham, "Restoration of Israel," 435-87.

137. Marshall, *Gospel of Luke*, 359-60; Bock, *Luke*, 1:829; Danker, *Jesus and the New Age*, 191; Nolland, *Luke*, 1:440-41; Schürmann, *Lukasevangelium*, 512-13.

138. Marshall, *Gospel of Luke*, 358. See also Nolland, *Luke*, 1:442; Schürmann, *Lukasevangelium*, 515.

promise.¹³⁹ The divine declaration "this is my Son" (v. 35) echoing Ps 2:7, recognizes Jesus as a Davidic royal figure, anointed by God.¹⁴⁰ Similarly, the divine injunction to "listen to him" (v. 35) casts Jesus as a new Moses (Deut 18:15) who, through his upcoming passion, will accomplish a new "exodus" (v. 31) by which he will bring about redemption and establish the kingdom for the remnant who will follow him.¹⁴¹ The transfiguration narrative sees dozens of OT images woven together, but one overriding implication is that God has established his kingdom through his Son in a manner reminiscent of, but greater than, his saving acts of the past.

Perhaps surprisingly, the inauguration of the kingdom, accompanied as it is with so many national symbols from Israel's Scriptures, is closely followed by an outward gaze beyond ethnic Israel. Intriguingly, after setting his face toward Jerusalem (v. 51), Jesus's first destination is a Samaritan village (v. 52). Despite their rejection of Jesus, they are shown mercy in anticipation, it seems, of their eventual acceptance (cf. Acts 8:8-25). It is also likely that the universal invitation is reflected in the twofold mission that brackets this passage (9:1-10; 10:1-12), for while the mission of twelve disciples is almost certainly symbolic of Israel's twelve tribes (9:1; cf. 22:30), Luke's addition of the sending of the seventy(-two) in such close proximity strongly suggests a foreshadowing of the mission to the nations.¹⁴² With the restoration of Israel comes a light to the nations (cf. Isa 49:6).

---

139. Though Luke probably does not intend this event to be the primary fulfillment of v. 27, the temporal indicator linking these two episodes shows that they are to be taken together, so that the transfiguration is in some way a revelation of the kingdom. On the issue of Luke's "eight days" (v. 28; cf. Mark 9:2), see esp. Marshall, *Gospel of Luke*, 382; Fitzmyer, *Luke*, 1:797; Bock, *Luke*, 1:865-66.

140. Pao and Schnabel, "Luke," 312; Edwards, *Gospel according to Luke*, 118; Marshall, *Gospel of Luke*, 387-88; Bock, *Luke*, 1:873-74; Tannehill, *Luke*, 162; *pace* Bovon, *Luke*, 1:379. Fitzmyer, *Luke*, 1:485-86, is right to caution against seeing sonship language exclusively in terms of a Davidic figure, for it also describes more broadly the "special relationship to God" which he enjoys. Nevertheless, it is difficult to deny some element of kingdom fulfillment here. On Luke's use of "chosen" (cf. Mark 9:7), see esp. Marshall, *Gospel of Luke*, 388.

141. Bock, *Luke*, 1:874; Marshall, *Gospel of Luke*, 388; Nolland, *Luke*, 2:502; Pao and Schnabel, "Luke," 312; Fitzmyer, *Luke*, 1:803; Edwards, *Gospel according to Luke*, 282. Note that the Lukan word order in v. 35 more closely reflects LXX Deut 18:15 (cf. Mark 9:7).

142. On the significance of seventy(-two), scholars point especially to the seventy (-two) nations listed in Genesis 10 (MT lists seventy, LXX lists seventy-two). See Tannehill, *Narrative Unity*, 232-33; Marshall, *Gospel of Luke*, 414-15; Stein, *Luke*, 304; Bovon, *Luke*, 2:26; Nolland, *Luke*, 2:549, 558; Evans, *Luke*, 169; cf. Danker, *Jesus and*

Conclusion

Luke 9 marks a major turning point in Luke's Gospel, one in which the true nature of Jesus's mission is fully revealed. As Jesus prepares to embark on a journey to Jerusalem, and thus to the cross, this mission takes center stage. At the same time, Luke's editorial decisions bring out the characteristically Elijianic aspects of Jesus's ministry. Even in those points where Jesus surpasses the OT prophet, he is unmistakably a prophet like Elijah. The reason for such an emphasis on Elijah at so crucial a juncture appears to be once again Luke's development of a theology of remnant. In his journey through death into renewed life, Jesus surpasses even Elijah as a quintessential remnant figure. His unique mission sets him apart as the only truly faithful Israelite. Those who fail to grasp the significance of the cross are effectively excluded from God's blessing, while the few who follow him in a cruciform discipleship join him in a renewal movement that grows out of a remnant of one into a glorious kingdom. These he sends in turn to all nations.

The Ascension (Luke 24:51; Acts 1:1–11)

The Elijah motif reemerges in the accounts of Jesus's ascension (24:50–52; Acts 1:1–11) after remaining in the background for most of the latter part of Luke's Gospel. This relative silence throughout the travel narrative is somewhat surprising, given the prominence of the motif in the first nine chapters of Luke (though cf. 17:11–17 [2 Kgs 5:8–19]).[143] This is due at least in part to the shift in the type of material contained in this section, for while the Elijah motif occurs primarily in narrative episodes, especially miracle accounts, the travel narrative contains predominantly parables and teaching.[144] Nevertheless, the introduction of this section

---

the New Age, 212; Pao and Schnabel, "Luke," 316–17, who also see an allusion to the seventy elders in Numbers 11 as likely. *Pace* Edwards, *Gospel according to Luke*, 303–4; Bock, *Luke*, 2:1015–16; Fitzmyer, *Luke*, 2:846, who do not see any symbolism present. On the text-critical question, see esp. Marshall, *Gospel of Luke*, 414–15; cf. Verheyden, "How Many Were Sent," 193–238; Jellicoe, "'Seventy(-Two),'" 319–21; Metzger, "Seventy or Seventy-Two," 299–306.

143. The healing of the Samaritan leper in 17:11–17 bears numerous similarities to the Naaman account, which space will not allow us to examine in depth (see Bruners, *Die Reinigung*, esp. 103–11).

144. Cf. Nolland, *Luke*, 2:527–31; Bock, *Luke*, 2:959–60. Brodie's suggestion that Luke's dependence on the Elijah-Elisha narratives is temporarily suspended in favor of

with reference to Jesus's coming ἀνάλημψις (9:51) allows the reader to anticipate the resumption of the Elijah motif at the dénouement of the Gospel narrative.[145]

Jesus's ascension is of obvious theological and narratival significance for the author of Luke-Acts, for not only does he narrate it twice (Luke 24:51; Acts 1:9-11), but he also references it in both Luke and Acts (Luke 9:51; Acts 1:22; cf. 2:32-36; 5:30-31; 13:31) so that both narratives point forward and back respectively to this critical moment.[146] By contrast, the other three Evangelists never narrate the ascension at all.[147] Among the other theological and practical reasons for Luke's interest in this event, it allows him to pattern Jesus's succession by his disciples after the scripturally familiar model of Elijah and Elisha.[148] We shall focus our attention on Acts 1:1-11 as not only the longer and more textually secure of the two accounts, but also the one with the clearest allusions to the Elijah narratives.[149] It is in the context of such a distinctly Elijianic event that Luke introduces a discussion on the coming of the kingdom of God and the future of Israel's remnant (Acts 1:7-8).

---

the book of Judges is unconvincing (Brodie, *Birthing of the New Testament*, 96).

145. Cf. Brodie, "Departure for Jerusalem," 107.

146. The last line of Luke 24:51 (καὶ ἀνεφέρετο εἰς τὸν οὐρανόν) is missing from some important MSS., but is generally accepted as authentic, due in large part to the testimony of 𝔓75. For this and other text-critical issues, see Fitzmyer, "Ascension of Christ," 409-40; de Jonge, "Chronology of the Ascension Stories," 151-71; Barrett, *Acts of the Apostles*, 1:65-69; Maile, "Ascension in Luke-Acts," 29-59; Parsons, *Departure of Jesus*, 125, 192-94; Parsons, "Text of Acts 1:2 Reconsidered," 58-71; Schille, "Die Himmelfahrt," 183-99; Stockhausen, "Luke's Stories of the Ascension," 251-63.

147. The description in Mark 16:19 is almost unanimously recognized as a later addition, and likely distilled from the Lukan narrative. Though they do not narrate the event, numerous other NT texts either refer to or assume it (e.g., John 20:17; Eph 4:10; 1 Tim 3:16; 1 Pet 3:22; Heb 4:14; 6:19; 9:24). See Zwiep, *Ascension of the Messiah*, 164-73, 189-90; Nolland, *Luke*, 2:1225; Fitzmyer, "Ascension of Christ," 410-20.

148. Pervo, *Acts*, 45-46; cf. Litwak, *Echoes of Scripture*, 148-49. For other theological reasons for Lukan interest in the ascension, see Maile, "Ascension in Luke-Acts," 55-59; Lohfink, *Die Himmelfahrt Jesu*, 251-75.

149. On the unity and distinction of Luke's two ascension accounts, see esp. Maile, "Ascension in Luke-Acts," 29-59; Tannehill, *Narrative Unity*, 1:298-301, 2:9-19; Stockhausen, "Luke's Stories of the Ascension," 251-63.

Elijah Motif

Acts 1:9-11 shares obvious structural elements in common with 2 Kgs 2:1-18, including the ascension of the hero into heaven, the presence of watching disciples, the appearance of something (cloud/chariot) to block their view, the bestowal of an empowering spirit, and the subsequent continuation of ministry by the disciples.[150] This parallel structure in itself would be sufficient to establish a literary parallel, even without the "impressive" verbal correspondence.[151] The verb ἀναλαμβάνω, used twice in this passage to describe Jesus's "going up" (vv. 2, 11; cf. v. 22), is used in the LXX especially to describe Elijah's ascension (2 Kgs 2:9, 10, 11; cf. Sir 48:9; 1 Macc 2:58).[152] Further verbal correspondence includes the use of the phrase "from you" (ἀφ'ὑμῶν/ἀπὸ σοῦ) in conjunction with ἀναλαμβάνω (v. 11; cf. 2 Kgs 1:9); the phrase "into heaven" (εἰς τὸν οὐρανόν) (vv. 10, 11; cf. 2 Kgs 2:11); and reference to "spirit" (πνεύματος) (v. 8; cf. 2 Kgs 2:9, 15).[153] Commentators also point to the reference to forty days (v. 3; cf. 1 Kgs 19:8) and the promise of Jesus's eventual return (v. 11; cf. Mal 3:23 [4:5]) as further echoes of the Elijah narratives, though of course the parallels are inexact.

In addition to these verbal echoes, these two narratives are linked thematically. Most notable is the theme of spiritual succession: Elisha faithfully remains beside his master until his departure, whereupon he inherits his spirit and is immediately seen to emulate him in powerful deeds (2 Kgs 2:13-15). In a similar fashion, after witnessing Jesus's ascension, the disciples remain in Jerusalem in order to receive the Holy Spirit (vv. 4-5, 8), whereupon they imitate Jesus in the Spirit-empowered miracles depicted throughout the rest of the book of Acts.[154] Tied to this

---

150. See Brodie, "Departure for Jerusalem," 99; Brodie, *Birthing of the New Testament*, 377-80; Pervo, *Acts*, 45-46; Keener, *Acts*, 1:713-20; Marshall, "Acts," 528; cf. Öhler, *Elia im Neuen Testament*, 203-15. For similarities with the assumptions of Enoch (cf. Gen 5:24) and Moses (cf. Deut 34:5-12), see Barrett, *Acts of the Apostles*, 82; Keener, *Acts*, 1:718-19.

151. Stockhausen, "Luke's Stories of the Ascension," 257.

152. By contrast, LXX Gen 5:24 uses μετατίθεμαι of Enoch, the only other OT figure to ascend into heaven (though cf. Sir 49:14).

153. Stockhausen, "Luke's Stories of the Ascension," 257-58; Marshall, "Acts," 527. Parsons, *Departure of Jesus*, 139, also mentions that the disciples "return" (ὑποστρέφω/ἐπιστρέφω) (v. 11; cf. 2 Kgs 2:13) after the event, as well as the use of the substantive "ascended" (ὁ ἀναλημφθείς) (v. 8; cf. Sir 48:12), though the latter is not found in the Kings account.

154. Stockhausen, "Luke's Stories of the Ascension," 260-61; Marshall, "Acts," 527;

theme is the motif of sight, for Elisha is told that seeing (ἐὰν ἴδῃς) his master ascend is a necessary condition for inheriting his spirit (2 Kgs 2:10). Thus, as Elijah was taken up, Elisha "kept watching [ἑώρα]" until "he could no longer see him [οὐκ εἶδεν αὐτὸν ἔτι]" (2 Kgs 2:12).[155] Likewise, sight is referenced no fewer than five times in Acts 1:9-11, making explicit that the disciples were eyewitnesses of the entire event from beginning to end.[156]

Remnant Theme

Removal through Unbelief

The opening scene of the book of Acts illustrates one of the critical issues in Lukan theology: even after the dramatic events in Jerusalem, the kingdom is not restored to Israel in the sense that the opening chapters of the Gospel would have us expect (cf. Luke 1:68-79).[157] Even if one were to spiritualize Israel's restoration entirely in terms of the repentance and faith preached by John and then Jesus, his crucifixion at the hands of the Jewish leaders bears testimony to the fact that few have truly received his message. Socially, politically, and even spiritually, Israel has remained a remnant, and there is no sign yet of restoration. The disciples' question—"Is this the time when you will restore the kingdom to Israel?" (v. 6)—implies the still-ruined state of the nation. Expectations remain unfulfilled. In the following chapters, it will be further underscored that this is still a "corrupt generation" (2:40; cf. Luke 9:41; Deut 32:5) guilty of having crucified the messiah (2:23, 36) and thus in need of repentance (2:38-39).[158]

Keener, *Acts*, 1:713.

155. See esp. Stockhausen, "Luke's Stories of the Ascension," 258, 260.

156. Βλεπόντων (v. 9), ἀπὸ τῶν ὀφθαλμῶν αὐτῶν (v. 9), ἀτενίζοντες (v. 10), ἐμβλέποντες (v. 11), ἐθεάσασθε (v. 11).

157. See esp. Bauckham, "Restoration of Israel," 435-87; Tannehill, "What Kind of King," 17-21; Tannehill, "Israel in Luke-Acts," 69-85; Wolter, "Israel's Future," 312-16; Wainwright, "Luke and the Restoration," 76-79; Ravens, *Luke and the Restoration of Israel*, 48-50; Turner, *Power from on High*, 297-303.

158. Scholars are divided on whether Luke places responsibility for Jesus's death on the Jewish nation as a whole (cf. 10:39-40), the Jerusalemites in particular (cf. 4:27), or only the religious leaders (cf. 13:27). See esp. discussion in Matera, "Responsibility for the Death of Jesus," 77-93; cf. Keener, *Acts*, 1:941, who rightly notes that 4:27 explicitly "shares Israel's guilt with the Gentiles." For our purposes it is sufficient to note that,

Remainder Empowered by the Spirit

Jesus's answer to the disciples' question about the kingdom (v. 7) implies that the timeline will be longer than they think: Israel will remain a remnant in need of restoration for at least a little while longer. Rather than focusing on chronology, which is the Father's sole prerogative, they are to devote themselves to the mission at hand, empowered by the Spirit. The sending of the Spirit cannot be the same as the restoration of the kingdom, if for no other reason than that Jesus has given a timeline for the one (v. 8) while he has just eschewed timelines for the other (v. 7). Nor is it, as some commentators suggest, a substitute or "spiritualization" of the kingdom, but rather a crucial piece and down payment of its restoration.[159] The OT prophecies that speak of this outpouring envision the Spirit of God poured out on remnant Israel like "water on thirsty ground" as a sign that her fortunes will be reversed (Isa 44:3; cf. Isa 32:15; Ezek 39:29; Joel 2:28; Zech 12:10).[160] The events at Pentecost will be a token of the kingdom's inaugurated presence, showing that, in some respect, the remnant is being restored (cf. esp. Acts 2:30–31), but they also function as the empowering force that will eventually bring about its greater fulfillment (v. 8).[161] Only with the advance of the gospel would times of greater restoration come (cf. Acts 3:19–21).

As they continue to hope for this restoration, the spirit-empowered disciples "will be [Jesus's] witnesses [ἔσεσθέ μου μάρτυρες]." Though Luke places importance on the disciples as observers of Jesus's earthly ministry (Acts 1:21–22; cf. Luke 1:2; 24:48) and especially his death and resurrection, from which they proclaim repentance and the forgiveness of sins (Luke 24:46–48; cf. Acts 2:32; 3:15; 5:31–32; 10:39–41; 13:31; 22:15;

---

wherever the responsibility is chiefly laid, the whole nation is warned of judgment and called to repentance, and the proclamation of the crucified messiah "leads to a division within Israel" such that hearers either repent or refuse to repent (Matera, "Responsibility for the Death of Jesus," 88).

159. Contra Conzelmann, *Acts of the Apostles*, 7, who famously writes that the Spirit is not the sign of the endtime kingdom "but its substitute." See Peterson, *Acts of the Apostles*, 110–11; McLean, "Did Jesus Correct the Disciples' View," 216; Maston, "How Wrong Were the Disciples," 169–78; Tiede, "Acts 1:6–8," 49.

160. See Keener, *Acts*, 1:682; Marshall, "Acts," 527; Pao, *Isaianic New Exodus*, 92–93; McLean, "Did Jesus Correct the Disciples' View," 216; Peterson, *Acts of the Apostles*, 110–11; Tiede, "Acts 1:6–8," 49. Additionally, the phrase "from on high" may point to Isa 32:15, which speaks of "the New Exodus restoration of Israel" through the outpouring of the Spirit (Turner, *Power from on High*, 300–301).

161. Tiede, "Exaltation of Jesus," 278.

26:16), the term has its roots in Isaiah 43–44 (esp. Isa 43:10 [γένεσθέ μοι μάρτυρες]; cf. 44:8).[162] Ironically, the "eyewitness" is blind (Isa 43:8)—a metaphor for the spiritual state of remnant Israel.[163] Yet this blind and battered remnant will be the ideal witness, for, rather than being impartial observers, they will experience God's saving work for themselves in a new exodus.[164] As Yahweh pours out his life-giving Spirit to restore the fortunes of this remnant (Isa 44:3), they will truly know him (Isa 43:10) and thus be qualified to attest to his unique divine power. That the disciples are "witnesses" in this sense implies that they too will undergo this sort of spiritual transformation. The kingdom will not be fully restored "at this time" (v. 6), but the spirit-empowered remnant will first experience and then begin to effect its restoration.

Restoration for Israel and beyond

The disciples' question about renewal (v. 6) is not, as some commentators suggest, "excruciatingly inept," or even "the last flicker" of their nationalistic misunderstanding.[165] Though he has no trouble elsewhere rebuking the disciples harshly for their lack of understanding regarding the kingdom (cf. Luke 24:25), the one correction Jesus here offers is not theological but chronological (v. 7). Indeed, the passage is filled with expectation regarding kingdom restoration—it is, above all, precisely "about the kingdom of God" that Jesus has been instructing the disciples over the past forty days (v. 3), as he instructs them to remain in Jerusalem and await the fulfillment of the Father's promise (v. 4–5).[166] The question is not whether Israel's remnant will be restored, but when and how. Thus Jesus instructs that his disciples bear witness to him first in Jerusalem,

162. See Keener, *Acts*, 1:694–707; Marshall, "Acts," 528; Fitzmyer, *Acts of the Apostles*, 206; Pao, *Isaianic New Exodus*, 93–94; Beers, *Followers of Jesus as the Servant*, 132; Peterson, *Acts of the Apostles*, 111.

163. Oswalt, *Isaiah*, 2:143–47; Goldingay and Payne, *Isaiah 40–55*, 283.

164. Goldingay and Payne, *Isaiah 40–55*, 1:282, note that, paradoxically, the servant/witness is called forward "not that any third party should be convinced of Yhwh's case but that the witnesses' own convictions should be built up." See also Oswalt, *Isaiah*, 1:147; Childs, *Isaiah*, 343.

165. *Pace* Pervo, *Acts*, 41; Bruce, *Book of the Acts*, 36; cf. Munck, *Acts of the Apostles*, 7. For a more positive reading, see Bock, *Acts*, 62; Keener, *Acts*, 683; Maston, "How Wrong Were the Disciples," 169–78; McLean, "Did Jesus Correct the Disciples' View," 215–27; Peterson, *Acts of the Apostles*, 108–10; Tiede, "Acts 1:6–8," 46.

166. Peterson, *Acts of the Apostles*, 107–8.

then Judea, Samaria, "and to the ends of the earth [ἕως ἐσχάτου τῆς γῆς]" (v. 8). This last phrase is drawn from Isa 49:6: "It is too light a thing that you should be my servant to raise up the tribes of Jacob and to restore the survivors of Israel; I will give you as a light for the nations, that my salvation may reach to the end of the earth [ἕως ἐσχάτου τῆς γῆς]" (cf. Acts 13:47). Here Isaiah describes the servant as Israel's representative (Isa 49:3) as well as the one sent to gather rebellious Israel (Isa 49:5-6).[167] As Israel's true representative within a nation under judgment, the servant is the remnant, but as the one who "restores" the scattered tribes, this remnant grows greater and greater, ultimately becoming the impetus for renewal.[168] This is also the pattern we have seen in Ben Sira's application of Isa 49:6 to Elijah (Sir 48:10).[169] In the same way, the disciples, succeeding Jesus as the core of Israel's remnant, become witnesses to the rest of their nation to effect the very restoration about which they had asked.[170] Yet even this is "too light a thing" (Isa 49:6).

In their capacity as the purified remnant, the Twelve were not merely to be witnesses to the rest of their nation but were also given Israel's mission to the nations.[171] How exactly these two tasks play out will be the subject of the rest of the book of Acts. Perhaps it is for this reason that Jesus eschewed timelines: Israel would, on the one hand, be renewed

---

167. See Childs, *Isaiah*, 383-86; Beers, *Followers of Jesus as the Servant*, 38; Knight, *Deutero-Isaiah*, 184; Moessner, "Ironic Fulfillment," 49-50.

168. On the overlap between the servant and the remnant in Isaiah, see discussion in ch. 2.

169. See esp. Lévêque, "Le Portrait d'Élie," 22. Blenkinsopp, *Isaiah*, 2:301, further connects this verse with Elijah's work in Mal 3:24[4:6] by noting the similar use of the Hiphil of שוב ("to restore"). The LXX of Isa 49:6 differs from the MT at several key points in this verse, the most pertinent for the present study is the use of διασπορά ("exiles") for נְצִיר ("survivors"). While this shifts the meaning slightly, the term nevertheless retains the sense of "remnant" in this context (see Goldingay and Payne, *Isaiah 40-55*, 2:165). On the other points of divergence, see esp. Karrer et al., "Das Lukanische Doppelwerk," 261-62.

170. Such an understanding of the restoration of Israel is confirmed in the next pericope (vv. 14-26) by the appointment of Matthias among the Twelve to complete their number. Though the disciples are distinguishable from Israel as a whole, they do nevertheless represent the renewed Israel. See Pao, *Isaianic New Exodus*, 123-27; Bauckham, "Restoration of Israel," 469; Fitzmyer, *Acts of the Apostles*, 220-21; Peterson, *Acts of the Apostles*, 119-20; Bock, *Acts*, 77; cf. Tannehill, *Narrative Unity*, 2:21-22.

171. Pao rightly suggests that the phrase ἐσχάτου τῆς γῆς is best understood in "theopolitical terms" rather than merely geographic or ethnic (*Isaianic New Exodus*, 93-95). Cf. Bock, *Acts*, 65-67; Beers, *Followers of Jesus as the Servant*, 132-33; Fitzmyer, *Acts of the Apostles*, 206; Keener, *Acts*, 1:704-8.

or restored in a few days with the outpouring of the Holy Spirit on the disciples as God's servants, but on the other hand, the restoration after which they were asking would not truly take place until they had carried out the mission program he outlined for them, and even then, it would far exceed the scope they had in mind.

The disciples are not wrong to ask after the restoration of Israel, and in fact, Jesus shares their concern. However, their interest in chronology betrays a level of ignorance as to the nature of the restoration after which they are asking. The timeline cannot be pinned down because, as with the remnant throughout salvation history, two timelines are in operation simultaneously. Once Jesus, the true remnant of Israel, departs, and his spirit is poured out on the Twelve as his spiritual successors, true Israel can be said to exist in them as the remnant. At the same time, it is only now that the work of restoration truly begins, for now they, like Elijah, are tasked with raising up the tribes of Jacob and restoring the survivors of Israel (Isa 49:6). Through their apostolic witness, Israelites will experience the renewal made possible through repentance and faith in Jesus. Jesus's answer also reveals that their sights are set too low: his program will not be satisfied with merely raising up the tribes of Israel, but the restored remnant will serve as a light to the nations, bringing salvation to the ends of the earth.

Summary and Conclusions

In his miraculous healings, his bold confrontations with political and religious authorities, his compassion towards outsiders, and his dramatic ascension into heaven, the Lukan Jesus is undeniably cast in the image of Elijah. From the very beginning, Jesus himself describes his ministry as one modeled after that of the Tishbite (Luke 4:25–26). His healing miracles are strongly reminiscent of those of the OT prophet (esp. Luke 7:1–17), and at the high point of his popularity the masses assumed that he was in fact Elijah returned (9:8, 19). Even in those instances in which his actions can be contrasted with those of Elijah (esp. Luke 9:52–56), his ministry is still thoroughly Elijianic in nature. Finally, the account of his ascension into heaven and subsequent bestowal of his spirit on his successors is clearly modeled after the Tishbite's departure.

We have seen that, whatever else these parallels communicate about Jesus, Luke employs them to advance and develop his theology of the remnant. Luke portrays Jesus himself as the true remnant—the only faithful Israelite who, like Elijah, becomes the nucleus around which a growing remnant gathers. In pronouncing both judgment and blessing, Jesus's sermons accomplish what they predict, driving away the hardened while drawing the humble, poor, and repentant to himself. In promising the Spirit to his twelve apostles, he establishes them as the core of a renewed Israel, sending them as witnesses to the rest of the nation. At the same time, as we shall see in the next chapter, he gives them Israel's mission to the nations, so that salvation will extend to the ends of the earth.

7

Elijah and the Disciples in Luke-Acts

BY FAR THE MOST overlooked aspect of the Elijah motif in Luke-Acts is Luke's appeal to Elijah in connection with the disciples. However, not only do these connections force us to move past the models of one-to-one correlation that has dominated the scholarly debate for so long, but they also bring to the fore the paradoxes of salvation present in Luke's conception of the church: that Israel is enjoying restoration and renewal, and yet is reduced to a remnant; that the gospel is the hope of Israel and yet is open to all nations; that God's work of salvation in Jesus Christ is in line with his saving acts of old, and yet is radically new. As Luke develops the Elijah motif in connection with Peter, Paul, and the other pillars of the church, he reveals the usefulness of the remnant theme for understanding the complexities of the people of God. This will be seen through one final cluster of verses from Luke's Gospel before attention is turned fully to the narrative in Acts.

Messengers Ahead of Him (Luke 9:52; 10:1-16)

The Elijah Motif: The Lord's Messenger

As the Gospel narrative shifts to the journey to Jerusalem, the messenger motif reemerges as Luke appeals to Mal 3:1 yet again, this time with reference to the disciples (9:52; 10:1).[1] The allusion in 9:52 is strongest, linked

---

1. ἰδοὺ ἐγὼ ἐξ <u>ἀποστέλλω</u> τὸν <u>ἄγγελόν</u> μου, καὶ ἐπιβλέψεται ὁδὸν [u] <u>πρὸ προσώπου</u> μου, καὶ ἐξαίφνης ἥξει εἰς τὸν ναὸν ἑαυτοῦ <u>κύριος</u>, ὃν ὑμεῖς ζητεῖτε, καὶ ὁ

by the use of ἀποστέλλω ("send") with ἄγγελος ("messenger"), as well as the phrase πρὸ προσώπου αὐτοῦ ("ahead of him").[2] We have already seen a high concentration of Elijah echoes in Luke 9 (cf. vv. 8, 10-17, 19, 30-33, 42, 52-56, 57-62), increasing the likelihood of a recurrence of the motif here. Most notably, v. 52 introduces an episode in which disciples attempt to imitate Elijah in summoning heavenly fire (vv. 52-56).[3] Coming so close after 9:52, the echo to Mal 3:1 in 10:1 is also clear, even without the use of ἄγγελος this time. Jesus, identified as "the Lord [ὁ κύριος]," sets apart other messengers to "send [ἀπέστειλεν]" them "ahead of him [πρὸ προσώπου αὐτοῦ]" to every place where he intended to "go [ἔρχεσθαι]." Additionally, Jesus's instructions to heal the sick (10:9) as well as to live off the hospitality of those who receive him (v. 7) recall Elijah's itinerant ministry (cf. 1 Kgs 17:17-24).[4] We have already seen Luke appeal to Mal 3:1 three times to describe John the Baptist's role (1:17, 76; 7:27), and certainly there is a sense in which the disciples are continuing John's work.[5] However, it might also be said that at this point the disciples are fulfilling Elijah's role more truly than John ever did, for they are quite literally preceding "the Lord [ὁ κύριος]" (10:1) on his way to Jerusalem and thus to the temple (cf. v. 51). Like John the Baptist before

---

ἄγγελος τῆς διαθήκης, ὃν ὑμεῖς θέλετε· ἰδοὺ ἔρχεται, λέγει κύριος παντοκράτωρ (Mal 3:1 LXX). Though it lacks explicit verbal links, 19:29 exhibits the same pattern of messengers preparing the way for Jesus, and thus may also draw from Mal 3:1.

2. Although all of these terms are relatively common in the LXX and the NT, they are found all together in only one other verse apart from Mal 3:1 (cf. 2 Kgs 6:32), and only in Malachi is this construction used to speak of making preparations for the "Lord" (κύριος). See Nolland, *Luke*, 2:535; Tannehill, *Narrative Unity*, 1:230-31; Fitzmyer, *Gospel according to Luke*, 1:828; pace Bock, *Luke*, 2:969, who calls the link "less than clear." Brodie's proposed echo of 2 Kgs 1:3, 5-6 is implausible ("Departure for Jerusalem," 104-5). On possible influence from Isa 40:3 for the use of ἑτοιμάζω in place of ἐπιβλέπω, see ch. 4 above.

3. Though this episode presents James and John as a negative foil for the Tishbite, part of the reason the comparison works is because the appeal to Mal 3:1 in v. 52 sets the reader to thinking about the disciples in terms of Elijah.

4. Bock, *Luke*, 2:999-1000; Danker, *Jesus and the New Age*, 215; cf. Öhler, *Elia im neuen Testament*, 299-300; Müller, *Mehr als ein Prophet*, 239-40. The instruction to "greet no one on the road" (v. 4) may even be an echo of Elisha's words to Gehazi (2 Kgs 4:29), illustrating the urgency of their mission (Pao and Schnabel, "Luke," 317; Nolland, *Luke*, 2:552; Stein, *Luke*, 305; Marshall, *Gospel of Luke*, 418; Danker, *Jesus and the New Age*, 214-15; cf. O'Hagan, "'Greet No One on the Way,'" 69-84).

5. Tannehill, *Narrative Unity*, 1:49, cf. 230-31.

them, Jesus's followers fulfill a vital preparatory function, extending the offer of repentance to the nation before the Lord's coming.[6]

The Remnant Theme

Removal of Many

Like John and Jesus before them, the disciples' ministry would be divisive, placing many under judgment for their refusal to believe (10:16). Jesus's instructions to his messengers suggest that rejection would be the rule, not the exception, for he sends them "like lambs into the midst of wolves" (v. 3).[7] The image of lambs among wolves is familiar from Jewish literature (cf. 1 En. 89:10-27), though in this case the wolves are not pagan nations but their fellow Jews who reject the message of the kingdom (cf. Ezek 22:27; Zeph 3:3).[8] Likewise, the act of shaking the dust from one's feet (9:5) would have symbolically marked the offending town as unclean: "The action treats Jewish communities that *act* pagan (i.e., like non-Jews rejecting the kingdom) as if they were pagan."[9] Jesus pronounces judgment on such towns that would rival that of Sodom and Gomorrah (vv. 12-15).[10] The kingdom is coming, regardless of one's response (v. 9, 11), but for those who have found themselves outside of the protection of the covenant because of their rejection of the message, its coming will mean judgment.

---

6. In addition to preaching, these preparations likely involved logistical arrangements for Jesus and his entourage (cf. 9:52b) (Nolland, *Luke*, 2:535, 537).

7. Fitzmyer, *Luke*, 2:847; Green, *Luke*, 411, 413; cf. Bovon, *Luke*, 2:26. Cf. O'Hagan, "Greet No One on the Way," 83, who suggests that the injunction to "greet no one on the way" (v. 4) was a sign of "positive hostility towards the inimical world of evil." Intriguing as this suggestion is, it probably has more to do with the urgency of the mission (cf. 2 Kgs 4:29) (Nolland, *Luke*, 2:552; Marshall, *Gospel of Luke*, 418).

8. Cf. Marshall, *Gospel of Luke*, 417; Fitzmyer, *Luke*, 2:847; Bovon, *Luke*, 2:26-27.

9. Keener, *Acts*, 2:2106. See also Fitzmyer, *Luke*, 1:754; Marshall, *Gospel of Luke*, 354; Bovon, *Luke*, 1:346, 2:29. See also Acts 13:51.

10. See esp. Green, *Luke*, 416; Danker, *Jesus and the New Age*, 209; Dochhorn, "Die Verschonung," 361.

Remainder of a Few

The workers are "few [ὀλίγος]" (10:2), and they are innocent and vulnerable like "lambs" (v. 3)—an image familiar in the OT for the remnant of Israel (esp. Isa 40:11; Mic 2:12).[11] Yet, as messengers, their task is to go in among the "wolves" and gather those who will join them. Here again, though the remnant is necessarily divisive, it is not static or elitist, but rather seeks to draw others in as well for the purpose of renewing the whole. This remnant of seventy(-two) messengers was to gather Israel's remnant like Elijah of old, granting a spirit of peace to those children of peace (υἱὸς εἰρήνης) (v. 6) who would receive the message of the kingdom.[12]

Hope of Renewal

Though the messengers could expect hostility, and though their converts would be few, nevertheless this remnant could hope for the restoration and renewal characteristic of the kingdom of God. Their presence would mean the shalom of God on all who receive them (v. 6), and their ministry of healing would not merely bring benefit to those in need, but would itself be a proclamation that the kingdom of God has drawn near (v. 9).[13] As in Jesus's ministry, the healing of the sick and the raising of the dead was a symbolic enactment of the restoration of the kingdom (cf. 4:18–21; 7:22; cf. Isa 61:1–2). Even when the message was rejected, the kingdom was no less present (v. 11), for the time for restoration had begun. The disciples' Elijianic ministry will develop dramatically in the book of Acts, but even here they are seen to gather the repentant remnant from

---

11. Pao and Schnabel, "Luke," 317; Bock, *Luke*, 2:996; Nolland, *Luke*, 2:551; Meyer, "Jesus and the Remnant," 130. See also 1 En. 89:10–27. Though ὀλίγος is frequently used in other contexts, it is often used to describe the remnant (Deut 4:27; Jer 49:2 LXX; 51:28 LXX; Ezek 5:3).

12. Nolland, *Luke*, 2:552–53, suggests that the use of ἐπαναπαύομαι "is meant to echo the use of the same idiom in the LXX of the spirit of Elijah resting upon Elisha" (Επαναπέπαυται τὸ πνεῦμα Ηλιου ἐπὶ Ελισαιε; cf. 2 Kgs 2:15), so that "the messenger in some way reproduces himself in the recipient as he passes on to him the peace of God." See also Klassen, "'Child of Peace,'" 488–506; Green, *Luke*, 414; Bock, *Luke*, 2:998; Marshall, *Gospel of Luke*, 419–20.

13. Nolland, *Luke*, 2:554; Bock, *Luke*, 2:1001–2; Green, *Luke*, 414–15; cf. Fitzmyer, *Luke*, 2:848–49.

among Israel before the time of judgment and in anticipation of future restoration.

Philip and the Ethiopian Official (Acts 8:26-40)

It is in the book of Acts that the disciples' connection with the Elijah motif comes to prominence. As seen in the previous chapter, the first few chapters of Acts record the explosion of the Jerusalem church at Pentecost and immediately after, as the disciples step into their role as witnesses to the risen Christ. Acts 8 serves as a major turning point in the narrative line of Acts, showing the gospel beginning to spread beyond Jerusalem and Judea. The Samaritan ministry, initiated by Philip (8:5-8), sanctioned by the apostolic commission (vv. 14, 25), and confirmed by the gift of the Holy Spirit (vv. 15-17), marks the first major boundary crossed. Immediately following this progression, Philip is sent from the Samaritan towns in the north to a desert road in the south, where he will breach yet another theopolitical barrier for the gospel. The narrative is dramatic, with its miraculous entrances and exits and exotic setting, and no less striking for its numerous links to the Elijah-Elisha narratives.[14]

The Elijah Motif

This narrative contains numerous echoes of the Elijah narratives: Philip receives instructions from the "angel of the Lord [ἄγγελος κυρίου]" to "get up and go" (v. 26; cf. v. 29), recalling the OT prophet's numerous similar angelic encounters (2 Kgs 1:3, 15; cf. 1 Kgs 18:1; 21:17-18). Likewise, his dramatic departure, snatched away by the "Spirit of the Lord [πνεῦμα κυρίου]" (v. 39) recalls Elijah's spiritual mode of travel (1 Kgs 18:12; 2 Kgs 2:16; cf. 2 Kgs 2:11).[15] Furthermore, like Elijah, Philip is

---

14. On the significance of this passage within Luke-Acts, see Tannehill, *Narrative Unity*, 2:107-12; Pao, *Isaianic New Exodus*, 140-42; Keener, *Acts*, 2:1534-96; O'Toole, "Philip and the Ethiopian Eunuch," 25-34; Parsons, "Isaiah 53 in Acts 8," 104-19; Shauf, "Locating the Eunuch," 762-75; Smith, "'Do You Understand,'" 48-70; Strelan, "Running Prophet," 31-38; Dunn, *Acts of the Apostles*, 113-16; Pervo, *Acts*, 219-20. For consistency with the text, we will still speak of the "Ethiopian" and "Ethiopia," though see Keener, *Acts*, 2:1550-65 on the exact referent of Αἰθίοψ. On textual issues in this passage, especially the addition of v. 37 in some MSS, see Fitzmyer, *Acts of the Apostles*, 414-15; Barrett, *Acts of the Apostles*, 1:433; Bock, *Acts*, 348.

15. Marshall, "Acts," 575; Pervo, *Acts*, 226-27; Barrett, *Acts of the Apostles*, 1:434;

seen running to overtake a "chariot [ἅρμα]" (vv. 29–30; cf. 1 Kgs 18:46).[16] Even the geography of the passage, in which Philip departs from Samaria, leaves his companions, and then travels south into the wilderness where he receives divine instructions (vv. 26–29), echoes Elijah's journey in 1 Kgs 19:3–8. Finally, that he was taken while the eunuch was watching, so "he saw him no more" (v. 39), may even echo Elijah's departure before Elisha, given the importance of sight in that account (cf. 2 Kgs 2:10–12).[17]

In addition, this episode shares numerous structural parallels with the Naaman account (2 Kgs 5:1–19), already seen to be a favorite for Luke (Luke 4:27; 7:1–10; 17:11–19; cf. Acts 10:1–48).[18] Both narratives concern a prominent gentile official in a pagan royal court (v. 27; cf. 2 Kgs 5:1).[19] Despite his wealth and power, the man is also marginalized socially (v. 27; cf. Deut 23:1; 2 Kgs 5:1). He departs from his homeland in a "chariot [ἅρμα]" to the land of Israel to inquire of Israel's God (vv. 27–28; cf. 2 Kgs 5:3–9). In a demonstration of faith and humility, he undergoes a ritual immersion (βαπτισθῆναι) (vv. 36, 38; cf. 2 Kgs 5:14).[20] Finally, he does not remain in Israel, but, just as Naaman is permitted to worship the God

---

Bock, *Acts*, 346; Dunn, *Acts of the Apostles*, 115.

16. On this and other links, see esp. Strelan, "Running Prophet," 32–35. The use of ἅρμα to describe a carriage used for long-range travel is unusual, and may have been selected specifically for the parallel with 1 Kings (Keener, *Acts*, 2:1579–80; Fitzmyer, *Acts of the Apostles*, 413; Pervo, *Acts*, 224; Brodie, *Birthing of the New Testament*, 416; cf. Barrett, *Acts of the Apostles*, 1:426–27).

17. Cf. Stockhausen, "Luke's Stories of the Ascension," 258, 260.

18. See esp. Schöpflin, "Naaman," 48–50; Strelan, "Running Prophet," 32–33; Marshall, "Acts," 575; Pervo, *Acts*, 220; Brodie, "Luke-Acts as an Imitation," 81–82; Brodie, *Birthing of the New Testament*, 402–16; cf. Witherington, *Acts of the Apostles*, 291–92; Keener, *Acts*, 2:1539–40. Numerous scholars also note parallels between this passage and Luke 4:16–30 (Keener, *Acts*, 2:1536; Smith, "'Do You Understand,'" 40), and this passage and Acts 10 (Pervo, *Acts*, 222; Tannehill, *Narrative Unity*, 2:110–11; Keener, *Acts*, 2:1538), both of which also appeal to Naaman. It is unlikely that this is mere coincidence.

19. On the status of the eunuch as a gentile, see Shauf, "Locating the Eunuch," 762–75; Keener, *Acts*, 2:1550–71; Barrett, *Acts*, 1:425–26; Tannehill, *Narrative Unity*, 2:110. *Pace* Fitzmyer, *Acts of the Apostles*, 410, 412; Bock, *Acts*, 338. See also Smith, "'Do You Understand,'" 48–70.

20. Naaman's washing, though obviously not a true baptism, nevertheless has ritual elements, most notably the sevenfold immersion (2 Kgs 5:10, 14; cf. Lev 14:7). Moreover, the LXX use of βαπτίζω may be sufficient to establish the link for Luke and his readers. On the Ethiopian's demonstration of humility, see esp. Smith, "'Do You Understand,'" 69; Shauf, "Locating the Eunuch," 772. On other possible links between these two stories, see Brodie, *Birthing of the New Testament*, 410.

of Israel in Syria, the eunuch returns on a chariot to his homeland with his newfound faith (v. 39; cf. 2 Kgs 5:15-19). An appeal to Naaman is particularly satisfying at this point in the storyline of Acts, for it anticipates the progress of the gospel to the ends of the earth.[21]

The Remnant Theme

Removal of the Proud

In his humble acceptance of the gospel, the Ethiopian, like Naaman, stands out as a foil for those who miss out on God's blessings in their pursuit of money and power (cf. 2 Kgs 5:20-27). This narrative follows a series of events in which the Jerusalem leadership, in a vain attempt to maintain power, executes several failed attempts to stifle the gospel (4:1-3; 5:17-18, 26-28, 33, 40; 6:11-15), and it is because of the resultant persecution that Philip leaves Jerusalem in the first place to go to Samaria and eventually to the desert road (8:1-5).[22] In contrast, this influential official is wealthy enough to own a scroll and educated enough to read it, yet he shows the humility to ask for a guide in understanding it and, still more, to seek a baptism of repentance.[23] More telling still, the official is returning from having spent significant time in Jerusalem, worshiping at the temple, and yet he bemoans that there is no one who is able to explain the Scriptures to him (v. 31).[24] That he is leaving Jerusalem with his questions about this text unanswered is a subtle critique of the temple establishment as (to use Jesus's words) "foolish" and "slow of heart to believe all that the prophets have declared" (cf. Luke 24:25).[25] The religious elite

---

21. See Hays, *Echoes of Scripture*, 29-32, on the criteria of "satisfaction" and "thematic coherence." On the function of this story within Acts, see esp. Shauf, "Locating the Eunuch," 773-75.

22. On the implicit contrast in the narrative between the Ethiopian and the religious leaders of Jerusalem, see esp. Smith, "'Do You Understand,'" 55, 60; Pervo, *Profit with Delight*, 18-21; cf. Brodie, *Birthing of the New Testament*, 402-16.

23. Keener, *Acts*, 2:1585; Smith, "'Do You Understand,'" 69; Shauf, "Locating the Eunuch," 772; Schöpflin, "Naaman," 48-49.

24. Given the length of his journey, he would have spent at least a month in Jerusalem, possibly longer if he stayed for both Passover and Pentecost (Keener, *Acts*, 2:1551-52).

25. On the several verbal and conceptual parallels between esp. v. 35 and Luke 24:25-27, 44-47, see Barrett, *Acts of the Apostles*, 1:428, 432; Pervo, *Acts*, 219; Kistemaker, *Acts*, 315; Bock, *Acts*, 344; O'Toole, "Philip and the Ethiopian Eunuch," 31-32.

of Israel are passed by in favor of an unclean gentile who is nevertheless humble enough to seek the truth.

The Humble Remainder

With an implicit judgment removing many of the elite of the nation, nevertheless many elements of this story imply a remainder. There are sufficient verbal connections in v. 26 to suspect echoes of Zephaniah 2–3, especially given Luke's penchant for drawing from the Minor Prophets.[26] The prophecy mentions Gaza (Γάζα) desolated (Zeph 2:4), a desert (ἔρημον) (Zeph 2:13), and noon (or the south) (μεσημβρίας) (Zeph 2:4), as well as people coming from Ethiopia (Αἰθιοπία), bringing sacrifices to worship Yahweh (3:10). After Yahweh's wrath is poured out on Israel and the surrounding nations (2:1–3:8), a humble and obedient remnant will be gathered (3:11–13). They will trust in Yahweh and will help people from all nations—specifically Ethiopia—to call on the name of Yahweh (3:9–10). In this case, Philip, in contrast to the Jerusalem leadership who are unable to interpret their Scriptures or instruct on them, appears as a remnant figure in the wilderness, enabling the Ethiopian to call on the Lord.[27]

Many commentators also see echoes of Isa 56:3–8, a text that speaks of worship of Yahweh by foreigners and eunuchs.[28] Far from being cut off from God's people, foreigners will be welcomed into the temple—"a house of prayer for all peoples" (Isa 56:7)—and eunuchs who obey the Lord will be given "a monument and a name better than sons and daughters" (Isa 56:5). The basis for this restoration is that the Lord "gathers the outcasts of Israel," and so will "gather others to them besides those already gathered" (Isa 56:8).[29] The restoration of Israel's remnant is thus the guarantee

---

On other possible elements of antitemple polemic in this passage, see Parsons, "Isa 53 in Acts 8," 113; Pervo, *Acts*, 224; cf. Dunn, *Acts of the Apostles*, 113.

26. Πορεύου κατὰ μεσημβρίαν ἐπὶ τὴν ὁδὸν τὴν καταβαίνουσαν ἀπὸ Ἰερουσαλὴμ εἰς Γάζαν, αὕτη ἐστὶν ἔρημος (Acts 8:26). Marshall, "Acts," 573; Pervo, *Acts*, 220–21; Keener, *Acts*, 2:1547; *pace* Barrett, *Acts of the Apostles*, 1:426. For a helpful survey of critical issues in Zephaniah, including the relationship between Zeph 2:4–3:8 and 3:9–20, see Sweeney, "Zephaniah," 119–45; cf. Smith, *Micah–Malachi*, 122–24.

27. Note a similar note of judgment on the Jerusalem leadership in Zeph 3:1–5.

28. Pao, *Isaianic New Exodus*, 140–42; Keener, *Acts*, 2:1540–41; Pervo, *Acts*, 222; Dunn, *Acts of the Apostles*, 113; Peterson, *Acts of the Apostles*, 291; Parsons, *Acts*, 120.

29. Hausmann, *Israels Rest*, 248–49, connects this passage with Isa 66:18–21 and

for the inclusion of outcasts and even foreigners; that a gentile eunuch is now depicted worshiping the God of Israel implies that this restoration has occurred or is underway. The restoration begun at Pentecost has already spread from Jerusalem and Judea into Samaria (Acts 8:5). Now Philip, as a Spirit-empowered disciple, and therefore a representative of the restored remnant of Israel, is sent on mission to reach the "ends of the earth," as represented by this Ethiopian eunuch, and the way is being opened for gentiles—as gentiles—to receive the blessings of the God of Israel, just as Naaman did. Though for now this expansion is an isolated incident, this too will soon change.

Peter with Tabitha and Cornelius (Acts 9:32–43; 10:1–48)

The conversion of Cornelius (Acts 10:1–48) is undoubtedly a turning point, if not quite the narrative center of the storyline of Acts.[30] It is told three times (10:1–48; 11:4–17; 15:7–9; cf. 10:30–32), thus rivaling even Paul's conversion for significance, and it is critical to the progression of the book, opening the door to gentile mission, serving as a transition between Peter's and Paul's ministries, and even anticipating the endpoint in Rome.[31] However, its relation to the raising of Tabitha (9:32–43), which immediately precedes it, is rarely given sufficient attention. The two are linked first of all geographically, for the first narrative occurs in Joppa (9:36), where Peter stays for a large portion of the second narrative, until he is called to Caesarea (9:43; cf. 10:5–8).[32] Additionally, both narratives depict Peter as a protagonist who is summoned to aid a person commended for charitable acts (ἐλεημοσύνη) (9:39; 10:2–4).[33] Most significantly for our purposes, the two pericopae are linked in that they

---

Zech 9:7, arguing that "Der Rest ist zwar nicht identisch mit dem Gottesvolk, doch wird die Einbeziehung fremder Völker in das Gottesvolk offensichtlich über den Restgedanken vollzogen." See also Pao, *Isaianic New Exodus*, 140–42. The term "outcasts" in Isa 56:8 (נדח; LXX διεσπαρμένοι) is also used in Isa 11:11–12 to describe the relationship of the remnant of Israel vis-à-vis the nations.

30. Barrett, *Acts*, 1:491; Bock, *Acts*, 381; Keener, *Acts*, 2:1728; Fitzmyer, *Acts of the Apostles*, 447; Acosta Valle, "Actes 10,1–11,18," 427.

31. Keener, *Acts*, 2:1727.

32. Pervo, *Acts*, 257.

33. See Witherup, "Cornelius" 49–50; Fitzmyer, *Acts of the Apostles*, 443; Tannehill, *Narrative Unity*, 2:127. Barrett, *Acts*, 1:477–78, suggests that the two narratives were already connected in Luke's sources.

appeal to the OT narratives of Elijah and the Zarephathite widow (1 Kgs 17:17-24), and Elisha and Naaman (2 Kings 5), respectively—two accounts which are of particular significance in the Lukan narrative, and which Luke has already linked together in his Gospel (Luke 4:25-27; 7:1-10, 11-17).

Although the OT parallels are plain enough, we shall see that Luke plays with the themes at this point in the narrative in order to accomplish his theological purposes. The account of Tabitha does not take place among gentiles, as with the widow of Zarephath, but rather in the Jewish town of Joppa. Likewise, though Cornelius, like Naaman, is considered "unclean," the episode is not a healing at all, but, if anything, a cleansing, as Naaman's leprosy is subsumed into his gentile-ness. Taken together, these two episodes depict that Israel is enjoying the inauguration of the promised restoration through a growing remnant of Jewish believers and that this remnant must now take up Israel's mission as a light to the nations.

The Elijah Motif

Tabitha (Acts 9:32-43)

Structurally, Peter's raising of Tabitha bears numerous similarities to Elijah's raising of the widow's son (1 Kgs 17:8-24).³⁴ (1) A man of God enters the city (vv. 38-39; cf. 1 Kgs 17:10); (2) he is summoned when an individual grows sick and dies (v. 38; cf. 1 Kgs 17:17-18; 2 Kgs 4:22-25); (3) the death causes grief to a widow/widows, who were supported by the deceased (v. 39; cf. 1 Kgs 17:10, 17-18); (4) the deceased is laid in an upper room (ὑπερῷον) (v. 37; cf. 1 Kgs 17:19); (5) the man of God is alone with the corpse (v. 40; cf. 1 Kgs 17:19); (6) he prays (v. 40; cf. 1 Kgs 17:20-21); (7) after the deceased revives, he presents her to the widow(s) alive (vv. 40-41; cf. 1 Kgs 17:22-23); and (8) as a result, people come to trust in the Lord (v. 42; cf. 1 Kgs 17:24).³⁵ In contrast to the OT

---

34. Stipp, "Vier Gestalten," 71-73; Tannehill, *Narrative Unity*, 2:126-27; Keener, *Acts*, 2:1710-11; Bovon, *Luke*, 1:267; Öhler, *Elia im neuen Testament*, 202-3; Dunn, *Acts*, 129; Bock, *Acts*, 375; Marshall, "Acts," 576-77; Pervo, *Acts*, 252, 254. Intriguingly, Tabitha is also associated with Elijah in the second-century document *Apoc. El. (C)* 4:1-6. See Wintermute, "Apocalypse of Elijah," 1:725; though cf. Frankfurter, "Tabitha," 13-25.

35. On other possible connections to the Elijah-Elisha narratives, see Tannehill, *Narrative Unity*, 2:126; Stipp, "Vier Gestalten," 71; Barrett, *Acts*, 1:485; Fitzmyer, *Acts*

narrative, Tabitha is neither a gentile nor a social outcast, but a Jewish "disciple [μαθήτρια]" (v. 36).[36] Nor is there any hint of the scandal implicit in Elijah's aiding a Sidonian woman (cf. Luke 4:25–26), or a crisis of faith within the community or amongst the widows (cf. 1 Kgs 17:18; 2 Kgs 4:27–28).[37] While Luke in his Gospel used this OT narrative to portray the posture of the remnant as poor and humble (7:11–17), he has transformed it here into a picture of restoration. Furthermore, the healing of this Jewish believer—this time not marginalized, but a valued member of the community—allows for an even starker contrast with the next episode and the conversion of a gentile.

Cornelius (Acts 10:1–48)

In light of the interest we have already seen Luke take in the OT account of Naaman (esp. Luke 4:27; 7:1–10; Acts 8:26–40), numerous parallels emerge in the present pericope. (1) It concerns a prominent gentile military officer who represents a nation oppressing Israel (v. 1; cf. 2 Kgs 5:1–2); (2) he is considered ritually unclean (v. 28; cf. 2 Kgs 5:1); (3) the officer is recommended to an Israelite man of God, in part through the mediation of his servants (vv. 3–8; cf. 2 Kgs 5:2–3); (4) he communicates with the prophet by means of messengers (vv. 17–23; cf. 2 Kgs 5:8, 10); (5) the prophet is aware of their coming before their arrival at the house (vv. 19–20; cf. 2 Kgs 5:8); (6) the officer displays humility before the prophet (v. 25; cf. 2 Kgs 5:10–14); (7) he is immersed (βαπτισθῆναι) (vv. 44–48; cf. 2 Kgs 5:14) and thus considered clean (ἐκαθάρισεν) (v. 15; 11:9; 15:9; cf. 2 Kgs 5:13–14); and (8) there is resistance because the figure is a gentile (11:1–3; cf. 2 Kgs 5:20–27).[38] Most significantly, this is an account of a gentile who, like Naaman, is permitted to worship the God of Israel as a

---

of the Apostles, 445.

36. Her Aramaic name is given, followed by its Greek translation for the benefit of the reader, indicating her Jewish ethnicity (Fitzmyer, *Acts of the Apostles*, 445; Barrett, *Acts*, 482–83).

37. Stipp, "Vier Gestalten," 75–76.

38. Shelton, "Healing of Naaman," 69–72; Kolasny, "Luke 4:16–30," 71; Crockett, "Luke 4:25–27," 181–83; cf. Pao and Schnabel, "Luke," 299. On other potential OT parallels also present in this passage, see Wall, "'Son' of Jonah," 79–90; Keener, *Acts*, 2:1730, 1769; Pervo, *Acts*, 255; Marshall, "Acts," 577–78. See also Acosta Valle, "Actes 10,1–11,18," 427–31.

gentile. It is this thematic coherence that makes Naaman a favorite figure for Luke.

The Remnant Theme

Tabitha (Acts 9:32–43)

Removal and Remainder

After the initial growth of the church in the first few chapters, a major strand of the narrative of Acts has depicted the first believers as an oppressed remnant, opposed by a hostile nation which, in betraying and murdering Jesus, has broken the law and the covenant which pointed to him (7:51–53; cf. 2:23; 4:27; 5:30–33).[39] This theme reached a climax with the persecution arising out of Stephen's stoning (8:1), yet with the conversion of Saul, the church's chief persecutor (9:1–22), it fades temporarily into the background. Though the attempts on Saul's life by "the Jews" presage a reemergence of hostilities (9:23, 29), at this point in the narrative, the church experiences a time of relative peace, as well as continued growth (v. 31).[40] There is the hope that the church's days as a remnant are soon to be over, and the promised restoration of Israel is at hand. "The followers of Jesus are being portrayed by Luke as true, messianic Jews, attempting to rescue other Jews so they might be a part of the righteous remnant of Israel."[41]

Renewal

In keeping with this optimism, the Tabitha episode depicts signs of the restoration carried out within the community of Jewish believers. We have already looked extensively at how the act of raising the dead is linked with the restoration of Israel's remnant (esp. Ezek 37:1–14; Hos 6:1–2). This understanding is further strengthened by the inclusion of Aeneas in this pericope (vv. 32–35).[42] Brief though it is, the account of

---

39. On this theme, see esp. Tannehill, *Narrative Unity*, 2:69–85.
40. Cf. Pao, *Isaianic New Exodus*, 129; Ravens, *Restoration of Israel*, 92n89.
41. Witherington, *Acts of the Apostles*, 163.
42. Although Aeneas is a Greek name, it was not unknown among Jews as well. At this point in the overall narrative, the fact that he is an accepted member of the Christian community (τοὺς ἁγίους) (9:32) makes it almost a certainty that he was

a lame man walking just before a report of the dead being raised brings to mind Jesus's appeal to these wonders as signs of the restoration that his ministry brings (Luke 7:22; cf. Isa 35:5–6; 61:1–2). This restoration is seen in the many more Israelites who turn to the Lord in faith as a result of these signs (vv. 35, 42). These two episodes in Acts 9:32–43 give one final glimpse at the explosive growth of the Jewish church before attention turns predominantly to the gentile mission for the remainder of the narrative.[43] With substantial numerical growth and with the miraculous healing and raising of the dead, the picture of the restoration of Israel that Luke has been sketching in the first chapters of Acts is now complete. The twelve apostles, symbolizing the reconstitution of Israel, and the thousands who join their ranks, are now witnessing the renewal and regrowth that is predicted by the prophets, modeled in the Elijah narratives, and outlined by Jesus himself (cf. 1:8).[44] Thus, while the drama to unfold in the next episode is a shock to Peter and the other actors in it, it should not be so for the readers. With the restoration of the remnant comes the mission to the gentiles (cf. esp. Isa 49:6).

Cornelius (Acts 10:1–48)

Removal

Peter's sermon to Cornelius (vv. 34–43) rehearses the progression of the remnant concept in Acts to this point. In his summary of Jesus's death, he draws on a theme of rejection that runs throughout the narrative of Acts (2:23; 3:14–15; 5:28; 7:52; 13:27–28). It is "they" (that is, those in Jerusalem and Judea) who put Jesus to death (v. 39)—a fact that Peter will not omit even when speaking to gentiles. In rejecting Jesus as messiah and seeking his death, many in Israel, especially the Jerusalem leaders, are themselves rejected and "destroyed from the people" (cf. 3:22–23).[45] Yet despite the large-scale removal of so many in Israel, some like himself are allowed to remain as "witnesses" of the resurrection (vv. 39–41).[46]

Jewish. See Keener, *Acts*, 2:1706–7; Dunn, *Acts of the Apostles*, 129.

43. Witherup, "Cornelius," 49–50; cf. Dunn, *Acts of the Apostles*, 128.

44. See esp. Pao, *Isaianic New Exodus*, 129.

45. Keener, *Acts*, 2:1805; Fitzmyer, *Acts of the Apostles*, 465; Dunn, *Acts of the Apostles*, 143; Matera, "Responsibility for the Death of Jesus," 85.

46. Notice esp. Peter's distinction in v. 41: "not to all the people, but to us...." See previous chapter on the remnant implications for the apostles as "witnesses" (cf. Acts

Remainder

Although this remnant of apostolic "witnesses" is select and initially small (vv. 39–41), it is hardly exclusive, for they are given the task of preaching restoration and forgiveness to the very people (τῷ λαῷ) who had rejected Jesus in the first place (vv. 42–43). Peter still appears to see the scope of apostolic preaching as limited to "the people" (τῷ λαῷ) (v. 42)—that is, Israelites—even after his dramatic vision and his willingness to enter Cornelius's house.[47] However, the events of the very next verse will reveal that his statement that "everyone who believes in him receives forgiveness of sins through his name" (v. 43) is much truer than he realizes. In restoring only the tribes of Israel, the apostles are aspiring to "too light a thing." The renewed remnant is meant to be a light to the nations (cf. Isa 49:6).

Renewal and Reaching out in Mission

The sudden, dramatic outpouring of the Holy Spirit at this point (10:44) confirms the legitimacy of the mission to the gentiles. The amazement of Peter and his companions (v. 45) is understandable, since, overwhelmingly, the prophetic passages that speak of the outpouring of God's Spirit do so in the context of the restoration of the remnant of Israel and the reconstitution of Israel as a nation (esp. Isa 32:15; 44:3; Ezek 39:29; Joel 2:28–32; Zech 12:10), rather than the conversion of the nations.[48] However, Joel 2, quoted in Acts 2 by Peter himself, poignantly states that the Spirit will be poured out on "all flesh" (Acts 2:17; cf. Joel 2:28), and that "everyone" who calls on the Lord will be saved (2:21; cf. Joel 2:32).[49] The

---

1:8; Isa 43:10). Cf. Fitzmyer, *Acts of the Apostles*, 466; Barrett, *Acts*, 1:527.

47. The term λαός is generally used of the people of Israel in the LXX, as well as in Luke-Acts up to this point (esp. 3:23; 4:10). Though it is true that the events about to take place will expand the people of God so that he will choose "a people [λαός] for his name from the Gentiles" (15:14), the astonishment that Peter experiences here (v. 45) indicates that he is still thinking in terms of an Israelite mission at the time of his sermon. "To the very Gentile audience to whom Peter here preaches, in fulfillment of the Lord's command, he mentions only Jesus's command to preach to Israel!" (Keener, *Acts*, 2:1807). See also Barrett, *Acts*, 1:525, 527; Bruce, *Book of Acts*, 215; Tannehill, *Narrative Unity*, 2:169–70, 280–81; Keener, *Acts*, 2:1806–7; pace Bock, *Acts*, 399.

48. See discussion in Keener, *Acts*, 2:1812.

49. Probably for Joel, and even for Peter at the time he quoted it, "all flesh" meant all types of people in Israel, though the phrase leaves open the possibility of "all

Lukan narrative capitalizes on this opening.⁵⁰ The gift that was given first to the remnant of Israel to revitalize the nation is now given to people of all nations who will repent and believe in Jesus so that they too may share in the blessings of eternal life (cf. 11:17-18; 15:8-9).

In light of this development, it is significant that the narrative in Acts 10 is the account not simply of Cornelius's conversion, but rather also of Peter's mission to Cornelius. Though the consequences of Cornelius's baptism ripple out into Acts 15 and beyond, the centurion himself fades from view, and Peter is clearly seen as the central figure. The Lukan narrative could well have followed the pattern of Paul's conversion: in the subsequent retellings, Paul's dramatic vision takes center stage, while Ananias, whose role parallels that of Peter here, eventually drops out entirely (26:9-18). By contrast, in the third telling of the Cornelius account, both his vision and Peter's are omitted entirely, the centurion himself is unnamed, and Peter's missionary role (along with the gift of the Holy Spirit) is primary (15:7-9).⁵¹ Luke's interest at this point in the narrative is not merely in gentile conversion as such, but in the mission of the Israelite church (i.e., the remnant) to the gentiles.⁵²

Later, after reflecting on Peter's experience in Caesarea (15:7-11, 14), the Jerusalem church came to this conclusion through an appeal to Amos 9:11-12 (15:15-18).⁵³ Though the theological implications of this

humanity" (cf. esp. Isa 40:3), which is the way the Lukan narrative eventually takes it. Bock, *Acts*, 113; Pao, *Isaianic New Exodus*, 232; Fitzmyer, *Acts of the Apostles*, 252; Keener, *Acts*, 1:881-82; cf. Tannehill, *Narrative Unity*, 2:30-31; Treier, "Fulfillment of Joel 2:28-32," 13-26.

50. Pao, *Isaianic New Exodus*, 231-33 argues that in deliberately ending the quotation where he does, before mention of judgment on the nations, as well as combining of this quotation with an allusion to Isa 57:19 (Acts 2:39), Luke transforms the prophecy in Joel to speak of mission to the gentiles.

51. On the rhetorical effect accomplished in the variations of the three accounts of Cornelius's conversion, see Witherup, "Cornelius," 45-66, esp. 54; Keener, *Acts*, 2:1728; Acosta Valle, "Actes 10,1-11,18," 427-31; Miller, "Men or the Menu?," 311-14. With regards to Paul's conversion, see Witherup, "Functional Redundancy," 67-86; Stockhausen, "Luke's Stories of the Ascension," 251-54.

52. Keener, *Acts*, 2:1728, calls this a "conversion" of the church to the agenda Jesus laid out in 1:8. Cornelius is not the first gentile convert (cf. 8:27-39), but the first to be recognized by the church community (cf. Tannehill, *Narrative Unity*, 2:134-37).

53. More properly, it is an appeal to "the prophets," since the quotation incorporates wording from Isa 45:21 and Jer 12:15 as well as thematic connections with numerous other prophetic texts (cf. Zech 2:11; 8:22; Isa 2:2; Hos 3:4-5). See Bock, *Acts*, 503; Bauckham, "James and the Gentiles," 165; Witherington, *Acts*, 459; Marshall, "Acts," 589-90; cf. Keener, *Acts*, 3:2246.

particular passage are vast and far reaching, it bears sufficient pertinence to our present discussion to merit some comment here. James, addressing the council, notes that Peter's experience in the home of Cornelius "agrees with the words of the prophets" (15:15). He then cites from Amos: "After this, I will return, and I will rebuild the dwelling of David, which has fallen; from its ruins I will rebuild it, and I will set it up, so that all other peoples may seek the Lord—even all the gentiles over whom my name has been called" (15:15–17; cf. Amos 9:11–12).[54] The tent of David, fallen and in ruins, is the nation of Israel as represented by the Davidic dynasty, which has been reduced to a remnant in Yahweh's judgment (cf. Amos 9:8–9).[55] Once the kingdom of Israel is re-established, the way is made for other nations to turn to Yahweh. In other words, the restoration of Israel, inaugurated by the outpouring of the Spirit on the witnesses of the resurrected Christ, is to be followed by mission to the nations, which is inaugurated by the outpouring of the same Spirit on gentiles who repent and believe. This is a turning point in the book of Acts, and, in the logic of Acts 15, a key piece to it is that the remnant of Israel is in fact enjoying restoration—that the tent of David has in fact been raised. In other words, Acts 10 must be preceded by Acts 9 (and with it, Acts 2).

---

54. The quotation most closely follows the LXX version, which differs from the MT in significant ways. The LXX version is certainly more amenable to James's argument, but many scholars hold that even the text as reflected in the MT can support his point, especially when read in light of related OT texts (e.g., Zech 2:11; 8:22). See discussion in Marshall, "Acts," 589–93; Keener, *Acts*, 3:2247–58; Bock, *Acts*, 503–5; Ådna, "Die Heilige Schrift als Zeuge," 1–23; Glenny, "Septuagint and Apostolic Hermeneutics," 1–25; Bauckham, "James and the Gentiles," 154–70. Cf. Barrett, *Acts*, 2:727–28; and Pervo, *Acts*, 375–76, who see the LXX reading as incompatible with that of the MT, and therefore not likely to have been adduced by James. Regardless of its relationship to the MT tradition, we shall focus our attention on Luke's theology of remnant as evidenced by the text as he cites it.

55. The reference to David likely has christological implications as well, but the primary referent is the restoration of Israel, of which Christ's resurrection is the foundational event. See Pao, *Isaianic New Exodus*, 136–38; Keener, *Acts*, 3:2255–57; Bock, *Acts*, 503–4; Jervell, *Luke and the People of God*, 51–54; cf. Barrett, *Acts*, 2:725–26. See also Bauckham, "James and the Gentiles," 165, who sees a reference to the people of God as the eschatological temple. Glenny, "Septuagint and Apostolic Hermeneutics," 4–6, esp. n12, notes other points in which the LXX of Amos 9 further emphasizes the national restoration of Israel through a righteous remnant.

Conclusion

The successive narratives of Tabitha and Cornelius, linked both thematically and geographically, draw from two of Luke's favorite episodes within the Elijah-Elisha narratives—the stories of the Zarephathite widow and of Naaman's cleansing (cf. Luke 4:25–27; 7:1–17). The allusions may be plain enough, but the narratives, incorporated as they are into the storyline of Acts, are not without adaptation. The story of Tabitha, together with the account of Aeneas preceding it, is less about mercy on a gentile outcast, and instead represents the eschatological restoration now experienced by the remnant of Israel. The community of Jewish believers is flourishing under the Spirit-enabled apostolic witness and has grown exponentially in Jerusalem, Judea, and Samaria (vv. 35, 42). The story of Cornelius draws upon the precedent set in the Naaman account, by which a gentile is permitted to worship the God of Israel as a gentile. Rather than a cleansing from leprosy, the episode concerns the spiritual cleansing of believing gentiles (v. 28; cf. v. 15). If the restoration of Israel's remnant is underway by means of the gift of the Spirit on the church in Jerusalem, Judea, and Samaria, then the way has been opened for "all the other peoples" to seek the Lord and enjoy the benefits of the people of God as gentiles (cf. Acts 15:16).

Paul and Eutychus (Acts 20:7–12)

Perhaps best known as a warning for long-winded preachers and heavy-lidded youths alike, the story of Eutychus is surprising (and perhaps a little humorous) in its brevity and matter-of-fact tone. However, this makes it no less important for the insight it gives into the character of Paul and the nature of his mission. Paul's weeklong stay in Troas, along with his subsequent testament to the Ephesian elders (vv. 17–38), falls within his journey to Jerusalem (cf. 19:21) and forms a double conclusion to his missionary travels as a free man.[56] This journey embodies the heart of Paul's ministry, promoting the full inclusion of gentile Christians in a unified church, for Paul is bringing a gift from the gentile churches he has visited (including, presumably, the one in Troas) to the Jewish churches in Jerusalem (cf. 24:17; Rom 15:25–27; 2 Cor 8:20–21). It is at this point

---

56. Kowalski, "Der Fenstersturz," 30–31; Stipp, "Vier Gestalten," 73–77.

that we see a brief glimpse of Paul as an Elijianic figure, and with it, the final development in Luke's theology of the remnant.

Paul and Elijah

The basic parallels between this narrative and the accounts of Elijah and Elisha, especially in light of Peter's earlier raising of Tabitha, are easily caught, and noted by most commentators.[57] The setting is again an "upper room [ὑπερῷον]" (v. 8; cf. 1 Kgs 17:19), and the deceased is a "boy [παῖς]" (v. 12; cf. 1 Kgs 17:21).[58] The community is grieved at his death (v. 10; cf. 1 Kgs 17:18, 20), yet Paul embraces the lad, apparently throwing himself on top of him (v. 10; cf. 1 Kgs 17:21), and subsequently his spirit (ψυχή) returns (v. 10; cf. 1 Kgs 17:17, 22).[59] The result is that Paul's prophetic authority is confirmed (cf. 1 Kgs 17:24).

As with the Tabitha narrative, a point of divergence from the Elijah-Elisha stories is that it portrays the community at peace with itself and with Paul. There is no hint of blame or of crisis of faith (cf. 1 Kgs 17:18; 2 Kgs 4:27).[60] Likewise, just as the Tabitha narrative showed a broadening in scope from an isolated widow to a community of believers that includes widows, the present passage focuses on the whole believing community—the event occurs during a gathering of the whole church in worship, with no mention of widows at all. In contrast to the Tabitha narrative (though in keeping with Elijah's sojourn in Sidon), the community in Troas appears to be predominantly gentile.[61] Thus, not only does this

---

57. Pervo, *Acts*, 512; Keener, *Acts*, 3:2959, 2977-78; Pervo, *Acts*, 512-13; Bock, *Acts*, 620; Fitzmyer, *Acts of the Apostles*, 668-69; Barrett, *Acts*, 2:954-55; Dunn, *Acts of the Apostles*, 268; Öhler, *Elia im neuen Testament*, 203, 231; Glavic, "Eutychus," 190-92; Stipp, "Vier Gestalten," 73-75; Trémel, "À propos d'Actes 20:7-12," 366.

58. On the identification of Eutychus as both a παῖς (v. 12) and a νεανίας (v. 8), see esp. Keener, *Acts*, 3:2975-76.

59. It is unclear whether Paul's statement (v. 10) means that Eutychus's spirit has returned or that, contrary to appearances, the boy is still alive. In either case, the account is narrated in the style of a miracle story, and as such should recall similar resuscitation miracles to the reader's mind. See Keener, *Acts*, 3:2977-79; Bock, *Acts*, 620; Pervo, *Acts*, 510; Barrett, *Acts*, 2:955; Kowalski, "Der Fenstersturz," 26-28; cf. Stipp, "Vier Gestalten," 74.

60. Stipp, "Vier Gestalten," 74.

61. The text does not specify the makeup of the church in Troas, either here or in Acts 16:8-11. The location strongly suggests a gentile majority, as does the name Eutychus, which recalls the Greek god of fortune. See Keener, *Acts*, 3:2334-35, 2963.

passage reflect on Paul as a prophet like Elijah, but, building off of the events of Acts 10, it gives hints towards the place of the gentile church in relation to Israel.

Paul and the Remnant

Removal through Unbelief

The scene at Troas takes on an ominous tone, despite its happy outcome, for it is situated within the context of increasing hostilities from "the Jews," who oppose Paul's Gospel (20:3, 19), thus removing themselves from its blessings. The period of peace enjoyed by the church in 9:31 is quickly overshadowed by resumed hostilities and persecution (cf. 12:3), most notably in Pisidian Antioch, where Paul accuses the Jews who oppose him of having "thrust aside" the word of God, thereby judging themselves "unworthy of eternal life" (13:46; cf. 18:6).[62] These tensions carry into the present episode, for the reason Paul is in Troas at all, and not in Jerusalem for the Passover, is because of a Jewish plot against his life (20:3).[63] The all-night meeting is an indication that this is Paul's last meeting with this community. Furthermore, in light of Paul's decisive journey to Jerusalem (19:21; cf. Luke 9:51) and the subsequent foreshadowing of his suffering there (20:23; 21:4, 11–13), the worship service at Troas comes to function as a sort of Last Supper.[64] Such parallels with Jesus's passion highlight the dangers Paul faces at every turn from the many who have "thrust aside" the word of God.

---

62. On the implications of this text for the Lukan narrative, as well as the use of Isa 49:6 in v. 47, see Tannehill, *Narrative Unity*, 2:172–75; Tannehill, "Rejection by Jews," 83–10; Barrett, *Acts*, 1:657; Pao, *Isaianic New Exodus*, 96–101; Fitzmyer, *Acts*, 520–21.

63. Later, in addressing the Ephesian elders, he speaks of similar "plots of the Jews" (v. 19). On the developing narrative tension in this scene, see Pervo, *Profit with Delight*, 30.

64. Note esp. the breaking of bread (vv. 7, 11) in an upper room (v. 8) around the time of the Passover (v. 6). See Tannehill, *Narrative Unity*, 2:250–51; Fitzmyer, *Acts of the Apostles*, 669; Pervo, *Acts*, 510; Stipp, "Vier Gestalten," 73–75; Kowalski, "Der Fenstersturz," 27, 31; though cf. Barrett, *Acts*, 2:950–51. For the parallels between Paul's and Jesus's journeys to Jerusalem, see esp. Keener, *Acts*, 3:2860–63; Tannehill, *Narrative Unity*, 2:239–40; Glavic, "Eutychus in Acts," 184–85.

Remainder of the Faithful

In contrast to his Jewish opponents and the opposition he faces at their hands, Paul remains a faithful Israelite, obedient to Israel's God and the mission he has been given. This can be seen especially in his concern for the Jewish festivals, which drives the chronology of this leg of his journey. His initial plans had been to sail for Jerusalem via Syria, arriving in time for the Passover (cf. v. 3), yet this plan was thwarted, ironically, by a plot from fellow Jewish pilgrims.[65] He then stops in Philippi to celebrate the festival, which is the reason for his late and hurried arrival in Troas (v. 6). A major reason, then, for his midnight sermon in Troas appears to be his determination to arrive in Jerusalem at least in time for Pentecost (20:16).[66] This attention to the festivals shows not only his piety, but also his Jewish solidarity, for Paul later describes the purpose of this trip as to "bring alms to my nation" (24:17), apparently a reference to the collection among the gentile churches for the Jewish Christians in need (cf. 2 Cor 8:1–9:15; Rom 15:25–27).[67] It may also be that his eagerness to be in Jerusalem for at least one of the festivals is due to a desire to preach the gospel to the many Jews who will gather in Jerusalem.[68] This portrayal of Paul as a true Israelite, faithful to Israel and to Israel's God, remains a consistent theme throughout the remainder of Acts.[69] It is in this capacity as a representative of Israel's remnant that Paul continues to fulfill Israel's mission as a light to the nations.

HOPE OF RENEWAL

Despite the ominous signs of increasing hostility, this episode provides a glimmer of hope. The resuscitation of Eutychus, like the other miraculous healings in Acts, serves as an indicator of the time of restoration inaugurated by Christ's resurrection and the coming of the Holy Spirit. Certainly, the death and restoration to life of a member of the believing community—on the first day of the week, no less (v. 7)—points back to

---

65. See Keener, *Acts*, 3:2951–53; Barrett, *Acts*, 2:946–47.

66. Glavic, "Eutychus in Acts," 188–90; Tannehill, *Narrative Unity*, 2:247; Keener, *Acts*, 3:2961–63.

67. Bruce, *Book of Acts*, 445; Keener, *Acts*, 3:2989; Dunn, *Acts of the Apostles*, 269; Bock, *Acts*, 693.

68. Keener, *Acts*, 3:2962; cf. Barrett, *Acts*, 2:960.

69. Tannehill, *Narrative Unity*, 2:247, esp. n6. Cf. esp. Acts 18:18.

Jesus's own death and resurrection.[70] The comfort this community found in the restoration of one boy (v. 12) is tied to the much deeper and greater comfort and hope in Christ's power over death. What is more, Paul, as a representative of faithful Israel, is seen bringing this hope and power into a gentile community.

Conclusion

Having seen Luke's interest in the account of Elijah and the Zarephathite widow (Luke 4:25–26; 7:11–17; Acts 9:32–43), echoes emerge here in the tragicomedy of Eutychus as well. Though this miraculous event sets Paul in the company of both Peter and Jesus, who also emulate the OT prophet, within the context of the storyline of Luke-Acts, it serves a greater function yet. This brief episode presents Paul as a faithful and pious Israelite, concerned both for the welfare of his nation as well as for Israel's mission to the nations, despite the hostilities he faces from his opponents. Situated as it is at this point in the storyline, the story of Eutychus forms a counterpoint with that of Tabitha.[71] The latter concludes Peter's recorded ministry and conveys the hopeful optimism of renewal that makes way for the remnant community to be "a light to the nations" (cf. Isa 49:6). Yet with this episode at the end of Paul's mission, the inverse also becomes clear: despite the growth it enjoys, the remnant is still a remnant, and will remain so a while longer. However, the gospel now bears fruit among the gentiles, and God's power over death, powerfully revealed in this moment, offers unshakeable hope to God's people as they continue to serve him in the advancement of the gospel among Jews and gentiles alike.

Summary and Conclusions

The parallels that Luke draws between Elijah and the disciples reveal most clearly that his use of the Elijah motif is not primarily tied to

---

70. "To deny that a short pericope describing a celebration of the Eucharist in an upper room on Sunday that climaxes in the return of a dead person in the morning has any symbolic reference would border on absurdity" (Pervo, *Acts*, 513). See also Kowalski, "Der Fenstersturz," 21, 32; Fitzmyer, *Acts of the Apostles*, 668.

71. On further points of comparison and contrast between these two stories, see Stipp, "Vier Gestalten," 71–77; Tannehill, *Narrative Unity*, 2:247–48.

typology or prophecy fulfillment, but rather serves a theological purpose. Just as John's fiery ministry removed the wicked from among true Israel, and Jesus's ministry promised hope to the humble who remained, the subsequent ministry of the disciples embodies the hope of renewal that the remnant enjoys because of the risen Christ. The outpouring of the Holy Spirit brings about new life for thousands of Israelites, thus marking the beginnings of renewal for the nation. Yet this is too small a thing. In keeping with the promise of the prophets, this renewed remnant becomes a light to the nations. However, in an unexpected development of the remnant theme, this universal mission becomes itself a cause of further hardening of the unrepentant. Those who reject the gospel for themselves and take offense at its being presented to others become persecutors of the remnant, thus further removing themselves from the benefits of the people of God.

The mission of Jesus's disciples as Elijianic messengers preparing the way for the Lord (Luke 9:52; 10:1) sets the stage for Jesus's climactic entrance into Jerusalem. Their testimony has a polarizing effect, revealing the opposition of the unrepentant—and treating them like unclean pagans—but also bringing blessing to the "children of peace" who will receive them.

Philip's mission to the Ethiopian eunuch (Acts 8:26–40) recalls the Elijah–Elisha narratives in several points, but especially with regards to the cleansing of Naaman. With the outpouring of the Holy Spirit causing the growth of the church in Jerusalem, Judea, and Samaria, the time is right to reach the ends of the earth. Though at this point the Ethiopian's conversion is an isolated incident, it symbolizes the eschatological renewal anticipated by Isaiah that now exists within the church. This picture is further developed with Peter's healing of Aeneas and Tabitha (Acts 9:32–43). In raising the dead (along with healing the lame), he is not merely following the pattern of Elijah's sojourn in Zarephath, but symbolically enacting the restoration that Israel enjoys (Luke 7:22; cf. Isa 61:1–2). The community of faith in Israel is now experiencing the eschatological blessings promised by the prophets to the restored remnant of Israel. It is at this point that, by divine direction, and in keeping with the prophets, sights are turned towards the gentiles so that "all other peoples may seek the Lord" (Acts 15:17; cf. LXX Amos 9:12). Peter's visit to Cornelius (Acts 10), another parallel to the Naaman account, shows that, with the restoration of the remnant of Israel, the time is right for gentiles, as gentiles, to enter into the people of God.

However, there will still be those who oppose the plan of God. Those Israelites who reject the offer of eternal life in Jesus find themselves opposing this remnant community and their universal mission. It is in the face of such opposition that Paul finds himself in Troas (Acts 20:7–12). Though a faithful Israelite, he is oppressed by his kinsfolk. Nevertheless, he is faithful in executing the mission of the remnant. Paul's raising of Eutychus recalls Elijah's miracle at Zarephath yet again, drawing attention to the remnant's mission to gentiles who will listen, rather than to the "many in Israel" (cf. Luke 4:25–27). The remnant is thus a polarizing force, repelling the hardened in Israel, even as it draws in many repentant ones from both Israel and the nations. It is perhaps this dynamic above all that makes Elijah such a powerful symbol of the remnant for Luke: he can be both *for* Israel and *against* her; he can be the only one faithful to the covenant, and yet be the one sent to those outside the covenant.

8

Conclusion

"At the appointed time, it is written, you are destined to calm the wrath of God before it breaks out in fury, to turn the hearts of parents to their children, and to restore the tribes of Jacob."—Sir 48:10

"I ALONE AM LEFT." Elijah's words standing alone before an apostate Israel on Mount Carmel (1 Kgs 18:22) and standing alone before God on Mount Horeb (1 Kgs 19:10, 14) mark him as a quintessential remnant figure. This image of the faithful but solitary prophet has endured through the centuries such that, whatever else Elijah has come to represent—the angelic defender, the revealer of mysteries, and the champion of the downtrodden—he is consistently associated with the remnant of Israel. We have seen that Luke has capitalized on this association for his own theological purposes.

Summary

In ch. 2, we attempted to bring some clarity to the concept of remnant in the OT. While recognizing the need for further study on the concept, we were able to establish a definition of remnant as the representative remainder that is preserved after a large portion is removed in judgment (often through death, but also at times through apostasy), offering hope for the renewal or rebirth of the whole. This renewal was often followed by a reaching out to the nations, especially in the Prophets. These three subthemes—removal, remainder, and renewal—served as our criteria for identifying the remnant theme throughout the rest of the study. In ch. 3, we applied these criteria to the Elijah narratives, noting that Elijah functions as the sole Israelite to remain faithful in the midst of an apostate nation. Yet on Mount Horeb he is promised that seven thousand faithful Israelites will be spared from the coming judgment (1 Kgs 19:18), making Elijah the nucleus around which the remnant of a purified Israel is gathered. This function of "turning the hearts" of the people back to God (cf. 1 Kgs 18:37) continues in Mal 3:23–24, which expects Elijah's eschatological return to gather a repentant remnant before the great and terrible day of Yahweh, thus preserving the nation from total destruction.

As we saw in ch. 4, this same perspective on Elijah remained consistent in subsequent generations leading into the NT era. Much of the STJ literature that references Elijah is literarily dependent upon Malachi 3 (esp. 4Q521; 4Q558; Sir 48:10), and the focus is generally on Elijah's role vis-à-vis the righteous remnant of Israel, as well as, at times, the gentile nations (esp. 1 En. 90:30–31, 37–38). Though not all NT texts mentioning Elijah are interested in the remnant concept specifically (Heb 11:32–38; Jas 5:17–18), Paul's appeal to Elijah bears remarkable similarities to the Lukan usage (Rom 11:1–6). Comparing himself to Elijah, Paul argues that, despite widespread Jewish rejection of the gospel, God has not forsaken Israel, for he has preserved a remnant (Rom 11:1–3). The existence of an Israelite remnant provides a theological apologetic for the gentile mission as well as the grounds for hope of the future salvation of Israel. Finally, the book of Revelation, though it shows subtle variations on the remnant theme, depicts eschatological figures cast after Moses and Elijah who, through faithful witness and a call to repentance, gather a repentant remnant in the last days (Rev 11:1–13).

In light of this consistent stream of thought that connects Elijah with the remnant, it is no surprise that Luke should make a similar move. Thus, ch. 5 shows that, though Luke certainly saw some manner of typological fulfillment in John the Baptist's coming "in the spirit and power of Elijah" (1:17), this association fits within the broader framework of Elijah's connection with the remnant. John's particular function as the Elijianic messenger is to prepare the way for the Lord by making ready "a people prepared for the Lord" (v. 17). The presentation of John's public ministry shows him, like Elijah, confronting the Ahabs of his day, and issuing a general call of repentance to the people (3:1–21). Those who failed to bear the fruit of repentance were no longer children of Abraham but a "brood of vipers" (3:7-9), cut off from the people. Though John's message was largely rejected by the fickle generation to whom he was sent (7:33-34), his ministry of preparation also held out the hope of renewal, for it pointed to the one coming after him, who would gather the remnant to himself (3:16).

The nature of this remnant, as ch. 6 shows, is seen especially in Jesus's own ministry. Ultimately it is Jesus alone who comprises the true remnant, yet he gathers around himself those who will follow him in cruciform discipleship. In his inaugural sermon, in which he explicitly describes his ministry through parallels with Elijah (4:25-27), he identifies the recipients of his good news as the "poor" and heartbroken who will come to him in repentance (4:18). His miracles are strongly reminiscent of those of Elijah, not only in the actions themselves, but in the humble nature of those who benefit (7:1-17; 9:10-17, 37-43). Luke's redactional decisions in 9:1-62 underscore the Elijah motif in those episodes. The transfiguration account in particular (9:28-36) recalls Elijah's experience on Mount Horeb. In the presence of Moses and Elijah, Jesus himself is distinguished as the remnant *par excellence*—the truly faithful one, who is left "alone" when all others fade away. Finally, Jesus parallels Elijah in his ascension into heaven, at which time he sends his Spirit on his disciples, who will succeed him. In so doing, he establishes them as the core of a renewed Israel.

In ch. 7, we saw that the Lukan narrative connects Elijah with the disciples as well, especially in Acts. The first followers of Jesus, in receiving the promised Holy Spirit, serve as the first fruits of a restored remnant. Philip's encounter with the Ethiopian eunuch (Acts 8:26-40)—recalling the healing of Naaman—shows that, despite the opposition they may be facing, this group of disciples is enjoying the restoration promised for the remnant (cf. Isa 56:3-8; Zeph 2:1-3:13). Peter's raising of Tabitha (9:32-43) similarly depicts the church in Israel enjoying the eschatological blessings of renewal. It is because of this renewal that attention can shift to the gentiles and Israel's task to be a light to the nations. Thus, the Tabitha narrative flows directly into Peter's visit to Cornelius (10:1-48)—another parallel to Naaman's cleansing—which shows that gentiles are now welcomed as gentiles to worship Israel's God. The raising of Eutychus towards the end of the narrative (20:7-12) casts Paul in the place of Elijah and shows God's blessings poured out on gentiles as well. Though many of Paul's fellow Jews remain hardened to the gospel, the remnant continues to thrive, carrying out Israel's mission to the nations. As the book of Acts draws to a close, it becomes evident that the remnant will remain a remnant for a little while longer. Yet these spirit-empowered witnesses are faithful to their mission to present the good news in Jerusalem, Judea and Samaria, and to the ends of the earth.

Implications

Our study has shown first and foremost that Luke's use of Elijah is far more complex and theologically rich than is often assumed. Though Luke appears to retain some conception of John the Baptist as a typological fulfillment of Mal 3:23–24, we have seen that his interests in Elijah should not be explained primarily in terms of typology or of a one-to-one correlation between Elijah and any one figure. Rather, in associating Elijah with each of his major protagonists, Luke thematizes the remnant concept in such a way that every major development in the theme is punctuated by references to Elijah. Though the three subthemes of remnant are present in some form with each instance of the Elijah motif, we have also seen a logical progression within the flow of the Lukan narrative: the birth narratives reflect the initial hope of renewal; John's ministry highlights the removal of wickedness; Jesus's ministry shows himself as the true remnant who gathers the humble and poor around him; the disciples in Acts reflect the inauguration of the hoped-for restoration as the church experiences the blessings of renewal and begins to reach out to the nations.

These findings have implications for our understanding of Luke's use of the OT more generally. A literary approach shows that his hermeneutical method is much more complex than mere "proof from prophecy."[1] Rather, in appealing to the figure of Elijah as a literary motif, he can access a dynamic theological concept that develops as the narrative unfolds. Moreover, we see that his interest in the Scriptures extends beyond matters of Christology. Unquestionably, Luke saw in the OT Scriptures a great wealth of evidence showing "that the Messiah is Jesus" (Acts 18:28; cf. Luke 24:25–27, 44–47), and his own use of Scripture certainly seeks to establish this point. However, flowing from this one point come numerous other issues of critical interest to Luke and his readers, such as the

---

1. See esp. Bock, *Proclamation*, 277–79.

mission to the nations, the nature of the people of God, and the fate of Israel—all of which must be evaluated by evidence from Scripture.

More significantly, our study has given further insights into the complex question of Luke's theology regarding Israel. We have seen that, despite the absence of technical vocabulary, remnant theology is prominent throughout the Lukan narrative as Luke capitalizes on the long-standing association of the person of Elijah with this important OT theme. In so doing, he is able to utilize a theology of remnant to hold otherwise contradictory concepts in theological tension. Throughout his narrative, Luke goes to great pains to show that the salvation that has come in Christ has continuity with and is in fact the fulfillment of the promises that God made in the OT (see esp. 1:46–55, 67–79). When more and more of the nation of Israel rejects this salvation, Luke's theology will not allow him to let go of God's faithfulness to his ancient promises of salvation, nor to the centrality of the nation of Israel within them. Rather, he draws on the OT concept of remnant, identifying those Jews who respond negatively with the apostate who are removed from God's blessing so that only the faithful remain. As the narrative progresses, the remnant concept focuses on Jesus himself as the only one truly faithful to God and his purposes. Seen through this lens, his death and resurrection serve as the ultimate expression of the remnant experience. Far from being a symbol of divine failure, the cross becomes the place where all the sins of God's people are gathered so that they can be once and for all removed. With Jesus's resurrection comes the renewal of Israel, first focused on the Twelve as the purified core of Israel, but rapidly growing by the thousands. Although the universal reach of salvation is already indicated (esp. 1:8; 2:21), the first third of the book of Acts still revolves around the Jewish nation, indicating the continuing importance of Israel within Luke's theology. As the book of Acts develops, it becomes evident that, because a large portion of the nation continues to oppose the gospel, Israel will remain a remnant for at least a little longer. Nevertheless, the dramatic reception in the initial chapters is sufficient to establish the renewal and restoration of the remnant. It is only because Israel's remnant is enjoying this restoration that the mission to the gentiles has its legitimacy, for, in keeping with the OT prophets, it is the restored remnant that is sent on mission to the nations (see esp. Isa 66:19). This reaching out to the nations, already present in OT texts, is developed significantly by Luke and given a very prominent place in his own remnant thought. Luke appeals both to prophetic expectation and the precedent from the Elijah narratives to show that, with Israel's restoration inaugurated, gentiles are to be welcomed as gentiles alongside believing Jews as recipients of God's blessings of salvation, even as hope is held out for the final restoration of Israel.

Although the question of Luke's relationship to Paul and Pauline writings is beyond the scope of this study, it is striking to note the several similarities between Luke's use of Elijah with respect to the remnant, and that of Paul in Rom 11:2–5.[2] Both authors are seeking to reconcile the apparent tension between OT expectations for the salvation of Israel and the lack of receptivity to the gospel among the Jews. In both cases, Elijah is referenced as the remnant of faithful Israel as well as the nucleus around which a growing remnant will be gathered, and in both cases, Paul himself, among other Jewish believers, is compared to Elijah. Additionally, both authors appeal to remnant theology in connection to the mission to the gentiles, showing that the presence of an Israelite remnant provides a theological apologetic for the gentile mission, even as the reduction of Israel to a remnant through widespread rejection of the gospel provides the historical occasion for it. A major difference between the two is that, while the Lukan narrative ends ambiguously, Paul appears very optimistic about Israel's future, apparently expecting widespread Jewish reception to the gospel at some point in the future. It may be that, if Luke's thought parallels Paul's with respect to Elijah and the remnant, he holds a similar hope for Israel's future, perhaps even expecting that the thriving gentile mission will be the means for arousing Israelite jealousy.[3] In this case, Luke's presentation of Israel would not be a "tragic history," as Tannehill suggests, but instead a hopeful tragedy—a story that ends at a low point but implies, through its persistent application of remnant theology, a happy resolution.[4]

Finally, our findings give insight into the *Sitz im Leben* of Luke-Acts. As Luke's readers were faced with an increasingly gentile church and mounting persecution, the remnant concept would have offered them theological assurance, ecclesial unity, and eschatological comfort. First, it would have provided theological assurance of the legitimacy of the Christian movement. Despite a dwindling Jewish presence, believers

---

2. Similar parallels between Rom 11:1–5 and the presentation of Paul in the Lukan narrative are discussed in Butticaz, "'Has God Rejected His People?,'" 148–64.

3. Though Luke does speak of Jewish jealousy in connection to evangelism of the gentiles, it is always in the negative sense (cf. Acts 5:17; 13:45; 17:5).

4. Cf. Tannehill, "Israel in Luke-Acts," 69–85.

could be assured of the continuity of their faith with OT Scriptures, for the remnant concept, especially in connection with Elijah, provides a scriptural precedent for the widespread Jewish rejection of the gospel. Second, despite the changing demographics of the church, Luke's readers would have been encouraged towards greater unity, for the model of a remnant preserves the salvation-historical priority of Israel while still affirming the legitimacy of gentiles as recipients of God's blessings of salvation and even the scriptural necessity of gentile mission. With a robust theology of remnant, neither group can despise the other. Third, it would have provided eschatological comfort in the face of persecution, for Luke's readers would have found in the remnant a model for their own experiences. Throughout the story of God's dealings with his people, the way to purification and renewal was through tribulation and diminution, just as surely as resurrection must be preceded by suffering and death. As the book of Acts comes to a close, it becomes clear that believers will have to wait a little longer yet for the kingdom to be restored to Israel, yet at the same time they can take comfort that the renewal and restoration now inaugurated will in due course be consummated.

Appendix

Possible Allusions to the Elijah-Elisha Narratives in Luke's Gospel

The following table lists possible references to Elijah or the Elijah narratives throughout Luke's Gospel, including direct references, echoes, and allusions. These are compiled from various commentators as well as the present author's own observations (see body text for citation information). Each entry includes comments, including suspected verbal links, if present (though see body text for more thorough argumentation). Additionally, entries are ranked according to whether, in the present author's estimation, they are (1) likely, (2) somewhat likely, or (3) somewhat less likely. Verses unique to Luke are marked with an asterisk (*). Although most of the references listed below—even some not mentioned in the body text—are in some way tied to the theme of remnant, it is not necessary to our overall thesis that every single echo points to this theme. Some echoes, for example, are too faint to function well as motifs, and merely serve to highlight Luke's deep interest in this OT figure.

APPENDIX

NT Reference	OT Reference	Referent	Comments	Ranking
*1:16–17	Mal 3:1, 22–23 LXX (EV 3:1; 4:5–6); cf. 1 Kgs 18:37	John	John will go before the Lord (cf. Mal 3:1) "in the spirit and power of Elijah" (v. 17). He will turn "the hearts of parents to their children" (καρδίας πατέρων ἐπὶ τέκνα/καρδίαν πατρὸς πρὸς υἱόν) (v. 17; cf. Mal 3:22–23)	1
*1:76	Mal 3:1	John	John is identified as a "prophet" who will prepare the "way" (ὁδούς) for the "Lord" (κυρίου).	1
3:2	1 Kgs 17:2, 8; 18:1; 19:9; 21:28 [20:28 LXX]	John	"The word of God came [ἐγένετο ῥῆμα θεοῦ]" to John (cf. use of λόγος generally in the Prophets)	2
3:2–3	1 Kgs 17:3–9; 19:4, 5; 2 Kgs 2:6–14; cf. 2 Kgs 5:10	John	The wilderness (ἔρημος) and the Jordan River (Ἰορδάνης) as significant locations for Elijah's ministry	2
3:19–20 (cf. 13:31–33; 23:6–12)	1 Kgs 16:31	John	Herod, like Ahab, was denounced for his many sins, including an illegitimate marriage	3
3:9, 16–17	Mal 3:19	John	John's sermon spoke of the cutting down and burning of a tree in judgment	2
3:16	Mal 3:1	John	John's ministry anticipated that of one who "is coming [ἔρχεται]"	2
4:1–2	1 Kgs 19:4–8	Jesus	Jesus experienced a forty-day (ἡμέρας τεσσεράκοντα) fast in the wilderness (ἔρημος).	2
*4:25–27	1 Kgs 17:17–24; 2 Kgs 5:1–14	Jesus	Jesus explicitly compared his own experience as a prophet to that of Elijah at Zarephath and Elisha with Naaman	1

5:1–11	1 Kgs 19:19–21	Jesus	Jesus called his disciples while they were plying their trade, causing them to leave behind the tools of their profession as Elisha did (cf. 9:61–62)	2
5:12–16 (cf. 17:11–19)	2 Kgs 5:1–14	Jesus	With a command (καθαρίσθητι), Jesus cleansed a man with leprosy	2
5:27–28	1 Kgs 19:19–21	Jesus	Jesus called Levi while he was plying his trade, causing him to leave behind the tools of his profession (cf. 9:61–62)	2
6:12–16	1 Kgs 19:19–21	Jesus	Jesus called disciples after descending from a mountain where he met with God. Note also the significance of the number twelve (v. 13; cf. 1 Kgs 19:19)	3
7:1–10	2 Kgs 5:1–14	Jesus	A respected Gentile officer sought healing. He communicates through messengers and the healing takes place at a distance. Cf. Luke 4:27.	1
*7:11–17	1 Kgs 17:17–24 (cf. 2 Kgs 4:18–37)	Jesus	Jesus raised a widow's dead son and gave him to his mother (καὶ ἔδωκεν αὐτὸν τῇ μητρὶ αὐτοῦ) (v. 16; cf. 1 Kgs 17:23)	1
7:18–19	Mal 3:1	John	John's messengers (ἀγγέλων, v. 24) asked if Jesus was the one who "is coming" (ἔρχεται). Note also the use of "send" (πέμπω) and "Lord" (κύριος). Cf. 7:27.	2
7:27	Mal 3:1	John	Jesus quoted Mal 3:1, applying it to John	1
*8:1–3	2 Kgs 4:8–10	Jesus	Jesus's needs were regularly provided for by wealthy women	3

APPENDIX

8:40–56 (cf. 7:11–17)	1 Kgs 17:17–24 (cf. 2 Kgs 4:18–37)	Jesus	Jesus raises a dead child. Note Luke's addition of "her spirit returned [ἐπέστρεψεν τὸ πνεῦμα αὐτῆς]" (v. 55; cf. ἐπιστραφήτω δὴ ἡ ψυχή, 1 Kgs 17:21)	3
9:8, 19	--	Jesus	Jesus's healing ministry (cf. esp. 8:40–56//1 Kgs 17:17–24) led to popular expectation that he was Elijah	1
9:10–17	2 Kgs 4:42–44 (cf. 1 Kgs 17:8–16; 2 Kgs 4:1–7)	Jesus	Multiplication of food. Note that Luke's redactional changes align this episode more closely with the 2 Kings account.	2
9:28–36	1 Kgs 19:9–18	Jesus	Appearance of Elijah in person. Jesus's transfiguration recalls Elijah's (and Moses's) own theophanic experiences on the mountain	1
*9:51	2 Kgs 9, 10, 11	Jesus	Jesus's departure is described in terms of his ἀνάλημψις	1
*9:52 (cf. 1:17, 76; 7:27)	Mal 3:1	Disciples	Jesus "sent messengers ahead of him [ἀπέστειλεν ἀγγέλους πρὸ προσώπου αὐτοῦ]" on his way to Jerusalem, and thus the temple	1
*9:52–56	2 Kgs 1:9–16	Disciples	The disciples attempted to call "fire to come down from heaven to consume them [πῦρ καταβῆναι ἀπὸ τοῦ οὐρανοῦ καὶ ἀναλῶσαι αὐτούς]" (v. 54; cf. 2 Kgs 1:10, 12, 14). Note also the addition of ὡς καὶ ἐποίησεν Ἠλίας in many mss.	1
*9:61–62 (cf. vv. 57–60)	1 Kgs 19:19–21	Jesus	Elijah's calling of Elisha is echoed in the disciples' offer to follow (ἀκολουθήσω) Jesus after first bidding farewell to family, as well as in Jesus's reference to a plow (ἄροτρον).	1
*10:1 (cf. 1:17, 76; 7:27; 9:52)	Mal 3:1	Disciples	Jesus sent (ἀπέστειλεν) messengers ahead of him (πρὸ προσώπου) to make preparations.	2

10:4	2 Kgs 4:29	Jesus	Jesus's instructions to "greet no one on the road" echoes those of Elisha to Gehazi. This phrase is a Lukan addition.	3
12:3	2 Kgs 6:12	--	What is spoken in private rooms (τὸ οὖς ἐλαλήσατε ἐν τοῖς ταμείοις) will be proclaimed. Cf. Matt 10:27 and Mark 4:22, which do not use ταμεῖον.	3
12:24	1 Kgs 17:4, 6	Disciples	Ravens (κόρακας) as a sign of God's provision (cf. πετεινά in Matt 6:26)	2
*12:49	1 Kgs 18:37–38; 2 Kgs 1:10 (cf. Sir 48:3)	Jesus	Jesus came to cast fire on the earth	3
*12:54	1 Kgs 18:43–44	--	A cloud coming from the west as a sign of rain.	3
*17:11–19	2 Kgs 5:1–14	Jesus	A man with leprosy cleansed after complying with Jesus's instructions. His faith is contrasted with that of Israelites.	2
19:41–44 (cf. 13:34–35)	2 Kgs 8:11–12	Jesus	Jesus wept over the destruction to befall Jerusalem.	3
*22:43	1 Kgs 19:5, 7	Jesus	Jesus was strengthened by an angel who appeared to him after his prayer of distress	3
*24:49–51 (cf. Acts 1:9–11)	2 Kgs 2:9–12	Jesus	Jesus gave his disciples instructions for receiving his Spirit before being separated (διέστη) from them and taken up into heaven (εἰς τὸν οὐρανόν) (though cf. text critical questions for v. 51).	1

BIBLIOGRAPHY

Acosta Valle, Martha Milagros. "Actes 10,1–11,18: Une intertextualité différée pour un lecteur davantage impliqué." *ScEs* 66 (2014) 427–31.
Ådna, Jostein. "Die Heilige Schrift als Zeuge der Heidenmission: Die Rezeption von Amos 9:11–12 in Apg 15:16–18." In *Evangelium, Schriftauslegung, Kirche: Festschrift für Peter Stuhlmacher zum 65. Geburtstag*, 1–23. Göttingen: Vandenhoeck & Ruprecht, 1997.
Albertz, Rainer. "Die 'Antrittspredigt' Jesu im Lukasevangelium auf ihrem alttestamentlichen Hintergrund." *ZNW* 74 (1983) 182–206.
Alexander, Loveday. "Reading Luke-Acts from Back to Front." In *Acts in Its Ancient Literary Context*, 207–30. New York: T. & T. Clark, 2005.
Allen, Leslie C. *The Books of Joel, Obadiah, Jonah, and Micah*. Grand Rapids: Eerdmans, 1976.
Allison, Dale C., Jr. *Constructing Jesus: Memory, Imagination, and History*. Grand Rapids: Eerdmans, 2010.
———. "Elijah Must Come First." *JBL* 103 (1984) 256–58.
———. *Intertextual Jesus: Scripture in Q*. Harrisburg, PA: Trinity, 2000.
———. "Rejecting Violent Judgment: Luke 9:52–56 and Its Relatives." *JBL* 121 (2002) 459–78.
Alter, Robert. *The Art of Biblical Narrative*. Rev. and updated. New York: Basic, 2011.
Andersen, Francis I., and David Noel Freedman. *Hosea: A New Translation with Introduction and Commentary*. AB 24. Garden City, NY: Doubleday, 1980.
Angel, Hayyim. "Hopping between Two Opinions: Understanding the Biblical Portrait of Ahab." *JBQ* 35 (2007) 3–10.
Ap-Thomas, D. R. "Elijah on Mount Carmel." *Palestinian Exploration Quarterly* 92 (1960) 146–55.
Assis, Elie. "Moses, Elijah and the Messianic Hope: A New Reading of Malachi 3,22–24." *ZAW* 123 (2011) 207–20.
Attridge, Harold W. *The Epistle to the Hebrews: A Commentary on the Epistle to the Hebrews*. Hermeneia. Philadelphia: Fortress, 1989.
Aune, David E. *Revelation 6–16*. Vol. 2. WBC 52B. Nashville: Thomas Nelson, 1998.
Baer, David A. "'It's All about Us!' Nationalistic Exegesis in the Greek Isaiah (Chapters 1–12)." In *"As Those Who Are Taught": The Interpretation of Isaiah from the LXX to the SBL*, edited by Claire Matthews McGinnis and Patricia K. Tull, 29–48. SBLSymS 27. Atlanta: Society of Biblical Literature, 2006.

Baker, Murray. "Paul and the Salvation of Israel: Paul's Ministry, the Motif of Jealousy, and Israel's Yes." *CBQ* 67 (2005) 469–84.

Bakon, Shimon. "The Day of the Lord." *JBQ* 38 (2010) 149–56.

Baldick, Chris. *Oxford Dictionary of Literary Terms*. 3rd ed. New York: Oxford University Press, 2008.

Barr, James. *The Semantics of Biblical Language*. Oxford: Oxford University Press, 1961.

Barré, Michael L. "New Light on the Interpretation of Hosea 6:2." *VT* 28 (1978) 129–41.

Barrett, C. K. *A Critical and Exegetical Commentary on the Acts of the Apostles*. 2 vols. ICC. Edinburgh: T. & T. Clark, 1994.

Barth, Karl. *The Epistle to the Romans*. Translated by Edwyn Clement Hoskyns. London: Oxford University Press, 1933.

Barth, Markus. "One God, One Christ, One People." *ExAud* 4 (1988) 8–26.

———. *The People of God*. JSOTSup 5. Sheffield: JSOT, 1983.

Bascom, Robert A. "Preparing the Way—Midrash in the Bible." In *Issues in Bible Translation*, 221–46. UBS Monograph Series 3. New York: United Bible Societies, 1988.

Bates, Matthew W. "Cryptic Codes and a Violent King: A New Proposal for Matthew 11:12 and Luke 16:16–18." *CBQ* 75 (2013) 74–93.

Bauckham, Richard. *The Climax of Prophecy: Studies on the Book of Revelation*. Edinburgh: T. & T. Clark, 1993.

———. "James and the Gentiles (Acts 15.13–21)." In *History, Literature, and Society in the Book of Acts*. Edited by Ben Witherington III, 154–84. New York: Cambridge University Press, 1996.

———. "The Martyrdom of Enoch and Elijah: Jewish or Christian?" *JBL* 95 (1976) 447–58.

———. "The Restoration of Israel in Luke-Acts." In *Restoration: Old Testament, Jewish, and Christian Perspectives*, edited by James M. Scott, 435–87. JSJSup 72. Boston: Brill, 2001.

Beale, G. K. *The Book of Revelation: A Commentary on the Greek Text*. NIGTC. Grand Rapids: Eerdmans, 1999.

———. *Handbook on the New Testament Use of the Old Testament: Exegesis and Interpretation*. Grand Rapids: Baker, 2012.

———. "Isaiah 6:9–13: A Retributive Taunt against Idolatry." *VT* 41 (1991) 257–78.

Beale, G. K., and Sean M. McDonough. "Revelation." In *Commentary on the New Testament Use of the Old Testament*, edited by G. K. Beale and D. A. Carson, 1081–162. Grand Rapids: Baker Academic, 2007.

Beentjes, Pancratius C. "'The Countries Marvelled at You': King Solomon in Ben Sira 47:12–22." In *"Happy the One Who Meditates on Wisdom" (Sir. 14,20): Collected Essays on the Book of Ben Sira*, 135–44. Contributions to Biblical Exegesis and Theology 43. Dudley, MA: Peeters, 2006.

———. "In Search of Parallels: Ben Sira and the Book of Kings." In *"Happy the One Who Meditates on Wisdom" (Sir. 14,20) Collected Essays on the Book of Ben Sira*, 187–200. Contributions to Biblical Exegesis and Theology 43. Dudley, MA: Peeters, 2006.

Beers, Holly. *The Followers of Jesus as the Servant: Luke's Model from Isaiah for the Disciples in Luke-Acts*. LNTS 535. New York: T. & T. Clark, 2015.

Beetham, Christopher A. *Echoes of Scripture in the Letter of Paul to the Colossians*. BIS 96. Boston: Brill, 2008.

Beker, J. Christiaan. "Echoes and Intertextuality: On the Role of Scripture in Paul's Theology." In *Paul and the Use of the Scriptures of Israel*, edited by Craig A. Evans and James A. Sanders, 64–69. JSNTSup 83. Sheffield: Sheffield Academic, 1993.

Bell, Richard. *Provoked to Jealousy: The Origin and Purpose of the Jealousy Motif in Romans 9–11*. WUNT 2/63. Tübingen: Mohr Siebeck, 1994.

Beyer, H. W. "ἐπισκέπτομαι, ἐπισκοπέω, ἐπισκοπή, ἐπίσκοπος, ἀλλοτριεπίσκοπος." In *TDNT* 2:599–621.

Bird, Michael F. "The Unity of Luke-Acts in Recent Discussion." *JSNT* 29 (2007) 425–48.

Blair, Hugh J. "Putting One's Hand to the Plough: Luke 9:62 in the Light of 1 Kings 19:19–21." *ExpTim* 79 (1968) 342–43.

Blenkinsopp, Joseph. *Ezra-Nehemiah: A Commentary*. OTL. Philadelphia: Westminster, 1988.

———. *Isaiah: A New Translation with Introduction and Commentary*. 3 vols. AB 19. New York: Doubleday, 2000–2003.

Block, Daniel I. *The Book of Ezekiel*. 2 vols. NICOT. Grand Rapids: Eerdmans, 1997.

———. *Judges, Ruth*. NAC 6. New York: Broadman & Holman, 1999.

Blomberg, Craig L. "Elijah, Election, and the Use of Malachi in the New Testament." *CTR* 2 (1987) 99–117.

———. "The Law in Luke-Acts." *JSNT* 22 (1984) 53–80.

Bock, Darrell L. *Acts*. BECNT. Grand Rapids: Baker Academic, 2007.

———. *Luke*. 2 vols. BECNT. Grand Rapids: Baker Academic, 1994.

———. *Proclamation from Prophecy and Pattern: Lucan Old Testament Christology*. JSNTSup 12. Sheffield: Sheffield Academic, 1987.

———. "Proclamation from Prophecy and Pattern: Luke's Use of the Old Testament for Christology and Mission." In *The Gospels and the Scriptures of Israel*, edited by Craig A. Evans and W. Richard Stegner, 280–307. JSNTSup 104. Sheffield: Sheffield Academic, 1994.

Böhlemann, Peter. *Jesus und der Täufer: Schlüssel zur Theologie und Ethik des Lukas*. SNTSMS 99. Cambridge: Cambridge University Press, 1997.

Böhm, Martina. *Samarien und die Samaritai bei Lukas: Eine Studie zum religionshistorischen und traditionsgeschichtlichen Hintergrund der lukanischen Samarientexte und zu deren topographischer Verhaftung*. WUNT 2/111. Tübingen: Mohr Siebeck, 1999.

Booth, Wayne C. *The Rhetoric of Fiction*. 2nd ed. Chicago: University of Chicago Press, 1983.

Borgman, Paul. *The Way according to Luke: Hearing the Whole Story of Luke-Acts*. Grand Rapids: Eerdmans, 2006.

Bovon, François. *Luke: A Commentary on the Gospel of Luke*. 3 vols. Hermeneia 3. Minneapolis: Fortress, 2002.

———. *Luke the Theologian: Fifty-Five Years of Research (1950–2005)*. 2nd ed. Waco, TX: Baylor University Press, 2006.

Braaten, Laurie J. "God Sows: Hosea's Land Theme in the Book of the Twelve." In *Thematic Threads in the Book of the Twelve*, edited by Paul L. Redditt and Aaron Schart, 104–32. Berlin: de Gruyter, 2003.

Braun, Roddy L. *1 Chronicles*. WBC 14. Waco, TX: Thomas Nelson, 1986.

Brawley, Robert L. *Luke-Acts and the Jews: Conflict, Apology, and Conciliation*. SBL Monograph Series 33. Atlanta: Scholars Press, 1987.

Brink, Laurie. *Soldiers in Luke-Acts: Engaging, Contradicting, and Transcending the Stereotypes*. WUNT 362. Tübingen: Mohr Siebeck, 2014.

Brodie, Thomas L. "The Accusing and Stoning of Naboth (1 Kgs 21:8–13) as One Component of the Stephen Text (Acts 6:9–14, Acts 7:58a)." *CBQ* 45 (1983) 417–32.

———. *The Birthing of the New Testament: The Intertextual Development of the New Testament Writings*. Sheffield: Sheffield Phoenix Press, 2004.

———. *The Crucial Bridge: The Elijah-Elisha Narrative as an Interpretive Synthesis of Genesis-Kings and a Literary Model for the Gospels*. Collegeville, MN: Liturgical, 2000.

———. "The Departure for Jerusalem (Luke 9:51–56) as a Rhetorical Imitation of Elijah's Departure for the Jordan (2 Kgs 1:1–2:6)." *Bib* 70 (1989) 96–109.

———. "Intertexuality and Its Use in Tracing Q and Proto-Luke." In *The Scriptures in the Gospels*, edited by C. M. Tuckett, 469–78. Leuven: Leuven University Press, 1997.

———. "Luke-Acts as an Imitation and Emulation of the Elijah-Elisha Narrative." In *New Views on Luke and Acts*, edited by Earl Richard, 78–85. Collegeville, MN: Liturgical, 1990.

———. "Luke the Literary Interpreter: Luke-Acts as a Systematic Rewriting and Updating of the Elijah-Elisha Narrative in 1 and 2 Kings." PhD diss., University of St. Thomas, 1981.

———. "Luke's Use of the Elijah-Elisha Narrative." In *The Elijah-Elisha Narrative in the Composition of Luke*, edited by John S. Kloppenborg and Joseph Verheyden, 6–29. LNTS 493. New York: T. & T. Clark, 2014.

———. "Luke 9:57–62: A Systematic Adaptation of the Divine Challenge to Elijah (1 Kings 19)." In *Society of Biblical Literature 1989 Seminar Papers*, edited by David J. Lull, 237–45. SBLSPS 28. Atlanta: Scholars, 1989.

———. "Reply to Robert Derrenbacker and David Barrett Peabody." In *The Elijah-Elisha Narrative in the Composition of Luke*, edited by John S. Kloppenborg and Joseph Verheyden, 61–64. LNTS 493. New York: T. & T. Clark, 2014.

Brown, Colin. "What Was John the Baptist Doing?" *BBR* 7 (1997) 37–49.

Brown, Raymond E. "Jesus and Elisha." *Per* 12 (1971) 85–104.

Brown, Schuyler. *Apostasy and Perseverance in the Theology of Luke*. AnBib 36. Rome: Pontifical Biblical Institute, 1969.

Bruce, F. F. *The Book of the Acts*. Rev. ed. NICNT. Grand Rapids: Eerdmans, 1988.

———. *The Epistle to the Hebrews*. Rev. ed. NICNT. Grand Rapids: Eerdmans, 1990.

Brueggemann, Walter. *1 and 2 Kings*. Smyth & Helwys Bible Commentary. Macon, GA: Smyth & Helwys, 2000.

———. "A Brief Moment for a One-Person Remnant (2 Kings 5:2–3)." *BTB* 31 (2001) 53–59.

———. *Isaiah 40–66*. Westminster Bible Companion. Louisville: Westminster John Knox, 1998.

———. *The Theology of the Book of Jeremiah*. Old Testament Theology. Cambridge: Cambridge University Press, 2007.

Bruners, Wilhelm. *Die Reinigung der zehn Aussätzigen und die Heilung des Samariters: Lk 17,11–19: Ein Beitrag zur lukanischen Interpretation der Reinigung von Aussätzigen*. Forshung zur Bibel 23. Stuttgart: Katholisches Bibelwerk, 1977.

Bruno, Christopher R. "'Jesus Is Our Jubilee' . . . But How? The OT Background and Lukan Fulfillment of the Ethics of Jubilee." *JETS* 53 (2010) 81–101.

Bryan, Steven M. *Jesus and Israel's Traditions of Judgement and Restoration*. Cambridge: Cambridge University Press, 2002.

Burnett, Clint. "Eschatological Prophet of Restoration: Luke's Theological Portrait of John the Baptist in Luke 3:1–6." *Neot* 47 (2013) 1–24.

Butticaz, Simon. "'Has God Rejected His People?' (Romans 11.1). The Salvation of Israel in Acts: Narrative Claim of a Pauline Legacy." In *Paul and the Heritage of Israel: Paul's Claim upon Israel's Legacy in Luke and Acts in the Light of the Pauline Letters*, edited by David P. Moessner et al., 148–64. New York: T. & T. Clark, 2012.

Cadbury, Henry J. *The Making of Luke-Acts.* 2nd ed. Peabody, MA: Hendrickson, 1999.

Campbell, Joseph C. "God's People and the Remnant." *SJT* 3 (1950) 78–85.

Campbell, William S. "The Freedom and Faithfulness of God in Relation to Israel." *JSNT* 13 (1981) 27–45.

———. *Paul and the Creation of Christian Identity.* LNTS 322. New York: T. & T. Clark, 2006.

———. *Paul's Gospel in an Intercultural Context: Jew and Gentile in the Letter to the Romans.* New York: Peter Lang, 1992.

———. "The Rationale for Gentile Inclusion and Identity in Paul." *CTR* 9 (2012) 23–38.

Carena, Omar. *Il resto di Israele: Studio storico-comparativo delle iscrizioni reali assire e dei testi profetici sul tema del resto.* Supplementi alla Rivista Biblica 13. Bologna: Edizioni Dehoniane, 1985.

Carlson, R. A. "Élie à l'Horeb." *VT* 19 (1969) 416–39.

Carroll, John T. *Luke: A Commentary.* NTL. Louisville: Westminster John Knox, 2012.

Carson, D. A. "Do the Prophets and the Law Quit Prophesying before John? A Note on Matthew 11.13." In *The Gospels and the Scriptures of Israel*, edited by Craig A. Evans and W. Richard Stegner, 179–94. JSNTSup 104. Sheffield: Sheffield Academic, 1994.

———. "James." In *Commentary on the New Testament Use of the Old Testament*, edited by G. K. Beale and D. A. Carson, 997–1014. Grand Rapids: Baker Academic, 2007.

Charlesworth, James H., ed. *Old Testament Pseudepigrapha.* 2 vols. Garden City, NY: Doubleday, 1983.

Childs, Brevard S. *The Book of Exodus: A Critical, Theological Commentary.* OTL. Philadelphia: Westminster, 1974.

———. *Introduction to the Old Testament as Scripture.* Philadelphia: Fortress, 1979.

———. *Isaiah.* OTL. Louisville: Westminster John Knox, 2001.

———. "On Reading the Elijah Narratives." *Int* 34 (1980) 128–37.

Chilton, Bruce. "Romans 9–11 as Scriptural Interpretation and Dialogue with Judaism." *ExAud* 4 (1988) 27–37.

Christensen, Duane L. *Deuteronomy 21:10–34:12.* WBC 6B. Nashville: Thomas Nelson, 2002.

Clark, D. G. *Elijah as Eschatological High Priest: An Examination of the Elijah Tradition in Mal. 3.23–24.* PhD diss., University of Notre Dame, 1975.

Clarke, Ernest G., trans. *Targum Pseudo-Jonathan: Deuteronomy.* ArBib 5B. Collegeville, MN: Liturgical, 1997.

Clarke, William K. L. "The Use of the Septuagint in Acts." In *The Beginnings of Christianity*, edited by F. J. Foakes Jackson and Kirsopp Lake, 2:66–105. London: Macmillan, 1922.

Clements, Ronald E. "'A Remnant Chosen by Grace' (Romans 11:5): The Old Testament Background and Origin of the Remnant Concept." In *Pauline Studies: Essays Presented to Professor F. F. Bruce on His 70th Birthday*, edited by Donald A. Hagner and Murray J. Harris, 106–21. Grand Rapids: Eerdmans, 1980.

Cogan, Mordechai. *1 Kings: A New Translation with Introduction and Commentary*. AB 10. New York: Doubleday, 2000.

Cogan, Mordechai, and Hayim Tadmor. *II Kings: A New Translation with Introduction and Commentary*. AB 11. Garden City, NY: Doubleday, 1988.

Collins, John J. "A Herald of Good Tidings: Isaiah 61:1–3 and Its Actualization in the Dead Sea Scrolls." In *The Quest for Context and Meaning: Studies in Biblical Intertextuality in honor of James A. Sanders*, edited by Craig A. Evans and Shemaryahu Talmon, 225–40. BIS 28. Leiden: Brill, 1997.

———. *The Scepter and the Star: The Messiahs of the Dead Sea Scrolls and Other Ancient Literature*. ABRL. New York: Doubleday, 1995.

———. "The Works of the Messiah." *DSD* 1 (1994) 98–112.

Collins, Terrence. *The Mantle of Elijah: The Redaction Criticism of the Prophetical Books*. The Biblical Seminar 20. Sheffield: JSOT, 1993.

Conroy, Charles. "Hiel between Ahab and Elijah-Elisha: 1 Kgs 16,34 in Its Immediate Literary Context." *Bib* 77 (1996) 210–18.

Conzelmann, Hans. *Acts of the Apostles: A Commentary on the Acts of the Apostles*. Hermeneia. Philadelphia: Fortress, 1963.

———. *The Theology of St. Luke*. Translated by Geoffrey Buswell. New York: Harper & Row, 1960.

Cook, Michael J. "The Mission to the Jews in Acts: Unraveling Luke's 'Myth of the "Myriads."'" *Luke-Acts and the Jewish People: Eight Critical Perspectives*, edited by Joseph B. Tyson, 102–23. Minneapolis: Augsburg, 1988.

Cortes, Juan B., and Florence M. Gattie. "On the Meaning of Luke 16:16." *JBL* 106 (1987) 247–56.

Cotter, Wendy J. "The Parable of the Children in the Market-Place, Q (Lk) 7:31–35: An Examination of the Parable's Image and Significance." *NovT* 29 (1987) 289–304.

Crenshaw, James L. *Joel: A New Translation with Introduction and Commentary*. AB 24C. New York: Doubleday, 1995.

Croatto, J. Severino. "Jesus, Prophet like Elijah, and Prophet-Teacher like Moses in Luke-Acts." *JBL* 124 (2005) 451–65.

Crockett, Larrimore C. "Luke 4:25–27 and Jewish-Gentile Relations in Luke-Acts." *JBL* 88 (1969) 177–83.

Cronauer, Patrick T. *The Stories about Naboth the Jezreelite: A Source, Composition, and Redaction Investigation of 1 Kings 21 and Passages in 2 Kings 9*. Library of Hebrew Bible/Old Testament Studies 424. New York: T. & T. Clark, 2005.

Cross, Frank Moore. *Canaanite Myth and Hebrew Epic: Essays in the History of the Religion of Israel*. Cambridge, MA: Harvard University Press, 1973.

Cuany, Monique. "'Physician, Heal Yourself!'—Jesus' Challenge to His Own." *NovT* 58 (2016) 347–68.

Cuffey, Kenneth H. *Literary Coherence of the Book of Micah: Remnant, Restoration, and Promise*. London: T. & T. Clark, 2013.

———. "Remnant, Redactor, and Biblical Theologian: A Comparative Study of Coherence in Micah and the Twelve." In *Reading and Hearing the Book of the Twelve*, edited by James D. Nogalski and Marvin A. Sweeney, 186–202. SBLSymS 15. Atlanta: Society of Biblical Literature, 2000.

Cunningham, Scott. *"Through Many Tribulations": The Theology of Persecution in Luke-Acts*. JSNTSup 142. Sheffield: Sheffield Academic, 1997.

Curkpatrick, Stephen. "'Real and Fictive' Widows: Nuances of Independence and Resistance in Luke." *LTQ* 37 (2002) 215–24.

Dabeck, P. "Siehe, es erschienen Moses und Elias." *Bib* 23 (1942) 175–89.

Damm, Alexander. "A Rhetorical-Critical Assessment of Luke's Use of the Elijah-Elisha Narrative." In *The Elijah-Elisha Narrative in the Composition of Luke*, edited by John S. Kloppenborg and Joseph Verheyden, 88–113. LNTS 493. New York: T. & T. Clark, 2014.

Danker, Frederick W. *Jesus and the New Age: A Commentary on St. Luke's Gospel*. Rev. ed. Philadelphia: Fortress, 1988.

———. "Luke 16:16: An Opposition Logion." *JBL* 77 (1958) 231–43.

Darr, John A. *Herod the Fox: Audience Criticism and Lukan Characterization*. JSNTSup 163. Sheffield: Sheffield Academic, 1998.

Davids, Peter H. *The Epistle of James: A Commentary on the Greek Text*. NIGTC. Grand Rapids: Eerdmans, 1982.

Davidson, Richard M. *Typology in Scripture: A Study of Hermeneutical ΤΥΠΟΣ Structures*. Berrien Springs, MI: Andrews University Press, 1981.

Davies, J. G. *He Ascended into Heaven: A Study in the History of Doctrine*. Bampton Lectures. London: Lutterworth, 1958.

Day, John. "Shear-jashub (Isaiah 7:3) and the 'Remnant of Wrath' (Psalm 76:11)." *VT* 31 (1981) 76–78.

de Jonge, Henk Jan. "The Chronology of the Ascension Stories in Luke and Acts." *NTS* 59 (2013) 151–71.

de Jonge, Marinus, and Adam S. van der Woude. "11Q Melchizedek and the New Testament." *NTS* 12 (1966) 301–26.

Dearman, J. Andrew. *The Book of Hosea*. Grand Rapids: Eerdmans, 2010.

Delling, Gerhard. "Τρεῖς, τρίς, τρίτος." In *TDNT* 8:216–25.

Dempster, Stephen. "From Slight Peg to Cornerstone to Capstone: The Resurrection of Christ on 'The Third Day' according to the Scriptures." *WTJ* 76 (2014) 371–409.

Denaux, Adelbert. "Old Testament Models for the Lukan Narrative: A Critical Survey." In *The Scriptures in the Gospels*, edited by C. M. Tuckett, 271–306. Leuven: Leuven University Press, 1997.

Denova, Rebecca I. *The Things Accomplished among Us: Prophetic Tradition in the Structural Pattern of Luke-Acts*. JSNTSup 141. Sheffield: Sheffield Academic, 1997.

Derrenbacker, Robert A., Jr. "A Response to Thomas Brodie, 'Luke's Use of the Elijah-Elisha Narrative.'" In *The Elijah-Elisha Narrative in the Composition of Luke*, edited by John S. Kloppenborg and Joseph Verheyden, 30–36. LNTS 493. New York: T. & T. Clark, 2014.

Derrett, J., and M. Duncan. "Herod's Oath and the Baptist's Head: With an Appendix on Mk 9:12–13, Mal 3:24, Micah 7:6." *BZ* 9 (1965) 49–59.

DeVries, Simon J. *1 Kings*. WBC 12. Waco, TX: Word, 1985.

———. *Prophet against Prophet: The Role of the Micaiah Narrative (1 Kings 22) in the Development of Early Prophetic Tradition*. Grand Rapids: Eerdmans, 1978.

DeYoung, James B. "The Function of Malachi 3.1 in Matthew 11.10: Kingdom Reality as the Hermeneutic of Jesus." In *The Gospels and the Scriptures of Israel*, edited by Craig A. Evans and W. Richard Stegner, 66–91. JSNTSup 104. Sheffield: Sheffield Academic, 1994.

Dharamraj, Havilah. *A Prophet like Moses? A Narrative-Theological Reading of the Elijah Stories*. Paternoster Biblical Monographs. Colorado Springs: Paternoster, 2011.

Dibelius, Martin. *James: A Commentary on the Epistle of James*. Translated by Michael A. Williams. Hermeneia. Minneapolis: Fortress, 1976.

Doble, Peter. *The Paradox of Salvation: Luke's Theology of the Cross*. SNTSMS 87. Cambridge: Cambridge University Press, 1996.

Dochhorn, Jan. "Die Verschonung des samaritanischen Dorfes (Lk 9.54–55) Eine kritische Reflexion von Elia-Überlieferung im Lukasevangelium und eine frühjüdische Parallele im Testament Abrahams." *NTS* 53 (2007) 359–78.

Duhaime, Jean. "Le messie et les saints dans un fragment apocalyptique de Qumrân (4Q521 2)." In *Ce Dieu qui vient: Études sur l'Ancien et le Nouveau Testament offertes au professeur Bernard Renaud à l'occasion de son soixante-cinquième anniversaire*, edited by Raymond Kuntzmann, 265–74. Paris: Cerf, 1995.

Dunn, James D. G. *The Acts of the Apostles*. Narrative Commentaries. Valley Forge, PA: Trinity, 1996.

———. "John the Baptist's Use of Scripture." In *The Gospels and the Scriptures of Israel*, edited by Craig A. Evans and W. Richard Stegner, 42–54. JSNTSup 104. Sheffield: Sheffield Academic, 1994.

———. *Romans 9–16*. WBC 38B. Dallas, TX: Word, 1988.

Dunn, James D. G., and Scot McKnight, eds. *The Historical Jesus in Recent Research*. Sources for Biblical and Theological Study 10. Warsaw, IN: Eisenbrauns, 2005.

Dupont, Jacques. "Ressuscité 'le troisième jour.'" *Bib* 40 (1959) 742–61.

Edwards, Calvin R. "The Hamlet Motif in Joyce's Ulysses." *Western Review* 15 (1950) 5–13.

Edwards, James R. *The Gospel according to Luke*. PiNTC. Grand Rapids: Eerdmans, 2015.

Egelkraut, Helmuth L. *Jesus' Mission to Jerusalem: A Redaction Critical Study of the Travel Narrative in the Gospel of Luke, Lk 9:51–19:48*. Europäische Hochschulschriften 23/80. Frankfurt: Peter Lang, 1976.

Eichrodt, Walther. *Theology of the Old Testament*. Vol. 1. Translated by J. A. Baker. OTL. Philadelphia: Westminster, 1961.

Elliott, M. W. "Remnant." In *New Dictionary of Biblical Theology*, edited by T. Desmond Alexander et al., 723–26. Downers Grove, IL: InterVarsity, 2006.

Elliott, Mark Adam. "Israel." In *Dictionary of Jesus and the Gospels*, edited by Joel B. Green and Scot McKnight, 356–63. 1st ed. Downers Grove, IL: InterVarsity, 1992.

———. *The Survivors of Israel: A Reconsideration of the Theology of Pre-Christian Judaism*. Grand Rapids: Eerdmans, 2000.

Emadi, Samuel. "Intertextuality in New Testament Scholarship: Significance, Criteria, and the Art of Intertextual Reading." *CBR* 14 (2015) 8–23.

Enslin, Morton S. "Luke and the Samaritans." *HTR* 36 (1943) 277–97.

Ernst, Josef. *Johannes der Täufer: Interpretation, Geschichte, Wirkungsgeschichte*. BZNW 53. Berlin: de Gruyter, 1989.

Evans, C. F. "The Central Section of St. Luke's Gospel." In *Studies in the Gospels: Essays in Memory of R. H. Lightfoot*, edited by D. E. Nineham, 37–54. Oxford: Blackwell, 1967.

Evans, Craig A. "'He Set His Face': Luke 9:51 Once Again." *Bib* 68 (1987) 80–84.

———. "Isa 6:9–13 in the Context of Isaiah's Theology." *JETS* 29 (1986) 139–46.

———. *Luke*. NIBCNT 3. Peabody, MA: Hendrickson, 1990.

———. "Luke's Use of the Elijah-Elisha Narratives and the Ethics of Election." *JBL* 106 (1987) 75–83.

———. "Messianic Hopes and Messianic Figures in Late Antiquity." *Journal of Greco-Roman Christianity and Judaism* 3 (2006) 9–40.

———. "Prophecy and Polemic: Jews in Luke's Scriptural Apologetic." In *Luke and Scripture: The Function of Sacred Tradition in Luke-Acts*, 171–211. Minneapolis: Fortress, 1993.

———. "Prophet, Sage, Healer, Messiah, and Martyr: Types and Identities of Jesus." In *Handbook for the Study of the Historical Jesus*, edited by Tom Holmen and Stanley E. Porter, 2:1217–44. Leiden: Brill, 2011.

Evans, Craig A., and James A. Sanders. *Luke and Scripture: The Function of Sacred Tradition in Luke-Acts*. Minneapolis: Fortress, 1993.

———, eds. *Paul and the Scriptures of Israel*. JSNTSup 83. Sheffield: JSOT, 1993.

Everson, Joseph A. "The Days of Yahweh." *JBL* 93 (1974) 329–37.

Faierstein, Morris M. "Why Do the Scribes Say That Elijah Must Come First?" *JBL* 100 (1981) 75–86.

Feldman, Ariel. *The Dead Sea Scrolls Rewriting Samuel and Kings: Texts and Commentary*. BZAW 469. Berlin: de Gruyter, 2015.

Fensham, F. Charles. *The Books of Ezra and Nehemiah*. NICOT. Grand Rapids: Eerdmans, 1982.

Finkel, Asher. "Jesus' Preaching in the Synagogue on the Sabbath (Luke 4.16–28)." In *The Gospels and the Scriptures of Israel*, edited by Craig A. Evans and W. Richard Stegner, 325–41. JSNTSup 104. Sheffield: Sheffield Academic, 1994.

Firth, David G., and H. G. M. Williamson, eds. *Interpreting Isaiah: Issues and Approaches*. Downers Grove, IL: IVP Academic, 2009.

Fitzmyer, Joseph A. *The Acts of the Apostles: A New Translation with Introduction and Commentary*. AB 31. New York: Doubleday, 1998.

———. "Aramaic 'Elect of God' Text from Qumran Cave IV." *CBQ* 27 (1965) 348–72.

———. "The Ascension of Christ and Pentecost." *TS* 45 (1984) 409–40.

———. "The Composition of Luke, Chapter 9." In *Perspectives on Luke-Acts*, edited by Charles H. Talbert, 139–52. Perspectives on Religious Studies, Special Studies Series 5. Danville, VA: Association of Baptist Professors of Religion, 1978.

———. "Further Light on Melchizedek from Qumran Cave 11." *JBL* 86 (1967) 25–41.

———. *The Gospel according to Luke: Introduction, Translation, and Notes*. Vol. 1. AB 28. New York: Doubleday, 1981.

———. "More about Elijah Coming First." *JBL* 104 (1985) 295–96.

———. *The One Who Is to Come*. Grand Rapids: Eerdmans, 2007.

———. *Romans: A New Translation with Introduction and Commentary*. AB 33. New York: Doubleday, 1993.

Flesher, Paul V. M., and Bruce Chilton. *The Targums: A Critical Introduction*. Waco, TX: Baylor University Press, 2011.

Fletcher-Louis, Crispin H. T. "Jesus as the High Priestly Messiah, Part 1." *Journal for the Study of the Historical Jesus* 4 (2006) 155–75.

———. "Jesus as the High Priestly Messiah, Part 2." *Journal for the Study of the Historical Jesus* 5 (2007) 57–79.

Frankfurter, David. *Elijah in Upper Egypt: The Apocalypse of Elijah and Early Egyptian Christianity*. SAC. Minneapolis: Fortress, 1993.

———. "Tabitha in the Apocalypse of Elijah." *JTS* 41 (1990) 13–25.

Franklin, Eric. *Luke: Interpreter of Paul, Critic of Matthew*. JSNTSup 92. Sheffield: Sheffield Academic, 1994.

Fretheim, Terence E. *First and Second Kings*. Westminster Bible Companion. Louisville: Westminster John Knox, 1999.
Friedrichsen, Timothy A. "Luke 9,22—A Matthean Foreign Body." *ETL* 72 (1996) 398-407.
———. "The Temple, a Pharisee, a Tax Collector, and the Kingdom of God: Rereading a Jesus Parable (Luke 18:10–14A)." *JBL* 124 (2005) 89–119.
Fuller, George C. "The Life of Jesus, after the Ascension (Luke 24:50–53, Acts 1:9–11)." *WTJ* 56 (1994) 391–98.
Fuller, Michael E. *The Restoration of Israel: Israel's Re-Gathering and the Fate of the Nations in Early Jewish Literature and Luke-Acts*. BZNW 138. New York: de Gruyter, 2006.
Fusco, Vittorio. "Luke-Acts and the Future of Israel." *NovT* 38 (1996) 1–17.
Gagnon, Robert A. J. "Luke's Motives for Redaction in the Account of the Double Delegation in Luke 7:1–10." *NovT* 36 (1994) 122–45.
———. "Statistical Analysis and the Case of the Double Delegation in Luke 7:3–7a." *CBQ* 55 (1993) 709–31.
García Martínez, Florentino, and Eibert J. C. Tigchelaar, eds. *The Dead Sea Scrolls Study Edition*. 2 vols. Leiden: Brill, 1997.
Garsiel, Moshe. *From Earth to Heaven: A Literary Study of Elijah Stories in the Book of Kings*. Bethesda, MD: CDL, 2014.
Gathercole, Simon. "The Heavenly Anatole (Luke 1:78–9)." *JTS* 56 (2005) 471–88.
Gerleman, Gillis. "Rest und Überschuss: Eine terminologische Studie." In *Travels in the World of the Old Testament: Studies Presented to Professor M. A. Beek on the Occasion of His 65th Birthday*, 71–74. Assen, The Netherlands: Van Gorcum, 1974.
Ginzberg, Louis. *The Legends of the Jews*. Translated by Henrietta Szold. Vol. 4. Philadelphia: Jewish Publication Society of America, 1909.
Glavic, Julie A. "Eutychus in Acts and in the Church: The Narrative Significance of Acts 20:6–12." *BBR* 24 (2014) 179–206.
Glazier-McDonald, Beth. *Malachi: The Divine Messenger*. SBLDS 98. Atlanta: Scholars, 1987.
Glenny, W. Edward. "The Septuagint and Apostolic Hermeneutics: Amos 9 in Acts 15." *BBR* 22 (2012) 1–25.
Glombitza, Otto. "Der dankbare Samariter: Luk. xvii 11–19." *NovT* 11 (1969) 241–46.
———. "Die Christologishe Aussage des Lukas in seiner Gestaltung der drei Nachfolgeworte Lukas IX 57–62." *NovT* 13 (1971) 14–23.
Glover, Neil. "Elijah versus the Narrative of Elijah: The Contest between the Prophet and the Word." *JSOT* 30 (2006) 449–62.
Goldingay, John, and David Payne. *A Critical and Exegetical Commentary on Isaiah 40–55*. 2 vols. New York: T. & T. Clark, 2006.
Goodacre, Mark. "Mark, Elijah, the Baptist and Matthew: The Success of the First Intertextual Reading of Mark." In *Biblical Interpretation in Early Christian Gospels 2: Gospel of Matthew*, edited by Thomas R. Hatina, 73–84. LNTS 310. New York: T. & T. Clark, 2008.
Gorman, Michael J. *Apostle of the Crucified Lord: A Theological Introduction to Paul and His Letters*. Grand Rapids: Eerdmans, 2004.
Gosse, Bernard. "Isaïe VI et la tradition isaïenne." *VT* 42 (1992) 340–49.
Goulder, Michael. "Elijah with Moses, or, a Rift in the Pre-Markan Lute." In *Christology, Controversy and Community: New Testament Essays in honour of David R.*

Catchpole, edited by David G. Horrell and Christopher M. Tuckett, 193–208. Boston: Brill, 2000.

Graham, Pat. "The Remnant Motif in Isaiah." *RQ* 19 (1976) 217–28.

Gray, John. *I and II Kings: A Commentary*. Rev. ed. OTL. Philadelphia: Westminster, 1970.

Green, Joel B. "From 'John's Baptism' to 'Baptism in the Name of the Lord Jesus': The Significance of Baptism in Luke-Acts." In *Baptism, the New Testament and the Church: Historical and Contemporary Studies in honour of R. E. O. White*, edited by Stanley E. Porter and Anthony R. Cross, 157–72. JSNTSup 171. Sheffield: Sheffield Academic, 1999.

———. "Good News to Whom? Jesus and the 'Poor' in the Gospel of Luke." In *Jesus of Nazareth: Lord and Christ: Essays on the Historical Jesus and New Testament Christology*, edited by Joel B. Green and Max Turner, 59–74. Grand Rapids: Eerdmans, 1994.

———. *The Gospel of Luke*. NICNT. Grand Rapids: Eerdmans, 1997.

———. "The Problem of a Beginning: Israel's Scripture in Luke 1–2." *BBR* 4 (1994) 61–86.

Green, William Scott. "Doing the Text's Work for It: Richard Hays on Paul's Use of Scripture." In *Paul and the Scriptures of Israel*, edited by Craig A. Evans and James A. Sanders, 58–63. JSNTSup 83. Sheffield: JSOT, 1993.

Gregory, Andrew. "The Reception of Luke and Acts and the Unity of Luke-Acts." *JSNT* 29 (2007) 459–72.

Gregory, Bradley C. "The Postexilic Exile in Third Isaiah: Isaiah 61:1–3 in light of Second Temple Hermeneutics." *JBL* 126 (2007) 475–96.

Gregory, Russell. "Irony and the Unmasking of Elijah." In *From Carmel to Horeb: Elijah in Crisis*, edited by Alan J. Hauser, 91–170. JSOTSup 85. Sheffield: Almond, 1990.

Guthrie, George H. "Hebrews." In *Commentary on the New Testament Use of the Old Testament*, edited by G. K. Beale and D. A. Carson, 919–96. Grand Rapids: Baker Academic, 2007.

Haag, Herbert. *Der Gottesknecht bei Deuterojesaja*. EdF 233. Darmstadt: Wissenschaftliche Buchgesellschaft, 1985.

Haenchen, Ernst. *The Acts of the Apostles: A Commentary*. Philadelphia: Westminster, 1971.

———. "Judentum und Christentum in der Apostelgeschichte." *ZNW* 54 (1963) 155–87.

Hafemann, Scott. "The Salvation of Israel in Romans 11:25–27: A Response to Krister Stendahl." *ExAud* 4 (1988) 38–58.

Hahn, Ferdinand. "Die Himmelfahrt Jesu: Ein Gespräch mit Gerhard Lohfink." *Bib* 55 (1974) 418–26.

Hamm, Dennis. "Praying 'Regularly' (Not 'Constantly') A Note on the Cultic Background of dia pantos at Luke 24:53, Acts 10:2 and Hebrews 9:6, 13:15." *ExpTim* 116 (2004) 50–52.

———. "What the Samaritan Leper Sees: The Narrative Christology of Luke 17:11–19." *CBQ* 56 (1994) 273–87.

Harbin, Michael A. "The Manumission of Slaves in Jubilee and Sabbath Years." *TynBul* 63 (2012) 53–74.

Harmon, William. *A Handbook to Literature*. 9th ed. Upper Saddle River, NJ: Pearson, 2003.

Hartin, Patrick J. *James*. Sacra Pagina 14. Collegeville, MN: Liturgical, 2003.
Hasel, Gerhard F. "Linguistic Considerations regarding the Translation of Isaiah's Shear-Jashub: A Reassessment." *AUSS* 9 (1971) 36–46.
———. *The Remnant: The History and Theology of the Remnant Idea from Genesis to Isaiah*. Andrews University Monographs 5. Berrien Springs, MI: Andrews University Press, 1972.
———. "Semantic Values of Derivatives of the Hebrew Root Š'R." *AUSS* 11 (1973) 152–69.
Hauck, F., and E. Bammel. "πτωχός, πτωχεία, πτωχεύω." In *TDNT* 6:885–915.
Hauser, Alan J. "Yahweh versus Death—The Real Struggle in 1 Kings 17–19." In *From Carmel to Horeb: Elijah in Crisis*, edited by Alan J. Hauser, 9–90. JSOTSup 85. Sheffield: Almond, 1990.
Hauser, Alan J., and Russell Gregory. *From Carmel to Horeb: Elijah in Crisis*. JSOTSup 85. Sheffield: Almond, 1990.
Hausmann, Jutta. *Israels Rest: Studien zum Selbstverständnis der nachexilischen Gemeinde*. Beiträge zur Wissenschaft vom Alten und Neuen Testament 124. Stuttgart: Kohlhammer, 1987.
Hays, J. Daniel. "'Sell Everything You Have and Give to the Poor': The Old Testament Prophetic Theme of Justice as the Connecting Motif of Luke 18:1–19:10." *JETS* 55 (2012) 43–63.
Hays, Richard B. *The Conversion of the Imagination: Paul as Interpreter of Israel's Scripture*. Grand Rapids: Eerdmans, 2005.
———. *Echoes of Scripture in the Letters of Paul*. New Haven, CT: Yale University Press, 1989.
Heil, John Paul. "From Remnant to Seed of Hope for Israel: Romans 9:27–29." *CBQ* 62 (2002) 703–20.
———. *The Transfiguration of Jesus: Narrative Meaning and Function of Mark 9:2–8, Matt 17:1–8 and Luke 9:28–36*. AnBib 144. Rome: Editrice Pontificio Istituto Biblico, 2000.
Herntrich, Volkmar Martinus, and Gottlob Schrenk. "λεῖμμα, ὑπόλειμμα, καταλείπω." In *TDNT* 4:194–214.
Hill, Andrew E. *Malachi: A New Translation with Introduction and Commentary*. AB 25D. New York: Doubleday, 1998.
Hobbs, T. R. *2 Kings*. WBC 13. Waco, TX: Word, 1985.
Hoffmann, Yair. "The Day of the Lord as a Concept and a Term in the Prophetic Literature." *ZAW* 93 (1981) 37–50.
Holladay, Carl R. "Luke's Use of the LXX in Acts: A Review of the Debate and a Look at Acts 1:15–26." In *Die Septuaginta und das frühe Christentum / The Septuagint and Christian Origins*. WUNT 277. Tübingen: Mohr Siebeck, 2011.
Holtz, Gundrun. "Zur christologischen Relevanz des Furchtmotivs im Lukasevangelium." *Bib* 90 (2009) 484–505.
Holtz, Shalom E. "A Comparative Note on the Demand for Witnesses in Isaiah 43:9." *JBL* 129 (2010) 457–61.
Holtz, Traugott. *Untersuchungen über die alttestamentlichen Zitate bei Lukas*. Berlin: Akademie-Verlag, 1968.
Horne, Charles M. "Meaning of the Phrase 'And Thus All Israel Will Be Saved' (Romans 11:26)." *JETS* 21 (1978) 329–34.

Horsley, Richard A. "'Like One of the Prophets of Old': Two Types of Popular Prophets at the Time of Jesus." *CBQ* 47 (1985) 435–63.
House, Paul R. *1, 2 Kings*. NAC 8. Nashville: Broadman & Holman, 1995.
———. "Dramatic Coherence in Nahum, Habakkuk, and Zephaniah." In *Forming Prophetic Literature: Essays on Isaiah and the Twelve in honor of John D. W. Watts*, 195–208. Sheffield: Sheffield Academic, 1996.
———. *Old Testament Theology*. Downers Grove, IL: InterVarsity, 1998.
———. "Suffering and the Purpose of Acts." *JETS* 33 (1990) 317–30.
———. *The Unity of the Twelve*. JSOTSup 97. Sheffield: Almond, 1990.
Huddleston, Jonathan. "What Would Elijah and Elisha Do? Internarrativity in Luke's Story of Jesus." *JTI* 5 (2011) 265–82.
Huebsch, Robert William. "The Understanding and Significance of the 'Remnant' in Qumran Literature: Including a Discussion of the Use of This Concept in the Hebrew Bible, the Apocrypha and the Pseudepigrapha." PhD diss., McMaster University, 1981.
Ishai-Rosenboim, Daniella. "Is YOM H' (The Day of the Lord) a Term in Biblical Language?" *Bib* 87 (2006) 395–401.
Iwry, Samuel. "*Massēbāh* and *Bāmāh* in 1Q Isaiaha 6:13." *JBL* 76 (1957) 225–32.
Jacob, Edmond. *Theology of the Old Testament*. Translated by Arthur W. Heathcote and Philip J. Allcock. New York: Harper & Row, 1958.
Janes, Regina. "Why the Daughter of Herodias Must Dance (Mark 6.14–29)." *JSNT* 28 (2006) 443–67.
Japhet, Sara. "The Concept of the 'Remnant' in the Restoration Period: On the Vocabulary of Self-Definition." In *From the Rivers of Babylon to the Highlands of Judah: Collected Studies on the Restoration Period*, 432–49. Winona Lake, IN: Eisenbrauns, 2006.
Jellicoe, Sidney. "St. Luke and the 'Seventy(-Two).'" *NTS* 6 (1960) 319–21.
Jeremias, Joachim. "Der Gedanke des 'Heiligen Restes' im Spätjudentum und in der Verkündung Jesu." *ZNW* 42 (1949) 184–94.
———. *The Prayers of Jesus*. Studies in Biblical Theology 6. Naperville, IL: A. R. Allenson, 1967.
———. "Ἠλ(ε)ίας." In *TDNT* 2:928–41.
———. "λίθος, λίθανος." In *TDNT* 4:268–80.
———. "παῖς θεοῦ." In *TDNT* 5:654–717.
Jervell, Jacob. "The Church of Jews and Godfearers." In *Luke-Acts and the Jewish People: Eight Critical Perspectives*, edited by Joseph B. Tyson, 11–20. Minneapolis: Augsburg, 1988.
———. "The Divided People of God: The Restoration of Israel and Salvation for the Gentiles." In *Luke and the People of God: A New Look at Luke-Acts*, 41–74. Minneapolis: Augsburg, 1972.
———. "God's Faithfulness to the Faithless People: Trends in Interpretation of Luke-Acts." *WW* 12 (1992) 29–36.
———. *Luke and the People of God: A New Look at Luke-Acts*. Minneapolis: Augsburg, 1972.
———. *The Theology of the Acts of the Apostles*. NTT. Cambridge: Cambridge University Press, 1996.
———. *The Unknown Paul: Essays on Luke-Acts and Early Christian History*. Minneapolis: Augsburg, 1984.

Jewett, Robert. *Romans: A Commentary*. Hermeneia. Minneapolis: Fortress, 2007.
Johnson, Dan G. "Structure and Meaning of Romans 9–11." *CBQ* 49 (1984) 91–103.
Johnson, Luke Timothy. *The Letter of James: A New Translation with Introduction and Commentary*. AB 37A. New York: Doubleday, 1995.
Jones, Barry Alan. *The Formation of the Book of the Twelve: A Study in Text and Canon*. SBLDS 149. Atlanta: Scholars, 1995.
Jost, François. "Introduction." In *Dictionary of Literary Themes and Motifs*, edited by Jean-Charles Seigneuret et al., 1:xv–xxiii. Westport, CT: Greenwood, 1988.
Joynes, Christine E. "A Question of Identity: 'Who Do People Say That I Am?': Elijah, John the Baptist and Jesus in Mark's Gospel." In *Understanding, Studying and Reading: New Testament Essays in honour of John Ashton*, edited by Christopher Rowland and Crispin H. T. Fletcher-Louis, 15–29. JSNTSup 153. Sheffield: Sheffield Academic, 1998.

———. "The Returned Elijah? John the Baptist's Angelic Identity in the Gospel of Mark." *SJT* 58 (2005) 455–67.

Juncker, Günther H. "Jesus and the Angel of the Lord: An Old Testament Paradigm for New Testament Christology." PhD diss., Trinity Evangelical Divinity School, 2001.
Jung, Chang-Wook. *The Original Language of the Lukan Infancy Narrative*. New York: T. & T. Clark, 2004.
Kaiser, Otto. *Isaiah 1–12: A Commentary*. 2nd ed. OTL. Philadelphia: Westminster John Knox, 1972.
Kaiser, Walter C., Jr. *Malachi: God's Unchanging Love*. Grand Rapids: Baker, 1984.

———. "The Promise of the Arrival of Elijah in Malachi and the Gospels." *GTJ* 3 (1982) 221–33.

Kaminsky, Joel. *Yet I Loved Jacob: Reclaiming the Biblical Concept of Election*. Nashville: Abingdon, 2007.
Karrer, Martin, et al. "Das Lukanische Doppelwerk als Zeuge für den LXX-Text des Jesaja-Buches." In *Florilegium Lovaniense: Studies in Septuagint and Textual Criticism in honor of Florentino García Martínez*, edited by Hans Ausloos et al., 253–74. BETL 224. Leuven: Peeters, 2008.
Käseman, Ernst. *Commentary on Romans*. Translated by Geoffrey W. Bromiley. Grand Rapids: Eerdmans, 1980.
Kazmierski, Carl R. "The Stones of Abraham: John the Baptist and the End of Torah (Matt 3,7–10 par. Luke 3,7–9)." *Bib* 61 (1987) 22–40.
Keener, Craig S. *Acts: An Exegetical Commentary*. 4 vols. Grand Rapids: Baker Academic, 2012–2015.
Kellermann, Ulrich. "Elia als Seelenführer der Verstorbenen oder Elia-Typologie in Lk 23,43 'Heute wirst du mit mir im Paradies sein.'" *BN* 83 (1996) 35–53.

———. "Zu den Elia-Motiven in den Himmelfahrtsgeschichten des Lukas." In *Altes Testament—Forschung und Wirkung: Festschrift für Henning Graf Reventlow*, 123–38. Frankfurt: Peter Lang, 1994.

Kessler, Rainer. *Maleachi*. HTKNT. Freiburg: Herder, 2011.
Kiddle, Martin. *The Revelation of St. John*. MNTC. London: Hodder & Stoughton, 1952.
King, Greg A. "The Remnant in Zephaniah." *BSac* 151 (1994) 414–27.
Klassen, William. "'A Child of Peace' (Luke 10:6) in First Century Context." *NTS* 27 (1981) 488–506.
Kleger, Roland. "Die Struktur der Jesaja-Apokalypse und die Deutung von Jes 26,19." *ZAW* 120 (2008) 526–46.

Klein, Ralph W. *1 Samuel*. 2nd ed. WBC 10. Nashville: Thomas Nelson, 2000.
———. *2 Chronicles*. Hermeneia. Minneapolis: Fortress, 2012.
Kline, Meredith G. "Death, Leviathan, and Martyrs: Isaiah 24:1–27:1." In *A Tribute to Gleason Archer*, edited by Walter C. Kaiser Jr. and Ronald R. Youngblood, 229–49. Chicago: Moody, 1986.
Kloppenborg, John S., and Joseph Verheyden, eds. *The Elijah-Elisha Narrative in the Composition of Luke*. LNTS. New York: T. & T. Clark, 2013.
Knibb, M. A. "2 Esdras." In *The First and Second Books of Esdras*, 76–306. CBCNEB. Cambridge: Cambridge University Press, 1979.
Knight, George A. F. *Deutero-Isaiah: A Theological Commentary on Isaiah 40–55*. New York: Abingdon, 1965.
Koester, Craig R. *Revelation: A New Translation with Introduction and Commentary*. Vol. 1. AB 38A. New Haven, CT: Yale University Press, 2014.
Koet, Bart J. "Elijah as Reconciler of Father and Son: From 1 Kings 16:34 and Malachi 3:22–24 to Ben Sira 48:1–11 and Luke 1:13–17." In *Rewriting Biblical History: Essays on Chronicles and Ben Sira in honor of Pancratius C. Beentjes*, 173–90. Deuterocanonical and Cognate Literature 7. Berlin: de Gruyter, 2011.
Kolasny, Judette M. "An Example of Rhetorical Criticism: Luke 4:16–30." In *New Views on Luke and Acts*, edited by Earl Richard, 67–77. Collegeville, MN: Liturgical, 1990.
Kowalski, Beate. "Der Fenstersturz in Troas (Apg 20,7–12)." *SNTSU* 30 (2005) 19–38.
Kurz, William S. "Intertextual Use of Sirach 48.1–16 in Plotting Luke-Acts." In *The Gospels and the Scriptures of Israel*, edited by Craig A. Evans and W. Richard Stegner, 308–24. JSNTSup 104. Sheffield: Sheffield Academic, 1994.
Kvalbein, Hans. "Die Wunder der Endzeit: Beobachtungen zu 4Q521 und Matth 11,5p." *ZNW* 88 (1997) 111–25.
Ladd, George Eldon. *A Commentary on the Revelation of John*. Grand Rapids: Eerdmans, 1972.
Lane, William L. *Hebrews 9–13*. WBC 47B. Dallas, TX: Word, 1991.
Leithart, Peter J. *1 and 2 Kings*. Brazos Theological Commentary on the Bible. Grand Rapids: Brazos, 2006.
Lévêque, Jean. "Le Portrait d'Élie dans l'Éloge des Pères (Si 48,1–11)." In *Ce Dieu qui vient: Études sur l'Ancien et le Nouveau Testament offertes au professeur Bernard Renaud à l'occasion de son soixante-cinquième anniversaire*, edited by Raymond Kuntzmann, 215–29. Paris: Cerf, 1995.
Levey, Samson H. *The Messiah: An Aramaic Interpretation*. Monographs of the Hebrew Union College 2. Cincinnati: Hebrew Union College Press, 1974.
Levin, Harry. *James Joyce: A Critical Introduction*. Rev. ed. New York: New Directions, 1960.
Levine, Nachman. "Twice as Much of Your Spirit: Pattern, Parallel and Paronomasia in the Miracles of Elijah and Elisha." *JSOT* 85 (1999) 25–46.
Lim, Bo H. "Which Version of the Twelve Prophets Should Christians Read? A Case for Reading the LXX Twelve Prophets." *JTI* 7 (2013) 21–36.
Litke, Wayne Douglas. *Luke's Knowledge of the Septuagint: A Study of the Citations in Luke-Acts*. Ann Arbor, MI: UMI Dissertation Services, 1993.
Litwak, Kenneth Duncan. *Echoes of Scripture in Luke-Acts: Telling the History of God's People Intertextually*. New York: T. & T. Clark, 2005.

Lo, Alison. "Remnant Motif in Amos, Micah, and Zephaniah." In *A God of Faithfulness: Essays in honour of J. Gordon McConville on His 60th Birthday*, edited by James A. Grant, Alison Lo, and Gordon J. Wenham, 130-48. New York: T. & T. Clark, 2011.

Lohfink, Gerhard. *Die Himmelfahrt Jesu: Untersuchungen zu dien Himmelfahrts- und Erhöhungstexten bei Lukas*. SANT 26. Munich: Kosel, 1971.

———. *Die Sammlung Israels: Eine Untersuchung zur lukanischen Ekklesiologie*. Studien zum Alten und Neuen Testament 39. Munich: Kosel, 1975.

Longenecker, Bruce W. *Eschatology and the Covenant: A Comparison of 4 Ezra and Romans 1-11*. JSNTSup 57. Sheffield: JSOT, 1991.

Longenecker, Richard N. *Introducing Romans: Critical Issues in Paul's Most Famous Letter*. Grand Rapids: Eerdmans, 2011.

Lucas, Alec J. "Assessing Stanley E. Porter's Objections to Richard B. Hays's Notion of Metalepsis." *CBQ* 76 (2014) 93-111.

Lust, Johan. "A Gentle Breeze or a Roaring Thunderous Sound?" *VT* 25 (1975) 110-15.

Lust, Johan, et al. *Greek-English Lexicon of the Septuagint*. Rev. ed. Stuttgart: Deutsche Bibelgesellschaft, 2003.

Luz, Ulrich. *Matthew: A Commentary*. 3 vols. Hermeneia. Minneapolis: Fortress, 2001.

Lyons, Michael A. "Paul and the Servant(s) Isaiah 49,6 in Acts 13,47." *ETL* 89 (2013) 345-59.

Macintosh, A. A. *A Critical and Exegetical Commentary on Hosea*. ICC. Edinburgh: T. & T. Clark, 1997.

Maile, John F. "The Ascension in Luke-Acts." *TynBul* 37 (1986) 29-59.

Malchow, Bruce V. "The Messenger of the Covenant in Mal 3:1." *JBL* 103 (1984) 252-55.

Mallen, Peter. *The Reading and Transformation of Isaiah in Luke-Acts*. LNTS 367. New York: T. & T. Clark, 2008.

Marcus, Joel. *The Way of the Lord: Christological Exegesis of the Old Testament in the Gospel of Mark*. Louisville: Westminster John Knox, 1992.

Marguerat, Daniel. "The Enigma of the Silent Closing of Acts (28:16-31)." In *Jesus and the Heritage of Israel: Luke's Narrative Claim upon Israel's Legacy*, edited by David P. Moessner, 284-304. Luke the Interpreter of Israel 1. Harrisburg, PA: Trinity, 1999.

———. *The First Christian Historian: Writing the "Acts of the Apostles."* Translated by Ken McKinney, Gregory J. Laughery, and Richard Bauckham. Society for New Testament Studies Monograph Series 121. Cambridge: Cambridge University Press, 2002.

———. "Jews and Christians in Conflict." In *The First Christian Historian: Writing the "Acts of the Apostles,"* 129-54. Cambridge: Cambridge University Press, 2002.

———. "Luc-Actes: Une unite à construire." In *The Unity of Luke-Acts*, edited by Joseph Verheyden, 57-81. BETL 142. Leuven: Leuven University Press, 1999.

Marshall, I. Howard. "Acts." In *Commentary on the New Testament Use of the Old Testament*, edited by G. K. Beale and D. A. Carson, 513-606. Grand Rapids: Baker Academic, 2007.

———. "Acts and the 'Former Treatise.'" In *The Book of Acts in Its Ancient Literary Setting*, edited by Bruce W. Winter and Andrew D. Clarke, 163-82. Carlisle: Paternoster, 1993.

———. *The Gospel of Luke: A Commentary of the Greek Text*. NIGTC 3. Grand Rapids: Eerdmans, 1978.

———. "The Hope of a New Age: The Kingdom of God in the New Testament." *Them* 11 (1985) 5–15.

———. "'Israel' and the Story of Salvation: One Theme in Two Parts." In *Jesus and the Heritage of Israel: Luke's Narrative Claim upon Israel's Legacy*, edited by David P. Moessner, 340–57. Harrisburg, PA: Trinity, 1990.

———. *Luke: Historian and Theologian*. Contemporary Evangelical Perspectives. Grand Rapids: Zondervan, 1970.

Martin, James D. "Ben Sira's Hymn to the Fathers: A Messianic Perspective." In *Crises and Perspectives: Studies in Ancient Near Eastern Polytheism, Biblical Theology, Palestinian Archaeology, and Intertestamental Literature: Papers Read at the Joint British-Dutch Old Testament Conference, Held at Cambridge, U.K., 1985*, 107–23. Oudtestamentische studiën 24. Leiden: Brill, 1986.

Maston, Jason. "How Wrong Were the Disciples about the Kingdom? Thoughts on Acts 1:6." *ExpTim* 126 (2015) 169–78.

Matera, Frank J. "Jesus' Journey to Jerusalem (Luke 9.51–19.46): A Conflict with Israel." *JSNT* 51 (1993) 57–77.

———. "Responsibility for the Death of Jesus according to the Acts of the Apostles." *JSNT* 39 (1990) 77–93.

Mays, James Luther. *Micah: A Commentary*. OTL. Philadelphia: Westminster, 1976.

McCartney, Dan G. *James*. BECNT. Grand Rapids: Baker Academic, 2009.

McComiskey, Thomas Edward. "Hosea." In *The Minor Prophets: An Exegetical and Expository Commentary*, edited by Thomas Edward McComiskey, 1:1–238. Grand Rapids: Baker Academic, 1992.

McLay, R. Timothy. *The Use of the Septuagint in New Testament Research*. Grand Rapids: Eerdmans, 2003.

McLean, John A. "Did Jesus Correct the Disciples' View of the Kingdom?" *BSac* 151 (1994) 215–27.

McNicol, Allan J. "Revelation 11:1–14 and the Structure of the Apocalypse." *RQ* 22 (1979) 193–202.

Mearns, Chris. "Realized Eschatology in Q: A Consideration of the Sayings in Luke 7:22, 11:20 and 16:16." *SJT* 40 (1987) 189–210.

Meek, James A. *The Gentile Mission in Old Testament Citations in Acts: Text, Hermeneutic and Purpose*. LNTS 385. New York: T. & T. Clark, 2008.

Meinhold, Arndt. *Maleachi*. BKAT XIV/8. Neukirchen-Vluyn: Neukirchener, 2000.

Metzger, Bruce M. "Seventy or Seventy-Two Disciples?" *NTS* 5 (1959) 299–306.

———. *A Textual Commentary on the Greek New Testament*. 2nd ed. Stuttgart: Deutsche Bibelgesellschaft, 1994.

Metzger, Wolfgang. "Der Horizont der Gnade in der Berufungsvision Jesajas: Kritische Bedenken zum masoretischen Text von Jesaja 6,13." *ZAW* 93 (1981) 281–84.

Meyer, Ben F. "Election-Historical Thinking in Romans 9–11, and Ourselves." *ExAud* 4 (1988) 1–7.

———. "Jesus and the Remnant of Israel." *JBL* 84 (1965) 123–30.

Meyer, Lester V. "Remnant." In *The Anchor Bible Dictionary*, edited by David Noel Freedman et al., 5:669–71. New York: Doubleday, 1992.

Meyer, Rudolf. "'Elia' und 'Ahab' (Tg. Ps.-Jon zu Deut. 33:11)." In *Abraham unser Vater: Juden und Christen im Gespräch über die Bibel, Festschrift für Otto Michel zum 60. Geburtstag*, 356–68. Leiden: Brill, 1963.

Meyers, Carol L., and Eric M. Meyers. *Haggai, Zechariah 1–8: A New Translation with Introduction and Commentary*. AB 25B. New York: Doubleday, 1987.

———. *Zechariah 9–14*. AB 25C. New York: Doubleday, 1993.

Miller, Chris A. "Did Peter's Vision in Acts 10 Pertain to Men or the Menu?" *BSac* 159 (2002) 302–17.

Miller, David M. "The Messenger, the Lord, and the Coming Judgement in the Reception History of Malachi 3." *NTS* 53 (2007) 1–16.

———. "Seeing the Glory, Hearing the Son: The Function of the Wilderness Theophany Narratives in Luke 9:28–36." *CBQ* 72 (2010) 498–517.

Miller, Merrill P. "Function of Isa 61:1–2 in 11Q Melchizedek." *JBL* 88 (1969) 467–69.

Miller, R. J. "Elijah, John, and Jesus in the Gospel of Luke." *NTS* 34 (1988) 611–22.

Minear, Paul S. "Luke's Use of the Birth Stories." In *Studies in Luke-Acts: Essays Presented in honor of Paul Schubert*, edited by Leander E. Keck and J. Louis Martyn, 111–30. Nashville: Abingdon, 1966.

Moberly, R. W. L. *At the Mountain of God: Story and Theology in Exodus 32–34*. JSOTSup 22. Sheffield: JSOT, 1983.

Moessner, David P., ed. "The Ironic Fulfillment of Israel's Glory." In *Luke-Acts and the Jewish People: Eight Critical Perspectives*, edited by Joseph B. Tyson, 35–50. Minneapolis: Augsburg, 1988.

———. *Jesus and the Heritage of Israel: Luke's Narrative Claim upon Israel's Legacy*. Luke the Interpreter of Israel 1. Harrisburg, PA: Trinity, 1999.

———. *Lord of the Banquet: The Literary and Theological Significance of the Lukan Travel Narrative*. Harrisburg, PA: Trinity, 1989.

———. *Luke the Historian of Israel's Legacy, Theologian of Israel's "Christ": A New Reading of the "Gospel of Acts" of Luke*. BZNW 182. Berlin: de Gruyter, 2016.

———. "Luke 9:1–50: Luke's Preview of the Journey of the Prophet like Moses of Deuteronomy." *JBL* 102 (1983) 575–605.

Moessner, David P., et al., eds. *Paul and the Heritage of Israel: Luke's Narrative Claim upon Paul and Israel's Legacy*. Luke the Interpreter of Israel 2. New York: T. & T. Clark, 2012.

Moo, Douglas J. *The Epistle to the Romans*. NICNT. Grand Rapids: Eerdmans, 1996.

———. *The Letter of James*. PiNTC. Grand Rapids: Eerdmans, 2000.

Moore, Thomas S. "'To the End of the Earth': The Geographic and Ethnic Universalism of Acts 1:8 in light of Isaianic Influence on Luke." *JETS* 40 (September 1997) 389–99.

Motyer, J. Alec. *The Prophecy of Isaiah: An Introduction and Commentary*. Downers Grove, IL: InterVarsity, 1993.

Mounce, Robert H. *The Book of Revelation*. Rev. ed. NICNT. Grand Rapids: Eerdmans, 1997.

Müller, Christoph Gregor. *Mehr als ein Prophet: Die Charakterzeichnung Johannes des Täufers im Lukanischen Erzählwerk*. Herders biblische Studien 31. Freiburg: Herder, 2001.

Müller, Werner. *Die Vorstellung vom Rest im Alten Testament*. Rev. ed. Neukirchen-Vluyn: Neukirchener, 1973.

Munck, Johannes. *The Acts of the Apostles*. AB 31. Garden City, NY: Doubleday, 1967.

———. *Christ and Israel: An Interpretation of Romans 9–11*. Philadelphia: Fortress, 1967.

Muraoka, Takamitsu. *A Greek-English Lexicon of the Septuagint*. Walpole, MA: Peeters, 2009.

———. *A Greek-Hebrew/Aramaic Two-Way Index to the Septuagint*. Walpole, MA: Peeters, 2010.

———. "Introduction aux Douze Petits Prophètes." In *Les Douze Prophètes: Osèes*, edited by Jan Joosten et al., 1:i–xiii. Paris: Cerf, 2002.

———. "Luke and the Septuagint." *NovT* 54 (2012) 13–15.

Myers, Jacob M. *I and II Esdras: Introduction, Translation and Commentary*. AB 42. Garden City, NY: Doubleday, 1974.

———. *Ezra, Nehemiah*. AB 14. Garden City, NY: Doubleday, 1965.

Neef, Heinz-Dieter. "Das Hoseabuch in Spiegel der Septuaginta: Aspekte der Deutung." In *Die Septuaginta und das frühe Christentum/The Septuagint and Christian Origins*, edited by Thomas Scott Caulley and Hermann Lichtenberger, 106–18. WUNT 277. Tübingen: Mohr Siebeck, 2011.

———. "Der Septuaginta-Text und der Masoreten-Text des Hoseabuches im Vergleich." *Bib* 67 (1986) 195–220.

Nelson, Neil D. "'This Generation' in Matt 24:34: A Literary Critical Perspective." *JETS* 38 (1995) 369–85.

Nelson, Richard D. *First and Second Kings*. Interpretation: A Bible Commentary for Teaching and Preaching. Louisville: John Knox, 1987.

Niccum, Curt. "One Ethiopian Eunuch Is Not the End of the World: The Narrative Function of Acts 8:26–40." In *A Teacher for All Generations: Essays in honor of James C. VanderKam*, edited by Eric F. Mason et al., 2:883–900. JSJSup 153. Boston: Brill, 2012.

Nickelsburg, George W. E. *1 Enoch 1: A Commentary on the Book of Enoch, Chapters 1–36; 81–108*. Hermeneia. Minneapolis: Fortress, 2001.

Niehaus, Jeffrey J. *God at Sinai: Covenant and Theophany in the Bible and Ancient Near East*. Studies in Old Testament Biblical Theology. Grand Rapids: Zondervan, 1995.

Noble, Paul R. "The Remnant in Amos 3–6: A Prophetic Paradox." *HBT* 19 (1997) 122–47.

Nogalski, James D. "The Day(s) of YHWH in the Book of the Twelve." In *Thematic Threads in the Book of the Twelve*, edited by Paul L. Redditt and Aaron Schart, 192–213. BZAW 325. Berlin: de Gruyter, 2003.

———. "Recurring Themes in the Book of the Twelve: Creating Points of Contact for a Theological Reading." *Int* 61 (2007) 125–36.

Nolland, John. "Classical and Rabbinic Parallels to 'Physician, Heal Yourself' (Lk 4:23)." *NovT* 21 (1979) 193–209.

———. *Luke*. 3 vols. WBC 35A–C. Dallas, TX: Word, 1989.

North, Christopher R. *The Suffering Servant in Deutero-Isaiah: A Historical and Critical Study*. 2nd ed. Eugene, OR: Wipf & Stock, 1956.

Oberhänsli-Widmer, Gabrielle. "Elija als Pate des Bundes, oder die Dynamik rabbinischer Rezeption." *Kontexte der Schrift* 1 (2005) 126–37.

O'Hagan, Angelo. "'Greet No One on the Way' (Luke 10,4B)." *SBFLA* 16 (1965) 69–84.

Öhler, Markus. *Elia im Neuen Testament: Untersuchungen zur Bedeutung des alttestamentlichen Propheten im frühen Christentum*. BZNW 88. Berlin: de Gruyter, 1997.

———. "The Expectation of Elijah and the Presence of the Kingdom of God." *JBL* 118 (1999) 461–76.

Olley, John W. "YHWH and His Zealous Prophet: The Presentation of Elijah in 1 and 2 Kings." *JSOT* 80 (1998) 25–51.
Olson, Daniel C. *A New Reading of the Animal Apocalypse of 1 Enoch: "All Nations Shall Be Blessed."* Studies in Veteris Testamenti Pseudepigrapha 24. Boston: Brill, 2013.
Osborne, Grant. *Revelation*. BECNT. Grand Rapids: Baker Academic, 2002.
Oswalt, John N. *The Book of Isaiah*. 2 vols. NICOT. Grand Rapids: Eerdmans, 1986.
O'Toole, Robert F. "Luke's Message in Luke 9:1–50." *CBQ* 49 (1987) 74–89.
———. "Philip and the Ethiopian Eunuch (Acts 8:25–40)." *JSNT* 17 (1983) 25–34.
Otten, Jeremy D. "The Bad Samaritans: The Elijah Motif in Luke 9:51–56." *JSNT* 42 (2020) 375–89.
Pao, David W. *Acts and the Isaianic New Exodus*. Grand Rapids: Baker Academic, 2002.
———. "Israel and Israel's Scriptures" (review of Craig S. Keener, *Acts: An Exegetical Commentary*). *TJ* 37 (2016) 47–56.
———. "Waiters or Preachers: Acts 6:1–7 and the Lukan Table Fellowship Motif." *JBL* 130 (2011) 127–44.
Pao, David W., and Eckhard J. Schnabel. "Luke." In *Commentary on the New Testament Use of the Old Testament*, edited by G. K. Beale and D. A. Carson, 251–415. Grand Rapids: Baker Academic, 2007.
Parsons, Mikeal C. *Acts*. PCNT. Grand Rapids: Baker Academic, 2008.
———. *The Departure of Jesus in Luke-Acts: The Ascension Narratives in Context*. JSNTSup 21. Sheffield: JSOT, 1987.
———. "Isaiah 53 in Acts 8: A Response to Professor Morna Hooker." In *Jesus and the Suffering Servant: Isaiah 53 and Christian Origins*, edited by William H. Bellinger and William R. Farmer, 104–19. Harrisburg, PA: Trinity, 1998.
———. *Luke: Storyteller, Interpreter, Evangelist*. Peabody, MA: Hendrickson, 2007.
———. "The Text of Acts 1:2 Reconsidered." *CBQ* 50 (1988) 58–71.
Parsons, Mikeal C., and Richard I. Pervo. *Rethinking the Unity of Luke and Acts*. Minneapolis: Fortress, 1993.
Peabody, David Barrett. "A Response to Thomas Brodie's Proto-Luke as the Earliest Form of the Gospel." In *The Elijah-Elisha Narrative in the Composition of Luke*, edited by John S. Kloppenborg and Joseph Verheyden, 37–60. LNTS 493. New York: T. & T. Clark, 2014.
Pervo, Richard I. *Acts: A Commentary*. Hermeneia. Minneapolis: Fortress, 2009.
———. "Israel's Heritage and Claims upon the Genre(s) of Luke and Acts: The Problems of a History." In *Jesus and the Heritage of Israel: Luke's Narrative Claim upon Israel's Legacy*, edited by David P. Moessner, 127–43. Luke the Interpreter of Israel 1. Harrisburg, PA: Trinity, 1999.
———. *Profit with Delight: The Literary Genre of the Acts of the Apostles*. Philadelphia: Fortress, 1987.
Petersen, David L. "A Thrice-Told Tale: Genre, Theme, and Motif." *BR* 18 (1973) 30–43.
———. *Zechariah 9–14 and Malachi: A Commentary*. OTL. Louisville: Westminster John Knox, 1995.
Peterson, David G. *The Acts of the Apostles*. PiNTC. Grand Rapids: Eerdmans, 2009.
Petterson, Anthony R. *Haggai, Zechariah and Malachi*. ApOTC 25. Downers Grove, IL: InterVarsity, 2015.
Pfaff, Heidi-Marie. *Die Entwicklung des Restgedankens in Jesaja 1–39*. Europäische Hochschulschriften 23/561. Frankfurt: Peter Lang, 1996.

Pitre, Brant. *Jesus, the Tribulation, and the End of the Exile: Restoration Eschatology and the Origin of the Atonement*. Grand Rapids: Baker Academic, 2005.
Poirier, John C. "The Endtime Return of Elijah and Moses at Qumran." *DSD* 10 (2003) 221–42.
———. "Jesus as an Elijianic Figure in Luke 4:16–30." *CBQ* 69 (2007) 350–63.
Pollard, Leslie N. *The Function of Loipos in Contexts of Judgment and Salvation in the Book of Revelation*. Berrien Springs, MI: Andrews University Press, 2007.
———. "The Function of ΛΟΙΠΟΣ in the Letter to Thyatira." *AUSS* 46 (2008) 45–63.
Poon, Wilson C. K. "Superabundant Table Fellowship in the Kingdom: The Feeding of the Five Thousand and the Meal Motif in Luke." *ExpTim* 114 (2003) 224–30.
Porter, Stanley E. "Allusions and Echoes." In *As It Is Written: Studying Paul's Use of Scripture*, edited by Stanley E. Porter and Christopher D. Stanley, 29–40. SBLSymS 50. Atlanta: Society of Biblical Literature, 2008.
———. "Mark 1.4, Baptism and Translation." In *Baptism, the New Testament and the Church: Historical and Contemporary Studies in honour of R. E. O. White*, edited by Stanley E. Porter and Anthony R. Cross, 81–98. JSNTSup 171. Sheffield: Sheffield Academic, 1999.
———. "The Use of the Old Testament in the New Testament: A Brief Comment on Method and Terminology." In *Early Christian Interpretation of the Scriptures of Israel: Investigations and Proposals*, edited by Craig A. Evans and James A. Sanders, 79–96. JSNTSup 148. Sheffield: Sheffield Academic, 1997.
Powell, Mark Allan. *What Is Narrative Criticism?* Guides to Biblical Scholarship. Minneapolis: Fortress, 1990.
Preuss, Horst Dietrich. *Old Testament Theology*. 2 vols. OTL. Louisville: Westminster John Knox, 1995.
Priest, J. "Testament of Moses (First Century A.D.) A New Translation and Introduction." In *Apocalyptic Literature and Testaments*, edited by James H. Charlesworth, 919–34. New Haven, CT: Yale University Press, 1983.
Proctor, Mark. "'After Three Days He Will Rise': The (Dis)appropriation of Hosea 6.2 in the Markan Passion Predictions." In *Biblical Interpretation in Early Christian Gospels 1: Gospel of Mark*, edited by Thomas R. Hatina, 131–50. LNTS 304. London: T. & T. Clark, 2006.
Propp, William H. *Exodus 19–40: A New Translation with Introduction and Commentary*. AB 2A. New York: Doubleday, 2006.
Puech, Émile. "Ben Sira 48:11 et la Résurrection." In *Of Scribes and Scrolls: Studies on the Hebrew Bible, Intertestamental Judaism, and Christian Origins, Presented to John Strugnell on the Occasion of His Sixtieth Birthday*, edited by Harold W. Attridge et al., 81–90. Lanham: University Press of America, 1990.
———. *La croyance des Esséniens en la vie future: Immortalité, résurrection, vie éternelle? Histoire d'une croyance dans le judaïsme ancien*. 2 vols. EBib 20–21. Paris: Gabalda, 1993.
———. "Une apocalypse messianique (4Q521)." *RevQ* 15 (1992) 475–522.
Pummer, Alfred. *A Critical and Exegetical Commentary on the Gospel according to S. Luke*. ICC. Edinburgh: T. & T. Clark, 1913.
Räisänen, Heikki. "The Redemption of Israel: A Salvation-Historical Problem in Luke-Acts." In *Challenges to Biblical Interpretation: Collected Essays, 1991–2000*, 61–84. Leiden: Brill, 2001.

Ramelli, Ilaria L. E. "Luke 16:16: The Good News of God's Kingdom Is Proclaimed and Everyone Is Forced into It." *JBL* 127 (2008) 737–58.

Ravens, David. *Luke and the Restoration of Israel*. JSNTSup 119. Sheffield: Sheffield Academic, 1995.

Redditt, Paul L., and Aaron Schart, eds. *Thematic Threads in the Book of the Twelve*. BZAW 325. Berlin: de Gruyter, 2003.

Reiser, Marius. *Jesus and Judgment: The Eschatological Proclamation in Its Jewish Context*. Translated by Linda M. Maloney. Minneapolis: Fortress, 1997.

Reiss, Moshe. "Elijah the Zealot: A Foil to Moses." *JBQ* 32 (2004) 174–80.

Renker, Alwin. *Die Tora bei Maleachi: ein Beitrag zur Dedeutungsgeschichte von Tora im Alten Testament*. Freiburger theologische Studien 112. Freiburg: Herder, 1979.

Rese, Martin. *Alttestamentliche Motive in der Christologie des Lukas*. SNT 1. Gütersloh: Gütersloher Verlagshaus, 1969.

Rice, Gene. "The Interpretation of Isaiah 7:15–17." *JBL* 96 (1977) 363–69.

———. *Nations under God: A Commentary on 1 Kings*. ITC. Grand Rapids: Eerdmans, 1990.

Rindoš, Jaroslav. *He of Whom It Is Written: John the Baptist and Elijah in Luke*. OBS 38. Frankfurt: Peter Lang, 2010.

Ringe, Sharon H. *Jesus, Liberation, and the Biblical Jubilee: Images for Ethics and Christology*. Eugene, OR: Wipf & Stock, 1985.

———. *Luke*. Westminster Bible Companion. Louisville: Westminster John Knox, 1995.

Robbins, Vernon K. "The Social Location of the Implied Author of Luke-Acts." In *The Social World of Luke-Acts: Models for Interpretation*, edited by Jerome H. Neyrey, 303–32. Peabody, MA: Hendrickson, 1991.

Robert, André. "Les attaches littéraires bibliques de Prov. I–IX." *RB* 43 (1934) 42–68.

———. "Littéraires (Genres)." In *Dictionnaire de la Bible. Supplément*, edited by Louis Pirot et al., 5:405–21. Paris: Letouzey et Ané, 1957.

Roberts, J. J. M. *First Isaiah: A Commentary*. Hermeneia. Minneapolis: Fortress, 2015.

Roberts, Kathryn L. "God, Prophet, and King: Eating and Drinking on the Mountain in First Kings 18:41." *CBQ* 62 (2000) 632–44.

Robertson, C. K. "Inheriting the Agitator's Mantle: Paul and the Nature of Apostleship in Luke-Acts." In *Jesus and Paul: Global Perspectives in honor of James D. G. Dunn for His 70th Birthday*, edited by B. J. Oropeza et al., 127–38. LNTS 414. New York: T. & T. Clark, 2009.

Robinson, Bernard P. "Elijah at Horeb, 1 Kings 19:1–18: A Coherent Narrative?" *RB* 98 (1991) 513–36.

Robinson, J. A. T. "Elijah, John and Jesus: An Essay in Detection." *NTS* 4 (1958) 263–81.

Robinson, William Childs. "Theological Context for Interpreting Luke's Travel Narrative." *JBL* 79 (1960) 20–31.

Roth, S. John. *The Blind, the Lame and the Poor: Character Types in Luke-Acts*. London: Bloomsbury, 1997.

Rowe, Christopher Kavin. *Early Narrative Christology: The Lord in the Gospel of Luke*. Grand Rapids: Baker Academic, 2006.

———. "Literary Unity and Reception History: Reading Luke-Acts as Luke and Acts." *JSNT* 29 (2007) 449–57.

———. *World Upside Down: Reading Acts in the Graeco-Roman Age*. Oxford: Oxford University Press, 2009.

Rowley, Harold H. "The Servant of the Lord in the Light of Three Decades of Criticism." In *The Servant of the Lord and Other Essays on the Old Testament*, 1–60. 2nd ed. Oxford: Blackwell, 1965.

Rusam, Dietrich. *Das Alte Testament bei Lukas*. BZNW 112. Berlin: de Gruyter, 2003.

Russell, Michael. "On the Third Day, according to the Scriptures." *RTR* 67 (2008) 1–17.

Salmon, Marilyn. "Insider or Outsider? Luke's Relationship with Judaism." In *Luke-Acts and the Jewish People: Eight Critical Perspectives*, edited by Joseph B. Tyson, 76–82. Minneapolis: Augsburg, 1988.

Sanders, E. P. *Jesus and Judaism*. Philadelphia: Fortress, 1985.

———. *Judaism: Practice and Belief, 63 BCE–66 CE*. Philadelphia: Trinity, 1992.

———. *Paul and Palestinian Judaism*. Philadelphia: Fortress, 1977.

———. *Paul, the Law, and the Jewish People*. Philadelphia: Fortress, 1983.

Sanders, Jack T. "The Jewish People in Luke-Acts." In *Luke-Acts and the Jewish People: Eight Critical Perspectives*, edited by Joseph B. Tyson, 51–75. Minneapolis: Augsburg, 1988.

———. *The Jews in Luke-Acts*. Philadelphia: Fortress, 1987.

Sanders, James A. "From Isaiah 61 to Luke 4." In *Christianity, Judaism and Other Greco-Roman Cults: Studies for Morton Smith at Sixty*, 1:75–107. SJLA 12. Leiden: Brill, 1975.

Schenker, Adrian. *The Septuagint in the Text History of 1–2 Kings*. Boston: Brill, 2010.

Schille, Gottfried. "Die Himmelfahrt." *ZNW* 57 (1966) 183–99.

Schlatter, Adolf. *Das Evangelium des Lukas*. Stuttgart: Calwer, 1960.

Schnabel, Eckhard J. *Early Christian Mission: Jesus and the Twelve*. Vol. 1. Downers Grove, IL: InterVarsity, 2004.

———. "Israel, the People of God, and the Nations." *JETS* 45 (2002) 35–57.

Schöpflin, Karin. "Naaman: Seine Heilung und Bekehrung im Alten und Neuen Testament." *BN* 141 (2009) 35–56.

Schreiner, Thomas R. *Romans*. BECNT. Grand Rapids: Baker, 1998.

Schürmann, Heinz. *Das Lukasevangelium*. HTKNT 3. Freiburg: Herder, 1969.

Schwemer, Anna Maria. "Lukas als Kenner der Septuaginta und die Rede des Stephanus (Apg 7,2–53)." In *Die Septuaginta und das frühe Christentum/The Septuagint and Christian Origins*, edited by Thomas Scott Caulley and Hermann Lichtenberger, 301–28. WUNT 277. Tübingen: Mohr Siebeck, 2011.

Segal, Samuel M. *Elijah: A Study in Jewish Folklore*. New York: Behrman's Jewish Book House, 1935.

Shauf, Scott. "Locating the Eunuch: Characterization and Narrative Context in Acts 8:26–40." *CBQ* 71 (2009) 762–75.

Shaw, David A. "Converted Imaginations? The Reception of Richard Hays's Intertextual Method." *CBR* 11 (2013) 234–45.

Sheinfeld, Shayna. "Who Is the Righteous Remnant in Romans 9–11? The Concept of Remnant in Early Jewish Literature and Paul's Letter to the Romans." In *Paul the Jew: Rereading the Apostle as a Figure of Second Temple Judaism*, edited by Gabriele Boccaccini and Carlos A. Segovia, 33–50. Minneapolis: Fortress, 2016.

Shelton, John. "The Healing of Naaman (2 Kgs 5.1–19) as a Central Component for the Healing of the Centurion's Slave (Luke 7.1–10)." In *The Elijah-Elisha Narrative in the Composition of Luke*, edited by John S. Kloppenborg and Joseph Verheyden, 65–87. LNTS 493. New York: T. & T. Clark, 2014.

Silva, Moisés. *Biblical Words and Their Meaning: An Introduction to Lexical Semantics.* Grand Rapids: Zondervan, 1983.

———. "ἐπίσκοπος." In *New International Dictionary of New Testament Theology and Exegesis,* 2:248–52. 2nd ed. Grand Rapids: Zondervan, 2014.

———. "λαός." In *New International Dictionary of New Testament Theology and Exegesis,* 3:88–93. 2nd ed. Grand Rapids: Zondervan, 2014.

———. "πτωχός." In *New International Dictionary of New Testament Theology and Exegesis,* 4:181–87. 2nd ed. Grand Rapids: Zondervan, 2014.

Skehan, Patrick W., and Alexander A. Di Leila. *The Wisdom of Ben Sira: A New Translation with Commentary and Notes.* AB 39. New York: Doubleday, 1987.

Sloan, Robert B., Jr. *The Favorable Year of the Lord: A Study of Jubilary Theology in the Gospel of Luke.* Austin, TX: Schola, 1977.

Smith, Abraham. "'Do You Understand What You Are Reading?' A Literary Critical Reading of the Ethiopian (Kushite) Episode (Acts 8:26–40)." *JITC* 22 (1994) 48–70.

Smith, Dennis E. "The Messianic Banquet Reconsidered." In *The Future of Christianity: Essays in honor of Helmut Koester,* edited by Birger A. Pearson, 64–73. Minneapolis: Fortress, 1991.

———. "Table Fellowship as a Literary Motif in the Gospel of Luke." *JBL* 106 (1987) 613–38.

Smith, Gary V. *Isaiah 1–39.* New American Commentary 15A. Nashville: B&H, 2007.

Smith, Ralph L. *Micah–Malachi.* WBC 32. Waco, TX: Word, 1982.

Snodgrass, Klyne. "Streams of Tradition Emerging from Isaiah 40:1–5 and Their Adaptation in the New Testament." *JSNT* 8 (1980) 24–45.

Snyman, S. D. "Once Again: Investigating the Identity of the Three Figures Mentioned in Malachi 3:1." *Verbum Et Ecclesia* 27 (2006) 1031–44.

Stanley, Christopher D. "The Significance of Romans 11:3–4 for the Text History of the LXX Book of Kingdoms." *JBL* 112 (1993) 43–54.

Stegemann, Ursula. "Der Restgedanke bei Isaias." *BZ* 13 (1969) 161–86.

Stendahl, Krister. *Paul among Jews and Gentiles and Other Essays.* Philadelphia: Fortress, 1976.

Stein, Robert H. *Luke.* NAC 24. Nashville: Broadman, 1992.

Steyn, Gert J. "Luke's Use of ΜΙΜΗΣΙΣ? Re-opening the Debate." In *The Scriptures in the Gospels,* edited by C. M. Tuckett, 551–57. Leuven: Leuven University Press, 1997.

———. *Septuagint Quotations in the Context of the Petrine and Pauline Speeches in Acta Apostolorum.* Biblical Exegesis and Theology 12. Kampen: Kok Pharos, 1995.

Stipp, Hermann-Josef. "Vier Gestalten einer Totenerweckungserzählung (1 Kön 17,17–24; 2 Kön 4,8–37; Apg 9,36–42; Apg 20,7–12)." *Bib* 80 (1999) 43–77.

Stockhausen, Carol L. "Luke's Stories of the Ascension: The Background and Function of a Dual Narrative." *PEGLMBS* 10 (1990) 251–63.

Stone, Michael Edward. *Fourth Ezra: A Commentary on the Book of Fourth Ezra.* Hermeneia. Minneapolis: Fortress, 1990.

Strauss, Mark. *The Davidic Messiah in Luke-Acts: The Promise and Its Fulfilment in Lukan Christology.* LNTS. Sheffield: Sheffield Academic Press, 1995.

Strelan, Rick. "The Running Prophet (Acts 8:30)." *NovT* 43 (2001) 31–38.

Stuart, Douglas K. "David's 'Lamp' (1 Kings 11:36) and 'a Still Small Voice' (1 Kings 19:12)." *BSac* 171 (2014) 3–18.

———. *Hosea-Jonah*. WBC 31. Waco, TX: Word, 1987.
———. "Malachi." In *The Minor Prophets: An Exegetical and Expository Commentary*, edited by Thomas Edward McComiskey, 3:1245–396. Grand Rapids: Baker Academic, 1992.
Sweeney, Marvin A. *I and II Kings: A Commentary*. OTL. Louisville: Westminster John Knox, 2007.
———. "A Form-Critical Reassessment of the Book of Zephaniah." *CBQ* 53 (1991) 388–408.
———. "Sequence and Interpretation in the Book of the Twelve." In *Reading and Hearing the Book of the Twelve*, edited by James D. Nogalski and Marvin A. Sweeney, 49–64. SBLSymS 15. Atlanta: Society of Biblical Literature, 2000.
———. *The Twelve Prophets*. Vol. 2. Berit Olam. Collegeville, MN: Liturgical, 2000.
———. "Zephaniah: A Paradigm for the Study of the Prophetic Books." *CurBS* 7 (1999) 119–45.
Syrèn, Roger. *The Blessings in the Targums: A Study on the Targumic Interpretations of Genesis 49 and Deuteronomy 33*. Acta Academiae Aboensis, Ser. A 64/1. Åbo: Åbo Akademi, 1986.
Tabor, James D. "'Returning to the Divinity': Josephus's Portrayal of the Disappearances of Enoch, Elijah, and Moses." *JBL* 108 (1989) 225–38.
Tannehill, Robert C. "'Cornelius' and 'Tabitha' Encounter Luke's Jesus." *Int* 48 (1994) 347–56.
———. "Israel in Luke-Acts: A Tragic Story." *JBL* 104 (1985) 69–85.
———. *Luke*. Abingdon New Testament Commentaries. Nashville: Abingdon, 1996.
———. *The Narrative Unity of Luke-Acts: A Literary Interpretation*. 2 vols. Fortress, 1986.
———. "Rejection by Jews and Turning to Gentiles: The Pattern of Paul's Mission in Acts." In *Luke-Acts and the Jewish People: Eight Critical Perspectives*, edited by Joseph B. Tyson, 83–101. Minneapolis: Augsburg, 1988.
———. "What Kind of King? What Kind of Kingdom? A Study of Luke." *WW* 12 (1992) 17–21.
Taylor, Joan E. *The Immerser: John the Baptist within Second Temple Judaism*. Studying the Historical Jesus. Grand Rapids: Eerdmans, 1997.
Thiel, Winfried. "'Es ist genug!': Untersuchungen zu I Reg 19,4b." *ZAW* 119 (2007) 201–16.
Thompson, Alan J. *The Acts of the Risen Lord Jesus: Luke's Account of God's Unfolding Plan*. New Studies in Biblical Theology 27. Downers Grove, IL: InterVarsity, 2011.
Thompson, Andrew. "Parallel Composition and Rhetorical Effect in Luke 7 and 8." *JSNT* 38 (2015) 169–90.
Tiede, David L. "Acts 1:6–8 and the Theo-Political Claims of Christian Witness." *WW* 1 (1981) 41–51.
———. "The Exaltation of Jesus and the Restoration of Israel in Acts 1." *HTR* 79 (1986) 278–86.
———. "'Glory to Thy People Israel': Luke-Acts and the Jews." In *Luke-Acts and the Jewish People: Eight Critical Perspectives*, edited by Joseph B. Tyson, 21–34. Minneapolis: Augsburg, 1988.
———. *Prophecy and History in Luke-Acts*. Philadelphia: Fortress, 1980.
Tiller, Patrick A. *A Commentary on the Animal Apocalypse of I Enoch*. SBLEJL 4. Atlanta: Scholars, 1993.

Treier, Daniel J. "The Fulfillment of Joel 2:28–32: A Multiple-Lens Approach." *JETS* 40 (1997) 13–26.

———. "Typology." In *Dictionary for Theological Interpretation of the Bible*, edited by Kevin J. Vanhoozer, 823–27. Grand Rapids: Baker, 2005.

Trémel, Bernard. "À propos d'Actes 20:7–12: Puissance du thaumaturge ou du témoin?" *RTP* 112 (1980) 359–69.

Trumblower, Jeffrey A. "The Role of Malachi in the Career of John the Baptist." In *The Gospels and the Scriptures of Israel*, edited by Craig A. Evans and W. Richard Stegner, 28–41. JSNTSup 104. Sheffield: Sheffield Academic, 1994.

Turner, Max. *Power from on High: The Spirit in Israel's Restoration and Witness in Luke-Acts*. Journal of Pentecostal Theology Supplement Series 9. Sheffield: Sheffield Academic, 1996.

Tyson, Joseph B., ed. *Luke-Acts and the Jewish People: Eight Critical Perspectives*. Minneapolis: Augsburg, 1988.

———. "The Problem of Jewish Rejection in Acts." In *Luke-Acts and the Jewish People: Eight Critical Perspectives*, edited by Joseph B. Tyson, 124–37. Minneapolis: Augsburg, 1988.

———. "Torah and Prophets in Luke-Acts: Temporary or Permanent?" In *SBLSP* 31 (1992) 539–48.

Uhlig, Torsten. "Too Hard to Understand? The Motif of Hardening in Isaiah." In *Interpreting Isaiah: Issues and Approaches*, edited by David G. Firth and H. G. M. Williamson, 62–83. Downers Grove, IL: IVP Academic, 2009.

VanderKam, James C. "Open and Closed Eyes in the Animal Apocalypse (1 Enoch 85–90)." In *The Idea of Biblical Interpretation: Essays in Honor of James L. Kugel*, 279–92. Leiden: Brill, 2004.

———. "Studies in the Apocalypse of Weeks (1 Enoch 93:1–10, 91:11–17)." *CBQ* 46 (1984) 511–23.

Vena, Osvaldo D. "Paul's Understanding of the Eschatological Prophet of Malachi 4:5–6." *BR* 44 (1999) 35–54.

Venema, Cornelius P. "'In This Way, All Israel Will Be Saved': A Study of Romans 11:26." *MAJT* 22 (2011) 19–40.

Verheyden, Joseph. "By Way of Epilogue: Looking Back at the Healing of Naaman and the Healing of the Centurion's Slave—in Response to John Shelton." In *The Elijah-Elisha Narrative in the Composition of Luke*, edited by John S. Kloppenborg and Joseph Verheyden, 153–60. LNTS 493. New York: T. & T. Clark, 2014.

———. "How Many Were Sent according to Lk 10,1?" In *Luke and His Readers: Festschrift A. Denaux*, edited by Reimund Bieringer, Gilbert Van Belle, and Joseph Verheyden, 193–238. BETL 182. Leuven: Leuven University Press, 2005.

———. *The Unity of Luke-Acts*. BETL 142. Leuven: Leuven University Press, 1999.

———. "The Unity of Luke-Acts: What Are We Up To?" In *The Unity of Luke-Acts*, edited by Joseph Verheyden, 3–56. BETL 142. Leuven: Leuven University Press, 1999.

Verhoef, Pieter A. *The Books of Haggai and Malachi*. NICOT. Grand Rapids: Eerdmans, 1987.

von Rad, Gerhard. *Old Testament Theology: The Theology of Israel's Historical Traditions*. Translated by D. M. G. Stalker. Vol. 1. OTL. Louisville: Westminster John Knox, 2001.

———. *Old Testament Theology: The Theology of Israel's Prophetic Traditions*. Translated by D. M. G. Stalker. Vol. 2. New York: Harper & Row, 1965.

Wagner, J. Ross. *Heralds of the Good News: Isaiah and Paul in Concert in the Letter to the Romans*. NovTSup 101. Leiden: Brill.
Wainwright, Arthur W. "Luke and the Restoration of the Kingdom to Israel." *ExpTim* 89 (1977) 76–79.
Wall, Robert W. "Peter, 'Son' of Jonah: The Conversion of Cornelius in the Context of Canon." *JSNT* 29 (1987) 79–90.
Walsh, Jerome. *1 Kings*. Berit Olam. Collegeville, MN: Liturgical, 1996.
Warne, Donald M. "The Origin, Development and Significance of the Concept of the Remnant in the Old Testament." PhD diss., University of Edinburgh, 1958.
Watts, James W. "The Remnant Theme: A Survey of New Testament Research, 1921–1987." *PRSt* 15 (1988) 109–29.
Watts, John D. W. "A Frame for the Book of the Twelve: Hosea 1–3 and Malachi." In *Reading and Hearing the Book of the Twelve*, edited by James D. Nogalski and Marvin A. Sweeney, 209–17. SBLSymS 15. Atlanta: Society of Biblical Literature, 2000.
———. *Isaiah*. 2 vols. Rev. ed. WBC 24. Nashville: Thomas Nelson, 2005.
Watts, Rikki E. *Isaiah's New Exodus in Mark*. Grand Rapids: Baker Academic, 2000.
Watts, Rikki E., et al. "Isaiah in the New Testament." In *Interpreting Isaiah: Issues and Approaches*, 213–33. Downers Grove, IL: IVP Academic, 2009.
Weatherly, Jon A. "Eating and Drinking in the Kingdom of God: The Emmaus Episode and the Meal Motif in Luke-Acts." In *Christ's Victorious Church: Essays on Biblical Ecclesiology and Eschatology in Honor of Tom Friskney*, 18–32. Eugene, OR: Wipf & Stock, 2001.
Webb, Robert L. *John the Baptizer and Prophet: A Socio-Historical Study*. JSNTSup 62. Sheffield: Sheffield Academic, 1991.
Wenham, Gordon J. *Genesis*. 2 Vols. WBC. Waco, TX: Word, 1987–1994.
Westermann, Claus. *Isaiah 40–66: A Commentary*. OTL. Philadelphia: Westminster, 1969.
Widmer, Michael. *Moses, God, and the Dynamics of Intercessory Prayer: A Study of Exodus 32–34 and Numbers 13–14*. FAT 2/8. Tübingen: Mohr Siebeck, 2004.
Wifstrand, Albert. "Luke and the Septuagint." In *Epochs and Styles: Selected Writings on the New Testament, Greek Language, and Greek Culture in the Post-Classical Era*, edited by Lars Rydbeck and Stanley E. Porter, 28–45. WUNT 179. Tübingen: Mohr Siebeck, 2005.
Wijngaards, J. "Death and Resurrection in Covenantal Context Hos 6:2." *VT* 17 (1967) 226–39.
Wilcox, Peter, and David Paton-Williams. "The Servant Songs in Deutero-Isaiah." *JSOT* 42 (1988) 79–102.
Wildberger, Hans. *Isaiah: A Commentary*. Translated by Thomas H. Trapp. 3 vols. Continental Commentary. Minneapolis: Fortress, 1991–2002.
Wink, Walter. *John the Baptist in the Gospel Tradition*. SNTSMS 7. London: Cambridge University Press, 1968.
Winn, Adam. *Mark and the Elijah-Elisha Narrative: Considering the Practice of Greco-Roman Imitation in the Search for Markan Source Material*. Eugene, OR: Pickwick, 2015.
Wintermute, O. S. "Apocalypse of Elijah (First to Fourth Century A.D.) A New Translation and Introduction." In *OTP*, edited by James H. Charlesworth, 1:722–54. New York: Doubleday, 1983.

Witherington, Ben, III. *The Acts of the Apostles: A Socio-Rhetorical Commentary.* Grand Rapids: Eerdmans, 1998.

Witherup, Ronald D. "Cornelius Over and Over and Over Again: 'Functional Redundancy' in the Acts of the Apostles." *JSNT* 15 (1993) 45–66.

———. "Functional Redundancy in the Acts of the Apostles: A Case Study." *JSNT* 48 (1992) 67–86.

Wold, Benjamin. "Agency and Raising the Dead in 4QPseudo-Ezekiel and 4Q521 2 ii." *ZNW* 103 (2012) 1–19.

Wolff, Hans Walter. *Haggai: A Commentary.* Translated by Margaret Kohl. Minneapolis: Augsburg, 1988.

———. *Hosea: A Commentary on the Book of the Prophet Hosea.* Translated by Paul D. Hanson. Hermeneia. Philadelphia: Fortress, 1974.

———. *Micha.* BKAT XIV/12. Neukirchen-Vluyn: Neukirchener, 1980.

Wolter, Michael. *Das Lukasevangelium.* HNT 5. Tübingen: Mohr Siebeck, 2008.

———. "Israel's Future and the Delay of the Parousia, according to Luke." In *Jesus and the Heritage of Israel: Luke's Narrative Claim upon Israel's Legacy,* edited by David P. Moessner, 307–24. Luke the Interpreter of Israel 1. Harrisburg, PA: Trinity, 1999.

Wong, Daniel K. "The Two Witnesses in Revelation 11." *BSac* 154 (1997) 344–54.

Wray Beal, Lissa M. *1 and 2 Kings.* ApOTC 9. Downers Grove, IL: InterVarsity, 2014.

Wright, Addison G. "Literary Genre Midrash." *CBQ* 28 (1966) 105–38.

———. "Literary Genre Midrash (Part Two)." *CBQ* 28 (1966) 417–57.

Wright, Benjamin G., III. "'Put the Nations in Fear of You': Ben Sira and the Problem of Foreign Rule." In *Praise Israel for Wisdom and Instruction: Essays on Ben Sira and Wisdom, the Letter of Aristeas and the Septuagint,* 127–46. JSJSup 131. Boston: Brill, 2008.

Wright, N. T. *Paul and the Faithfulness of God.* Christian Origins and the Question of God 4. Minneapolis: Fortress, 2013.

Wyatt, Stephanie. "Jezebel, Elijah, and the Widow of Zarephath: A Ménage à Trois That Estranges the Holy and Makes the Holy the Strange." *JSOT* 36 (2012) 435–58.

Xeravits, Géza G. *King, Priest, Prophet: Positive Eschatological Protagonists of the Qumran Library.* Studies on the Texts of the Desert of Judah 47. Boston: Brill, 2003.

———. "Some Remarks on the Figure of Elijah in Lives of the Prophets 21:1–3." In *Flores Florentino: Dead Sea Scrolls and Other Early Jewish Studies in Honour of Florentino García Martínez,* edited by Anthony Hilhorst, Emile Puech, and Eibert J. C. Tigchelaar, 499–508. JSJSup 122. Leiden: Brill, 2007.

York, Anthony D. "The Dating of Targumic Literature." *JSJ* 5 (1974) 49–62.

Zeller, Dieter. "Die Bildlogik des Gleichnisses Mt 11,16f/Lk 7,31f." *ZNW* 68 (1977) 252–57.

———. *Juden und Heiden in der Mission des Paulus: Studien zum Römerbrief.* FB 1. Stuttgart: Katholisches Bibelwerk, 1973.

Zeller, Johannes. *Der Brief an die Römer.* Göttingen: Vandenhoeck & Ruprecht, 1989.

Zoccali, Christopher. "'And So All Israel Will Be Saved': Competing Interpretations of Romans 11.26 in Pauline Scholarship." *JSNT* 30 (2008) 289–318.

Zwiep, A. W. *The Ascension of the Messiah in Lukan Christology.* NovTSup 87. Leiden: Brill, 1997.

Author Index

Acosta Valle, Martha Milagros, 147, 149, 153
Ådna, Jostein, 154
Albertz, Rainer, 103, 104
Alexander, Loveday, 12
Allison, Dale C., 13, 119
Alter, Robert, 6, 7
Andersen, Francis I., 126
Assis, Elie, 45, 49
Attridge, Harold W., 65
Aune, David E., 67, 68
Baker, Murray, 64
Bakon, Shimon, 47
Baldick, Chris, 6
Bammel, E., 103, 104
Barr, James, 16
Barrett, C. K., 131, 132, 143, 144, 145, 146, 147, 148, 149, 152, 154, 156, 157, 158
Barth, Markus, 64
Bascom, Robert A., 46, 81, 82
Bauckham, Richard, 54, 56, 67, 68, 69, 77, 88, 128, 133, 136, 153, 154
Beale, G. K., 2, 13, 14, 20, 21, 67, 68, 90
Beentjes, Pancratius C., 52, 53
Beers, Holly, 22, 135, 136
Beetham, Christopher A., 13, 14
Beker, J., 13
Bell, Richard, 64
Beyer, H. W., 113
Bird, Michael F., 12
Blair, Hugh J., 121

Blenkinsopp, Joseph, 20, 21, 22, 99, 136
Block, Daniel I., 23
Bock, Darrell L., 2, 4, 71, 73, 74, 75, 76, 77, 79, 81, 82, 84, 85, 86, 87, 88, 89, 91, 92, 93, 94, 98, 99, 109, 110, 111, 112, 113, 115, 116, 117, 118, 120, 121, 122, 123, 124, 125, 126, 128, 129, 130, 135, 136, 140, 142, 143, 144, 145, 147, 148, 152, 153, 154, 156, 158, 165
Böhm, Martina, 124
Booth, Wayne C., 39
Bovon, François, 13, 73, 75, 76, 77, 78, 84, 86, 88, 89, 93, 94, 95, 98, 104, 109, 111, 113, 114, 115, 118, 119, 120, 121, 127, 129, 141, 148
Brawley, Robert L., 10
Brink, Laurie, 87, 108
Brodie, Thomas L., 4, 5, 97, 108, 118, 119, 120, 130, 131, 132, 140, 144, 145
Brown, Colin, 85, 86, 87
Brown, Raymond E., 3, 90, 109
Bruce, F. F., 65, 135, 152, 158
Brueggemann, Walter, 23, 105, 106
Bruners, Wilhelm, 130
Bruno, Christopher R., 104, 105, 106
Bryan, Steven M., 26
Burnett, Clint, 73, 80, 85
Butticaz, Simon, 11, 167
Cadbury, Henry J., 12
Campbell, William S., 63, 64

AUTHOR INDEX

Carena, Omar, 17, 18, 24, 104
Carlson, R. A., 36, 37, 43, 44, 72, 99
Carroll, John T., 77, 79, 83, 90
Charlesworth, James H., 58, 60
Childs, Brevard S., 20, 21, 22, 35, 37, 40, 41, 43, 45, 49, 54, 88, 104, 135, 136
Chilton, Bruce, 60, 64
Clark, D. G., 4, 56
Clarke, Ernest G., 60
Clarke, William K. L., 13
Clements, Ronald E., 21
Cogan, Mordechai, 31, 32, 33, 35, 36, 37, 39, 41, 67, 109, 121
Collins, John J., 56, 99, 100, 104, 106
Conzelmann, Hans, 2, 3, 71, 78, 83, 92, 114, 134
Cook, Michael J., 9
Cotter, Wendy J., 94
Croatto, J. Severino, 4
Crockett, Larrimore C., 149
Cross, Frank Moore, 41
Cuany, Monique, 101
Dabeck, P., 109, 110, 118
Danker, Frederick W., 44, 79, 80, 83, 87, 90, 92, 99, 101, 114, 116, 119, 120, 121, 123, 128, 129, 140, 141
Darr, John A., 79, 80, 83, 115, 123
Davids, Peter H., 66
Davidson, Richard M., 2
de Jonge, Marinus, 106, 131
Dearman, J. Andrew, 126
Dempster, Stephen, 126
Denova, Rebecca I., 5
DeVries, Simon J., 33, 34, 36, 40, 121
DeYoung, James B., 82
Dharamraj, Havilah, 31, 32, 33, 35, 37, 38, 40, 41, 56
Di Leila, Alexander A., 53, 54
Dibelius, Martin, 66
Dochhorn, Jan, 119, 141
Dozeman, Thomas B., 37
Duhaime, Jean, 56
Dunn, James D. G., 62, 63, 64, 80, 81, 85, 86, 88, 143, 144, 146, 148, 151, 156, 158
Dupont, Jacques, 126

Edwards, Calvin R., 7
Edwards, James R., 115, 116, 118, 124, 129, 130
Elliott, Mark Adam, 26, 38, 60
Emadi, Samuel, 13
Ernst, Josef, 71
Evans, C. A., 5, 6, 21, 98, 99, 101, 109, 119, 123, 129
Evans, C. F., 118
Everson, Joseph A., 47
Faierstein, Morris M., 57, 59
Feldman, Ariel, 57
Fitzmyer, Joseph A., 3, 13, 57, 63, 71, 72, 73, 75, 78, 79, 81, 82, 83, 84, 86, 87, 88, 89, 90, 91, 92, 93, 94, 98, 99, 101, 105, 109, 110, 111, 112, 114, 115, 116, 117, 118, 119, 120, 121, 123, 124, 126, 129, 130, 131, 135, 136, 140, 141, 142, 143, 144, 147, 148, 149, 151, 152, 153, 156, 157, 159
Flesher, Paul V. M., 60
Frankfurter, David, 60, 148
Freedman, David Noel, 126
Fretheim, Terence E., 32, 34, 41, 44, 106, 121
Fuller, Michael E., 86
Fusco, Vittorio, 10
Gagnon, Robert A. J., 108, 109
García Martínez, Florentino, 55
Garsiel, Moshe, 31, 32, 33, 35, 37, 39, 41
Gathercole, Simon, 77
Gerleman, Gillis, 16, 18
Ginzberg, Louis, 1
Glavic, Julie A., 156, 157, 158
Glazier-McDonald, Beth, 45, 46, 48, 49, 81, 82
Glenny, W. Edward, 154
Glover, Neil, 31, 39
Goldingay, John, 22, 135, 136
Gorman, Michael J., 64
Gosse, Bernard, 21
Graham, Pat, 7, 21
Gray, John, 42, 121
Green, Joel B., 12, 72, 73, 75, 77, 79, 80, 81, 83, 84, 85, 86, 87,

88, 90, 91, 92, 93, 94, 95, 98,
101, 103, 104, 105, 108, 109,
110, 111, 112, 113, 114, 115,
117, 120, 122, 123, 124, 125,
127, 141, 142
Green, William Scott, 13
Gregory, Russell, 12, 31, 35, 36, 39,
41, 104, 105, 106
Haag, Herbert, 22
Haenchen, Ernst, 9, 10
Hafemann, Scott, 62, 63, 64
Harmon, William, 6
Hasel, Gerhard, 16, 17, 18, 19, 20,
21, 23, 24, 25, 31, 32, 36,
44, 127
Hauck, F., 103
Hauser, Alan J., 39
Hausmann, Jutta, 16, 18, 23, 43, 146
Hays, J. Daniel, 103
Hays, Richard B., 13, 14, 90, 145
Heil, John Paul, 116, 125
Herntrich, Volkmar Martinus, 16
Hill, Andrew E., 45, 46, 48, 49, 81,
82
Hobbs, T. R., 106
Hoffmann, Yair, 47
Holtz, Gundrum, 110, 112
Holtz, Traugott, 13
Horne, Charles M., 64
Horsley, Richard A., 59, 86
House, Paul R., 23, 41, 47
Huebsch, Robert William, 25, 26, 37
Ishai-Rosenboim, Daniella, 47
Iwry, Samuel, 20
Jacob, Edmond, 104
Janes, Regina, 79
Japhet, Sara, 18, 24
Jellicoe, Sidney, 130
Jeremias, Joachim, 20, 44, 88, 104
Jervell, Jacob, 10, 154
Jewett, Robert, 62, 63
Johnson, Dan G., 62, 64
Johnson, Luke Timothy, 66
Jones, Barry, 23, 45, 48
Jost, François, 6
Juncker, Günther H., 46, 77, 82
Jung, Chang-Wook, 72
Kaiser, Walter C., 4

Karrer, Martin, 136
Käseman, Ernst, 62
Keener, Craig S., 11, 132, 133, 134,
135, 136, 141, 143, 144, 145,
146, 147, 148, 149, 151, 152,
153, 154, 156, 157, 158
Kessler, Rainer, 45, 46, 47, 48, 49, 82
Kiddle, Martin, 68
Kistemaker, Simon J., 145
Klassen, William, 142
Kleger, Roland, 21
Kline, Meredith G., 21
Kloppenborg, John S., 5
Knibb, M. A., 60
Knight, George A., 22, 136
Koester, Craig R., 67, 68, 69
Koet, Bart J., 48, 51, 53
Kolasny, Judette M., 149
Kowalski, Beate, 155, 156, 157, 159
Kurz, William S., 73
Kvalbein, Hans, 56, 104
Ladd, George Eldon, 68
Lane, William L., 65
Leithart, Peter J., 33, 35, 36, 40, 41
Lévêque, Jean, 52, 53, 54, 55, 136
Levin, Harry, 7
Lim, Bo H., 23
Litwak, Kenneth Duncan, 5, 131
Lohfink, Gerhard, 10, 131
Longenecker, Bruce W., 60
Lucas, Alec J., 13
Luz, Ulrich, 83, 92, 94
Macintosh, A. A., 126
Maile, John F., 131
Malchow, Bruce V., 45, 46
Marcus, Joel, 82, 86
Marguerat, Daniel, 9, 10, 11, 12
Marshall, I. Howard, 3, 4, 10, 12,
13, 71, 72, 73, 75, 76, 77, 79,
81, 82, 83, 84, 86, 87, 88, 89,
90, 91, 92, 93, 94, 95, 98, 99,
100, 101, 102, 109, 110, 114,
115, 116, 117, 118, 119, 120,
122, 123, 124, 125, 126, 128,
129, 130, 132, 134, 135, 140,
141, 142, 143, 144, 146, 148,
149, 153, 154
Martin, James D., 54

Maston, Jason, 134, 135
Matera, Frank J., 133, 134, 151
Mays, James Luther, 24
McCartney, Dan G., 66
McDonough, Sean M., 67
McLean, John A., 134, 135
McNicol, Allan J., 68
Meinhold, Arndt, 45, 46, 48, 49
Metzger, Bruce M., 91, 130
Metzger, Wolfgang, 21
Meyer, Ben F., 104, 142
Meyer, Rudolf, 60
Meyers, Carol L., 24
Meyers, Eric M., 24
Miller, Chris A., 153
Miller, David M., 4, 53, 56, 80, 81
Miller, R. J., 71, 73, 81, 82, 92, 119
Minear, Paul S., 3
Moberly, R. W. L., 43
Moessner, David P., 7, 10, 11, 95, 114, 136
Moo, Douglas J., 62, 63, 64, 66
Motyer, J. Alec, 54, 55, 104
Mounce, Robert H., 67, 68
Müller, Christoph Gregor, 3, 71, 72, 76, 78, 83, 85, 87, 91, 109, 140
Müller, Werner E., 17, 18, 23, 24, 30, 31, 104
Munck, Johannes, 62, 63, 64, 135
Myers, Jacob M., 60
Nelson, Neil D., 94
Nelson, Richard D., 31, 35, 36, 39
Nickelsburg, George W. E., 58, 59
Niehaus, Jeffrey J., 37, 40, 41
Nogalski, James D., 47, 48
Nolland, John, 5, 73, 79, 84, 85, 86, 87, 90, 91, 92, 93, 94, 98, 99, 101, 102, 105, 109, 110, 111, 113, 116, 117, 118, 119, 122, 123, 124, 125, 126, 128, 129, 130, 131, 140, 141, 142
North, Christopher R., 22
O'Hagan, Angelo, 140, 141
Öhler, Markus, 5, 35, 54, 57, 59, 60, 61, 63, 65, 66, 67, 69, 72, 80, 81, 82, 86, 92, 99, 114, 115, 117, 118, 119, 121, 132, 140, 148, 156
Olson, Daniel C., 58, 59
Osborne, Grant, 67, 68, 69
Oswalt, John N., 20, 21, 22, 82, 88, 103, 104, 107, 135
O'Toole, Robert F., 114, 143, 145
Otten, Jeremy D., 120
Pao, David W., 7, 11, 22, 46, 73, 76, 77, 81, 82, 86, 87, 88, 92, 98, 99, 105, 108, 109, 112, 115, 119, 120, 123, 125, 129, 130, 134, 135, 136, 140, 142, 143, 146, 147, 149, 150, 151, 153, 154, 157
Parsons, Mikeal C., 12, 131, 132, 143, 146
Paton-Williams, David, 54
Payne, David, 22, 135, 136
Pervo, Richard I., 10, 12, 131, 132, 135, 143, 144, 145, 146, 147, 149, 154, 156, 157, 159
Petersen, David L., 45, 46, 48
Peterson, David G., 134, 135, 136, 146
Petterson, Anthony R., 45, 46, 48, 81, 82
Pfaff, Heidi-Marie, 20, 21, 55
Plummer, Alfred, 75, 124
Poirier, John C., 35, 56, 99, 100
Pollard, Leslie N., 67, 68
Poon, Wilson C. K., 7
Porter, Stanley E., 13, 87
Powell, Mark Allan, 12
Preuss, Horst Dietrich, 22
Proctor, Mark, 126
Propp, William H., 37
Puech, Émile, 54, 56, 100
Räisänen, Heikki, 9
Ravens, David, 133, 150
Reiss, Moshe, 35, 39
Rese, Martin, 13
Rice, Gene, 21, 41
Ridderbos, Herman, 64
Rindoš, Jaroslav, 3, 71, 73, 75, 77, 79, 80, 81, 84, 85, 86, 88, 91
Ringe, Sharon H., 98, 101, 105, 108
Robbins, Vernon K., 1

Robert, André, 5
Roberts, J. J. M., 21
Roberts, Kathryn L., 33, 34, 42
Robinson, Bernard P., 36
Robinson, J. A. T., 3, 81
Rowe, Christopher Kavin, 3, 12, 73, 81, 83, 86, 91, 110, 117, 119, 124
Rowley, Harold H., 22
Russell, Michael, 126
Sanders, E. P., 25, 26, 27
Sanders, Jack T., 9, 10, 98, 101, 103
Sanders, James A., 101
Schille, Gottfried, 131
Schnabel, Eckhard J., 73, 77, 81, 86, 88, 92, 99, 105, 108, 109, 112, 115, 119, 120, 123, 125, 129, 130, 140, 142, 149
Schöpfin, Karin, 106, 144, 145
Schrenk, Gottlob, 16
Schürmann, Heinz, 79, 115, 116, 123, 124, 125, 126, 128
Shauf, Scott, 143, 144, 145
Shaw, David A., 13
Shelton, John, 107, 108, 149
Silva, Moisés, 16, 103, 104, 113
Skehan, Patrick W., 53, 54
Sloan, Robert B., Jr., 101, 105
Smith, Abraham, 143, 144, 145
Smith, Dennis E., 7
Smith, Gary V., 21
Smith, Ralph L., 24, 45, 46, 48, 146
Snodgrass, Klyne, 73, 74, 77, 81, 82
Snyman, S. D., 45, 46
Stanley, Christopher D., 43
Stegemann, Ursula, 18, 20, 21
Stein, Robert H., 98, 101, 115, 118, 124, 129, 140
Stendahl, Krister, 64
Stipp, Hermann-Josef, 148, 149, 155, 156, 157, 159
Stockhausen, Carol L., 131, 132, 133, 144, 153
Stone, Michael Edward, 60
Strauss, Mark, 11
Strelan, Rick, 143, 144
Stuart, Douglas K., 48

Sweeney, Marvin A., 31, 32, 36, 40, 45, 48, 49, 146
Syrèn, Roger, 60, 61
Tadmor, Hayim, 67
Tannehill, Robert C., 1, 10, 11, 12, 38, 76, 89, 98, 101, 102, 105, 108, 109, 110, 112, 113, 115, 117, 118, 119, 121, 123, 124, 128, 129, 131, 133, 136, 140, 143, 144, 147, 148, 150, 152, 153, 157, 158, 159, 167
Taylor, Joan E., 84, 87
Thiel, Winfried, 35, 36, 37
Tiede, David L., 10, 97, 134, 135
Tigchelaar, Eibert J. C., 55
Tiller, Patrick A., 58, 59, 60
Treier, Daniel J., 2, 153
Trémel, Bernard, 156
Trumblower, Jeffrey A., 80, 81, 83, 84, 86
Turner, Max, 81, 85, 133, 134
Tyson, Joseph B., 9
van der Woude, Adam S., 106
VanderKam, James C., 59
Verheyden, Joseph, 5, 12, 108, 130
Verhoef, Pieter, 46, 48, 49
von Rad, Gerhard, 20, 32, 36, 41, 44
Wainwright, Arthur W., 133
Wall, Robert W., 149
Walsh, Jerome, 31, 33, 34, 36, 37, 39, 41, 42
Watts, James W., 25, 67
Watts, John D. W., 21
Watts, Rikki E., 82
Weatherly, Jon A., 7
Webb, Robert L., 79, 83, 84, 85, 86, 87
Westermann, Claus, 22, 82, 104
Wifstrand, Albert, 72
Wilcox, Peter, 54
Wildberger, Hans, 20, 21, 22
Wink, Walter, 2, 3, 5, 71, 72, 73, 77, 78, 90, 91, 92, 119
Wintermute, O. S., 148
Witherington, Ben, III, 144, 150, 153
Witherup, Ronald D., 147, 151, 153
Wold, Benjamin, 56

Wolff, Hans Walter, 24, 126
Wolter, Michael, 118, 122, 133
Wong, Daniel K., 67
Wray Beal, Lissa M., 31, 33, 34, 39, 41, 121
Wright, Addison G., 5
Wright, Benjamin G., III, 52
Wright, N. T., 62
Xeravits, Géza G., 56, 57
York, Anthony D., 60
Zeller, Dieter, 94
Zoccali, Christopher, 64
Zwiep, A. W., 118, 131

Scripture Index

OLD TESTAMENT

Genesis
5:24	132
5:24 (LXX)	132
7:23	19
9:1	19
11:30	74
12:2	19, 37
15:5	37
15:8	75
16:10–12	72
17:1	74
17:15–22	72
17:17	75
17:19	75
18:10	75
18:11	74
18:11–12	74
21:17	35
22:17	37, 62
25:21–23	72
32:8	37, 38
32:11	37, 48
32:12	21, 37, 48
45:7	19

Exodus
3:16	112
4:31	77, 112
6:6	77
16:1–36	37
19:2	37
19:6	22, 107
20:5	35
22:13	23
22:24	103
23:20	46, 82, 92
23:22–24	46
23:23	47
24–34	36, 37
24–32	41
24	33, 41
24:1–11	37
24:3	33
24:4	33
24:5	33
24:7–8	33
24:9–11	34
24:11	33
24:18	37
32–34	41
32:1–6	33, 37
32:7–14	35, 37
32:10	19, 36, 37, 47, 125
32:12–13	38
32:13	37
32:26–29	43
32:31	41
32:32	37, 125
33:2	46
33:12	41
33:12–16	37
33:18–34:9	37
33:22	37, 41

Exodus (continued)

34	43
34:4	37
34:6–7	38
34:8	37
34:14	35
34:28	37
35:22	48

Leviticus

14:7	144
25	104, 105
25:9–10	104
25:10	104
25:10 (LXX)	105
25:23–24	105
25:23–34	104
25:35–55	104
25:38	105
25:42	105
26:36	19
26:39	19

Numbers

11	130
14	19
14:12	19
25:1–9	35
25:6–13	56
25:11	35
25:13	35
31:8	48
33:55	16

Deuteronomy

2:34	19, 47
3:11	16, 19
4:27	19, 142
5:2	49
7:20	19, 47
9:14	19, 37
11:13–17	34
11:16–17	102
15	104
18:15	40, 67, 129
18:15 (LXX)	129
23:1	144
28:24	102
28:62	19
29:1	49
32	123
32:5	94, 123, 133
32:16	35
32:20	94, 123
32:21	35, 64
33:10	107
34:5–12	132

Joshua

3:1–17	85
5:2–7	86
8:17	19
8:22	19
10:28	47
10:37	47
10:39	47
10:40	47
15:18	35

Judges

1:14	35
13:3–5	72
18:3	35

1 Samuel

9:14	16
11:11	19

2 Samuel

14:5	35
17:12	24

1 Kings

1:3	143
1:5	34
1:16	35
8:9	49
16:29–30	79
16:30–34	79
16:31	79
16:31–33	36

17–19	8	18:20–46	30
17	109, 118	18:21	32, 33, 41, 42, 44, 92
17:1	30, 39, 45, 102	18:21b	32
17:2	39, 79	18:22	7, 19, 30, 31, 32, 36, 55, 162
17:3	80	18:23	32, 33
17:3–9	80	18:24	32
17:5	39	18:30	32, 41
17:7–16	108	18:31	32, 33, 39
17:8	39, 79	18:31–38	56
17:8–16	116	18:36–37	74
17:8–24	14, 30, 109, 148	18:37	33, 49, 87, 163
17:10	109, 148	18:38	33
17:12 (LXX)	109	18:39	33, 39, 41
17:13 (LXX)	109	18:40	30, 34
17:16	39	18:41	33, 34
17:16 (LXX)	109	18:41–42	37
17:17	109, 117, 156	18:41–45	34
17:17–18	148	18:41–46	42
17:17–24	56, 65, 90, 107, 115, 117, 140, 148	18:42–44	66
17:18	149, 156	18:46	34, 99, 144
17:19	148, 156	19	37, 39, 42
17:19–23	109	19:1	30, 37, 42
17:20	156	19:1–2	92
17:20–21	148	19:1–4	34
17:21	115, 156	19:1–18	29, 34
17:22	156	19:3–4	80
17:22 (LXX)	109	19:3–8	144
17:22–23	148	19:4	37, 80, 92
17:23	117, 128	19:5–7	37
17:23 (LXX)	110	19:8	37, 49, 80, 99, 132
17:23–24	41	19:8–9	65
17:24	39, 106, 109, 118, 148, 156	19:9	34, 37, 39, 79
18	34, 41	19:9–10	34
18:1	39, 66, 67, 79, 102, 143	19:10	7, 19, 26, 30, 31, 32, 34, 35, 36, 37, 39, 40, 42, 51, 53, 55, 63, 65, 92, 125, 127, 162
18:3–4	39	19:10–18	37
18:4	30, 31, 65	19:11	34
18:10	30	19:11–13	37, 41
18:12	99, 143	19:13	37, 67
18:13	30, 31, 65	19:14	7, 19, 26, 30, 31, 32, 34, 35, 36, 37, 39, 40, 42, 47, 51, 53, 55, 63, 65, 125, 127, 162
18:16–46	29		
18:17	50, 67, 94, 99		
18:17–18	102		
18:19	30, 31, 41		
18:19–20	42		
18:20	32, 41		

1 Kings (*continued*)

19:15	56, 80, 121
19:15–18	30, 34, 40, 43, 93
19:16	99
19:17	53, 99
19:17–18	43
19:18	19, 36, 49, 68, 163
19:19	67, 120, 121
19:19–21	120
19:21	120, 121
20:16 (LXX)	42
20:25 (LXX)	42
20:28 (LXX)	79
21:5–7	42
21:17	39
21:17–18	143
21:21–22	30
21:25 (MT)	42
21:27–29	42
21:28	39, 79

2 Kings

1:2	119
1:3	119, 120, 140
1:5–6	140
1:6	119
1:8	67
1:9	102, 120, 132
1:9–16	119
1:10	67, 119, 120
1:12	67, 119, 120
1:14	119
1:15	119, 120, 143
1:16	119, 120
1:17	39
1:18	78
2:1	118
2:1–18	132
2:6–14	80
2:8	67
2:9	44, 72, 132
2:9 (LXX)	118, 132
2:9–15	80
2:10	133
2:10 (LXX)	118, 132
2:10–12	144
2:11	67, 99, 132, 143
2:11 (LXX)	118, 132
2:12	133
2:13	67, 132
2:13–15	132
2:14	67
2:15	7, 40, 44, 72, 132, 142
2:16	99, 143
4	116
4:1–7	116
4:8	109, 116
4:14–17	117
4:18–37	65, 109
4:22–25	148
4:25–37	117
4:27	156
4:27–28	149
4:29	140, 141
4:31	118
4:32–37	90
4:42	116
4:42 (LXX)	116
4:42–44	115
4:43	16, 116
4:44	116
5	109
5:1	108, 144, 149
5:1–2	149
5:1–14	90, 107, 108
5:1–16	108
5:1–19	144
5:2–3	149
5:3	108
5:3–6	108
5:3–9	144
5:5–10	108
5:6	108
5:7–8	110
5:8	103, 149
5:8–19	130
5:10	144, 149
5:10–14	149
5:13–14	149
5:14	80, 108, 144, 149
5:15	106
5:15–19	145
5:17	106
5:17–18	106

SCRIPTURE INDEX 213

5:20–27	145, 149
5:25–27	110
6:28	35
6:32	140
8:12	40
8:18	79
8:27	79
9:6–10	44
9:15	30
9:36	39, 44
10:10	39, 44
10:11	30
10:14	30
10:17	30, 39, 44
10:19	30
10:21	30
10:25	30
10:26–28	40
10:32	40
13:3	40

3 Kingdoms

19:13	65
19:19	65

4 Kingdoms

2:8	65
2:13–14	65

Ezra

9:1–2	21
9:8–9	24
9:10–15	24
9:13–15	38

Nehemiah

7:71	24
10:29	24
11:1	24
11:20	24

Esther

5:3	35

Psalms

1:4	85
2:7	129
22	127
72:5	24
78:8	94
78:58	35
79:15 (LXX)	113
80:14	113
105:4 (LXX)	112
106:4	112
106:10 (LXX)	77
107:10	77
118:26	81

Isaiah

1:8–9	20
1:9	11, 38, 62
1:19–20	38
1:22–26	20
2:2	153
4:2	22
4:2–6	21
6	76
6:1	76
6:1–2	72
6:2	76
6:4	76
6:5	76
6:8–13	76
6:9–10	76
6:9–13	76
6:11	20
6:13	20, 68, 76
6:13 (LXX)	63
6:13a–b	20
7:3	21
9:1 (LXX)	77
9:2	77
10:12	21
10:19	21
10:20	78
10:20–21	21, 87
10:22	21, 27, 62
10:22–23	11, 37, 62
11:1	22
11:10	64

Isaiah (continued)

11:11	22, 103
11:11–12	147
13:19–22	103
14:22 (LXX)	63
14:30 (LXX)	63
15:9 (LXX)	63
17:3 (LXX)	68
25:6	128
25:8	21
26:14–19	21
26:19	56, 68, 100, 128
28:5–6	21
32:15	134, 152
34:8–17	103
35:1–2	21
35:1–10	85
35:5–6	56, 151
35:5–10	22
37:30–32	21
37:31–32	27
40	78, 87, 88, 89
40:1	106
40:1 (LXX)	88
40:1–9	88
40:2	77, 87
40:2 (LXX)	82
40:3	46, 72, 74, 77, 82, 86, 87, 140, 153
40:3 (LXX)	82, 86, 88
40:3–5	81, 82, 85, 86, 88, 89
40:5	89
40:9	88
40:11	142
41:15–16	85
42	126
43–44	135
43:8	135
43:8–13	22
43:10	135, 152
43:16–21	85
44:3	134, 135, 152
44:8	135
44:17	16
44:19	16
45:21	153
49	54
49:1–6	22
49:3	136
49:3–5	54
49:5–6	136
49:6	22, 54, 55, 64, 73, 107, 129, 136, 137, 151, 152, 157, 159
49:6 (LXX)	136
49:19–21	27
49:20–21	22, 112
49:21	54
49:21 (LXX)	112
49:22	22
51:1–2	75, 84
51:1–3	37, 88
51:3	88
55:7	77
56:3–8	22, 146, 164
56:5	146
56:7	146
56:8	146, 147
56:17	89
57:14	82
57:19	153
58:6	105
59:10	126
60:21	104
60:21–22	103
60:22	95, 105
61	54, 56, 95, 100, 103, 104, 105, 106, 107, 112
61:1	56, 99, 100, 104, 106, 110
61:1 (LXX)	105
61:1–2	56, 100, 103, 128, 142, 151, 160
61:1–3	22, 99
61:1–5	100
61:3	104
61:4	22, 95, 103, 104
61:5	107
61:6	106, 107
61:8	105
61:9	95
62:10	82
66:18–21	146

66:19	22, 64, 69, 107, 166

Jeremiah

1:1 (LXX)	79
1:2	79
6:9	23
12:15	153
21:7	38
23:3	23
23:5	22
23:5 (LXX)	77
24:1–10	27
24:5–7	23
24:8–10	23
29:17	23
31:2–3	85
31:2–6	23
31:7–9	23
33:15	22
34:8	104
34:15	104
34:17	104
40:11	23
40:15	23
42:10–12	23
42:17	23
44:7	23
44:14	16
49:2 (LXX)	142
50:20	23
51:28 (LXX)	142

Ezekiel

5:1–4	43
5:3	23, 142
6:8–10	23, 87
6:12	54
7:16	16
9:1–8	23
11:13	23
11:14–19	23
11:15	23
12:15–16	23
12:16	43
14:22–23	23
20:33–38	85
21:2–6	123
22:27	141
36:26	89
37:1–14	21, 23, 68, 112, 128, 150
37:5 (LXX)	68
37:10 (LXX)	68
37:11	68, 126
39:29	134, 152
40:1–6	68
42:20	68
46:17	104

Daniel

7:25	66, 102
8:16	75
9–10	75
9:20	75
9:20–21	75
9:21	75
9:23	75
10:12	75
12:7	66, 102

Hosea

1:1	79
1:10	37, 62, 75
2:14–23	85
2:23	62
3:4–5	153
5:14	126
6	126
6:1–2	68, 112, 126, 150
6:1–3	24
6:2	126, 127, 128
6:5	126
10:14	48

Joel

1:1	79
1:4	23
1:15	47
2:28	48, 134, 152
2:28–32	152
2:32	24, 152

Joel (continued)

3:14	47
4:14 (MT)	47

Amos

3:12	16, 23, 24, 126
3:15	48
5:3	20, 23, 27, 68
5:14–15	78, 87
5:15	24
5:18–20	47
6:9	23, 38
9 (LXX)	154
9:1	23, 38
9:8	16
9:8–9	154
9:9	85
9:10	23
9:11	24
9:11–12	153, 154
9:12 (LXX)	160

Obadiah

15	47
17	24
21	24

Jonah

1:1	79

Micah

1:1	79
2:12	24, 142
4:6–7	27
5:7	24, 69
5:8	24
7:6	48
7:8	24

Zephaniah

2–3	146
2:1—3:8	146
2:1—3:13	164
2:3	78, 87, 103
2:4	146
2:4—3:8	146
2:7	113
2:13	146
3:1–5	146
3:3	141
3:9–10	146
3:9–20	146
3:10	146
3:11–12	104
3:11–13	146
3:12	103
3:12–13	24

Haggai

1:12	24
1:14	24
2:2	24
2:14	24

Zechariah

2:5	68
2:11	153, 154
3:8	22
3:8 (LXX)	77
3:11–12	46
6:12	22
6:12 (LXX)	77
8:22	153, 154
9:7	147
12:10	134, 152
13:4	67
13:8–9	43
14:16	24

Malachi

1:1 (LXX)	77
2:1–4 (MT)	84
2:2 (MT)	77
2:4–8 (MT)	56
2:6 (MT)	73
2:7 (MT)	73, 82
3 (MT)	56, 73, 74, 78, 80, 163
3:1	72
3:1 (LXX)	72, 140

3:1 (MT)	3, 5, 8, 15, 45, 46, 56, 72, 73, 74, 76, 77, 81, 82, 86, 90, 91, 92, 99, 100, 119, 139, 140	3:7	83
		8:5–10	108
		8:18–22	120
		11:2–3	91
		11:5	56, 100
3:1–2 (MT)	47	11:10	73, 100
3:2 (MT)	47	11:14	1, 2, 92
3:3 (MT)	22	11:14–15	92
3:4 (MT)	22	11:16	94
3:5 (MT)	46	11:18–19	94
3:7 (MT)	48	14:14	128
3:17 (MT)	73	16:22–23	124
3:18 (MT)	47, 56, 73	17:9–13	1
3:19 (MT)	47, 53, 81	17:10–13	2, 92
3:20 (LXX)	77	17:13	117
3:20–21 (MT)	47		
3:22 (LXX)	4	**Mark**	
3:22 (MT)	45, 49	1:1–8	78
3:22–23 (LXX)	45, 72	1:2	73, 82, 86
3:22–24 (MT)	45, 116	1:2–3	74
3:23 (LXX)	73	1:3	89
3:23 (MT)	45, 46, 47, 56, 132	1:6	1, 2, 67, 78
3:23–24 (MT)	8, 29, 44, 45, 47, 51, 53, 59, 76, 77, 81, 99, 100, 163, 165	6:1–6	98
		6:14–29	79
		6:30–34	128
		6:37–38	116
3:24 (LXX)	45	6:44	116
3:24 (MT)	24, 33, 47, 48, 53, 54, 55, 56, 57, 60, 73, 74, 87, 136,	6:45—8:26	114, 115
		8:31	114, 122, 127
		8:32	126
4:2	77	8:32–33	124
4:4–6	116	9:1	128
4:4–6 (MT)	67	9:2	129
4:5	132	9:7	129
4:5–6	45, 72, 76, 77	9:9–13	2
4:6	53, 73, 74, 87, 136	9:10–13	92
		9:11–13	1, 117
		9:30	114

∽

NEW TESTAMENT

Matthew

3:1–12	78
3:3	89
3:4	67, 78

9:38	114
16:19	131

Luke

1–2	3, 75, 83, 88
1	72, 75
1:2	134
1:5	76, 80

Luke (continued)

Reference	Pages
1:5–17	71
1:5–23	77
1:5–25	108
1:6	74
1:7	74
1:9–10	75, 76
1:11	76
1:11–12	76
1:13	75
1:13–17	72
1:15–17	76
1:16	73, 74, 75, 86
1:16–17	75
1:17	2, 3, 5, 8, 15, 45, 48, 71, 72, 74, 76, 77, 78, 80, 81, 82, 86, 89, 91, 92, 95, 119, 140, 163
1:17b	73
1:18	74, 75, 76
1:18–20	38
1:19	75
1:20	76
1:22	39
1:26	75
1:26–48	72, 108
1:33	128
1:46–55	5, 166
1:52	83
1:53	7
1:55	74
1:66	77
1:67–79	76, 77, 166
1:68	77, 112, 113
1:68–69	5
1:68–79	72, 133
1:69	77
1:71	77
1:72–73	74, 77
1:74	77, 78
1:76	3, 5, 8, 15, 45, 72, 74, 76, 78, 81, 82, 86, 89, 91, 92, 95, 119, 140
1:77	77, 106
1:78	77, 112
1:79	77, 78
1:80	80
2:19	77
2:25–26	126
2:25–36	108
2:30	89
2:33	97
2:36–38	108
2:51	77
3	83, 88, 92
3:1–2	79, 84
3:1–6	78
3:1–17	89
3:1–20	8, 78
3:1–21	163
3:2	78, 79, 80, 102
3:2–3	78
3:3	80, 87, 102, 106
3:4	86
3:4–6	74, 82, 88, 102
3:4–14	98
3:6	89
3:7	81, 83, 84, 87, 102
3:7–9	111, 164
3:8	84, 87, 88
3:9	81, 83
3:10	84
3:12	84, 87
3:13	87
3:14	80, 83, 84, 87
3:15	84, 88
3:16	3, 46, 81, 91, 95, 164
3:16–17	81
3:17	81, 83, 85
3:18	84, 85, 106
3:18–20	78, 95
3:19	79, 80, 83
3:19–20	4, 78, 79, 83, 92
3:20–21	5
3:21	84, 87, 92
3:22	99
4:1	99
4:2	99
4:14	99, 102
4:14–15	72
4:16–27	98

SCRIPTURE INDEX 219

4:16–30	78, 98, 99, 119, 144	7:2	108, 112
4:17	99	7:3	108
4:18	98, 99, 103, 105, 106, 110, 164	7:3–5	108
		7:4–5	108
		7:5	113
4:18b	105	7:5–6	110
4:18e	105	7:6	113
4:18–19	98, 99, 102, 107, 123	7:6–7	111, 113
		7:6–8	111
4:18–21	142	7:6–9	108
4:18–30	103	7:8	111
4:21–25	97	7:9	97, 110, 111, 113
4:22	102, 105	7:10	108, 112
4:23	98, 102	7:11	109, 116
4:23–27	2, 122	7:11–12	109
4:24	99, 101, 102	7:11–16	2
4:25	66, 67, 102, 106	7:11–17	14, 90, 97, 107, 109, 117, 148, 149, 159
4:25–26	14, 109, 137, 149, 159		
4:25–27	5, 7, 8, 98, 99, 100, 106, 107, 110, 120, 123, 148, 155, 161, 164	7:12	109, 112, 117
		7:13	91, 111
		7:14	112
		7:15	109, 112
4:26	99	7:16	77, 109, 110, 112, 113, 115, 128
4:27	14, 80, 106, 144, 149		
		7:18	90
4:28–30	126	7:18–19	90
4:31	101	7:18–20	100
4:31–41	98	7:18–27	90
4:40–41	111	7:18–35	89
5:30–32	7	7:19	3, 81, 91, 92
6:11	126	7:19–29	81
6:16	126, 127	7:20	46, 81, 90, 91
6:20	103, 110	7:21	95, 99
6:20–23	110	7:21–22	128
6:20–49	110	7:22	56, 95, 99, 100, 103, 107, 112, 142, 151, 160
6:24–26	110		
6:26	101		
6:32–36	110	7:23	93
7	128	7:24	90
7:1	110	7:24–26	92
7:1–10	14, 80, 90, 104, 107, 108, 144, 148, 149	7:26	92
		7:27	3, 4, 5, 8, 15, 46, 73, 82, 90, 91, 96, 100, 119, 140
7:1–17	5, 8, 90, 99, 100, 107, 108, 110, 137, 155, 164		
		7:29	93, 95
		7:29–30	83, 90, 93, 94
7:1–50	90	7:30	93, 97, 111, 122

Luke (continued)

7:31	123
7:31–35	93
7:33	94
7:33–34	90, 94, 164
7:33–35	93
7:34	94
7:35	94, 95
8:3	80
8:10	76
8:13	127
8:40–42	115
8:49–56	115
8:51	124
9	114, 121, 122, 124, 125, 127, 128, 130, 140
9:1	115, 124, 128, 129
9:1–2	128
9:1–6	114
9:1–10	129
9:1–62	8, 114, 115, 164
9:2	128
9:3	124
9:5	120, 141
9:6	115, 128
9:7	80, 115
9:7–9	72, 92, 115, 116, 123
9:7–18	5
9:8	3, 5, 110, 137, 140
9:9	80, 123
9:10	114, 116, 124
9:10–17	115, 140, 164
9:11	128
9:11–17	128
9:12	128
9:13	116, 124
9:13–14	116
9:14	116
9:16	116
9:17	114, 116
9:18	114
9:18–20	124
9:19	3, 5, 110, 115, 116, 137, 140
9:20	115
9:20–22	124
9:22	114, 122, 123, 126, 127
9:22–27	122
9:23	127
9:23–27	124
9:24	128
9:24–26	125
9:27	127, 128, 129
9:28	114, 124, 128, 129
9:28–36	116, 125, 128, 164
9:30	114
9:30–33	140
9:31	117, 118, 123, 126, 129
9:33	124
9:33–34	124
9:34–35	124
9:35	126, 129
9:37	114
9:37–43	117, 128, 164
9:38	117
9:40	118, 120, 124
9:41	94, 123, 124, 133
9:42	117, 140
9:43	114, 118
9:43–44	124
9:44	122, 126
9:45	120, 125, 127
9:46	120, 124
9:46–48	127
9:49	114, 120, 124
9:49–50	127
9:51	3, 114, 118, 123, 124, 129, 131, 140, 157
9:51–56	114, 123
9:51–62	114
9:52	4, 5, 8, 15, 82, 119, 120, 129, 139, 140, 160
9:52b	141
9:52–56	3, 119, 137, 140
9:53	119, 120
9:54	119, 124
9:54–55	120, 125
9:55	115, 119, 120
9:56	119, 120

9:57	114, 220
9:57–62	120, 127, 140
9:59	120
9:60	128
9:61	120
9:61–62	114
9:62	120, 121, 125, 128
10:1	4, 5, 8, 15, 119, 139, 140, 160
10:1–12	114, 129
10:1–16	139
10:2	142
10:3	141, 142
10:4	140, 141
10:6	142
10:7	140
10:9	128, 140, 141, 142
10:10–12	120
10:11	141, 142
10:12–15	141
10:16	141
11:29–32	123
11:50–51	123
11:57–62	123
13:29	7
13:31	80
13:31–32	123
13:33–34	101
14:12–14	110
14:13	103
14:15	7
14:21	103
14:21–24	7
16:20	103
16:22	103
17:11–17	130
17:11–19	144
18:22	103
19:1–10	94, 104
19:10	119
19:29	140
19:31–33	126
22:30	94, 129
22:69	118
23:6–12	79, 123
23:7–15	80
23:8	80
24:6–7	126
24:25	135, 145
24:25–27	145, 165
24:26	125
24:44–46	126
24:44–47	145, 165
24:46–48	134
24:47	106
24:48	134
24:50–52	130
24:50–53	118
24:51	3, 130, 131

John

6:31–34	116
9:34	68
9:35	68
12:31	68
20:17	131

Acts

1:1–11	130, 131
1:2	3, 118, 132
1:2–9	8
1:3	132, 135
1:4–5	132, 135
1:6	133, 135
1:6–8	69
1:6–11	118
1:7	134, 135
1:7–8	131
1:8	72, 132, 134, 136, 151, 151–52, 153, 166
1:9	133
1:9–11	3, 131, 132, 133
1:10	132, 133
1:11	118, 132, 133
1:14–26	136
1:21–22	134
1:22	78, 118, 131, 132
2	152, 154
2:14–36	98
2:17	152
2:21	152, 166
2:23	93, 128, 133, 150, 151

Acts (continued)

2:30–31	134
2:32	134
2:32–36	131
2:36	133
2:38	106
2:38–39	133
2:39	153
2:40	133
2:41	10
2:47	10
3:14–15	151
3:15	134
3:15–16	128
3:19–21	134
3:21	118
3:22–23	151
3:23	10, 152
4:1–3	145
4:4	10
4:10	128, 152
4:27	80, 133, 150
4:28	93
4:33	72
5:17	167
5:17–18	145
5:26–28	145
5:28	151
5:30–31	131
5:30–33	150
5:31	106
5:31–32	134
5:33	145
5:40	145
6:11–15	145
7:1–53	83
7:48–50	83
7:51–53	150
7:52	101, 102, 151
8	143
8:1	150
8:1–5	145
8:5	147
8:5–8	143
8:8–25	129
8:14	143
8:15–17	143
8:25	143
8:26	143, 146
8:26–29	144
8:26–40	8, 14, 143, 149, 160, 164
8:27	144
8:27–28	144
8:27–39	153
8:29	143
8:29–30	144
8:31	145
8:35	145
8:36	144
8:37	143
8:38	144
8:39	143, 144, 145
9	154
9:1–22	150
9:2	86
9:23	150
9:29	150
9:31	150, 157
9:32	150
9:32–35	150
9:32–43	4, 14, 147, 148, 150, 151, 159, 160, 164
9:35	151
9:36	147, 149
9:36–43	8
9:37	148
9:38	148
9:38–39	148
9:39	147, 148
9:40	148
9:40–41	148
9:42	148, 151
9:43	147
10	144, 153, 154, 157, 160
10:1	149
10:1–48	4, 8, 14, 80, 144, 147, 149, 151, 164
10:2	113
10:2–4	147
10:3–8	149
10:5–8	147
10:15	149, 155

10:17–23	149	15:17	160
10:19–20	149	16:8–11	156
10:22	113	17:5	167
10:25	149	18:6	157
10:28	149, 155	18:7	113
10:30–32	147	18:18	158
10:34–43	151	18:28	165
10:35	155	19:4	87
10:37	78	19:9	86
10:39	151	19:21	155, 157
10:39–40	133	19:23	86
10:39–41	134, 151, 152	20:3	157, 158
10:41	151	20:6	157, 158
10:42	152, 155	20:7	157, 158
10:42–43	152	20:7–12	14, 155, 161, 164
10:43	106, 152	20:7–16	8
10:44	152	20:8	156, 157
10:44–48	149	20:10	156
10:45	152	20:11	157
11:1–3	149	20:12	156, 159
11:4–17	147	20:16	158
11:9	149	20:17–38	155
11:17–18	153	20:19	157
12:4	157	20:23	157
12:17	103	21:4	157
13:1	80	21:11–13	157
13:16–41	98	21:18	103
13:24	78, 87	21:20	10
13:24–25	81	22:4	86
13:27	133	22:15	134
13:27–28	151	24:4	86
13:31	131, 134	24:17	155, 158
13:38	106	24:22	86
13:45	167	25:13—26:32	80
13:46	64, 157	26:9–18	153
13:47	136, 157	26:16	135
13:51	141	26:18	106
15	153, 154	28:25–28	10
15:7–9	147, 153	28:26–27	76
15:7–11	153	28:28	89
15:8–9	153		
15:9	149		
15:13	103		
15:14	152, 153		
15:15	154		
15:15–17	154		
15:15–18	153		
15:16	155		

Romans

9–11	62
9:1–5	62
9:6	26, 62
9:7–13	62
9:16	62

Romans (continued)

9:24	62
9:25–29	62
9:27	17
9:27–29	11
9:30—10:21	63
11	38, 62
11:1	63, 64
11:1–3	163
11:1–5	7, 167
11:1–6	8, 62, 163
11:1–13	163
11:2–4	63
11:2–5	62, 167
11:3	61, 63
11:4	63, 68
11:5	17, 64, 69
11:5–6	63
11:8	63
11:11	64
11:11–12	64
11:13–14	64
11:14	64
11:15	64
11:16–32	64
11:17–24	64
11:25	64
11:26	64
15:25–27	155, 158

1 Corinthians

15:3–4	126

2 Corinthians

8:1—9:15	158
8:20–21	155

Ephesians

4:10	131
6:17	89

1 Timothy

3:16	131

Hebrews

4:14	131
6:19	131
9:24	131
11:32–38	8, 65, 163
11:34	65
11:34–37	65
11:35	65, 66
11:35–38	61
11:37	65
11:38	65

James

5:16	66
5:17	61, 66, 67, 102
5:18	66
5:13–14	66
5:15–16	66
5:17–18	8, 65, 66, 163
5:19–20	66

1 Peter

3:22	131

Revelation

1:20	67
2:20–24	67
2:24	17, 68
3:2	68
8:13	68
9:20	68
11:1	68
11:1–2	68
11:1–11	61
11:1–13	8, 67
11:2	68
11:3	67
11:3–6	66
11:4	67
11:5	67
11:6	67
11:7	67
11:7–12	67
11:10	67

11:13	68	16:9	68
12:17	17, 68	19:21	68
14:7	68	20:5	68
15:4	68		

Extra-Biblical Index

OLD TESTAMENT APOCRYPHA

Sirach

44:1—50:24	51
44:10	51
47:22	52
48:1	67
48:1–10	8
48:1–11	51, 52–53, 53, 55
48:2	53
48:2–3	66
48:3	53, 54, 56
48:5	53
48:6	53
48:6–7	54
48:7	53
48:9	53, 118, 132
48:10	1, 7, 48, 53, 54, 73, 81, 136, 162, 163
48:11	56
48:12	7, 44, 132
48:15	52
48:15–16	52
49:14	132

1 Maccabees

2:58	118, 132

2 Esdras

7:109	66

OLD TESTAMENT PSEUDEPIGRAPHA

Apocalypse of Elijah

4:1–6	148
4:7–19	60
5:30–32	60

1 Enoch

10:17–22	59
85–90	57
89:10–27	141, 142
89:50	58
89:51–52	57, 58
89:52	58
90:7	58
90:9–15	58
90:24–27	58
90:30	58, 59
90:30–31	163
90:31	57, 58, 59, 60, 67
90:31–38	65
90:37–38	58, 163
91:12–17	59
93:1–10	59
93:4	60
93:8	59

4 Ezra
6:24–26	8
6:25–26	60
6:26	59
13:13	60

Psalms of Solomon
4:18	118

QUMRAN/DEAD SEA SCROLLS

4Q382	57
frags. 43, 45	57
4Q390	26
4Q481a	57
4Q521	8, 54, 55, 56, 61, 100, 163
2 II	100, 104
2 II 1	56
2 II 5	56
2 II 12	56, 112
2 III 2	55
2 III 4	56
7 I 4–6	56
7 I 12–13	56
14 I 2	56
4Q558	8, 46, 57, 163
1 II 4	57
1 II 5	57
3 II 3	57
11QMelch	104, 106
II 6	106

CD
1:4–5	26
2:11–12	26
3:12–15	26
19:9–10	104

RABBINIC WORKS

Rabbah Deuteronomy
4:11	82

Rabbah Numbers
4:11	82

Baba Ḳamma (b. Kam.)
60b	1

TARGUMIC TEXTS

Targum Pseudo-Jonathan
on Exod 6:18	56, 60
on Exod 40:10	56, 60
on Num 25:12	100
on Deut 30:4	56, 60, 61
on Deut 33:11	59, 60
on Deut 34:3	60

JOSEPHUS

Jewish Antiquities
13.282–83	76
18.2.3	79
18.117	87
20.97–98	86

APOSTOLIC FATHERS

1 Clement
17:1	65

www.ingramcontent.com/pod-product-compliance
Lightning Source LLC
Chambersburg PA
CBHW051638230426
43669CB00013B/2353